PEOPLE'S PEACE

Syracuse Studies on Peace and Conflict Resolution
Robert A. Rubinstein and Çerağ Esra Çuhadar, *series editors*

SELECT TITLES IN SYRACUSE STUDIES ON PEACE
AND CONFLICT RESOLUTION

For a full list of titles in this series, visit https://press.syr.edu/supressbook
-series/syracuse-studies-on-peace-and-conflict-resolution/.

People's Peace

Prospects for a Human Future

■ ■ ■

Edited by
Yasmin Saikia *and* Chad Haines

Syracuse University Press

For a listing of books published and distributed by Syracuse University Press,
visit https://press.syr.edu.

ISBN: 978-0-8156-3657-1 (hardcover)
       978-0-8156-3661-8 (paperback)
       978-0-8156-5486-5 (e-book)

Library of Congress Cataloging-in-Publication Data
Names: Saikia, Yasmin, editor. | Haines, Chad, editor.
Title: People's peace : prospects for a human future / edited by Yasmin Saikia and
    Chad Haines.
Description: First edition. | Syracuse, New York : Syracuse University Press, 2019. |
    Series: Syracuse studies on peace and conflict resolution | Includes bibliographical
    references and index. | Summary: ""People's Peace: Prospects for a Human Future" is a
    collection of essays highlighting the everyday and ordinary acts of peace committed by
    people living in community. The essays span a range of humanities disciplines: history,
    philosophy, theology, anthropology, cultural studies, and peace studies. Putting these
    approaches and methods in dialogue with each other produces a theoretical intervention
    that aims to shift the study of peace away from high organizations and institutions
    and locate it within people's lives and lived culture. Each essay in this book provides
    an important instance of people's peace where individuals defy authority or overcome
    cultural stigmas to assert the value of peaceful relations with others and their own
    personal dignity. People look for peace, they make peace, and, in doing so, make us
    aware that common people on their own have always worked and continue to work
    toward resolution rather than division"— Provided by publisher.
Identifiers: LCCN 2019035274 (print) | LCCN 2019035275 (ebook) | ISBN 9780815636571
    (hardcover) | ISBN 9780815636618 (paperback) | ISBN 9780815654865 (epub)
Subjects: LCSH: Peace—Social aspects. | Conflict management—Social aspects.
Classification: LCC JZ5538 .P46 2019 (print) | LCC JZ5538 (ebook) | DDC 303.6/6—dc23
LC record available at https://lccn.loc.gov/2019035274
LC ebook record available at https://lccn.loc.gov/2019035275

Contents

Acknowledgments

Every research project and publication are the product of many more contributions and levels of support than what can be indicated on any title page. This work is the second of three planned edited volumes on people's peace, and we are particularly indebted to the Arizona State University (ASU) Center for the Study of Religion and Conflict (CSRC). The CSRC provides a dynamic scholarly environment that allowed us to grow our ideas and pursue a diversity of conceptual questions and social issues with a varied group of colleagues. We are deeply appreciative of Linell Cady, former CSRC director, and John Carlson, current interim director, for their support, encouragement, and guidance. In particular, we are thankful for the financial support provided by Ann Hardt, a retired ASU professor of education whose vision and dedication made peace studies at ASU a reality. She generously donated the initial funds to create the Hardt-Nickachos Endowed Chair in Peace Studies, which provides support for the many programs we are able to organize and participate in. We are appreciative of the further support provided by ASU president Michael Crow, who enhanced Ann Hardt's initial donation, making peace studies a living legacy of his own vision for the place of the university in the world today. President Crow also supported the program we developed on global engagement in the Muslim world, which provided the foundation for furthering our knowledge through a variety of international dialogues and contributing to our own ideas about people's peace.

We are particularly thankful for the thought-provoking ideas shared by the many contributors to this volume. We all came together in a conference hosted by the CSRC in April 2016. Their engaging contributions and insights as well as their patience brought this volume to fruition. In organizing the conference and in putting together this edited volume, we are deeply indebted to the various CSRC staff members, in particular Carolyn Forbes, assistant director, and Matt Correa, who has patiently and diligently provided so much daily support. We also thank Laurie Perko and Sarah Lords for their administrative assistance and Dominique Reichenbach for the research and editing assistance she provided.

We feel very fortunate that we were able to forge a relationship with Syracuse University Press and are indebted to our editor, Suzanne Guiod, and her very helpful staff. We appreciate the interest taken by the press's Studies in Peace and Conflict Resolution series editors as well as the thoughtful suggestions made by the anonymous reviewers, which strengthened the final product.

Without the guidance and support of Mary Lou Bertucci, this volume would not be what it is. We cannot thank her enough for her editing and formatting of the volume as well as for her contributions to strengthening and making it cohere.

We also are appreciative of the support from Abid Hasan, artist of the painting used for the cover, and the director and staff of Gallery 6 in Islamabad, Pakistan, for facilitating communication with the artist.

Although so many have contributed to the realization of this volume, whatever errors and shortcomings remain are ours.

PEOPLE'S PEACE

Editors' Introduction

YASMIN SAIKIA AND CHAD HAINES

We live in a troubled time in which peace is more elusive than ever before. Political and religious leaders; activists; local, national, and international organizations; and governments have generated multiple theories and strategies for peace, but at the same time the theater of violence and war has expansively grown.[1] Despite different guarantees of peace and even "wars waged for peace," peace remains unattained and undefined. Peace through war is one of the greatest contradictions we face today; peace, a utopian promise for a shared human future, is more evident in discourse than in action. And this discourse keeps changing between friends and foes, enacting violence to make peace.

By any standards of objective evaluation, for many people in our world today the promise of peace made by those in power appears romantic and abstract. It has acquired the unreality of a dream. Yet we cannot walk away and abandon that dream, even though we understand its dim prospects in our world. A people's endeavor for peace is crucial to move forward together, to become a human community. In this book, we call this encompassing possibility "people's peace." People's peace, we suggest, is not merely a concept but a living history that we have to understand to realize the true potential of peace. At the same time, we must believe in the power of peace to inspire us to imagine a better human future. The essays in this book blend these ideas, highlighting peace as people's efforts in ordinary circumstances *and* an aspirational ideal to guide us to a better world.

People's peace is not a stand-alone concept but is also connected to and emerging from political, social, and religious experiences. People's power of imagining peace has produced a variety of metaphors and interpretative frames; different communities understand peace differently. Despite these differences, living peacefully as a community and with neighbors beyond one's own group is a primary concern of the majority of people. We find that people's understanding of peace reaffirms one of the Old English words for peace, *frith*, the root word for *friend* and *free*.[2] Peace prevails in a community of friends and in an environment of freedom, affirming the Judaic and Islamic values of peace (shalom and salam) as holistic communal harmony, welfare, and submission; it is a social value as well as a personal greeting among friends and strangers. Settling disputes using common sense, community practices, and cultural traditions plays a critical role in people's agency for peace in their communities. The intimacy of this kind of peace allows for a certain level of accommodation and attention to experiences, making peace a community endeavor. Everyday negotiations bring people closer to peace. The social and cultural foundations facilitate the process: the multiple experiences that enable people's agentic actions, the mutual understanding of social support, and ethical values produce a people's peace that is at the heart of this book.

The topography of people's peace at the local level can be varied, based on specific needs and circumstances, actors, and available resources. Local peace is variable and immediate, an intimate experience for the community. Mahatma Gandhi advanced this idea as both political philosophy and direct action in his vision for nonviolent anticolonial activism.[3] Peace can also be an expansive, aspirational horizon, a far-reaching goal for the entire human community, as Jacques Derrida has argued.[4]

In this book, we view peace as being both an intimate experience and a capacious longing that involve individuals and communities in a common endeavor. The lived narratives of peace that we explore are not romantic. We highlight the practical, everyday ways people live in peace, establishing the foundation of a people's peace. Thus, we emphasize ordinary people as the main actors; people create the discourse of peace, transforming it from something generated by external and powerful organizations into a language they have developed to effect change in their communities. People's peace embodies and expresses a new episteme of peace.

In taking this approach to peace as an intimate experience and an expansive horizon, we are proposing people's peace as the site of a new "political humanity." This term was first coined by Jonas Hanway, the eighteenth-century philanthropist and celebrated English traveler.[5] In his efforts for the Marine Society, "political humanity" took the form of a disciplined ordering within the naval community in which the officers took care of orphans and the destitute and transformed them into "useful" members of society. Religion played an important role in this commitment. Thus, "political humanity" signaled the formation of community based on humanistic ethics inspiring change for improvement. We take this view of ethics combined with politics for advancing the cause of peace. Hannah Arendt calls this combination "ethicopolitics," which we develop further to stress the exercise of ethics as a conscious human politics for ensuring and safeguarding peace. Secular and religious values help turn the principles of peace into action for developing humane approaches. Achieving peace at the level of local and national community can generate human-centered methods to establish relationships with others beyond "our" borders to resolve sticky political issues. Drawing on Michel Foucault's theory of discipline and punishment,[6] we assert that disciplining people through violence and wars waged by powerful states against the less powerful cannot bring peace. Rather, the humane approach of relationship building between people of different communities is essential for peace.

The humane approach benefits individuals and nations morally and politically, as we show in this book. It is also a more grounded strategy that makes peace a practical way of living. This changed episteme of peace may well lead to transformative outcomes. It promotes human allegiance to one another and moves humanity forward together toward a peaceful horizon. People's peace posits a human future based on individual and collective humane actions rooted in the ethics of living together.

Peace Traditions and Scholarship

Peace scholarship, broadly speaking, has emerged from two foundations: Western and Eastern political thought. But these foundations do not form a binary divide. Religious and secular perspectives inform both, illuminating different assumptions about the human, time, and history that shape the imaginings of peace. Together, these perspectives reveal peace as the noblest human aspiration and the most urgent need of humanity.

Within the Western tradition, one of the earliest perspectives on peace came from the ancient Greek view of *eirene*, or the establishment of order. In the *Republic*, Plato emphasizes peace as a pact for maintaining order. The "philosopher-king" would establish the pact on behalf of the citizens for their well-being. The Roman concept of *pax* and the verb *pacifari* (to pacify) convey the justification of political domination for peace. The Roman emperor Augustus (27–14 BCE) described his military conquests and subjugation of rivals as the advent of peace. Both *eirene* and *pax* thus express the understanding of peace as an agreement or conquest after the submission of the defeated or weaker group. Clearly, such peace involves asymmetrical power relations and shapes social and political hierarchical relationships among humans. The Roman state's turn to Christianity brought the concept of God into the story of peace: God is the fountainhead of peace. As God's representative, a king or ruler, in turn, grounds heavenly peace on earth by subjugating enemies and creating order in his domain so that heavenly peace and worldly peace suffuse in an ontological scheme of multiple hierarchies. Augustine of Hippo (354–430 CE) distinguishes between "eternal peace," which can be realized only in God, and earthly, "temporal peace" as a human possibility in a well-ordered polity. Human peace, temporal in its very nature, is always fragile and threatened by the risk of conflict.[7] During the Christian Reformation in the fifteenth century, the Dutch theologian Desiderius Erasmus (1466–1536) in *A Complaint of Peace* chastises European monarchs for engaging in war, which he asserts is against the tenets of God and nature. Unity among people is God's desire because all humanity (read: European humanity) is dependent on one "common Father."[8]

To keep conflict in check, both kings and subjects were required to recognize the arrangement of power. The duty of kings was to maintain order; subjects had to obey the ruler (in modern terminology, citizens were required to obey their governments). Failure to do so justified the ruling authority's use of force to subjugate the defiant. In his classic work *Leviathan*, Thomas Hobbes (1588–1679) argues in favor of a central authority delivering peace based on a social contract with citizens. Without a social contract, in his opinion, human beings, governed by irrational animal passions, will engage in violence and destruction, leading to a state of chaos and disorder. For enforcing the social contract, rulers or constitutional governments have the legitimate right to use force. Peace, according to the Hobbesian perspective, is a political act intimately connected to the state's use of force.

Thus, from Alexander to Julius Caesar to Napoleon to today's so-called war on terror, the belief that peace can be secured by force has been a prevalent approach to manage the hierarchy of nations and people. The lack of effective social and political organizations at times makes war necessary, as Hobbes and, following him, many others have argued. The jubilation of victory and the bending of the defeated to the victor become the means to make a pact for peace. The coercive politics behind peace is really a compromise more than a relational understanding. Western governments, in particular that of the United States, have adhered to this way of peacemaking for establishing themselves as powerful states who deliver peace to their non-Western rivals.

The question of what kind of war is the best means for peace became the foundation for the theory of "just war." Augustine and Thomas Aquinas (1225–74) are considered the authors of the just-war theory. This framework has persisted to this day, reinvented as humanitarian intervention and invasion for "regime change," as witnessed in Iraq, Afghanistan, and many other places since the 1990s.

However, there is another strain of thought in the Western peace tradition. Baruch Spinoza (1632–77) believed the human potential for peace to be a constant but war to be a disruptive interlude in human history.[9] To Spinoza, peace is an ever-present constitutive, natural power that does not promote servility to a contract but is the bedrock for civil peace through social contract in a commonwealth. Spinoza's approach echoes Hobbes's political thought on social contract, and his belief in the fixity of peace as human potential influenced the Kantian approach of *pax perpetua*, or "perpetual peace."

The growing emphasis in Europe on civil peace controlled and managed by powerful forces does not indicate the disappearance of God from peace discourse. The monotheistic religions—Christianity, Judaism, and Islam, but Christianity and Judaism in particular, which have informed much of Western cultural traditions—continue to assert God's position in maintaining peace in the human community. Adherence to a "covenantal relationship" and obedience to rules enjoined by God according to these religions are important for peace.[10] The Old Testament term *shalom* and the Christian notion of peace in Christ, particularly as expressed in the Sermon on the Mount, continue to influence Western thinking about peace. The Islamic term *salam*, which denotes "peace" but also means "submission to God," and the two pillars *zakat* (alms giving) and Ramadan (the month of fasting) are foundational concepts for cultivating social justice and equity for peace within community. In the monotheistic religions, submission to God may require fighting in defense of the faith, whether it be the Christian concept of crusade, the Jewish understanding of offensive and defensive war, or the Islamic idea of smaller jihad. Religious war, in this understanding, is not violence, but a harbinger of peace for "believers."

Thus, whether one adopts a religious or a secular viewpoint, in Western thought waging war is acceptable for establishing peace. However, this narrow view of peace does not address the underlying causes at the root of tensions and problems in a community that lead to violence and war, or nonpeace. Johan Galtung, one of the founders of modern peace theory, labels peace through force as "negative peace."[11] Negative peace is unstable and fragile because it is based on shifting configurations of power within the complex political systems of national states and international relations. The breakdown of diplomacy can lead to war and negative peace.

There is a more hopeful and broader approach to peace that Galtung calls "positive peace." Positive peace focuses on the development and fulfillment of individuals in a society where harmony, prosperity, social justice, and good governance enable human advancement and serve as the bedrocks for peace. This state represents the "good life" or "perpetual peace," as Immanuel Kant (1724–1804) defined it. Post-Enlightenment political history in Europe after the Treaty of Westphalia (1648) idealized the Kantian approach to peace. In its broadest sense, positive peace in the twentieth century included all human development as the desired goal. Taking the view that all humans can achieve this peace also means adopting a global approach. The promoters of "liberal peace" advocate economic and political liberalization. But they also fear that the positive peace achieved in Western countries and intricately connected with economic advancement and political freedom could be threatened by the less-peaceful and fragile non-Western states unless these states are made like the West, democratic and liberal. There has been extensive criticism of this elite view for reinforcing the West's global dominance. How to achieve positive peace by adopting an inclusive and democratic approach continues to be much discussed and debated in peace studies scholarship. By way of adopting new approaches for achieving positive peace, scholars are beginning to pay attention to the role of empathy, compassion, friendship, relationship to strangers, hospitality, and a host of everyday, informal social practices that people use to overcome violence and give shape to positive peace in the contexts of their community.[12] Religious values and aspects of religion that people draw upon to overcome violence are new areas for peace research.[13] Can religious pluralism enable peace in diverse communities? Rejecting stereotypes and hate and allowing local people to figure out their own needs and workable practices, Oliver Richmond asserts, are the ways forward beyond liberal peace.[14]

Unlike Western traditions that focus on the public sphere as the site of peacemaking, Asian cultural traditions emphasize the individual's internal efforts. In India, the Sanskrit word *shanti* refers to "peace of mind" and "tranquility" achieved by an individual who follows the path of nonviolence. The Chinese word for peace, *ho p'ing* or *p'ing ho*, refers to a social order that harmonizes individuals with a community, creating the necessary balance for peaceful living. The Japanese word *heiwa* is similar to *p'ing ho*.[15] Thus, positive human relationships are foundational for building a harmonious community. Kinship, dialogical self-realization, and balance play integral parts in the Asian traditions of peace.

Communitarian ethics rooted in semblances of kinship and social relationships is key in the Confucian tradition.[16] Similar ideas developed in Islamic concepts of social ethics and peace, where the *ummah*, community, is understood in terms of familial relationships, an understanding most pronounced in South Asian Islamic culture. Another trend in Asian traditions of peace and ethics is a distinct understanding of the self as engaged in a constant process of self-realization. This is different from the fixed ego in the Western, liberal tradition. The dialogical social dynamic opens up distinct ethical relationships of respect between self and others that go beyond mere tolerance.

A third aspect of Asian traditions of peace is balance. In Buddhism, this is the Middle Path. In Islam practiced in Asia, the emphasis is on *wassatiyya*. Balance as an expression of peace is not an inherent act of nonviolence, but a recognition that violence itself must be balanced within ethical norms, duties and responsibilities, and social justice. Peace, therefore, is not a cessation of violence, but rather a societal movement toward balance.

Thus, we see that in the Asian view of peace, social tranquility is primary, and it is possible when community and political systems are in accord with one another, not in competition. Gandhi emphasized this understanding in his strategy of nonviolence and civil disobedience, which involved both an internal struggle, or *satya-graha* (struggle for truth), and a reordering of the external power for creating moral governance, which he imagined would lead to Ram Rajya, or the perfect system of rulership by the mythical Hindu god-king Lord Rama. The Indian Muslim peace thinker Maulana Wahi-duddin Khan recommends that individual Muslims must always try to establish peaceful relations with others and not pursue the dream of "Islamic rule" because that goes against the primary purpose of "availing opportunities for the Da'wah mission, the mission of inviting people to God's path."[17] He recommends an approach of compromise and accommodation for maintaining harmony between Muslims and others because without peace there cannot be normalcy in human life or the pursuit of happiness that is possible in and through religion. The Dalai Lama, the famed religiopolitical figure of Tibetan Buddhism, calls for love and compassion for developing an attitude of universal human responsibility and acknowledging the interconnected relationship between people, which is the path forward for peace.

Today, these Asian concepts of peace have become tools among Western peace thinkers who struggle for civil rights. Nonetheless, the dominance of the Western approach of using war for peace is the most readily accepted approach by governments in general. Not unlike the monotheistic religions' perspective, in the nonmonotheistic religions of Asia the role of God as the giver of peace, creating *shanti* in community, is a popularly accepted notion. In Asian traditions, rather than submission to a covenantal arrangement, different rituals become the means to propitiate the gods. In Hindu tantric practices, even human sacrifice was used to propitiate the gods to herald *shanti* and get through periods of personal and community turmoil, natural disasters, and other inauspicious events.

The definitions of peace, thus, are varied. The Western approach to peace, mostly outward looking, emphasizes maintaining political order with force, if necessary, whereas Eastern traditions turn the gaze inward, focusing on individual tranquility or "inner peace." However, at the heart of both traditions is concern for ending the conflict that destroys human community. Despite this exclusive focus on human well-being, whether West or East, Global North or Global South, peace is not a constant in our lives. In fact, because of the exponential increase in warfare and violence, peace has become a dream for all of humanity. Western countries have historically created a state of turmoil and unpeacefulness in the non-Western world through colonialism and in the postcolonial period through multiple "ghost wars."[18] The twentieth century is referred to as "a century of wars,"[19] and the twenty-first century is closer to realizing perpetual war rather than perpetual peace.

The proliferation of war in the twentieth century also produced the opposite effect of intense peace thinking, however. Peace writing has focused on how to control the spread of war and limit its destructive effect, as is evident in the four *Peace Studies* volumes.[20] After World War II, particularly during the Cold War, the threat of nuclear warfare alarmed peace thinkers and generated new scholarship for investigating the role of citizens in ending the Cold War crisis. In the United States, the Vietnam War became a turning point for citizens' involvement in ending the war.[21] Alternative approaches to peacebuilding in Europe and the United States in the second half of the twentieth century led to an impressive production of books and articles. On the one hand, this scholarship developed along the lines of conflict resolution and was linked empirically to the study of war, even though it also pushed for a wider vision for understanding human experiences and reinforcing human development for positive peace. This approach, in turn, spawned research in related fields of labor and social issues, social justice, gender and minority rights, and so on, producing new scholarship on peace history.[22]

In Europe in 1964, Johan Galtung founded the International Peace Research Institute. Sweden and Germany opened their own peace and conflict-resolution programs, and many more followed in Europe. Today, every university in Europe and the United Kingdom has a peace research institute. Beyond the programmatic mainstreaming of peace studies in European universities, the International Peace Research Institute launched the *Journal of Peace Research* in 1964.

For the past fifty-five years, this journal has produced scholarship on a range of topics related to negative and positive peace and has developed niche themes such as liberal peace and democratic peace, environmental change and conflict, military spending, nonviolence, and human rights.[23] One of the important debates in this journal was on democratic peace. Some favored the expansion of democracy in nondemocratic countries for the foundation of liberal peace, whereas others criticized this position as "elite" and "territorial," calling it "capitalist peace." These debates notwithstanding, the journal has continued to encourage methodological approaches and interdisciplinary studies for developing new thinking on peace research and peacebuilding. The journal currently focuses on nonviolence and international mediation to solve both human and environmental conflicts.

In the United States, a pioneering effort for peace study and research was undertaken at the University of Michigan's Center for Research on Conflict Resolution, led by Kenneth Boulding, Elise Boulding, and David Singer, among others. The 1970s witnessed a growth in peace research in several new centers across university campuses. The Consortium of Peace Research, Education, and Development was founded in Boulder, Colorado, in 1970; the International Peace Academy in New York was inaugurated in 1973; and the Kroc Institute for International Peace Studies at Notre Dame University was established in 1986. The US government, too, became involved in peace studies with the founding of the United States Institute of Peace in 1984.[24] At Arizona State University, the Center for the Study of Religion and Conflict was founded in 2003, and in 2010 the Hardt-Nickachos Endowed Chair in Peace Studies was inaugurated within the center. Today, more than a dozen university centers and programs and many private think tanks work on peace issues in the United States. Even the newly established centers and institutes of peace study and peace research in Asia and Africa have adopted the Western model. Peace studies have developed along three vectors: peace education, peacebuilding and conflict resolution, and peace research. At the Arizona State University Center for the Study of Religion and Conflict, we combine the three main paths to peace study with an emphasis on innovative peace research.

Imagining and producing knowledge on peace to make the world a safer place without war are the common goals of academic and private efforts. How do we get there? Galtung approached the issue by dividing violence into two categories: personal and structural, with the corresponding concepts of negative peace and positive peace. In building the idea of positive peace, he probed the underlying social and political issues that produce structural violence and offered a rethinking of peace by addressing concerns of justice and equity. Opposing the US Department of Defense–funded Project Camelot, designed to "predict and influence political aspects of social change in underdeveloped nations,"[25] which he viewed as "scientific colonialism," Galtung suggested that for real change to take place, human development should be the priority for national and international policies.[26] He and others called for a reduction in the arms race and disarmament as a significant step toward improving international relationships. Most prominently in the United States, the scholars involved in the Institute of World Order—Harold Lastwell at Yale University, Greenville Clark and Louis Sohn at Harvard, Richard Falk at Princeton, and Saul Mendlovitz at Rutgers, among others— have pressed forward along this line of peace research.

Institute of World Order scholars have covered a wide area of work and actors involved in political and community peace processes, human and social rights, peacekeeping, and ecological and environmental stability. They suggest the need to alter international institutions such as the United Nations and call for a new "coherent management" that views the world in its global dimensions for treating the problems in the current system of nation-states. An alternative world organization that addresses issues of worldwide disarmament and carries out certain other global tasks based on "world-order values," the Institute of World Order emphasizes, is the way forward for coherent management. The group has produced a wide variety of written works on possible alternative futures, participation and change, and peace education. Although the World Order scholars have broadened the scope of peace studies, they have not advanced the concept beyond what Galtung formulated as positive peace.

Outside the United States, many scholars and writers have accounted for new ways of peace thinking from different sites of literature and the study of social movements. Paulo Freire in Brazil (1921–97), the Frantz Fanon in Algeria (1925–61), Rajni Kothari in India (1928–2015), and many more grassroots activists and thinkers exposed the disempowerment of people during Western colonial rule and its continuation under oppressive postcolonial governments; they demanded fairer and more transparent politics and policies for improving the condition of the common person. Their pro-people approach, built on the concept of positive peace, conceptualized long-term and sustainable peace involving national and international actors and policies.

Peace, however, is not merely ending violence and creating conditions for social justice. It must take into consideration emotions and attitudes that are not measurable but that give shape to a moral awareness, enabling humans to reach beyond the boundaries of their community and to respond to the needs of the other.[27] Values that cultivate fellow feeling and humanitarian ethics drawn from different cultures and communities can have far-reaching outcomes for human development. Ethical thought that includes the concept of human life and its potentials are important for peace. In addition, understanding different cultural and political positions is vital to making the peace project work on the ground.

For developing multidimensional and inclusive approaches, cosmopolitanism and global citizenship form a current scholarly perspective on peace. Kwame Anthony Appiah, Akeel Bilgrami, Bhikhu Parekh, Michael Ignetieff, and Homi Bhaba, to name a few scholars, promote encounters with others and engagement with differences in today's diverse world as essential for peace. A cosmopolitan attitude and a sense of responsibility toward others, they opine, allow for experiencing the world as a community of friends, not for seeing others as competitors and rivals. Critics of the cosmopolitan approach question who has the privilege to "know" the world in its borderless dimension. Elite, globetrotting travelers have the luxury of such exposure, whereas the majority of the world populace do not have this privilege, many argue. To be at home in the world, aware of the diversity of possibilities, cultures, traditions, and realities that real people face, is certainly a gateway for improved human engagement. But how can we encourage this way of thinking without reducing cosmopolitanism and global citizenship to a pleasurable or economic pursuit? The academy has the task of fostering awareness of global responsibilities and enabling reflexive openness. For this task, multidisciplinary studies are essential. Mainstreaming peace studies in the university curriculum can build awareness and make global citizenship a lived experience. Both conceptual knowledge and empirical research are essential for developing such a holistic view of peace.

Also crucial for increased understanding are people's everyday and ordinary ways of achieving peace, a kind of everyday cosmopolitanism. In place of a focus on external institutions and organizations that produce abstract policies, accounts of real people who create conditions for living peacefully open space for trusting the moral caliber of ordinary people. Such accounts help overcome the top-down approach and erase the division of peace into West and non-West, stable and unstable, liberal and illiberal. This approach also negates the strategy of using force and instead highlights more refined non-violent methods for advancing peace. Oliver Richmond suggests that to "move beyond the installation of a hegemonic peace, and move towards an everyday notion of peace sensitized to the local as well as [to] the state, regional and global[,] . . . resting upon a just social order," is necessary for emancipation from received notions that no longer serve the purpose of peace in modern times.[28] David Roberts refers to Richmond's approach as "fourth-generation" scholarship in peace studies. Fourth-generation scholarship "advances concepts including greater emancipation from structural violence, indigenous autonomy in determining peacebuilding priorities and the idea of the 'everyday' as a focal point for 'post-Liberal' or fourth generation peacebuilding."[29]

Building on the idea of recognizing people's ownership of peace, the contributors to this volume probe ways people generate peace in their everyday lives. We recognize that the peace people live and create is not without problems and tensions. We investigate these tensions along with the tactics, strategies, and ethical values people use to overcome conflict and to create conditions for peaceful living. Our approach may resonate with "popular peace," which Roberts describes as "the outcome of hearing, centering and responding to everyday needs enunciated locally as part of the peacebuilding process . . . enabled by global actors with congruent interests in stable peace."[30] People's peace, as we understand it, is also different. It assumes the primacy of people's ownership of the peace process, but it also recognizes that solving issues alone does not bind and limit that process. History, religion, social culture, and lived experiences play important roles in shaping an ethics for fostering human responsibility and changing people's attitude from a fixation on war to a search for actions for expressing ethics. This kind of peace is neither vague nor loosely defined, although it is fluid, varied, and constantly in motion. Neither static nor final, it is not an end product, like a closing, an absolute and total thing. There is no end of peace, and it is not a value in itself existing outside the fluctuations of human life.[31] We interpret people's peace as a way of living in a nonviolent way and in amity and trust with others.

Because we emphasize the living dimensions of people's peace, we are also aware that conflict, war, and violence can easily disrupt peace in a community. In today's world, war and violence have a longer life span than peace. At the same time, we also observe that people's ethics and capacity to live in harmony with others can give rise to a moral vision that becomes an everyday activity. This potential allows for re-creating peace after the disruption from violence. Imbued with a kinetic energy, people's peace repeatedly offers the possibility of regeneration and new emergence. Such peace is by its nature heterogeneous, rejecting the view that one way of being peaceful works for everyone. There is no single, universal approach:

different people's and different perspectives' context-specific needs produce the ethical awareness to work for peace. People are the actors, architects, and partners in peacemaking in their own communities. The awareness of problems and the ability to solve them peacefully become the foundation of a political humanity in which positive human relationship nurtures peaceful living with neighbors and strangers. People's peace makes possible the realization of a human life for achieving the potentials of our humanity.

Organization of the Book

This volume brings together twelve essays in the many voices of people together forging a broad understanding of people's peace. The volume covers a wide range of cases from around the world, highlighting local, social, and cultural practices authored by everyday people who strive to maintain harmony with others and create an unself-conscious environment of peace. Such peace is not an event but a process that survives beyond and despite war and violence. For investigating and explaining on-the-ground workings of such a concept, the essays take a humanities approach and highlight the role of the humanities in advancing peace studies.

The twelve essays are divided into two parts. Part one comprises essays on religious and philosophical interpretations and applications of people's peace; part two is composed of case studies from diverse times and places. The book covers a broad chronology and multiple global sites, from ancient Israel, sixteenth-century Spain, and nineteenth-century United States to contemporary Indonesia, India, Pakistan, Philippines, Bosnia, El Salvador, Egypt, Israel/Palestine, and the United States.

In the twenty-first century, when people have become spectators to tumultuous wars and conflict, everyday encounters and interactions, too, have been reshaped. Fear, distrust, even hatred of others are naturalized. But the fact is that the majority of people do not participate in the theater of war; they resist the confrontational approach and continue to respect and dignify those who are different from themselves. They strive to achieve harmony, seek justice for those who are oppressed and suffering, and find value in their cultural practices of living in communities with diverse others. The twelve essays show this lived aspect of people's lives. They show that people have a common understanding of peace as a right and cultivate this consciousness through the moral values of harmony, justice, respect, and dignity. This "ground-up" view of peace shows the importance of solidarity and alliances in everyday activities as well as in organizational networks. Solidarity and peace between people are often difficult because international politics and the rigid boundaries set up between nation-states undermine people-to-people interaction, so that the consciousness of people's peace remains confined within the boundaries of one's own community. Nonetheless, people's ability to transform their violent external world into something peaceful internally is a remarkable achievement, as the essays show.

Understanding people's efforts to make peace in their communities requires multidisciplinary studies, as represented in this volume. The historical essays help us understand how and why we have a global crisis of peace in local, national, and international arenas; the anthropological and ethnographic methods adopted in several essays dig deep into human experiences and meanings in the struggle for peace; and the theological and philosophical essays search for human understanding of peace and examine religious values for peace. Putting these approaches and methods in dialogue with each other produces a theoretical intervention that shifts the study of peace from official organizations and institutions to people's lives and lived culture. It also offers a multidisciplinary methodology to study peace as a contesting vision with a range of possibilities created by human activities.

Each chapter provides an important instance of people's peace, where individuals defy authority or overcome cultural stigmas to assert the value of both peaceful relations with others and their own personal dignity. Ordinary people do not wait for the authorities to issue prescriptions; rather, they have always attempted to "work things out" with their neighbors. They succeed at times; at other times, they fail, and people's peace is undone, as is seen in the essay on Assam, India. Yet the search for people's peace continues even in conflict. As the various chapters show, people look for peace and make peace, and each chapter provides a means for studying and interpreting the diverse expressions of a people's peace and for understanding how people speak back to power that limits and denies community and agency.

The chapters demonstrate the plurality of the notion of people's peace. Whether we investigate how ancient Jews strove to achieve communal justice or how black and white citizens in Ferguson, Missouri, and Muslims and Jews in Israel and Palestine are working to achieve racial and ethnic harmony, we find that people's peace is not a fixed concept practiced in a static place. Rather, it is a constantly unfolding, continuous process of refinding harmony and balance. Understanding diverse structures of power, divisive politics, and disequilibrium is significant both for unmasking the ways power erases and hides peaceful practices and yearnings as well as for finding avenues for disrupting power and fostering spaces of peace. The challenges to people's peace are in particular evident where nationalism and religion combine to divide rather than unite people, as the case in Assam, India, reveals.

Part one, "Religion in Action," opens with Lisa Sowle Cahill's essay "Inspiring Peace: Religious Peacebuilding from Local to Global." Cahill shows what religious groups and individuals can accomplish toward ending conflict and establishing peace. The relation between peacebuilding activities and religious identity moves in two directions: a certain kind of religious identity gives birth to practices that favor peace, but engagement in peacebuilding activities also enlarges and enriches the human experience of the divine. The peacebuilders she discusses share how interreligious work for peace deepens and expands their sense of God. Human relationship is the cornerstone for improving spiritual conviction, she concludes.

David Cortright's chapter "The Power of Peace: The Moral and Political Advantages of Nonviolence" engages a more worldly concern for social justice and peace. Tracing the religious roots and political implications of nonviolent action, he examines how the core concepts of Gandhian nonviolence evolved into an effective strategy used widely around the world today as a means of achieving social change. He examines the religious and philosophical principles of nonviolence as well as the practical benefits of nonviolent action as a means of overcoming injustice and oppression. He argues that nonviolence is not only the right choice morally but also the most effective action politically, more likely than the use of military force to achieve justice, to fight against repression and dictatorship, and to produce democracy and an open society. When a resistance movement picks up arms, its chances of success diminish, he argues. He cites the tragedy of the Syrian revolution for understanding the power of nonviolent resistance to advance justice and peace.

Donald L. Fixico's chapter "The Spiritual Balance of Peace in the Red Stick War, 1813–1814," probes the quest for spiritual balance in Indigenous tribes. Fixico argues that this awareness begins with self-discovery because our identity, although it may be individual, is intimately connected to our relatives. In the Indigenous world, the understanding of relationships with other people and nonhumans allows for achieving balance. This "spiritual peace" requires a relationship with all entities. In particular, he examines the peace narratives of one Indigenous tribe, the Mvskokes, and shows how those narratives both sustained and divided them during the Red Stick War against the United States in the early nineteenth century.

Taking this view of peace as people's struggle to strike balance within one's self and with others, Bruce B. Lawrence's essay "Exegeting Peace from Nagpur" examines the work of the Qur'anic Arabic Classes (QAC), in particular the work of Dr. Shahina Khatib, who mobilizes Muslim efforts for peaceful interaction with other faith-based communities. For Dr. Khatib, as for others in the QAC, the best resource for peace is faith-committed groups working together, who can then lead their communities on behalf of peace initiatives. Although the QAC's faith-based approach has not yet transformed into a public culture, its initiative aims to instill a shared vision that comes from multiple scriptural sources, with the Qur'an in translation as the guidepost for Muslim participants. The QAC's greater effort is to make the Qur'anic themes of peace understandable to non-Muslims in India.

Furthering the concept of religious perspectives on peace, Joel Gereboff examines in "Peace, Reconciliation, and Forgiveness: Early Rabbinic Stories and Their Implications for People's Peace," the relationship among notions of peace, reconciliation, and forgiveness as well as the varied understanding of these concepts in Judaic traditions. Drawing on early rabbinic sources, especially a number of stories in the Babylonian Talmud, Gereboff argues that these accounts point to structural and complex emotional factors that frequently occasion conflicts. Successful reconciliations must address these multiplicities of approaches. He combines a discussion of several rabbinic stories with information about forgiveness and reconciliation from ancient Greece and draws out the implications of these views, which come from cultural, social, and political worlds far different from Judaic origins. The cross-pollination of ideas, he suggests, can be useful for peace and conflict-resolution studies and for efforts at achieving reconciliation and peace.

In Chad Haines's chapter "Coming Together in Peace: Community and Informality in Cairo," we see the possibility of another kind of transcendence. Haines brings to light Muslim cultures of community formation and informal acts of resistance in light of the January 25 Revolution in Egypt in 2011. He argues that community is a form of coming together, moving beyond identitarian politics to organizing in a moment laden with political and ethical meaning. This Muslim imaginaire of community provides a basis for forging informal relationships and fostering dialogical encounters that make people's peace a living reality.

Freedom of religion and the related idea of religious toleration are broadly held today to be a human right. Stuart B. Schwartz's chapter "The Iberian Empires: Religious Tolerance in Intolerant Places and from Unexpected People" explores the ideas of freedom of religion and conscience as well as the related concepts of toleration (official policy) and tolerance (lived attitude) in the context of Spain and Portugal and their empires in the premodern period. This approach opens a new dimension of understanding European history beyond the familiar narrative and cast of characters—Erasmus, Spinoza, Hobbes, Locke, Bayle, Voltaire—all of whom are represented as advocates of social harmony and charity. The characters in Schwartz's narrative are common folk as well as theologians, philosophers, and judges. By concentrating on "tolerance," or attitudes of religious acceptance or indifference based on common folk's lived experience and hopes, Schwartz probes the popular reception of these expressions of tolerance. This is a new approach because few historians have considered the possibility that an attitude of tolerance was shared by the general population in this period or even may have been generated by them.

The chapters in part two, "People in Action," offer understanding of how religious and cultural power are used and expressed in action that give a certain legitimacy to lived ethics for framing people's peace. "'US out of El Salvador!' The Maryknoll Sisters and the Transnational Struggle for Human Rights" pushes a new boundary for understanding Christian foreign mission as a catalyst for human rights mobilizations. Over the second half of the twentieth century, religious organizations with missionary roots established a pivotal presence in transnational activist networks. Amanda Izzo recounts the experience of one such group, the Maryknoll Sisters of St. Dominic, in the complex history of religious participation in the global human rights movement. Her essay reexamines the US Roman Catholic religious order's mobilization of activist resources in the wake of an international incident in 1980 in which security forces in El Salvador executed two Maryknoll sisters and two fellow US Catholic missioners. The decades-long quest to hold the women's killers accountable provides a compelling case study in people's peacemaking, a process that radiated out from the community level of interpersonal relations to mass protest directed at the US government and then ultimately to engagement with international law.

The synergy between people and place creates new possibilities for people's peace in Jackie Smith's chapter "Human Rights City Initiatives as a People's Peace Process." Smith gives the term *agency* a new meaning in which a city becomes the agent of change and the collectivities of people actualize its possibility. She examines the work of residents of Pittsburgh (including herself) to advance human rights in that city, which became the fifth Human Rights City in the United States in 2011. She considers how the work of Human Rights Cities to advance "dignity and justice for all residents" serves as a model for building a people's peace that can reduce violence and foster justice in communities.

Linking divided borders and communities, the chapter "Is Ferguson the Same as Gaza? Diaspora Grassroots Activism and Intersectional Alliances" highlights how American Jewish Palestine-solidarity activists embody and practice a form of people's peace in various ways, connecting and threading together seemingly disparate sites of injustice and conflict zones: from Ferguson, Missouri, where racism against African Americans is pronounced, to Gaza, an embodiment of Palestinian resilience and resistance despite decades of Israeli occupation. First, as author Atalia Omer shows, these activists articulate their agenda in terms of peacebuilding, aspiring for a just peace in Palestine/Israel to redress past injustices and transform the logic that enables the Israeli occupation of Palestinians. Second, Jewish American critics of Israeli policies and Zionism constructively develop a post-Zionist religiosity that is deeply multivocal, challenging the Jewish establishment from below while also prefiguring a new paradigm for Jewish American collective identification. Third, Jewish–Palestinian solidarity often intersects with other justice issues, such as racism, homophobia, militarism, and neoliberalism. This chapter unpacks the proposition that Jewish American critics of Israeli policies and Zionism who partake actively in Palestine-solidarity work exemplify people's peace in being a part of a broader global Palestine-solidarity social movement that can also be explained as a grassroots social movement that aims to transform and redefine American Judaism. Finally, the chapter grapples with the limits of intersectionality analysis and conceptions of coresistance as peacebuilding mechanisms.

Leslie Dwyer takes us to another zone of contact and confrontation leading to reconciliation in her chapter "Peacemaking at the

Intersection of the Local and Global in Bali." This study explores themes of local peacemaking in the context of postgenocidal Bali, Indonesia, where multiple generations have worked, often in quite different ways, to address the legacies of mass violence in the 1960s. For a younger generation seeking to build bridges between the children and grandchildren of perpetrators and victims, languages of reconciliation, conflict transformation, and transitional justice have provided compelling frames for reworking histories of violence. An older generation, especially women who lived through the violence and now serve as family and community ritual experts, communicates with murdered ancestors through trance and ceremonial offerings, reimagining social relationships and the karmic nature of justice. At the same time, national and international organizations continue to press for the implementation of globalized transitional justice models, including fact-finding projects, state accountability, and a truth-and-reconciliation commission. Drawing on long-term ethnographic research in Indonesia, Dwyer explores the tensions and possibilities that emerge from this landscape, asking how a people's peace may be forged through and across entangled visions of social and political repair and showing how "local" peacemaking efforts are rarely bounded by local imaginations.

Yasmin Saikia's chapter "People's Peace at Stake: An Assamese Experience" probes the relationship between people's peace and the lived culture in Assam, India. How did a culture of people's peace become a site for people's violence based on religious politics? How can victim and perpetrator communities overcome their distrust and renew the commitment to people's peace? Through a historical investigation of culture, community, and politics, Saikia explores the success and failure of people's peace in the region. From the perspective of the Assamese culture, people's peace is underscored by the spirit of coexistence, enabled by the river Brahmaputra, which promotes *xamonnoy* (a union of people and ecology) and produces *xanmiholi* (a blended culture). Today, however, this peace is contested by exclusivist and divisive religious politics. As a culture, people's peace along the riverbanks expands and includes new communities and is always in the making. But the rise of a new religious politics excludes some people from the realm of peace. Saikia concludes that because this politics of exclusion is bound to a political chronology, there is hope that it will be limited and temporary and that the process of people's peace will be renewed.

Overall, the twelve chapters show how ordinary people come together to generate peaceful relations in ordinary and extraordinary times of tension. They relate historical and contemporary incidents wherein people resisted and are resisting the impulse to hate others of different religions, races, nationalities, and so on, even while their governments wage wars with those others. These collected chapters open up a range of fields for studying and mapping humane actions along four broad approaches.

First, the chapters focus on the theme of direct action by many individuals and groups struggling for peace and social justice around the world. Direct action is often a mode of confronting representatives, forms, and structures of power with intention and demanding social transformation. It is not always confrontational, though. Drawing upon the values of ethical engagement, direct action as an expression of people's peace takes the form of nonviolence (Cortright), awareness-raising campaigns (Smith and Saikia), and transnational social movement networks (Omer). Cahill provides conceptual insights into the power of Christian ideas in informing peace activism in Bosnia-Herzegovina and the Philippines. Izzo shows the powerful work of Christian nuns working for justice for the violated and the vulnerable.

Second, the chapters show people's peace as a form of praxis—intentional acts of fostering and creating new kinds of community or disrupting normative modes and structures of power or both. Such acts are not necessarily directed against existing systems of violence, oppression, marginalization, and inequality but rather are directed toward creating alternative ways of being in the world. People's peace praxis draws upon a variety of inspirations, including religious values, in building peaceful and just communities. This is evident in Lawrence's chapter, which provides an example from India of Islamic values and practices creating new kinds of social interactions. Similarly, Gereboff draws attention to the Jewish values of people's peace praxis, reflecting on how medieval texts can be read in today's world. From Indonesia, Dwyer provides examples of how survivors of the brutal anti-Communist pogroms of the 1960s and 1970s employ values of compassion to protect the environment. Omer and Smith show how people cross the boundaries of their groups to forge new relationships and express the power of intersectionality for broadening the benefits of community rights.

Third, the chapters demonstrate concern for the recognition of everyday men and women, who are usually overlooked as important actors in the narrative of achieving local peace. We see this concern particularly in Omer, Lawrence, and Izzo's chapters, in which women are salient in forging peace in their communities. Schwartz's chapter, though, looks at how men who were marked as subordinates in the high politics of peace disturbed the status quo of the existing system by articulating a different narrative and showing the human capacity for ethical relationships.

Fourth, these chapters raise an often overlooked topic in studies of peace—the lived, everyday acts of people in negotiating difference and grappling with social inequalities, even while going about their daily routines. These acts are usually undertaken without an intention of deep impact but have resounding effects in transforming the world. Here are the silent acts of care, compassion, brotherliness, neighborliness, hospitality, and giving that make up the vast majority of ways in which people actually live in the world. Saikia's chapter provides an example from Assam in northeastern India of the embedded culture of union sustaining "fellow feeling," which constitutes the historical and cultural fabric of the place but which is torn apart by the politics of hate and religious nationalism. People's peace is undone by the high actors of regional and national politics. Haines similarly analyzes the values and practices of everyday community in Muslim society, with a focus on Egypt, while Fixico draws our attention, significantly, to the spiritual values of interconnectedness found in Indigenous belief systems of North America. Schwartz provides a historical example of everyday people's peace from the Iberian Peninsula, where many, despite persecution, latched on to values of diversity.

Because of extremely limited scholarly engagement with the agency of ordinary people in creating and maintaining peace, the view of people's peace that we offer is an invitation to find new ways for thinking about peace and a celebration of everyday people who claim peace to transform their own communities. Knowing and learning about people's peace from a variety of locations and cultures speak of the same human desire: peace is our hope and must be our future as a human community.

PART ONE

Religion in Action

1

Inspiring Peace

Religious Peacebuilding from Local to Global

LISA SOWLE CAHILL

Introduction: Religion, Theology, and Peacebuilding

I am a Christian theologian—an academic, not an activist.[1] As a theological ethicist, I have written about violence and the Bible, just-war theory, pacifism, and peacebuilding. This work has given me the privilege to reflect with and learn from those who work directly in conflict situations and who tirelessly and courageously serve the cause of peace. I have witnessed some of their activities firsthand.[2] My specific religious touchstone in this essay is Christianity, not because I (or the peacebuilders I mention) believe that God approaches humanity only through this tradition, but because it is my own tradition and thus the tradition I can represent most credibly.

As the introduction to this volume points out, "people's peace" resides in the hopes, dreams, and visions of everyday, ordinary people and is part of their "lived experiences." The lived experiences, hopes, and visions of ordinary peacebuilders are more often than not nourished in religious communities and expressed in religious terms. To understand people's peace, therefore, it is important to enter empathetically into the religious dimensions that are basic to peacebuilders' identities and to their construals of the world and its possibilities.

Others may consider religion from the standpoint of the social sciences or show concretely what religious groups and individuals can accomplish toward ending conflict and establishing peace. My approach is somewhat different because it concerns the "insider" content of the religious experiences and ideals whose power inspires peacebuilders. The relation between peacebuilding activities and religious identity moves in two directions: a certain kind of religious identity naturally gives birth to practices that favor peace, but engagement in peacebuilding activities also enlarges and enriches the human experience of the divine. The peacebuilders I discuss share how interreligious work for peace deepens and expands their sense of God.

In many peacebuilders' view, action for peace and justice is a test of the authenticity and truth of their convictions about God. For religious peacebuilders, religious identity is inherently a social and political identity; an authentic experience of God carries with it a distinctive way of life in which that experience is communally embodied. Their God is a God of compassion, mercy, and reconciliation, who not only judges evil but also sustains healing, forgiveness, and the restoration of life. That way of life expands beyond the faith community in the form of interreligious alliances and demands for structural change.

In the words of the Salvadoran theologian of liberation Jon Sobrino, SJ, the "actual life" of Christians must bear witness to the fact that "Jesus was something unique, ultimate and radical." Today, states Sobrino, there are persons and structures—"political, economic, and military—that tyrannize and oppress." Yet believers in Latin America and elsewhere "have proclaimed the lordship of Christ through their deeds . . . not in a fundamentalist way, but in the real way, through truth and justice," risking imprisonment, torture, and murder.[3] Through these actions, they make Christ present in history. In other words, it is for religious and theological reasons, not only for pragmatic and political ones, that a successful peace process must be a "people's peace."

The specific focus of my reflections is Bosnia-Herzegovina, and Mindanao, the Philippines, both of which have experienced conflicts between Catholics and Muslims. Two Catholic peacebuilders who have worked in Sarajevo and Mindanao, respectively, and whom I have met personally put a human face on the challenge of interreligious peacebuilding. The first is Father Ivo Markovic, a Croatian Franciscan priest working in Sarajevo. During the sectarian conflict that followed the breakup of the former Yugoslavia in 1992, Father Ivo reached out across divisions among Croats (Catholic), Serbs (Orthodox Christian), and Bosniaks (Muslim), often at great personal risk. He formed the interreligious chorale Pontanima after the Dayton Peace Accords of 1995, which brings together Muslims and Christians to perform religious songs and prayer from both traditions and now gives more than thirty concerts a year.[4]

The second peacebuilder is Myla Leguro, who works for Catholic Relief Services (CRS) in Mindanao. Committed to peacebuilding work since she was a teenager, she founded the Mindanao Peacebuilding Institute in 2000, which annually brings together grassroots leaders to engage in and spread peace training and education. The institute also conducts ongoing community-building activities.[5]

Speaking of her work with CRS, Leguro stresses the importance of building bridges and fostering relationships, so that if conflict does arise, there will be a way to resolve it without resorting to violence. CRS is promoting peace education in the schools and madrassas as well as in the public media, starting with small peacebuilding activities as "catalysts" for larger ones. She reports that it has been especially hard to engage the military in such processes, but in 2005 CRS invited a military officer to a peace-training program, which he attended and then became an advocate for the peace process within the military structure. Another focus of CRS is to make sure that "village-level development plans account for the concerns of the most vulnerable groups in the community, which often include Muslims, indigenous people, women, and youth."[6]

Father Ivo is living in the midst of a long-standing conflict that, although now supposedly resolved, has left a legacy of stereotyping, competition, and resentment. In my opinion, this legacy is especially evident in the way some of the Catholic Croats still talk about coexistence with their Bosniak Muslim neighbors. The Franciscan order of priests in the region has a long record of trying to foster better relations; however, the Croatian Catholic Church will not permit Ivo's chorale, the Pontanima—with both Muslim and Christian members, singing pieces from both traditions—to perform in any of its churches. Other members on the board for the journal *Concilium* and I heard this wonderful group sing in a Catholic church in Sarajevo. According to Father Ivo, the Catholic clergy who attack Pontanima are "more nationalistic than religious: God ha[s] been removed from their faith and replaced with the Nation."[7]

Nevertheless, Pontanima demonstrates that one of the most profound sources of religious experience as well as of cross-cultural communication and human unity is art. Father Ivo states, "Christianity doesn't destroy any religion or culture. . . . Through their artistic expressions especially, we discover other religions as something beyond our prejudices, and other religions' experiences not as alien phenomena, but as occasions we can embrace because we find a trace of God's grace in them."[8] Leguro's and Ivo's stories illuminate six religious and theological premises or themes that shed light on the broader challenges of peacebuilding, whether taken up under religious auspices or not:

1. Ideals of *peace*, compassion, and reconciliation are at the heart of the human experience of God.

2. Human beings are united at a basic level by their divine source, by the similar needs and aspirations they share, and in mutual responsibility for one another. Christians, Jews, and Muslims express this unity by saying that human beings are created in the *image of God*; the same idea is expressed in saying that we all are God's children or that we all are one human family.

3. Religion and theology identify the realities of human-caused evil as *sin*. It includes violence perpetrated in the name of religion.

4. *Eschatology*—typically a Christian term that means "the last things"—is popularly thought of as the end of the world and the beginning of eternal life. Eschatology is here interpreted to mean the actual effects of God's reign in human history.

5. Committed collective action is a source of *hope* for historical change.

6. The reality of *suffering* threatens human and religious meaning and drives the quest for peace, yet suffering is also an inevitable part of committed and successful peacebuilding.

Before exploring these ideas further, I want to emphasize two important preliminary points. First, we cannot begin to talk about religious ideals of peace without first confronting the all-too-pervasive reality of violence perpetrated by religious people, even in the name of religion. Just as any genuine and lasting peace must engage the people and be sustained by broad-based popular "buy-in" and benefits, similar social formations can also be effective sustainers of violence. This may be especially true of ethnic and class conflict that is promoted with religious rhetoric.

The director of the Kroc Institute, Scott Appleby (a Catholic social scientist and peacebuilding theorist), aptly titled a widely noted book *The Ambivalence of the Sacred*. Appleby sees religion as deeply and inherently ambivalent toward violence; thus, the role of religious peacebuilders is to magnify and implement the peaceful over the violent manifestations of religion: "*Religious violence* occurs when extremist leaders, in reaction to perceived injustices in the structural environment of the society, successfully employ religious arguments designed to mobilize religious (or ethnoreligious) actors to retaliate against their enemies." They "fuse ethnic, nationalist, and religious grievances in order to justify retaliatory violence." But the very ambivalence of religion provides an openness to tolerance. Religions "are strikingly accomplished in developing their own traditions of peace-related practices and concepts," which are to be celebrated and empowered, according to Appleby.[9]

A question here is whether religion is as naturally inclined to violence as it is to peace. I would say that it is not, but it can easily be conscripted for that end. As the American Protestant theologian Reinhold Niebuhr so persuasively argues, a prevalent motivator of social evil is "collective egotism," by which individuals' self-interest is harnessed to a group's supposedly transcendent value, purposes, and mission, lending finite, relative, and even perverse goals a magnitude and absoluteness that they could never claim on their own.[10] Even if peace and violence are not equally inherent and valid meanings of religion, it is important to underline that religion is responsible for violence, not just for peace. Hence, to seek or embody a "people's peace" often requires undermining and overturning a religiously reinforced "people's violence" that gives reach and staying power to violent movements and structures.

The second and closely related preliminary point is that peacebuilding involves much more than identifying and transmitting "ideals." Ideas and ideals, whether violent or peaceable, are always embedded in practices, validate those practices, and are validated by them. Again to cite Jon Sobrino, orthodoxy (right belief) always has to be tested by orthopraxis (right action) and by the justice of the larger social practices and institutions that shape and control behavior.[11] As a theologian from the Philippines says, reflecting on the Mindanao situation, "The way to justice and reconciliation lies beyond conciliatory 'talk' and dialogue. It involves . . . a work of everyday cultural practice and even primary socialization from childhood. . . . [C]onflicts are not mere interpersonal skirmishes; they are deeply-embedded structural asymmetries."[12]

A major practical and strategic question for religious peacebuilders is whether a conflict-torn society has within itself relatively strong and preexisting religious and cultural institutions, other institutions of civil society, democratic traditions, and at least an embryonic peace movement. This was the case in Northern Ireland, for example. However, in Rwanda all the political, cultural, and religious institutions were marked by the country's colonial history. Religious institutions lacked courageous and independent top-level leadership, and religious illiteracy was high among the people. In the former and probably rare case, as in Northern Ireland, peacebuilding proceeds in what Appleby (following the Mennonite John Paul Lederach[13]) calls a "saturation" mode: peacebuilders gather strength and multiply from within. In the latter and most cases, however, as in Rwanda, an interventionist or "elicitive" mode is required: external religious actors, usually at the invitation of parties to the conflict, initiate the peacebuilding process, with the goal of eventually "saturating" the society with a peacebuilding momentum from within.[14] This differentiation of strategies highlights the crucial point: practices of peace have to move from ideals to reality and must take hold broadly at the practical level in order to have long-term traction with "the people" throughout a society.

This is an opportune time to flag another closely related aspect of "people's peace": it needs multilayered and intersecting practices, initiatives, and infrastructures that connect grassroots efforts to midlevel actors; to key leaders of governments or competing groups or both; and even to international governmental, economic, and religious institutions and leadership. Successful peacebuilding needs the people and may be inspired by the people. But intransigent conflicts are virtually always fed and exploited by larger forces that benefit from them in some way. A more comprehensive effort is needed to protect and expand the "people's peace." As Lederach frequently comments, an unmatched asset of the Roman Catholic Church is that it has authority, representation, and participation at multiple local, regional, and global levels. In his view, it is often the midrange leaders who are the best positioned to lead long-term peace efforts, even though it is also true that "the people" are the ones who must ultimately believe in and practice peace if peace is to take hold as a stable social reality.

Grassroots leadership is usually pressured by survival needs and "operates in a reactive mode, on a day-to-day basis."[15] Meanwhile, top-level religious and government leaders are further removed from the suffering caused by conflict and are frequently more concerned with maintaining stability and preserving their own power, particularly after the agreements that will end conflict. Midrange religious leaders participate in networks connected to conflict settings, may be able to communicate with leaders in civil society and government at their own level, and also have access to higher-level religious leaders and other key players in business, government, and cultural organizations. At the broadest level, international agreements, United Nations resolutions, world economic institutions, and transnational nongovernmental organizations are all necessary to sustain peace. But without "people's peace" and the midrange people and institutions that extend and consolidate it, no number of treaties or accords on paper will actually transform conflict into cooperative social life.

Religious Convictions behind Peacebuilding

As noted earlier, the six religious premises of peacebuilding are *peace, image of God, sin, eschatology, hope,* and *suffering.* These terms indicate something about the basic experience of God that drives peacebuilding. Each term may also be interpreted theologically; it constitutes a point of theological understanding of religiously inspired peace. Among the six, *eschatology* is the most explicitly theological term rather than one that most believers would readily use to describe their religious experience.

Peace

Peace, love, compassion, forgiveness, and mercy—virtually every religious believer in the mainstream of every religious tradition would claim these ideals to be central. Examples from Christianity are readily visible and well known. Key among them is the "double-love command" found in all four Gospels as well as in the Hebrew Bible (Christian Old Testament): "You shall love the Lord your God with all your heart and with all your soul and with all your mind . . . [and love] your neighbor as yourself" (Matt. 22:34–40; see also Mark 12:28–34, Luke 10:25–28, John 4:7–8 and 15:17, Deut. 6:5, and Lev. 19:18).

The so-called hard sayings in the Gospel of Matthew intensify this command: "Love your enemies and do good to those who persecute you, that you may be children of your Father in heaven" (Matt. 5: 44–45). The Gospels also give us the example of Jesus, whose ministry of the reign of God included outreach to sinners and outcasts and inclusive table fellowship. The parables of the Good Samaritan (Luke 10:25–36) and the Prodigal Son (Luke 15:11–32) as well as

Jesus's instruction to forgive one's brother "seventy times seven" (Matt. 18: 21–22) demonstrate what Christian love and peace look like in action.

Despite the biblical centrality of sayings and narratives commending love, forbearance, and reconciliation, it must be acknowledged that the Christian (and Jewish) scriptures also contain texts commending violence, including killing, war, and destruction in God's name (Exod. 20:3, 5; Deut. 20:1–18; Psalms 9:2, 6, and 21:9–10). It is difficult to argue that Jesus advocated or condoned violence against other persons (despite his overturning tables in the "cleansing" of the temple in Jerusalem [Mark 11:15–19, 11:27–33; Matt. 21:12–17, 21:23–27; Luke 19:45–48, 20:1–8; John 2:13–16]). Yet the last book in the New Testament, Revelation, is replete with violent images, promising a violent end for the enemies of God and of God's people (18:21).

Though this essay is not the place for an extended treatment of biblical hermeneutics, a brief discussion is in order. No interpretation of the Bible is a "pure" reading from the page or a simple communing with the mind of a biblical author, much less with the mind of a divine author considered to have inspired the Bible's contents. Any later reader of these ancient texts will necessarily bring his or her own existential screen to their meaning and will most likely not be reading them in the original biblical languages. Interpretation is therefore a process that involves locating a text in its particular biblical setting, considering how it is balanced with other biblical texts and narratives, relating it to the experience and culture of the reader and the reader's community, and situating it against various theological and doctrinal expressions of Christian faith that have evolved over time.

Biblical fundamentalism and literalism are really creations of the modern period, when scientific and empirical criteria of truth and validation inspired a desire for similar standards of clarity and irrefutability in other fields of knowledge. But the heart of the Christian tradition, since at least the Middle Ages, has recognized that the Bible is a complex narrative whose authors aimed to communicate perennial truths about God and humanity's relation to God rather than primarily to narrate a factual account of past historical details. Patristic and medieval authors incorporated a variety of strategies for interpreting the "true" meaning of biblical texts that seemed implausible or erroneous on moral or religious grounds. The four different categories of biblical meaning were the literal, the typological (connecting the Old and New Testaments), the moral, and the anagogical (looking ahead to future events).

Biblical interpretation seeks readings that cohere with the basic message of the Gospels and with "the rule of faith," while also challenging later cultures and empowering resistance to evil. From the perspective of a critical Christian biblical hermeneutics, biblical texts must be reinterpreted, given less priority, or even rejected as authoritative in light of one key criterion: the basic message of Jesus Christ. That message is love of God, love of neighbor, mercy, forgiveness, and inclusion of all in a new family of brothers and sisters in Christ (Gal. 3:26–29).

Importantly for peacebuilders, Christian love does not stop at the family of believers. Although the early Christian mission reached across religious and ethnic boundaries to embrace gentiles, Jesus himself saw his mission as primarily to Israel. Contemporary peacebuilders, however, envision God's love as all-inclusive (a view that official Catholic teaching has endorsed since the Second Vatican Council in 1962–65). Today, the ideals of inclusion, love, forgiveness, and peace are extended to all religions and ethnicities. As Myla Leguro has expressed, "I have come to realize that to concretize our faith . . . is to embrace Muslims and Indigenous people as our neighbor, as our brother and sister."[16] In a similar way, during the Bosnian war, Father Ivo "was grounded in his belief in the power of religion for 'purification, healing, awareness, and peace.'"[17]

Image of God

The expansive nature of Christian peacebuilding is supported by the idea that all human beings are created in the image of God, a view supported by the story of creation shared by Jews, Christians, and Muslims. According to the first creation story in Genesis, "God created man in his own image, in the image of God he created him; male and female he created them" (Gen. 1:26–27). To affirm humanity's creation in the image of God is to see all other persons and communities as having been given a dignity that reflects the divine. Creation in God's image also signifies that human beings have a sense of the moral and social commandments of God, known to all though reason or conscience (Rom. 2:5). The love command and the ideal of loving one's enemy appeal to the Christian's particular identity as a follower of Jesus Christ, but the image of God references fellow humanity and is an equally or more effective basis on which to build a common, tradition-spanning commitment to peace and justice.

What aspect of humanity reveals God's image? Although the theological tradition's answer has centered on unique human capacities such as reason and free will, biblical scholars have in recent decades turned to a more social and less-individualistic approach: God's image is found in human relationships.[18] The fundamental reality is that humans are created in multiples to be partners and helpers to one another. Even the sequential creation of the first human and that creature's "one flesh" partner and companion, narrated in the second creation story (Gen. 2:7, 18–23), is not satisfactory to God or complete until humanity is differentiated into woman and man. Humans are social from the first, made for relationships with God and with one another. Moreover, humans are set into a natural universe, whose potential is to be a beneficent environment that they together are called to protect and cultivate. An equally basic mandate is to cooperate in bringing forth future generations of human beings: families, kin groups, and political societies (Gen. 1:28).

Humanity's multiplicity, unity, and relationship disclose in a special way the presence of God, who remains "wholly other."[19] The image of God consists in relationship to God, as immediately entailing relationships to other creatures, especially relationships of shared responsibility with and for other humans and for creation as a whole. The essence of humanity's nature and vocation is relationship, a "kind of nurturing rule done on God's behalf."[20] The Hebrew Bible expresses the content of this rule in terms of covenant, obedience to God's commandments, and generosity toward the widow, the orphan, the poor, and stranger in the land, all of whom are owed justice and the fulfillment of basic needs (Exod. 22:22; Deut. 10:18, 24:14; Ezek. 22:29, among many other texts).

For contemporary peacebuilders, the premise of God's image in human beings implies the possibility of cutting through and across differences, of agreeing on what basic needs are, and of acknowledging the equality of all in relation to such needs, including stable and just social institutions that uphold cooperative life. Leguro and Markovic's work embodies this possibility as they reach across religious and ethnic boundaries, appealing to interreligious understanding and a common effort toward peace. The positive responses they elicit show that their trust can be matched by other partners in the peace process. The image of God in humanity means that humans are responsible for restoring and maintaining relationships of peace.

To do so requires some overarching or even "universal" moral truths and values, expressed cross-culturally, for example, in prohibitions against murder, rape, torture, lying, and theft. These values can be given positive expression and legal recognition by means of the "public" vocabulary of human rights, for example. The articulation of such values or rights and especially their inculturation in different societies and legal systems must be achieved through broad dialogue and consultation among a variety of thinkers, stakeholders, organizations, and movements.[21] There will probably never be a conclusive list of universal needs, values, or rights to which all cultures and religions agree without qualification. However, this does not invalidate the need for some global vision of basic justice, the possibility of achieving a working definition, or the ongoing efforts to do so, as validated by the biblical story of the creation of all in the image of God.

Sin

Sin is easy to define: it is the violation of all of the ideals of well-being and relationship captured by the ideals of peace, love, and forgiveness and by the vocation of humans to embody God's image in personal and social relations. For Christians (and others), sin is especially identified with the failure to help those most in need, as we see in the parable of judgment that concludes Matthew's Gospel. The first "judgment" concerns those whose love is blessed by God.

> Come, you that are blessed by my Father, inherit the kingdom that was prepared for you from the beginning of the world; for I was hungry and you gave me food, I was thirsty and you gave me something to drink, I was a stranger and you welcomed me, I was naked and you gave me clothing, I was sick and you took care of me, I was in prison and you visited me. (Matt. 25:34–36)

Those who, in contrast, have turned away the needy reject Christ himself: "Depart from me, you cursed, into the eternal fire prepared for the devil and his angels. For I was hungry and you gave me no food, I was thirsty and you gave me no drink" (Matt. 25:41).

If the nature of sin is so clear and the consequence so dire, then why does evil happen? This question could be given a sociobiological, psychological, or sociological answer, and approaches from the social sciences do shed valuable light on the dynamics that encourage violence and diminish the commitment to peace.[22] But for present purposes, we may consider two ways, positive and negative, in which theological ethicists account for the phenomenon of violence.

Sometimes violence is justified as the "lesser of two evils," thereby taking it out of the category of moral wrong or sin and placing it in the category of last resort or tragic necessity. Examples are self-defense, just war, armed peacekeeping, and humanitarian intervention. Some would say such defenses of violence already open the door to the rationalization of unjust and extreme violence, and this may be true. But at least the categories of justified violence assume a moral framework, which also provides the tools to hold ostensible justifications to account, to identify illegitimate justifications, and to restrain exercises of violent force.

Even more pervasive and dangerous, however, is simple aggression justified in moral terms, usually the transcendent value of one's own group and the unworthiness of others. Augustine described this drive as the *libido dominandi* (lust for rule or domination),[23] captured in more recent times by Reinhold Niebuhr as "collective egotism," described earlier.

A perfect and perfectly frightening example of this drive is Serbian Christoslavism, detailed by Atalia Omer and Jason Springs in *Religious Nationalism*. In the Balkans, groups that were actually quite similar magnified their differences in a murderous ethnoreligious, nationalist mythology, which was promoted especially by Serbian president Slobodan Milošević. This ideology revolves around a selective and exploitative interpretation of the fourteenth-century Battle of Kosovo, featuring the legendary Serbian prince Lazar. Lazar was killed in battle but resurrected in the national memory as one who accepted total defeat in exchange for God's promise that the Serbs would one day vanquish the Muslim adversaries and grant Serbs a glorious national future. Prince Lazar historically became a sort of Christ symbol used to justify murderous opposition to Muslims and the creation of a Serbian Zion.[24]

Here, as in virtually all religiously validated conflicts, much more than religious identity is at stake: the interdependence of material and political competition, long-standing practices forming group members in hatred and xenophobia, and the formation of religious identity in exclusive, violent, nationalistic terms. This is also certainly the case in Mindanao, where the marginalization of indigenous and Muslim peoples with respect to rights to ancestral land has driven conflict under ethnic-religious ideologies. What peacebuilders have to get at and counteract are long-entrenched practices and habits, not just erroneous ideas about what a text such as the Bible or the Qur'an really says.

The Christian doctrine of sin offers four more resources to understand such practices and the reform they require.

First, Christianity (unlike Judaism) portrays the human proclivity to evil with the religious symbol and theological concept of "original sin." Although this concept is sometimes criticized for offering an unduly pessimistic and guilt-producing view of human nature, its virtue is that it confronts the fact—all too evident from the frequency and intractable nature of violent conflict—that all human beings have selfish and destructive desires, desires that are all too easily manipulated and rationalized into direct violence. This reality must be realistically appreciated, and humility and self-criticism are essential when trying to transform conflict.

Second, to call something "sin" is to make a statement about a larger reality of good against which we are offending. To resort to violence for political ends is not just another ordinary tool of statecraft or just "the way things are." Violence can be judged a perversion of a higher or more original order that is more reflective of ultimate reality or "God."

Third, the word *sin* carries with it a judgment of a moral and religious nature. We are *responsible*. Violence is not only a perversion. It is one we are responsible to counteract; we *can* do so, and we are *blameworthy* if we do not.

Finally, sin is not only personal but also inheres in the practices in which we are immersed, taking the form of *structural sin*: evil is perpetuated by the institutions humans have created. Free agents have a hand in keeping sinful structures in existence and at full operational capacity. The notion of structural sin calls us to social and political action to make social structures and institutions more just, more inclusive, and less violent.

More specifically in the case of peacebuilding, a long-lasting peace requires far-reaching structural changes. These changes go beyond peace agreements and reconciliation processes directly related to the conflict. It is also necessary to ensure restorative justice in the form of legal and practical guarantees of just institutions and human security. Restorative justice includes retributive justice in the sense of sanctions for offenders, the end of any ethos of impunity, and a police force and courts that are trustworthy and fair.

Eschatology

This concept may seem difficult to grasp for those who are not Christians, not theologians, or not religious. The word *eschaton* (pl. *eschata*) means "the last thing" in Greek, the language of the New

Testament. Our historical reality will never completely reflect the ideal order, God's will, or the perfection of the original creation. Therefore, God will complete and transform the historical process at the end of time or through a special divine intervention.

But eschatology, going back to the New Testament and as manifest in Christian social ethics, also has a broader meaning that is historically relevant. Eschatology refers to the fact that God's grace, the transforming power of the divine reality, is already breaking into the present order of things. Biblical scholars refer to the fact that the kingdom or reign of God preached by Jesus (Mark 1:14) is already becoming a reality in his ministry. The kingdom of God is both "present" and "not yet," to come in the future and yet in a sense already "realized."

A speaker at the Mindanao Peacebuilding Institute's annual training program in 2014 rendered the concept of eschatology in very practical terms when she delivered an "impassioned message, each word of which resonated to the very core of those present": "What does it mean to desire to be a peacebuilder? Simply being here for the training will not change you or the world. You must know why you are here. You must cultivate a hope and a belief that it's true, you can be part of the change in this world."[25] The power of the in-breaking reign of God is also manifest in the courage of the Pontanima choir as they embody in their music a new reality into which they invite their audiences.

Hope

"*You must cultivate a hope*"—How is that done? Sometimes the Christian virtue of hope is portrayed as an unexpected gift of God, an interior transformation of the soul that springs up despite all exterior indications to the contrary. Yes, hope is a gift of grace, but it is not a magic interior change of heart. The gift of hope is mediated by solidaristic action to combat evil, from risky and courageous initiatives to stand up and be counted. This does not mean that it simply is a human creation, but that God is, in fact, present and at work within human compassion, commitment, and solidarity.

My friend Danny Pilario (a fellow member of the *Concilium* board) has talked about his experiences in Mindanao, where conflict is rooted in long-standing structural injustices. He observes that paralysis and hopelessness set in when conflict keeps endlessly perpetuating itself despite any number of high-level peace consultations, government programs, and public hearings. These top-down efforts are little more than window dressing, not actually mitigating the grievances that led to conflict in the first place. They do not affect the reality people are living. Replacing personal and social sin with mutual recognition and peace must start with the concrete realities people face on a daily basis.

One example of such a start is the creation of "zones of peace," usually small territorial spaces set apart by Muslims and Christians in a village—people who have had enough of the violence that has made ordinary life impossible. Villagers agree on rules for the peace zones, such as the prohibition of firearms, the establishment of curfews, and the prompt resolution of any disputes. According to Pilario, "the message of peace zones is quite simple: 'if both sides still want to keep fighting, then please don't do it here.'" Children are included in similar initiatives in schools, where Muslims and Christians learn together. For example, children who get into arguments or fights in the classroom are asked to sit at "peace tables" until they resolve their problems. In order that a "people's peace" may take effect, "the actual cultural struggle to bring down the 'invisible wall' of prejudice and animosity is played on the ground in people's everyday lives."[26] Women are often the most active grassroots peacemakers because they care about the necessary activities of daily life, especially about their children.

Suffering

A central and sacred image of Christianity is one of suffering: Christ on the Cross. However, even though Christian faith and theology are unanimous on the fact *that* we are saved by Christ's Cross, there is no one "official," orthodox, or dominant belief or theology about *how* we are saved by the Cross.[27] One prevalent traditional Cross-centered theology and piety, "penal substitution," sees Christ's death as his vicarious acceptance of the human penalty for sin. This theology has recently fallen into disfavor because it supposes an unforgiving God whose anger can be appeased only by the death of an innocent man. Relevant to the discussion of peace, this view also presents God as someone who wants, plans, and is pleased by violence and death.

Political and liberation theologies offer an increasingly well-accepted alternative interpretation: the Cross is God's solidarity with human suffering. God does not intend or cause suffering but enters into it (in the person of Christ, both human and divine) in order to transform and heal it. What redeems and saves is not suffering but love. However, love, peace, mercy, and reconciliation are often risky, especially in the case of violent conflict. Suffering is the risk the peacebuilder must take.

Just as Father Ivo illustrates that reaching out to adversaries brings hope, he shows just as clearly that doing so can be dangerous. By the time the Dayton Peace Agreement ended hostilities in the former Yugoslavia in 1995, almost ninety-six thousand people had been killed.

> Friar Ivo tried to stop the horrors by reaching out across religious and ethnic lines to Croats (generally Catholic), Serbs (generally Orthodox Christians), and Bosniaks (generally Muslims). These efforts often put his life at risk. Once, in the middle of battle, Friar Ivo insisted upon going into a Muslim village by crossing the Croat forces' line of fire. Threatened with being shot if he went any further, he nonetheless continued onward to speak to the imam on the other side. Eventually, they negotiated a meeting between the local commanders, who agreed to stop the fighting.[28]

Similar examples abound; here are a few from the Philippines. In 2011, an Italian missionary priest, Fausto Tentorio, was killed in Mindanao after living there for thirty-two years when the Philippine military accused him of being an agent of the New People's Army rebels. He had backed the Indigenous people in the fight to protect their ancestral lands from loggers, land developers, and mining corporations.[29] In 2012, similar accusations were made against two religious sisters, one of whom created Benedictines for Peace, giving local efforts greater visibility by connecting them to the reputation and moral authority of an international religious order. Both of the nuns had worked for the defense of the natural environment and had called for the withdrawal of military forces.[30] A larger, social dimension of the riskiness of peacebuilding is its political fragility. For example, the peace agreements reached in Mindanao in 2014 were violated within one year when Muslim rebels—who were to disarm as part of the agreement—killed forty-four police commandos engaged in an antiterror raid. Nevertheless, CRS and the Mindanao Peacebuilding Institute continue their work with as much commitment as ever. Along with Leguro and Ivo, they accept that "the price of peace is to offer one's life."[31]

Conclusion

Three threads in the religious aspects of a "people's peace" may be highlighted here in conclusion. First, there is the definition of peace. For religious actors, peace must be holistic and inclusive; it must be a peace with justice, not merely an enforced social order that simply conceals ongoing exclusions and aggressions. Just as importantly, religious activists—who are the majority—regard the possibility of a just and inclusive peace as having a transcendent basis and sustaining power that lie outside the methods of the social sciences.

Second, although this understanding of peace is hardly new, a further aspect illumined by religious and theological categories deserves emphasis: the pervasiveness and attraction of practices and ideologies of violence, also belonging to the politics and religion of "the people." The vocabulary of personal and social sin is extremely useful in identifying the intransigent nature of conflict. A successful people's peace must involve widespread social practices that provide opportunities and incentives to turn away from violence because defeating it will not be easy.

Third, in order to accomplish broad social transformation, practitioners of a people's peace must work with the masterminds and executives of conflict because these leaders have constituencies among "the people" who are in some way benefitting from the status quo. Though peacebuilding may begin with commitment and action by local communities, the "people's peace" must be multilayered—elite, midlevel, and grassroots. For example, Father Ivo directly challenged both military leaders and obstructionist members of the Roman Catholic hierarchy. Leguro has made efforts to include military leaders who can relay the peace message upward on the social spectrum.

Yet, despite these efforts and their real success throughout society, the long-term prospects of peace require constant investment and renewal. Causes of conflict are difficult to eradicate, and they often grow into new sources of tension and bloodshed. Mindanao continues to be an unsettled region. Reaching for the roots of violence between the government and Moro rebels, Catholic Relief Services and its partners have implemented a project to alleviate land conflict, adapting local solutions to actual circumstances in communities. A basic issue is that when the postcolonial government resettled Christian populations to Mindanao, it displaced Muslim residents and Indigenous peoples and opened the door to commercial interests. Moreover, traditional systems of collective land ownership clash with Western models of individual property rights. A report coauthored by Leguro shows that civil society and a grassroots, ground-up approach to local land policy have the potential to resolve seemingly intractable land disputes and to give lasting peace a chance.[32] Traditional and religious leaders can act as mediators. The project builds long-term relationships through healing individual trauma, improving understanding within identity groups, and building bridges of trust among identity groups.

Bosnia-Herzegovina has seen a backsliding of relationships since the peace accords that followed the conflicts of the 1990s.[33] Today there is even less interfaith understanding than before those conflicts, a lack of faith that is embodied in the new segregation of classrooms and curricula for Muslim, Catholic, and Orthodox students. No national reconciliation or trust-building process was ever implemented. The present social reality, abetted by social inequality and threats to women's rights, is one in which the threat of new outbreaks of violence is real. Thus, interfaith dialogue among young people and joint projects by youth of different faiths have a tremendous role to play in increasing and consolidating peace. In a Youth for Peace project sponsored by Care International, young people from Srebrenica held a series of interfaith meetings and events, including Muslim–Serbian religious dialogues, a concert by Pontanima, talks by prominent Bosnian theologians from different faith traditions, and trips to different religious spaces. "The potential of such small steps should not be missed," for their effect on the citizens and leaders of tomorrow has been "genuinely transformative," according to Gorazd Andrejc.[34]

Despite inevitable setbacks, the people's ideal of peace can transform the reality of conflict. As Leguro reminds us, "Peacebuilding can be a decades-long process. You have to appreciate small victories, cultivate the aptitude for creating relationships, and have the commitment to stay in it for the long haul."[35] Hope is nurtured by solidarity, accompaniment, action, and faith in divine presence in human history. The "people's peace" is embodied in the ordinary heroism and the extraordinary power of small steps taken and "small victories" celebrated in the gradual forging of a trust that turns adversaries into neighbors.

2

The Power of Peace

The Moral and Political Advantages of Nonviolence

DAVID CORTRIGHT

The religious roots and political implications of nonviolent action are reflected in the writings and practices of Mahatma Gandhi, Martin Luther King Jr., Barbara Deming, and other advocates for social justice and peace. Some of the core concepts of Gandhian nonviolence and its evolution over the decades can be traced as an effective strategy used widely around the world today to achieve social change. Nonviolent action not only involves religious and philosophical principles but also has practical benefits as a means of overcoming injustice and oppression. Nonviolence is thus both the right choice morally and the most effective action politically. Nonviolent methods are more likely than the use of military force to achieve justice, to fight against repression and dictatorship, and to produce democracy and an open society. When a resistance movement picks up arms, its chances of success diminish. The arguments and evidence in support of these propositions have implications for the tragedy of the Syrian revolution and for understanding the power of nonviolent resistance to advance justice and peace.

Gandhi's Truths

Gandhi's philosophy and method of nonviolent action as well as his ideas and actions have had worldwide influence. New social science evidence confirms his belief that nonviolent action is the most potent means of struggling for justice. Gandhi was not a theorist. He was quintessentially a man of action. "My message is my life," he often said. He wrote more than a hundred volumes in total, but his strongest statements came through the actions he undertook personally and in the actions of the millions he inspired and organized. Many extol Gandhi's greatness, but few grasp the deeper meaning and revolutionary significance of his nonviolent philosophy and method. Gandhi's thinking was deeply radical and sought to transform the root structures of social, economic, and political oppression. He overturned outdated hierarchies and shattered outmoded assumptions. He altered our way of being and doing in the world.

Gandhi's core message was nonviolence, *ahimsa*, the refusal to injure another. He was deeply influenced by the Hindu and Jain religious traditions in the Gujarat region of western India, where he was raised. The Jains believe that the way to fulfillment and meaning in life is through the renunciation of earthly wants and desires and the commitment to avoid harm to others. Selflessness, asceticism, and nonviolence are the hallmarks of the Jain philosophy and way of life, based on practices of vegetarianism and pacifism. *Ahimsa* is the principle of protecting life and avoiding harm to other living things. As interpreted by Gandhi, *ahimsa* is not a passive concept but includes an active commitment to uphold and protect the right to life of all other living beings. It is better to suffer injury personally than to impose suffering on others, he believed. He defined *ahimsa* as "action based on the refusal to do harm," an act of positive love to prevent injury to others.[1] The principle of noninjury leads to the necessity of harmonizing ends and means, one of Gandhi's most important contributions to moral philosophy. Ends and means are not separate realities or modes of thinking but are intimately intertwined and interdependent. One cannot achieve just ends with unjust means, he emphasized: "If one takes care of the means, the end will take care of itself."[2]

Gandhi forged these ideas and beliefs into an action strategy that he called *satyagraha*, a term that can be loosely translated as "social action to uphold truth." It is a method of nonviolent action to resist injustice and oppression and to seek higher truth through reconciliation and greater social equality. He espoused tolerance and respect for all persons, especially the most marginalized and oppressed. Gandhi emphasized the necessity of striving for justice through nonviolent means, thereby breaking the cycle of violence. By refusing to extend the chain of vengeance, he insisted, we create new possibilities for social progress. Hate and violence only generate more hate and violence. It is necessary to step outside of that vicious cycle. We get rid of the enemy by getting rid of enmity, he believed. Respect for the other is necessary to build relationships and find common solutions.

Gandhian nonviolence is often equated with pacifism, but this is a misperception. Gandhi developed the nonviolent method as a means of fighting for justice, not as a solution to the problem of war. He fought tenaciously against political oppression, but he did so with nonviolence, which he considered the most effective "weapon" for achieving success. Gandhi developed his method as a third way, an alternative to violence or to quiescence. We must resist injustice, he insisted, but must use methods that do not create new forms of violence and oppression.

Gandhi showed the power and effectiveness of nonviolence through the success of India's freedom movement. His colleagues adopted his methods because they considered them the most effective way of achieving their political goals. Few fully accepted Gandhi's philosophy of absolute nonviolence, but they all understood the social power of the mass noncooperation techniques he developed. As Jawaharlal Nehru wrote, "[We] accepted that method . . . not only as the right method but as the most effective one for our purpose."[3] The same has been true for nonviolent freedom fighters in struggles across the world, including in the United States.

Gandhi's philosophy and method greatly influenced Martin Luther King Jr. and the civil rights movement. King was impressed especially by Gandhi's ability to achieve freedom for the people of India without stirring hatred and rancor among his British adversaries. King understood that African Americans would have to do likewise and that nonviolent methods of struggle would allow them to live in harmony with their white brothers and sisters in the post-segregationist society they sought to create. Gandhi's religiously inspired nonviolent philosophy helped King better understand the social meaning of the commandment to love at the heart of his own Christian belief system. Gandhi also deeply influenced Cesar Chavez, who founded the United Farm Workers Union and played an important role in lifting the condition of America's poorest and most exploited workers. Chavez spoke of his great admiration for this "little half naked man without a gun," a person of color like himself who could stand up to race prejudice and overcome the power of a great empire.[4] Chavez found many things to admire in Gandhi: his success in winning Indian independence, his uncompromising commitment to nonviolence, his use of the boycott, and his fasting. Chavez found similarities between his own efforts to overcome racial prejudice and poverty and Gandhi's attempts to empower the down-trodden. In Gandhi, he found a leader who could inspire people to challenge the rich and powerful, a formula of obvious relevance to oppressed migrant workers facing wealthy landowners.

The Strength of Nonviolence

Political realists often dismiss nonviolence as naive and unworkable. Tyrants and terrorists only understand the message of violence, we are told. The historian Martin Ceadel writes that nonviolence "takes too utopian a view of the enemy" and can succeed only when opponents are relatively humane, as were the British in India.[5] The ethicist Michael Walzer argues that nonviolence is powerless against adversaries who employ brutal methods and in such settings is merely "a disguised form of surrender."[6] These criticisms reflect a misunderstanding of how nonviolence works. They incorrectly assume that nonviolence depends solely on moral persuasion to achieve success. They fail to see the underlying power dynamics and strategic impacts that account for the method's success.

Nonviolent action attempts to win over the oppressor, but its effectiveness does not depend on an appeal to conscience. Rather, nonviolent resistance seeks to transform political dynamics by sowing disaffection in the ranks and winning sympathy from third parties, thereby eroding the oppressor's power base. Nonviolence exerts coercive pressure through social and political action: boycotts, civil disobedience, and other forms of noncooperation. It does not depend on face-to-face persuasion but achieves its effectiveness through the force of mass action. Direct dialogue is often necessary to negotiate a settlement, as Gandhi and King emphasized, but this stage of the struggle usually comes after direct action and mass noncooperation have created conditions conducive to successful bargaining. Nonviolent action succeeds when it undermines the public consent that sustains power.

In his ineffable "Letter from a Birmingham Jail," King offers a guide to the strategy of effective nonviolent action. He describes the essential four steps of a nonviolent campaign, which can be paraphrased as follows: collect and present the facts, engage in negotiation and dialogue with the adversary, be prepared for sacrifice and struggle, and take direct action.[7] Demonstrations, blockades, sit-ins, and other forms of nonviolent pressure impose costs on the adversary. When the adversary resorts to repression against a disciplined nonviolent opposition, the authority of the adversary diminishes and that of the opposition grows. The result is a power shift that lays the foundation for a negotiated solution or, in rare cases, the collapse of corrupt power.

No one has done more to analyze and explain the underlying power dynamics of nonviolent action than the American scholar Gene Sharp. Author of the classic three-volume work *The Politics of Nonviolent Action*, Sharp has published dozens of books and pamphlets outlining the strategy and tactics of Gandhi's method.[8] Especially important is his book-length essay *From Dictatorship to Democracy*.[9] Sharp's works have been published in many languages and have provided the basis for training and education programs on nonviolent action in dozens of countries. His emphasis on the practical dimensions of Gandhian nonviolence is embodied in the work of the International Center on Nonviolent Conflict based in Washington, DC, and in similar education and training centers on nonviolence in other countries.

Critics claim that nonviolence has been tried and found wanting. The writer and nonviolent activist Barbara Deming argues to the contrary: "It has not been tried. We have hardly begun to try [it]. The people who dismiss it . . . do not understand what it could be."[10] Gandhi said at the end of his life that the "technique of unconquerable nonviolence of the strong has not been discovered as yet."[11] Organized nonviolence is a new and still undeveloped method of achieving political change. Only during the twentieth century, with Gandhi's disobedience campaigns in South Africa and India, did mass nonviolent action begin to emerge as a viable means of social change.

In recent decades, the methods of strategic nonviolent action have been applied and enlarged on with increasing frequency in a growing number of countries. Examples of major nonviolent successes are many, but perhaps the most dramatic is the nonviolent transformation of central and eastern Europe in the late 1980s, the "velvet revolution" that swept away Communist dictatorship without firing a shot and ended the Soviet Union. The "people power" movement of the Philippines ended the dictatorship of Ferdinand Marcos in 1986. Nonviolent resistance was decisive in the latter stages of the South African freedom movement, helping to end the hated apartheid regime. Nonviolent movements swept through Latin America in the 1980s and 1990s, ending military dictatorship in Chile and democratizing governments throughout the continent. Nonviolent power inspired the Serbian youth group Otpor! (Resistance!), which sparked the movement to overthrow Slobodan Milošević in 2000. Mass civil disobedience in Nepal overthrew the monarchy in April 2006 and laid the basis for the creation of a democratic republic. Civil resistance brought down the Ben Ali dictatorship in Tunisia in December 2010. The methods of nonviolent resistance have achieved significant political change and social transformation on every continent.

The Gandhian method does not always work, of course. Examples of failure exist, including the Tiananmen Square massacre of 1989 in China as well as the isolation and collapse of the Kosovar nonviolent resistance struggle in the early 1990s. Countless attempts to use nonviolent methods to resist occupation in the Palestinian Occupied Territories have failed so far to alter the structures of oppression. The mass uprising in Egypt in January–February 2011 showed the extraordinary power of unarmed revolution and seemed to vindicate the power of civil resistance, but the return to military dictatorship in 2013 shattered those hopes.

The overall record of success is nonetheless impressive. Walter Wink wrote in the early 1990s, "Never before have citizens actualized this potential [for nonviolent action] in such overwhelming numbers or to such stunning effect."[12] The use of mass nonviolence has introduced a new, more constructive, and more creative form of revolutionary power in the world that makes a decisive break with the traditional method of violent revolution.

The dissidents of eastern and central Europe who brought down communism in the 1980s rejected violence because they wanted a more radical and effective way of overcoming oppression. They rejected violence not because it was too radical, Václav Havel wrote, "but[,] on the contrary, because it does not seem radical enough." They believed that "a future secured by violence might actually be worse than what exists now . . . [and] would be fatally stigmatized by the very means used to secure it." Havel described the dissident movement as an "existential revolution" that would provide hope for the "moral reconstitution of society . . . [and] the rehabilitation of values like trust, openness, responsibility, solidarity, love."[13] As Jonathan Schell observes, both Havel and Gandhi made truth the touchstone of their philosophy. They shared the conviction that "the prime human obligation is to act fearlessly and publicly in accord with one's beliefs."[14] The revolution in which Havel participated was the most sweeping demonstration in history of the power of nonviolent action to achieve political change.

Evidence of Success

Recent empirical studies confirm the superiority of nonviolent action as a method of achieving significant social change. In their landmark study *Why Civil Resistance Works*, Erica Chenoweth and Maria J. Stephan examine 323 historical examples of civil resistance campaigns that occurred over a span of more than one hundred years to compare the relative effectiveness of nonviolent and violent methods.[15] Each case involved an intensive political conflict, sometimes lasting several years, in which sociopolitical movements struggled to change regimes or gain major concessions from government adversaries. Overall, nonviolent campaigns were successful 53 percent of the time, compared to a 26 percent success rate when violence was the principal means of resistance.[16] Nonviolent methods were found to be equally successful in repressive dictatorships as in democratic regimes.

Nonviolent action is not only more effective than armed struggle in achieving political change but also more likely to expand opportunities for democracy and political freedom. This is the conclusion of an important study in 2005 that examined sixty-seven political transitions over the previous decades, many in previously closed or authoritarian governments. The study asked whether violent or nonviolent methods were used to achieve change and evaluated the regimes resulting from these transitions according to the standard Freedom House ratings of "free," "partly free," or "not free." The study found that nonviolent civic resistance was a driving factor in fifty of the sixty-seven transitions. In those fifty cases, nearly all the resulting regimes (92 percent) were more democratic. Nonviolent movements were three times more likely than armed struggles to produce sustainable political freedom. The key variable in achieving greater democracy was identified as the presence of a "people power" effect—a bottom-up nonviolent resistance movement. "The stronger and more cohesive the nonviolent civic coalition," the study concluded, "the deeper the transformation in the direction of freedom and democracy." The presence of a robust civic coalition has a statistically significant effect on increasing the level of freedom.[17] Chenoweth and Stephan use a different methodology but reach a similar conclusion: the use of civil resistance methods is much more likely than the use of armed struggle to produce a democratic society.[18]

The most important factor in the success of nonviolent action, Chenoweth and Stephan find, is what they call the "participation advantage": nonviolent methods' ability to mobilize mass participation in political struggle. "Large campaigns are much more likely to succeed than small campaigns," they argue. As membership increases, so does the probability of success. Mass participation "can erode a regime's main sources of power when the participants represent diverse sectors of society."[19]

Mass participation also helps explain why nonviolent movements are more likely to produce democratic outcomes. Nonviolent movements are by their very nature mass-based, participatory expressions of free will. In Poland, for example, the power of the Solidarity movement flowed from the ten million members it represented and the support it received from virtually every segment of society. The same was true of the United Democratic Front in South Africa in the 1980s. With the participation of churches, trade unions, community organizations, and the African National Congress, the United Democratic Front was able to mobilize millions and could rightly claim to speak for the majority population in challenging apartheid.

In an armed struggle, by contrast, the resistance is carried out by a smaller, specialized cadre of fighters. An armed struggle must operate according to military discipline, and its success may depend on the rigidity and impregnability of its command structure. In the heat of battle, there is no room for debate or dissent. Armed movements are less able to accommodate factions and may turn on themselves in violent purges. Most of the armed revolutions of the twentieth century produced repressive and dictatorial regimes. Those who win by the gun tend to rule by the gun.

An expansion of democracy reflects the very essence of nonviolence. As Schell observes, nonviolence is inseparably linked to democracy. The spread of democracy extends the arena of human affairs in which political disputes are resolved without violence. Democracy embodies free expression, political cooperation, and mutual accommodation of interests. Nonviolence "is written into liberalism's genetic code," writes Schell. "In this basic respect, the long march of liberal democracy is a 'peace movement'—possibly the most important and successful of them all."[20]

According to Stephan and Chenoweth, loyalty shifts are a key mechanism of nonviolent change, occurring in more than half the successful nonviolent campaigns studied.[21] Hierarchical power systems depend on followers' obedience and loyalty. When that loyalty falters, the command system's oppressive power begins to erode. Resistance movements that generate disaffection in the opponent's ranks greatly increase their chances of political success. This was a key to the initial success of the unarmed revolution in Egypt (although the army subsequently turned against the revolution), and it has been evident in many other historic campaigns. In East Germany in 1989, soldiers of the Communist regime refused to fire on candlelight protestors in Leipzig, which opened the door to further massive protests and the fall of the Berlin Wall. During the military coup in Moscow in 1991, Boris Yeltsin famously climbed aboard a tank and successfully persuaded soldiers not to attack their own people. During the overthrow of Slobodan Milošević in Serbia and the Orange Revolution in Ukraine, resistance leaders negotiated with and reassured senior commanders and thereby kept the military on the sidelines. This ability to encourage loyalty shifts in the military is essential to the political power of nonviolent revolution.

Chenoweth and Stephan updated their research findings in an academic blog post in 2016.[22] Their latest research shows lower success rates for both violent and nonviolent struggles but a continuing significant effectiveness advantage for nonviolent campaigns. During the period 2011–15, nonviolent resistance struggles achieved success 30 percent of the time, compared to a success rate of only 12 percent for campaigns employing violent means. The proportional success gap between nonviolence and violence is actually wider now than in earlier decades.

The argument is sometimes made that so-called violent flanks are helpful to mass social movements. This question is often addressed under the euphemistic heading "diversity of tactics," with anarchists contending that limited forms of violence such as fighting with the police and trashing stores strengthen social resistance campaigns. Chenoweth and others have used comparative data to study this question and have found that limited uses of violence undermine the strategic effectiveness of social campaigns rather than helping them.[23] Street violence may attract media attention and allow protesters to "blow off steam," but the resulting press coverage often diverts attention from issues of justice and focuses on images of anarchist mayhem. Violent rampages tend to reduce levels of mass participation, which are crucial to political success. The use of violent tactics also tends to increase levels of state repression and can lead to greater political support for political candidates who employ law-and-order policies that undermine civil and human rights.[24]

Facing Repression

Nonviolent campaigns are better able than violent campaigns to withstand government repression. Opposition campaigns that seek to overthrow or reform a regime are likely to face violent repression from their government adversaries. In authoritarian and corrupt regimes especially, those in power will resist movements that challenge their authority. That resistance is often violent. In most of the campaigns studied by Chenoweth and Stephan, the regime in power used violence to suppress nonviolent challengers.

When repression occurs and the opposition refrains from retaliating in kind, the regime's use of violence tends to be counterproductive and may give a moral and political advantage to the challengers. Violent repression against unarmed protesters often creates a backfire effect. It generates a sympathetic reaction among third parties that increases support for the protesters while undermining the regime's legitimacy. The result is a greater likelihood of loyalty shifts and defections among government officials and within the security forces. As social consent diminishes, the repressive regime's power begins to erode.

Many practitioners and scholars of nonviolence have noted and commented on this third-party effect. Cesar Chavez referred to it as the "strange chemistry" of nonviolent action. Whenever the adversary commits an unjust act against nonviolent protesters, said Chavez, "we get tenfold paid back in benefits."[25] Barbara Deming describes this effect as the "special genius" of nonviolent action.[26] Unjustified repression against disciplined nonviolent action can spark a sympathetic reaction among third parties and in the ranks of the adversary. This may spark loyalty shifts and increase support for the nonviolent campaigners, while undermining the legitimacy of the adversary. The theologian Reinhold Niebuhr writes that excessive brutality against nonviolent action "robs the opponent of the moral conceit" of serving the common good. He describes this effect as the "most important of all the imponderables in a social struggle."[27] Nonviolent campaigners' willingness to risk and accept repression without retaliation is fundamental to the political success of the Gandhian method. It alters political dynamics and tips the balance of sympathy and political support against the adversary and toward the nonviolent movement.

These findings on the efficacy of nonviolent resistance challenge traditional realist assumptions about the primacy of military force and the nature of political power. They raise doubts about political revolutionaries' assumption that armed struggle is the most potent weapon in the fight against oppression. Nonviolent means can shape the exercise of power and perceptions of legitimacy and are more likely than armed struggle to achieve political objectives.

The Fate of Syria

The relative inferiority of violent methods in relation to nonviolence helps explain the tragic outcome of the revolution in Syria. The movement against the Bashar Assad regime that began in the wake of the Egyptian revolution in 2011 was initially peaceful and nonviolent. When government forces arrested and brutalized a group of young boys in Daraa for spraying antiregime graffiti on the walls of a school, people gathered in the streets to protest their mistreatment. The police responded by opening fire on the crowd, killing several nonviolent demonstrators. This was an early spark of the revolution and led to further protests and more violent responses from the government. The movement remained mostly nonviolent despite the mounting repression, with protests occurring in many cities, including a huge protest in Hama in July 2011.[28] As the repression intensified, however, with both thugs and progovernment militias attacking the movement, the scale of peaceful protest gradually diminished. By the end of 2011 and early 2012, armed resistance was spreading, and foreign fighters were arriving. The revolution became an armed struggle, which descended in ever-deepening spirals of violence into a horrific civil war that has continued to the present, causing hundreds of thousands of deaths, the forced migration and displacement of some eleven million people (approximately half the prewar population), and the destruction of vast regions of the country.[29]

Sitting safely here in North America, I am not in a position to judge those who pick up arms to fight against the vicious tyranny of the Assad regime. A people's ability to suffer violent repression and remain peaceful has limits. It is understandable that many opponents of the regime feel they had no choice but to join the military struggle. In so doing, however, they put themselves in a difficult dilemma. They had to calculate their fate against a much stronger and ruthless military opponent and rely on the faint hope, ultimately unrealized, that they might be saved by foreign military intervention. They put themselves at the mercy of extremist forces ready to exploit the crisis in Syria and the chaos of war to advance their separatist agendas. The Syrian resistance also failed to anticipate the massive support Iran and Hezbollah would provide to Assad's Alawi regime and Russia's later military intervention. Contrary to the revolutionary movement's hopes, the Syrian army has held firm for the most part. Defections occurred among conscripts and some officers in the early months, but most of the Syrian army has remained loyal and has continued to fight for the government even during the bitterest phases of the civil war. This scenario fits the empirical evidence that nonviolent campaigns are better able to induce regime defections.

When rebels pick up the gun and choose armed struggle, their chances of winning diminish. This is the cold fact that history teaches and empirical evidence confirms. Military measures are less effective than nonviolent resistance in overcoming dictatorship and repression. This is not to suggest that continuing the protests in Syria in 2011 and beyond would have brought down the government. Some regimes are willing to resort to the most pitiless persecution and may be able to crush even the strongest resistance movement, at least for a time. In some instances, movements have been forced underground, as Solidarity was in Poland after martial law was declared, or must wait many decades to achieve even small steps toward reform, as in the democracy movement in Burma. It may be necessary at times to suspend public protest and to consider tactics for registering public opposition that do not subject so many people to the risk of death. Sharp and other strategists emphasize the need for a diversity of methods and have cataloged a long list of tactics for challenging corrupt and repressive regimes.[30] Campaigns for significant political change often require a long-term horizon, with fundamental change emerging slowly, but if nonviolent means are applied, the chances of eventual success are greater.

Conclusion

Gandhi's commitment to nonviolence emerged from his religious convictions and the teachings of the Jain tradition of Hinduism. He interpreted the Buddhist/Hindu concept of *ahimsa*, noninjury, in a proactive manner to include preventing harm against others and struggling against injustice. This religious commitment to overcoming violence and oppression was linked to an ethics of equivalence between ends and means. To serve the end of avoiding violence, we must use means that are nonviolent. To achieve just purposes, we must employ just means. From these religious and ethical principles, Gandhi forged a method of nonviolent action, *satyagraha*, that enabled people to fight against oppression without succumbing to the evils of violent revolution. He pioneered a new form of mass nonviolent resistance that proved successful in achieving freedom for India and that was subsequently applied by Martin Luther King Jr., Cesar Chavez, and others in the United States and around the world in struggles against injustice. As Sharp, Deming, and others have argued, the Gandhian method offers a way of fighting against oppression while remaining true to one's religious and moral beliefs.

Nonviolence is not only a religious principle but also a pragmatic choice, a more effective means of achieving justice and overcoming oppression. Empirical evidence and historical experience confirm that nonviolent means are more likely than the use of arms to achieve political objectives and create more democratic societies. Campaigns that follow this approach are better able to seize and hold the moral high ground and to gain greater political and social support. The internal political and social dynamics that account for the success of nonviolent action depend on a disciplined commitment to non-violence. In practice, it can be difficult to maintain this discipline, especially when murderous regimes, such as in Syria, gun down unarmed protesters and brutalize those who challenge their policies. Nonviolent protest is not always successful, and resisters may be tempted to pick up the gun in self-defense, but in so doing they incur grave responsibilities. They face both a lower probability of success and the prospect of massive death and destruction spreading from insurgency and civil war. The choices for those suffering persecution and oppression are often excruciatingly difficult, with no easy path toward justice, but peaceful approaches and nonviolent practices are superior morally *and* practically, and over the long run they are more likely to achieve just outcomes.

3

The Spiritual Balance of Peace in the Red Stick War, 1813–1814

DONALD L. FIXICO

During a humid summer night in 1813, a Mvskoke war leader in his late forties stood on the bank of the Tallapoosa River. Named Menawa, meaning "Great Warrior" in his people's language, he lived in a town called Okfuskee. Born from the marriage of a white deer-skin trader and a Mvskoke woman, Menawa chose to live the Mvskoke Way. Two other individuals joined Menawa at the edge of the river. Monohe was an *owalla* (prophet), almost as old as Menawa, and the other was a young man in training to become a *hillis haya*, a medicine maker. All three Mvskokes had arrived at the newly built town of Tohopeka to celebrate the Green Corn harvest, the most important Mvskoke ceremony. Menawa asked the prophet and young medicine maker what they thought about the noted Shawnee war leader Tecumseh and his bold speech at Tuckabatchee town. Tecumseh wanted the Mvskokes to join him to destroy the Americans for encroaching on Shawnee homeland north of the Ohio River. If the Americans were not stopped, he warned they would invade the homeland of the Mvskokes. The young medicine maker remained silent as Menawa looked toward Monohe for a response. The prophet gazed at the stars. Menawa asked the prophet if there would be war in the near future. The bright stars were like the many fires of Indian nations throughout the land. Studying the stars, the prophet slowly nodded "yes" and responded that a great victory for the Mvskokes would happen at the Tallapoosa. Menawa grimaced—for there to be peace, there first must be war.

Peace begins with how we understand it, how it is achieved, and how we understand ourselves. Spiritual balance begins with self-discovery as a part of life because our identity informs us who we are and reminds us of the connections to our relatives. All of these connections are relevant to our spiritual well-being. Yet everything in the Indigenous world is about understanding relationships with other people and nonhumans. This means that to achieve a "spiritual peace" is to understand one's relationships with all entities. Within the Indigenous realm, peace is a spiritual balance. Each relationship is mutual and needs a healthy symbiosis with all other relationships. Our life's mission is to seek the balance not only within ourselves and with people but also with our surroundings. The ultimate objective of finding this balance is discovering inner peace. True balance equates peace with our spiritual existence inside us and in our communities.

Many Indian groups such as the Cheyenne, Iroquois, Navajo, Lakota, and Mvskoke Creek philosophize about a righteous "way" to live in order to achieve spiritual balance. Many tribes have a philosophy for living that translates into *balance* and *spiritual peace*. The Cheyennes of the Plains have a long tradition of peace chiefs. In the Great Lakes region, the League of the Iroquois exercised the Great Peace philosophy among their six nations. Prophets such as Sweet Medicine of the Cheyenne and Handsome Lake of the Iroquois shared divine messages with their peoples about a way of life that encouraged peace and how to achieve it. In the Southeast of the present-day United States, the Mvskoke Confederacy had a dual system, red towns of war and white towns of peace, and the period from the origin of the Mvskokes to the end of the Creek War has been called the "Redstick prophetic movement of 1812–14."[1]

To explain the red-and-white town system of the Mvskoke Creeks, two narratives in the oral tradition must be told that set the foundation for understanding the Mvskoke approach to peace and war. As the Mvskokes grew in power during the late sixteenth century, they expanded to include fifty-five towns called *etvlwv*s. Each town acted independently, and the town leaders, called *mekko*s, exercised tremendous power, *yekcetv*. The Mvskokes were known as people who lived in swampland areas and were later called Creeks after British traders began to refer to the people who lived near creeks and streams. The Mvskoke Confederacy expanded to cover present-day Alabama, Georgia, and central Florida. Once a year during the harvest of corn, the town leaders (*etvlwv mekko*s) met at the central or principal town, Ocmulgee, near present-day Macon, Georgia. At Ocmulgee, the town leaders decided whether to ally with other Indigenous groups, what other towns could join the confederacy, and who the Mvskokes would go to war against and when. If going to war were decided, runners would deliver the news, and the Mvskoke red towns could easily put a thousand warriors called Red Sticks on the battlefield. By the early 1800s, as many as twenty-five thousand people belonged to the Mvskoke Confederacy, a grand alliance with a humble beginning.[2]

The first narrative explains the origin of the Mvskoke people. A very long time ago the Mvskoke people lived as one group in total darkness and cold. Their hands felt damp walls as the people continued to move along in the dark. The Mvskokes realized they were moving upward and felt a dark mist on their faces that shrouded their eyes; they were filled with fear. The wind blew the mist away, and for the first time the people could see. They saw the earth and strange beings called animals of many kinds and observed the animals with intent curiosity; some could even fly. To the south, the Mvskoke saw a yellow fire in the distance. To the west, the people saw a black fire. A white fire burned at a distance in the east, while to the north a red fire was aflame. The Mvskokes learned to respect fire for its light and warmth.[3]

The Mvskokes then witnessed the sun above them. They regarded the sun as an elemental power and a gift. Rain fell, and lightning during a storm struck a tree, making a fire. After overcoming their fear of the lightning, the people made a small fire on the ground from the burning tree and called it the sun's little brother. The Mvskokes decided to celebrate the importance of the fire with a ceremony, so they danced around it. The Mvskoke people studied the sun, moon, earth, and stars. Groups of Mvskokes also began to study certain animals and devoted their lives to learning about the strange new beings.

Animals and plants became a central part of the Mvskoke world-view. The Mvskoke Medicine Way involved observing signs and symbols as well as receiving guidance from nonhumans, such as plants and animals. Clans play an integral part of life among the Indigenous peoples of the eastern woodlands. Animals in particular but also some plants and the wind became clan totems. Among the Mvskoke Creeks, the Wind Clan was the highest-ranked among a dozen clans. More clans would be added later as the Mvskokes expanded their knowledge to other plants and animals. Following the Wind Clan, the Bird Clan was important because of birds' ability to fly and oversee everything from above. Members of the Bird Clan made sure the people obeyed the community's laws, which were based on the laws of nature.

The Bear Clan emerged as another significant group for making medicines from plants. The Wolf Clan consisted of those people who were fast runners and were strong, like wolves. The Beaver Clan included innovative individuals who could work as a group, practicing effective diplomacy.[4] To this day among the Mvskokes, everyone is a member of his or her family and of the clans. Children inherit clan membership from their mother, making the Mvskokes matrilineal.

The Mvskokes' philosophical approach toward peace and war relates to their origin narrative, but a separate story also explains how the Mvskokes differentiate between peace and war. Following the people's emergence from Mother Earth, twin brothers were born, but they had no parents to raise them. Childhood became a time of discovery and sorting out important issues. Among the rest of the Mvskokes, chaos reigned. As the twin brothers grew, they realized that some sort of order had to be established because their Mvskoke world was new, and many unknowns existed. The First Twin was enthusiastic and wanted to explore the unknown and to find other people. The Second Twin was calm, reflective, and cautious. Both twin brothers agreed they should go in different directions, find out what they could, and meet back where they were at a certain time to share their new knowledge.[5]

The First Twin in his excitement offered to go in the direction of the black fire, the dark direction recorded in Mvskoke memory. In this direction, the mist began to fall again as it did when the Mvskoke first emerged from Mother Earth. The First Twin reasoned that the opposite direction to the east and the white fire would be safer because it was easier to see in that direction. The Second Twin accepted his brother's offer, so the First Brother set off toward the west and the black fire, and the Second Brother set off toward the east and the white fire.

The First Twin brother traveled in the dark mist; the unknown enticed him as he studied animals and plants along the way. He talked to them until he reached a group of spirits who looked like people. They wanted to know if the animals and plants talked back to him. He had learned about medicine from them in the earth of the dark direction of the black fire. The spirits challenged the First Twin to join them in their games of competition, including their stickball game, which they called the "Little Brother of War." He proved his superiority in running faster, jumping farther, and playing stickball better than they, so the spirits wanted him to stay and tried to stop him from leaving. The First Twin managed to escape, returning back to the place where he and his brother agreed to meet.

The Second Twin journeyed in the direction of the mist of the white fire until he arrived at a town. The town was full of spirits who reflected about the life of plants and animals as well as about life in general. They preferred to negotiate instead of going to war, yet they were strong because they did not allow their emotions to lead them into dangerous situations. They wanted the Second Twin to stay with them, but he kept repeating that he had to return to meet his brother. Finally, the Second Twin left so that he could rendezvous with his brother.

The twins met at the agreed site and shared their knowledge from their journeys. They decided to share their knowledge with the spirits of the two different directions to establish order among the Mvskoke people. Peace and war were a natural part of life. Red represented war because red was the color of blood, which carried life throughout all Mvskokes and all living humans and animals. White represented peace because it was a neutral color that did not provoke people's emotions. White symbolized stability, calm, strength, and order in life—all of the attributes of peace.

The Mvskokes instituted the red-and-white philosophy into their way of life. Red towns produced warriors, while white towns produced civil officials and individuals who were medicine people. In the Mvskoke worldview, the personalities of young boys and girls were introverted or extroverted. Their parents and other elders observed them and encouraged them, especially boys, to become trained as warriors or to learn about medicine.[6] The Mvskokes realized that all children had traits of war and peace in them, but they learned that it was best to encourage extroverted boys to become warriors and be recognized as Red Sticks. Elders encouraged introverted boys to become medicine makers, or White Sticks.

James Adair, an early British ethnographer, traveled in Mvskoke country in 1775 and observed that the Mvskokes

> have few enemies, and the traders with them have taught them to prevent the last contagion from spreading among their towns, by cutting off any communication with those who are infected, till the danger is over. Besides, as the men rarely go to war till they have helped the women to plant a sufficient plenty of provisions, contrary to the usual method of warring savages, it is so great to help propagation, that by this means also, and their artful policy of inviting decaying tribes to incorporate with them, . . . they have doubled in number in the space of thirty years past.[7]

The Mvskoke Way was a good one, and smaller Indigenous communities found that the Mvskokes welcomed them to join. Other groups' towns and even entire communities joined the Mvskoke Confederacy. Shawnees, Natchez, Hitchitis, Yuchis, Tuckabatchees, Alabamas, and other communities became a part of the growing confederacy. The new peoples, such as the Tuckabatchees, retained their original identities and maintained their towns. New arrivals to the town Tuckabatchee made it the largest Mvskoke town.[8] It was one of the earliest Mvskoke towns, along with Coweta, Cussita, and Abika; these four large early towns were called "mother towns."[9]

The towns interacted regularly, with people visiting friends, attending dances, and playing stickball. The Little Brother of War, the stickball game, was highly competitive but with only a few rules. Two towns would put the same number of players on the ball field, and the objective was to carry a small leather ball trapped between two ball sticks and to hit a goal post at the end of the field that the other team defended, each hit scoring one point. Each ball stick was about three feet long and curved at the end to form a small leather web. Both teams agreed when the game would start and end; no player could use his hands, only his pair of ball sticks, and the sticks could be used in any manner. Fights often broke out, causing broken bones, but the team with the most points scored at the end of the game was declared the winner.

Certain towns such as Coweta and Cuseta of the Lower Mvskokes became red towns because of the predominant number of Red Stick warriors in them. The others, such as Abihka and Coosa of the Upper Mvskokes, became white towns owing to the fact that a majority of the boys and men were White Sticks.[10] Everyone in the Mvskoke Confederacy knew which towns were red or white, and sometimes a red town became a white town and vice versa based on the shifting of the majority of males from red to white or white to red.

The fact that red towns represented war and white towns represented peace provides insight into the Mvskoke Creeks and the Seminoles, an offshoot of Mvskokes who migrated to northern and central Florida. In the Mvskoke language, the name "Seminole" means "those who camp at a distance." The Mvskoke Creeks and the Seminoles share the same culture and same language.

In the Mvskoke–Seminole worldview, peace and war were and remain a natural dichotomy among multiple dichotomies. Male/

female, light/dark, happy/sad, good/bad, left/right, right/wrong, up/
down, and other opposites are "spiritual constants" and the natural
laws of the universe. These constants cannot be changed; they exist
in perpetuity. The laws of nature, such as peace and war, go back
centuries to the origin of the Mvskokes and the Twin Brothers' narrative of oral tradition.

It was natural for a person, male or female, to negotiate his
or her life's journey between the spiritual constants. Each person
learned the instinct of his or her clan animal, which helped guide
the individual in life. For example, the wolf spirit would remind the
individual of the Wolf Clan what was right and what was wrong in
making a decision. Decision making every day, from insignificant to
important choices, dictated life's journey and negotiated the spiritual
constants from childhood to adulthood to old age. On life's journey,
there were attractions and distractions, temptations and responsibilities, and the unexpected and the predictable tugged at the Mvskokes' hearts as they pressed forward to walk the good road. But
there were unavoidable roadblocks—tangents, crossroads, panic,
and self-doubt.

For all of us, the effort to maintain spiritual balance within oneself is ongoing, a process more relevant to learning about peace than
to the journey's outcome. Life is a contiguous labyrinth with temptations, desires, goals, and distractions that become a culmination of
personal and business experiences. In this daily quest, four kinds of
balance challenge all of us: balance within one's self (the most difficult), balance with family, balance with society or clan (including
groups of non-Indian friends), and balance with community, which
is a balance with the natural environment in the Mvskoke order of
life, where all that is known and unknown is called "Ibofanga."[11]

In this Native paradigm, a person is never alone because the clan
totem is with him or her. The totem—for example, a wolf (*yaha*)—
acts as a spiritual guide; this spirit connects with the person when he
actually sees a wolf or encounters the presence of the animal, such
as a paw print. Among the Mvskokes and Seminoles, it is said that
you are never alone; for example, the Wolf Clan spirit shadows you

when you are traveling and is with you especially in time of need. It is important to believe that the clan totem is endowed with the power of generations of its own kind.

The communal belief is that the people of the Wolf Clan know the animal's strengths and weaknesses. They know the wolf's traits, and their own personality is like the wolf's, such that there is a symbiotic relationship between a Wolf Clan member and wolf animal. Those of the wolf can easily recognize another wolf relative.

The good life is finding a spiritual balance as a person deals with the spiritual constants on a daily basis. Indecision can lead to confusion and danger. Hence, the unknown presented a challenge to the Twin Brothers traveling to unknown lands to the east and west. Not knowing can cause self-destruction, like being caught in a void, which the Mvskoke Creek and Seminole call a kind of hell or state of confusion, *ehosa*. Such calamity occurs when a person is alone and lost in a spiritual void and sometimes hears his or her name being called from different directions as he or she wanders in the void. For mainstream Western-thinking minds, *ehosa* is similar to the "third space" that Homi Bhabha addresses in his work *The Location of Culture*.[12] In the third space, which is the overlap of two competing ideologies, a hybrid identity or compromised ideology emerges as a combination of the two originals. In *ehosa*, there is no emergence until an intervening force extracts the lost soul or a powerful medicine maker rescues the individual by removing the spell on the person.

Ehosa is forever present, and it must be avoided. It is also the state of indecision or confusion between war and peace. Strong minds and belief in the Mvskoke Medicine Way empowered the Red Stick warriors. Clan powers—from the swiftness of the wolf to the strength of the bear and the strengths of other clan animals—were a part of the warfare of the Mvskoke warriors in the eighteenth and early nineteenth centuries.

The Mvskokes' military strength impressed enemies, but this greatness hung on the premise that all the Mvskoke towns, or at least a majority of them, comprehended the advantage of belonging to the powerful confederacy. The towns had ranged far enough so that those along the Chattahoochee and Flint Rivers in present-day Alabama were called the Lower Mvskokes. The Upper Mvskokes were more isolated from European traders and were more traditional than the Lower Mvskokes, whose towns rested along the Coosa and Tallapoosa Rivers and their tributaries.[13]

As the leaves began to fall from trees in 1749, Mvskoke Red Sticks from the upper towns became angry at the British when the warriors visited Charlestown and returned sick. Indeed, some of the Red Sticks died on the journey home. French traders urged all Mvskokes not to trust the British, who courted the Cherokee leaders. The Cherokees had allowed the Senecas from the north to pass through Cherokee land and intrude into Mvskoke territory, which violated the Charlestown Treaty of 1749. An attack by some Cherokee and Senecas on several Lower Mvskoke hunters and the capturing of their women and children provoked a response. Malatchi, a noted war leader, led 500 Red Stick warriors from the lower towns against the Cherokees. The Red Sticks burned two Cherokee towns to ashes, and Malatchi and his warriors returned home fully satisfied that the brethren hunters and their families had been vindicated.[14]

The spring months of 1751 brought Cherokee war parties into Mvskoke lands, and the Red Stick towns of the upper and lower towns launched counterattacks. Attacks on the other people's hunters in the woods continued on both sides until negotiations led by white-town leaders ended the Cherokee–Mvskoke War in 1752.[15]

The war with the Cherokees subsided for only a few months, however. The previous hostilities lingered. In northern present-day Georgia, hunters from both the Cherokees and Mvskokes seized opportunities to kill hunters from the other group. In 1753, killings in the wilderness led to raids by both sides. Surprise attacks and ambushes were carried out, largely affecting the Lower Mvskokes in present-day Georgia. One of the main Mvskoke Red Stick towns, Coweta,[16] sent its Red Sticks into the Tennessee Valley and northern Georgia area to attack Cherokee towns. In 1755, however, the Cherokee–Mvskoke War ended as both sides now had to contend with the expansion of European Georgia settlers coming into Mvskoke and Cherokee homelands.

In the years that followed the war with the Cherokees, the Mvskokes encountered pressure from the Choctaws to the west. The two sides went to war in 1765, raiding and attacking each other intensively for five years. John Stuart, a British agent, intervened by providing guns and ammunition to the Choctaws to prevent the Mvskokes from sending Red Sticks against the British Georgia colony. The war with the Choctaw subsided in 1776, when the British colonies rebelled in what became the American Revolution.[17]

The rise of the United States caught the attention of the Mvskokes, especially Alexander McGillivray, a mixed-blood Mvskoke who owned large plantations. By the 1780s, McGillivray used his influence to unite the Mvskoke towns, especially in negotiations with the British and the new United States.[18] At this stage, Mvskoke country encountered external politics at a greater rate than before when European traders exchanged their material goods for pelts from the Mvskokes. In 1796, President John Adams appointed Benjamin Hawkins a US agent to the Mvskokes. Hawkins had the responsibilities of keeping peace among the Mvskokes, obtaining more of their land, and helping "civilize" the Mvskokes to live like white settlers.[19] Hawkins observed strife developing between traditional Mvskokes and those kinsmen who were friendly toward Americans and enjoyed their trade goods. In the following years, the division increased between the two kinds of Mvskokes. Agent Hawkins warned General Andrew Jackson and US officials about the influence of Mvskoke prophets to agitate all Mvskokes to destroy both Americans and friendly Mvskokes who were loyal to the United States,[20] so Jackson simultaneously courted the loyalty of friendly leaders, Big Warrior of the Mvskokes and Pathkiller of the Cherokees. Both leaders supplied warriors to Jackson against the Red Sticks.[21]

The Mvskokes felt the growing pressure of more whites pushing into their homelands. Whites, the "Americans" of the newly established United States, had pushed into the Ohio Country, and this alarmed Tecumseh, the Shawnee war leader in the early years of the nineteenth century. The Shawnee leader developed a master plan to unite as many Indian nations as he could, including the Mvskokes. On a trip to the South, he gave a magnificent speech at Tuckabatchee. Tecumseh had a natural tie to the Mvskoke because his mother was Mvskoke, and he was of the Panther Clan. Tecumseh envisioned fighting the Americans with as many Indian nations in the Ohio area as would join his cause. He allied his many warriors with the British in the War of 1812. In making his final stand at the Thames River in Canada, Tecumseh died on the battlefield, ending his dream of all Indian nations taking their homelands back from white settlers. He had predicted settler encroachment into Mvskoke territory, and the acceleration of this encroachment sparked the Red Stick War, which began with the Mvskokes making war on the whites but proceeded with the settlers trying to exterminate all of the Mvskokes.[22]

As the end of July 1813 approached, Peter McQueen led a large group of Red Sticks to Pensacola, Florida, to buy ammunition for their guns from the Spanish governor. McQueen had new guns and ammunition loaded on pack horses to transport back to Red Stick towns. Hearing about McQueen's pack train at Fort Mims, Colonel James Caller and Captain Dixon Bailey led an Alabama militia to intercept it. Caller and Bailey's soldiers surprised the Indians with an attack at dusk on July 27 and captured McQueen's pack horses. The Red Sticks scattered into the swamp area of Burnt Creek in southern Alabama but did not panic. McQueen regrouped the Red Sticks, and they counterattacked; Caller and Bailey's men scattered in retreat.[23] Until now, Mvskoke prophets had threatened the lives of those Mvskokes friendly to whites but had not threatened whites.[24] In fact, with the guns purchased, the Red Sticks had planned to attack Coweta, a Mvskoke town friendly to Agent Hawkins and US trade relations.[25] Almost all of the Upper Mvskoke towns joined the Red Stick movement. With the impending war, Red Sticks compelled the children of interracial marriages to follow the traditional Mvskoke ways.[26]

Fort Mims stood as a thorn in the side of the Mvskokes, located forty miles north of Mobile on the upper east bank of Tensaw Lake.

Named after a wealthy settler, Samuel Mims, the fort had started out as Mims's house. Prior to 1813, Mims's place, consisting of the main house, seventeen outbuildings, a blockhouse, and a log palisade, had become known as "Fort Mims." In early August, rumors of the Red Sticks' war activities convinced an estimated 550 settlers and slaves in the area to gather within Fort Mims. Ironically, some of the settlers were part Mvskoke through intermarriage.[27]

From Baton Rouge, Brigadier General Ferdinand L. Claiborne of the Mississippi Territorial Militia was responsible for protecting settlers in the Mississippi Territory. Claiborne sent one of his best friends, Major Daniel Beasley, to defend Fort Mims, but Beasley was a lawyer with no military experience. Major Beasley led 170 militiamen to Fort Mims, where he ordered 40 of them to reinforce Fort Pierce on Pine Lodge Creek, located two miles south of Fort Mims. William Weatherford, a Red Stick leader, watched them from a distance. Weatherford was part Mvskoke and part white, had learned to speak English, and had adopted many of the white ways. He owned a lot of land as well as slaves and cattle. He also had several wives. Weatherford preferred wearing his hair short, wore a black broadcloth jacket with a vest, and black boots and a hat.[28] He dressed like a white man, but his heart was Mvskoke.

William Weatherford, known as Red Eagle, and a mixed-blood prophet named Paddy Welsh hid in the wilderness with several hundred Red Stick warriors. On the eve of August 30, the fort's doors were left open to allow a periodic breeze to break the summer's humidity. Two young slaves tending to cattle outside the palisade saw the hidden warriors and reported this to Beasley. But Beasley did not believe them and had them whipped for lying and trying to sow panic among the settlers. On the morning of the fateful day, Beasley wrote in a letter to Claiborne that all was peaceful. Beasley dismissed a second warning when a scout, James Cornells, rode his horse through the fort's gates and shouted to Beasley that he had seen Mvskokes in the woods. Beasley ordered Cornells to be arrested, but the scout rode out of the fort, leaving the commander and the 550 settlers and slaves to suffer their fate.[29]

From the woods, Red Eagle and Welsh watched the fort; their restless warriors waited impatiently less than four hundred yards away. As predicted, a drummer sounded the call to mess. The soldiers and settlers gathered for the midday meal. Red Eagle ordered the Red Sticks to attack; the Mvskokes stormed the fort, flooding through the opened gates. *Hadjo* (crazy without fear) Red Sticks met the enemy first to confuse them with fear (*ehosa*). Welsh shouted to the *hadjo* warriors to use only their red war clubs.[30] In the second wave, *fixico* (heartless in battle) warriors followed. Three hours later, the fighting continued in the worst humidity of the day. The Red Sticks set fire to most of the buildings, and the fort's powder magazine in one of the cabins exploded. Three miles away, Lieutenant Andrew Montgomery, in charge of 40 soldiers and roughly 150 settlers, could hear the massacre at Fort Mims. The lieutenant reckoned that his small force could not save those at Fort Mims. By five o'clock, the massacre was over; the Red Sticks took most of the African American slaves as captives. At noon the next day, Montgomery sent a small force to investigate Fort Mims. The soldiers returned to report the massacre of burned and mutilated bodies. Montgomery ordered Fort Pierce to be abandoned and led his soldiers and settlers to safety at Mobile. The rest of Mississippi Territory would not forget the Fort Mims massacre of 250 settlers.[31]

During this time, the Mvskoke prophet Josiah Francis established Econochaca, Holy Ground, a fortified Red Stick town on the high bank of the Alabama River. Francis promised William Weatherford and other Red Sticks that white men would die when they touched the sacred ground of Econochaca. In December, General Claiborne led roughly 850 men, and Pushmataha, the Choctaw leader, promised that 150 of his warriors would join the Americans to crush Weatherford and the Red Sticks. On December 23, 1813, Claiborne led his starved men in three columns against Weatherford and more than 300 Red Sticks. When the deaths of the white men that Francis had predicted did not occur, the Red Sticks panicked and broke from their town defense and fled. One of the last to leave the battle,

Weatherford was forced to ride his gray stallion over a cliff twenty feet down into the Alabama River to escape.[32]

Red Stick raids provoked Andrew Jackson to personally lead a force against the Mvskokes. The Mvskokes had known about the noted Indian fighter Jackson, who had earned the name "Old Hickory" from his men. The Mvskokes called him "Jacksa Chula Harjo," which meant "Old Mad Jackson."[33]

On March 27, 1814, Jackson led an estimated 2,500 troops, mostly Tennessee militiamen, in his march against the Lower Mvskoke towns. Jackson was on a revenge mission to pay the Red Sticks back for the Fort Mims massacre. During his march into Mvskoke Country, he gave orders for the construction of Fort Strother on the Coosa River. This strategic location established Jackson's large force only fifteen miles from Tallushatchee, a town with a large number of Red Stick warriors.

Jackson ordered his best officer, General John Coffee, to attack the Red Sticks at Tallushatchee. On November 3, 1813, General Coffee led an estimated 900 dragoons against Tallushatchee. Coffee divided his men into two forces: one group circled around behind the town, while Coffee led another group in a frontal attack. Coffee's men outnumbered the Red Sticks, who retreated while trying to defend their women and children. The retreating Red Sticks fell into Coffee's trap, however, as the second force behind the town opened fire, catching the warriors in a crossfire. Davy Crocket claimed, "We shot them like dogs."[34] Coffee won a decisive victory: about 180 Red Sticks were killed, with only five of his own men lost and about forty soldiers wounded. In the course of the battle, Jackson saw Mvskoke women killing their babies because they believed the soldiers would mutilate them. One Mvskoke woman was dead but continued to hold her baby in her arms. Jackson took the baby boy from her, and he and his wife, Rachel, would name the child Lincoya and raise him until he died at the age of sixteen from tuberculosis.[35]

Coffee's victory incited the Red Sticks with revenge against all settlers, soldiers, and even friendly Mvskokes who had sided with the

Americans. Jackson and his 2,500 men were camped at Ten Islands on the Coosa River. The general received a report that Red Eagle and an estimated 700 Red Sticks were besieging Talladega, a town with about 150 White Sticks. Jackson ordered his men to prepare for the march, arriving at Talladega on November 9, 1813. Jackson and his force of 1,200 infantry and 800 cavalry immediately engaged Red Eagle and his Red Sticks. Within two hours, they drove the Red Sticks from the battlefield. The soldiers killed about 300 Red Sticks and wounded another 100. Jackson lost about 15 men in the battle, with about 85 wounded.

This major defeat convinced two major Red Stick towns, Hillabee and Fish Pond, to surrender to Jackson for lack of ammunition.[36] But also important was the continual deserting of Jackson's soldiers. December's winter convinced soldiers to leave for their homes as the time for the enlisted men had run out. Jackson returned to Fort Strother to wait for more enlisted men, while the Red Sticks found refuge in white towns for medicine makers to heal their wounds and revive their spiritual strength. Jackson knew that the Red Sticks were treating their wounded and were held up for the winter. Red Eagle received reports that Jackson's men were deserting him. With insufficient supplies, Jackson had only one regiment left, and their enlistments expired in mid-January. The situation became a question of who could regroup faster. Instead of waiting for new enlistments to arrive at Fort Strother in mid-February, Jackson decided to march against the Red Sticks, while hoping to gain reinforcement from the Georgia Militia.

During January 1814, Jackson, Coffee, and their small force marched farther into Mvskoke land and camped twelve miles from Emuckfaw town. The Red Sticks were watching. In early dawn on January 22, 1814, the Red Sticks attacked Jackson's camp. Jackson's men fought back, finally driving away the Red Sticks. To win a quick victory, Jackson ordered Coffee to take his men and burn down the Red Sticks' camp. Coffee arrived near the camp but realized that he was badly outnumbered and returned to report to Jackson.

Jackson had grossly underestimated the Mvskokes; he would not do this again. He reluctantly decided to return to Fort Strother but anticipated that the Red Sticks would follow and attack. Because Jackson had trouble crossing Emuckfaw Creek, he had to take a longer route, crossing at Enitachopco Creek. On the morning of January 24, Jackson and his men entered the freezing water when the Red Sticks attacked. He was right in assuming that the Red Sticks had been following them. Jackson ordered his advance guard to move to the rear to meet the Red Stick charge. Chaos (*ehosa*) reigned when Jackson's rear guard panicked. For whatever reason, the Red Sticks did not attack, allowing Jackson and his men to cross Enitachopco Creek safely in their pell-mell retreat to Fort Strother at Ten Islands on the Coosa River.

The Red Sticks did not take advantage of the opportunity to defeat Jackson while he and his men were most vulnerable. Nor did the Red Sticks follow Jackson to Fort Strother to deliver a decisive blow. Both sides chose instead to treat their wounded and wait out the remaining cold months until spring. News finally reached the Mvskokes that Tecumseh, the legendary Shawnee war leader, had refused to retreat and was killed on the battlefield at the Thames River on October 5, 1813.

Jackson did not wait for spring to bring warm weather. He received reports that the Red Sticks led by Red Eagle were gathered at Tohopeka town on the Tallapoosa River. Red Eagle had learned by now that Jackson enjoyed bringing the fight to the enemy. Red Eagle hoped to decide where the battlefield would be and to use the terrain of the swamp area as an advantage. For whatever reason, Red Eagle was not to be at the final battle of the Red Stick War.

During early March, Jackson received new enlisted men at Fort Williams. His force contained 2,500 soldiers, plus 500 Cherokees and about 100 Lower Mvskokes who had been influenced by Indian agent Benjamin Hawkins to fight the Upper Mvskokes. Some Mvskokes claimed it was wrong for Mvskokes to spill the blood of other Mvskokes. Upon hearing from Hawkins about the factionalism

among the Mvskokes, Jackson decided this was the best time to strike
against the enemy. Within a week, he began his march with more
than 3,000 soldiers and Indian allies deep into Mvskoke homeland.

Tohopeka town on the Tallapoosa River was the target. Medicine makers had moved the ceremonial fire from Okfuskee town to
build Tohopeka the previous year.[37] The *mekko* (chief) Menawa pre-
sided over the Red Sticks to fortify Tohopeka, covering twenty acres
of thirty to fifty lodges.[38] Jackson camped his large force near the
Mvskoke town, and news of the large number reached Menawa. The
Red Sticks prepared to defend their community, which was located
on an extension of land where the Tallapoosa River circled it like a
horseshoe. Jackson had devised his plan of attack, the same one that
General John Coffee had used at Tallushatchee on March 24. Jackson divided his men into two groups; one group of about 1,300 led
by Coffee crossed the river to attack the Red Sticks from behind. In
anticipating an attack on Tohopeka, Menawa had his people build a
wall of logs more than a thousand feet long in front of the town. The
wall stood five feet high, eight feet in some places, and it impressed
Jackson.

A little after ten o'clock at eighty yards away, Jackson fired two
cannons at the Red Sticks. Jackson's 100 friendly Mvskokes began
to rub their bodies with charred wood to make them black.[39] The
powers associated with red, representing life for the Red Sticks, and
black, symbolizing death for Jackson's Mvskokes, would help each
side's warriors. For two hours, the shooting went back and forth,
with soldiers and Red Sticks being only slightly wounded. Jackson
waited to hear from Coffee that his men had crossed the river and
were in position to fire at the Red Sticks should they try to escape
by fording the river. Jackson ordered Colonel John Williams to lead
the Thirty-Ninth Infantry Regiment in a bayonet charge over the
wall of logs. The soldiers and Indian allies engaged the Red Sticks,
firing muzzle to muzzle. As the sun's journey reached its end, the
hand-to-hand combat began to pile up Red Stick bodies. The dark
meeting the day's end did not alter the battle, the turning point of
the battle promised by Monohe, the prophet. Disgusted with the

prophet, Menawa fought on. Jackson, however, lost about 50 men. On the defensive, the remaining Red Sticks fell into the Tallapoosa as Coffee's men fired at them. About 200 Red Sticks managed to escape. Menawa refused to surrender. In anger, he killed Monohe, the prophet, because of the loss. When a prophecy is wrong, the prophet is responsible, and the Red Sticks killed two other prophets of their own that day.[40] Menawa received seven gunshot wounds; he was thought to be dead but floated downriver at night to escape.[41] Jackson declared the Battle of Horseshoe Bend a final victory over the Mvskokes.

The Treaty of 1814 officially ended the Red Stick War.[42] The Mvskokes were forced to agree to "a permanent peace" with the United States and with the Cherokees, Choctaws, and Chickasaws. A total of thirty-one Mvskoke leaders signed the treaty, but not Mekko Menawa.[43] With the absence of Menawa, the Mvskoke tradition was followed that a Red Stick leader of a town could not negotiate peace, which was the responsibility of White Stick leaders. Other Red Stick leaders representing other towns were forced to sign the treaty. US officials led by Major General Andrew Jackson and Benjamin Hawkins had learned about Mvskoke medicine ways and the dangerous role of prophets. Article 6 of the treaty also called for the surrender of all Mvskoke prophets and instigators of the war. The Mvskokes ceded fourteen million acres of their homeland to the United States.[44] The treaty led to the beginning of the removal of the Mvskokes from their traditional homelands to Indian Territory, which became Oklahoma.

The fall of the Mvskoke Confederacy had already started well before the Battle of Horseshoe Bend. One factor in this fall was the growing outside influence of Benjamin Hawkins and the Mvskoke desire for guns and material goods that traders offered. Another factor was the loose membership of many Indigenous groups in the Mvskoke Confederacy, which became a key factor in the factionalism that pitted the Upper Mvskokes against the Lower Mvskokes. Some people called it a civil war of Mvskokes. The spiritual balance eluded the entire Mvskoke community because the greater number of individuals, with relationships fluctuating all the time, made it more difficult to find peaceful harmony. This spiritual energy, where a group of people feel a single emotion, has been called patriotism and peoplehood or community feeling.

Yet although the spiritual balance of peace had been destroyed by war, the idea of it persisted and continues today among the Mvskoke people. Between good and bad is "balance" that calms individuals' emotions. This spiritual balance is the purpose of life. Although the Mvskokes stress the importance of peace among communities and within the community, they also focus equally on the spiritual peace within the person.

From the Mvskoke spiritual imbalance in the Red Stick War, we learn that Mvskoke philosophy is an important lesson for the rest of the world. But to understand other people's struggles for peace, the first step is to know who we are as individuals. Last, there are two observable contexts of peace. The first is the spiritual balance of peace in our personal journeys, which involves psychology, philosophy, and the study of other Indigenous people's practices of self-examination. The second context is outside the individual person, politics, as presented by the other chapters in this volume, which examine case studies of geopolitical peace and the suffering manifested from war, violence, trauma, and diaspora.

4

Exegeting Peace from Nagpur

BRUCE B. LAWRENCE

In the fall of 2013, I visited Nagpur, India. Even though Nagpur is the third-largest city in Maharashtra and renowned for its tiger reserves, it is off the beaten path for anyone interested in cultural or peace studies. After all, despite tigers and superhot *sabji* cuisine, Nagpur is more about high-tech education and right-of-center politics than it is about cultural activities. The city boasts a number of national research universities that relate mostly to technology, engineering, mining, and agriculture; historically, it has been renowned as the headquarters of Rashtriya Swayamsevak Sangh (RSS), a right-wing, Hindu nationalist paramilitary volunteer organization (its name means simply "National Volunteer Organization"). In fact, the RSS was founded by a medical doctor who lived in colonial Nagpur when it was still under British rule (1925).

For three days in 2013, I was sent by the US Department of State to speak at various venues with disparate audiences in Nagpur. The highlight came on Monday, September 8, when I led an interactive discussion with more than seventy people under the auspices of Qur'anic Arabic Classes (QAC). To my surprise, the discussion was scheduled at the India Peace Centre (IPC). It was chaired by a renowned scholar, Abdul Ghafoor Parekh, the son of a world-famous Qur'an translator, Abdul Karim Parekh, a close friend of Abul-Hasan Ali Nadwi, the founder of Nadwat al-Ulama (Assembly of Muslim Scholars, a major Muslim educational institution dating back to the late nineteenth century). The session began with a Qur'an recitation from Dr. Shahina Khatib, who also gave an address prior to the interactive discussion.

Since that event and my trip to India, I have remained in contact with Dr. Khatib. She has educated me about peace endeavors in India, all emanating from and relating to Nagpur. To the extent I know anything about Muslim efforts to pursue peace from below in modern-day India, I have been inspired and assisted by this remarkable woman, a scholar and professional who is also a social activist residing in Nagpur.[1]

The QAC as a Framework and Catalyst for Peace

Since the election of Narendra Damodardas Modi, the leader of the right-wing Hindu nationalist Bharatiya Janata Party (BJP, Indian People's Party), as prime minister in 2014, India has experienced a proliferation of anti-Muslim violence. Prior to the BJP's rise to power, Muslims retaliated against Hindus when attacked, but they are now cowed down and frightened. As a consequence, there has been an overall expansion of Hindu violence against Muslims. Generally speaking, the prevailing mood remains tense, and there is growing Muslim insecurity. Nagpur contains a majority Hindu population with a sizeable yet politically weak Muslim minority. The RSS, which is ideologically connected to the BJP, is headquartered in Nagpur. Because of this connection, one would expect Hindu–Muslim tensions to be especially heightened there. However, Dr. Khatib has not allowed this seemingly tense political situation in Nagpur to impede her from peacebuilding initiatives through the QAC.

For Dr. Khatib, as for others in the QAC, the best resource for peace is faith-committed groups working together, collectively seeking to mobilize others from their communities on behalf of peace initiatives. It is not quite a common people's ethos because these groups' activities have not yet been forged as a public culture,[2] but the QAC initiative does aim to instill a sense of shared vision that comes from multiple scriptural sources.

Dr. Khatib explains that "the basic work of the QAC is to make all aware of the original text of holy scripture, so that any mediator in between is not able to corrupt or deform or twist the meaning of divine words according to his mindset or wish."³ She takes an interdisciplinary approach to analyzing Qur'anic passages by committing to rendering the *meaning* of select passages into accessible English for wider dissemination among IPC activists, most of whom are not Muslim.

There are three key elements in Dr. Khatib's efforts: (1) recognizing the singular importance, the primal meaning, attached to the Qur'an in Arabic; (2) committing to rendering the meaning of select Qur'an passages into accessible English to achieve the QAC's greater effort of (3) making Qur'anic themes of peace understandable to Muslims and non-Muslims alike throughout India and the rest of the world. For Dr. Khatib and others in the QAC, a shared understanding of Qur'anic themes of peace will help alleviate Hindu–Muslim tensions, which pose an immediate threat to cultural and political stability in India. Thus, an interdisciplinary approach to exhorting social peace and building communities of shared faith and understanding is born.

Abdul Ghafoor Parekh stresses the grassroots nature of the IPC's appeal to the Qur'an. After noting that the translation of meaning is a human effort and therefore that "we don't promote any translation, nor do we condemn any," he observes that

> the Qur'an is, of course, available throughout the globe in almost all Muslim homes. It has been impossible to spread one or many translations throughout the world in centuries; rather, we concentrated on spreading the *meanings* of the words appearing in the Holy Book. It worked like a wonder! Hence we started the two-hundred-hour course, and, by the grace of the Almighty, it is working in the country on thousands. We came to the conclusion that the Qur'an is revealed in heavenly Arabic and is exceptionally easy to learn, understand, and realize. . . . As it says in Q 54:17: "Indeed, WE made this Qur'an easy to understand and remind. Who is now willing to take it to heart?"⁴

Yet this plea for access to the Qur'an also conceals a crucial point: an English translation of the Qur'an, like that of any scriptural resource, must be particular and carefully framed to properly provide the guidance needed for an inclusive movement directed toward peace. And so the QAC's threefold aim reflects a two-stage approach: (1) to choose the right passages and (2) to provide the right accents for these passages.[5]

In looking for the "right" parts of the Holy Qur'an to spread their message, QAC's leaders also have the mandate to find the most inclusive translation. Despite the assertion that the QAC does not "promote any translation," I discovered in Nagpur last fall and since then in extensive email exchanges with Dr. Khatib that there does exist a strong proclivity for Muhammad Asad's revisionist translation—at once bold and eccentric. His translation is titled *The Message of the Qur'an* (originally published in 1980 and reissued in 2003). In addition to these two editions, there are three India-specific editions, all produced during the past decade. They are locally available and widely distributed in Nagpur under the name "Adam Eisabhai."[6]

However, Dr. Khatib is careful to stress that students are not pressured to embrace Asad's translation; rather, through presenting this translation among others, the QAC enables students to "open the human thinking process with the help of divine verses, and a fruitful student will regard fellow beings with a peaceful mindset. He or she comes to realize the difference between default religion and God-ordered religion through pondering the original texts of Qur'an."

As I tried to explore the impact of Dr. Khatib's peace initiative through the QAC, I was put in touch with others outside her cohort. Although her own immediate circle at the QAC is mainstream Sunni in membership, outlook, and practice, she also connects to Shi'i Muslims and numerous non-Muslims: twenty-five Hindus, some twenty Christians, as well as Buddhists and Sikhs. Clearly, the range and insight of Dr. Khatib's civic discourse on behalf of peacemaking and justice seeking are extraordinary: she has a presence on the Internet but even more of one on the ground not only throughout India but also, above all, in Maharashtra and Nagpur. (The QAC's pragmatic impact is discussed later.)

I am *not* suggesting Dr. Khatib is the only or the best Muslim waging peace in contemporary India. There are others who are more renowned, such as the late Asghar Ali Engineer, the Dawoodi Bohra activist from Mumbai; Maulana Wahiduddin Khan, a modern-day Gandhian whose son, Saniyasnain Khan, founded Goodword Books (1996) and later coordinated with the Centre for Peace and Spirituality (2001), while his daughter, Fareed Khanam, assisted in his widely disbursed translation of the Qur'an (2009).

As notable as these giants of modern-day Hindustani Islam are, both Engineer and Wahiduddin Khan are professionally trained scholars (the former in the Bohra priesthood, the latter as a Sunni scholar and journalist). Dr. Khatib, although far from an autodidact, has continued her life as a scientist and teacher while using the QAC to wage peace in several settings. She has male role models and teachers. Among those who have inspired and assisted her is the American peace activist Mohamad Bashar Arafat.[7] Yet there is a distinctive female tone about her work. Is it also feminist? That question requires brief consideration before looking at other aspects of her labor and influence.

Dr. Shahina Khatib's Distinctive Approach

Although Dr. Khatib is a tireless female activist, she is not an Indian Muslim feminist who is engaged with the Qur'anic passages that occupy most Euro-American feminists. Dr. Khatib does not revisit the same "tired" issues of female inequality or uxorial degradation that are common fare for Euro-American feminists, whether Muslim or non-Muslim. Consider Q2:228 (men a degree above women), 4:1 (the creation verse), 4:3 (multiple wives), and 4:34 (wife remonstrating). Traditional feminists debate and engage with these sections of the Qur'an and ultimately propagate a feminist jihad to reconcile social justice with scriptural authority in the real and virtual world of the twenty-first century.

Dr. Shahina Khatib is well aware of these "dark" verses in the Qur'an and is alert to social justice as paramount for Muslims. For instance, when I spoke to her about the translation of the term *daraba* in Q4:34, which discusses men's right to punish women by "beating them lightly," as it is inclusively translated by Abdullah Yusuf Ali,[8] she agreed at once that it was a huge problem. "Prof. you are right," she wrote in an email message to me in April 2015; "no translation gives the exact meaning of *daraba*. Nobody can justify that the Creator of a *woman* has given permission to beat her to another creation *man*. NO. NO. NO."[9] However, although she is aware of these issues, she is not occupied with them in her public addresses, and she does not exploit them to pursue a feminist jihad.

Dr. Khatib instead pursues a mental jihad privileging common sense over gender in her approach to the same issues. She uses her QAC platform to mobilize Muslim women and involve them in peacebuilding initiatives. She annually arranges to give lectures to final-year theology students, and among the favorite topics are women and the Qur'an, peace from a Qur'anic perspective, gender equity, jihad, divorce in the Qur'an, and the technology of consciousness. She has also assembled nearly eighty-five Muslim women for a feed-the-poor movement in which wealthy Muslim women are dedicated to feeding the needy. The movement is said to have created a harmonious atmosphere observable at the city level between the Nagpur Municipal Corporation of Hindu women and these eighty-five Muslim women. Dr. Khatib's "female" approach thus creates harmony without calling for a physical feminist jihad.

Dr. Khatib's bent, like that of Abdul Ghafoor Parekh and others linked to the QAC, is to consider scripture as a rational instrument for peacebuilding: in short, to pursue a pragmatic jihad on behalf of social justice and global peace. As far back as 2005, when she came to the United States on a guided study tour of US religious education, Dr. Khatib gave a talk titled "The Qur'an Confirms the Rational Doctrine of All the Prophets." One can detect a clear line of argument and advocacy from this talk to many of her later interventions. They all relate to the Noble Book, the Holy Qur'an, but always to its bridge-building and peace-waging potential. For example, her talk "Consider the Women in Peacebuilding," delivered at the Interfaith Coalition for Peace Journey to Bhubaneshwar in August 2013, concerned the equality of men and woman as it is presented in scripture. The crucial citation to the Qur'an reads as follows: "O men! Behold, WE have created you all out of a male and a female, and have made you into nations and tribes, so that you might come to know one another. *Verily, the noblest of you in the sight of ALLAH is the one who is most deeply conscious of HIM.*[10] Behold, ALLAH is all-knowing, all-aware" (Q49:13, emphasis added).

The Role of Translation

In a later section of this essay, I assess the QAC's practical import, but first it is important to understand its intellectual origin and theological agenda. In many ways, it caters to Islamic modernism—and some would also say to neo-Mu'tazili rationalism—which is at the core of the pluralist/judicial equity struggle that animates Dr. Khatib. Owing to this connection, neither she nor any of her associates concealed from me their admiration for Muhammad Asad and his endeavor to utilize the English Qur'an to rethink and revive Islamic ethos. It is no accident, then, that Dr. Khatib accepts Asad's unique translations of key terms (especially *taqwa* and *muttaqi* as "God consciousness" and "the one conscious of God") because his translations highlight the positive content of the Qur'an in a reliable and comprehensible manner, which is particularly helpful for the QAC's purpose of appealing to non-Muslims and non-Arabic speakers. As an example of his positive translation, Asad explains in the very first usage of *muttaqi* in Q2:2 that the translation "God conscious" is to be preferred to

> the conventional translation of *muttaqi* as "God-fearing" (which) does not adequately render the *positive* content of this expression—namely, the awareness of His all-presence and the desire to mold one's existence in the light of this awareness; while the interpretation adopted by some translators, "one who guards against evil" or "one who is careful of his duty," does not give more than one particular aspect of God-consciousness.[11]

Yet in keeping with the QAC's insistence that it will not "promote any translation or condemn any," Dr. Khatib occasionally modifies

Asad on minor points, and she demurs on one major point: she does not accept "Allah" as a translatable name of the Supreme, Absolute Other. For her, Allah remains "ALLAH," always untranslated, always in caps throughout.

And this distinction gives a very different tone to many passages, such as Q33:35:

> Verily, for all men and women who have totally submitted themselves unto ALLAH, and all believing men and believing women, and all truly devout men and truly devout women, and all men and women who are true to their words and all men and women who are patient in adversity, and all men and women who humble themselves (before ALLAH) and all men and women who spend in charity, and all self-denying men and self-denying women, and all men and women who are mindful of their chastity, and all men and women who remember ALLAH unceasingly: for (all of) them has ALLAH readied forgiveness of sins and a mighty reward.

Here, even though "ALLAH" is not translated as "God," His message is expanded, not reserved for Muslims alone, as it is in Yusuf Ali's rendition, where "Allah" is consistently rendered as "God." The role of ALLAH/God in both the original Asad translation and the modification by Dr. Khatib contrasts starkly with Yusuf Ali's rendition from 1938:

> For Muslim men and women—for believing men and women, for devout men and women, for true men and women, for men and women who are patient and constant, for men and women who humble themselves, for men and women who give in Charity, for men and women who fast (and deny themselves), for men and women who guard their chastity, and for men and women who engage much in God's praise—for them has God prepared forgiveness and great reward.[12]

In other words, Yusuf Ali and others who translate the first phrase as "*Muslim* men and women" rather than "*all* men and women" are not just anachronistic but exclusionary in their reading of the Arabic text of the Word of God because in their translations this opening descriptor applies only to Muslims.

Individuals such as Dr. Khatib instead utilize inclusive translations of this section and others of the Qur'an with the intention of making it applicable to a wider audience. As Asad carefully explains in the foreword to his translation, "When his [Muhammad's] contemporaries heard the words *islam* and *muslim*, they understood them as denoting man's 'self-surrender to God' and 'one who surrenders himself to God,' without limiting these terms to any specific community or denomination."[13] And so it is crucial to underline that for Asad and for others who follow his lead, including Dr. Khatib and Abdul Ghafoor Parekh, God is addressing all—all men and all women—who submit to Him, all who believe in Him, all humankind, in effect, as a composite group "made ready for forgiveness of sins and a mighty reward."[14] Furthermore, Dr. Khatib's refusal to replace "Allah" with "God" or any other name and her selection of translations that appeal to a wider audience demonstrate more plainly that the name "Allah" and the Qur'an by extension belong within rhetoric aimed at peacebuilding regardless of one's personal religion or belief system. Utilizing and modifying inclusive translations is an integral part of using holy scripture to appeal to a wider audience for peacebuilding purposes, and the QAC has mastered the art of doing so.

Major Impacts of the QAC

What distinguishes QAC activists and the large peace community with which they align themselves is the common affirmation that all scripture is eternal truth, but elided with that axiom is a further commitment to using the Qur'an as pragmatic truth—that is, to apply selected verses from the Qur'an as truth in the service of collective pursuits, involving different Muslims but also non-Muslim others with shared ideals. And so the QAC project does not rely solely on the Qur'an or even on one translation in every venue for every audience.[15]

Especially pivotal for peacebuilding are the contexts for development of public space and citizenship in the modern era. It is difficult to map out the exact impacts Dr. Khatib and the QAC have had on communal life in Nagpur because their faith-based approach has not yet transformed into a public culture of peace. However, while the rest of India has been plagued with a rise of violent clashes of Hindus against Muslims since Modi's election, in Nagpur these QAC classes have helped create stable Hindu–Muslim relations by bridging peace between different belief systems.

Dr. Khatib is acutely aware that "it takes little time to corrupt and distort, but grassroots-level work of reformation takes a long time. The stable Hindu–Muslim relationship itself is a positive sign of awareness about nonviolence." She credits "periodic and frequent public lectures and . . . participation at all religious festivals, seminars, workshops, lectures, meetings, and representation of the QAC at local and national levels" for maintaining nonviolent relations between Hindus and Muslims in Nagpur.

Thus far, the most impressive and evident impact of the QAC and its other activities has been its ability to maintain peace by demonstrating to Hindus (and other religious groups) that the biased and oft-misunderstood "dominant image of Islam and its heavenly revealed commands are poles apart from each other." It is also worth mentioning that the QAC has extended beyond just the borders of Nagpur, with classes all over India, from Mumbai, Pune, and Surat to Calcutta, Chennai, and Manipur, among many other places.

Furthermore, Dr. Khatib's ability to craft non-Qur'anic presentations of Qur'anic principles has also led non-Muslims to enlarge their perceptions of Islam. For instance, in 2011 she addressed a group of RSS members about crucial Qur'anic principles. She omitted the name "Allah" from the opening invocation, cloaking it in a pronoun, "in His name the Most Exalted," and, as in her talks to largely Christian audiences in India or to mixed audiences in the United States, here she adopted a universal register to which even hard-core RSS members could relate. Non-Muslims then become more receptive to translations of the Qur'an and its divine messages and verses as instruments for waging peace. This is no small feat in an era of Islamophobia throughout Western, Christian nations and Hindu virulence in India. Dr. Khatib's ability to appeal to wider audiences with Islamic principles proves that the QAC's impact is far-reaching.

Shortcomings of the QAC Approach and Praxis

Dr. Khatib's approach also has certain tensions and occasional contradictions, whether in her use of Asad or in her fluctuation between Asad and other Qur'an translators-interpreters. These challenges became evident in two talks, one by her mentor and coworker at the QAC, Abdul Ghafoor Parekh, and the other by her. Parekh titled a speech delivered to a group of civil servants and magistrates "An Eye for an Eye Will Make the World Blind." After quoting Gandhi's popular dictum, he then developed its meaning for all who revere and quote from "the Heavenly Scriptures." Though the final appeal clearly was "to understand the scriptures in [their] original language and spirit[, then] apply [them] accordingly," no other "heavenly" scriptures are mentioned, but Allah is not cited as the name of the Creator, nor is reference made to God Almighty. An excerpt from this talk provides an example:

> Finally, I invite *all the people of the Book, people in power, officers, and every individual* to personally study the various aspects of the all-encompassing guidance, including that of the judiciary, and ponder its various aspects of mercy and the development of human character. This we must adopt in our lives and convey the message throughout the world.
>
> But yes, if the laws are hijacked by citizens and they decide the matters on their own, using such heavenly injunctions as a tool for vengeance among them, all on the earth will become blind due to such terror. May Almighty save us with such and may HE help us in understanding the scriptures in its original language and spirit and apply it accordingly!

Like Abdul Ghafoor Parekh, Dr. Khatib switches back and forth in her reference to the divine when she is trying to appeal to a mixed audience. In the case of a detailed explanation of "time," she appeals to all who, like her, share a scientific engagement with the modern world yet want to ascribe its original and ultimate purpose to a higher force. In the following passages, note especially the seamless, unmarked shifting back and forth of the name used for the ultimate referent: "Sustainer," "Lord," "Almighty God," "God Almighty," but then "Allah":

Most of the people underestimate the powers of their Sustainer, and are not ready to give a second thought to their independent life style. Instead of submitting to the Lord, they repeatedly raise doubts, and stubbornly ask questions about the occurrence of the day of reckoning and punishment, honor and reward, as presage by the Almighty God. They ask when this chastisement will occur?

To let us wake up from our deep slumber and to warn us, the Creator of this Universe sends upon us chastisements like earth quakes [sic], tornados and tsunamis. On those moments despite so much scientific progress, we are helpless in front of the power and strength of Nature. But despite so many notices and warnings, we are not prepared to mend. We prefer to live in our own world of imaginations and illusion and ignorance. We think that the whole Universe is moving on as per our own calculation of speed of the day and night. Fourteen centuries ago, our Lord invited us from the state of ignorance to the world of wisdom, that the planet we are habituating is bound to come to an end. The information about this transitory world and its resources is revealed by the Originator of the Universe in the Holy Qur'an, chapter 6 verse 32:

"And the life of this world is not more than but a play and a passing delight; and the life in the hereafter is by far the better for all who are conscious of ALLAH. Will you not, then, use your reason?"[16]

Then, again in chapter 3 verse 14 it is said:

"Alluring temptation and craze are kept for mankind in the fanciful desires of women, children, manpower, accumulated stocks and treasures of bullion and silver, and mode of conveyance like pedigreed horses, live-stock and lands. All these are not more than consumables of this world only—while with ALLAH, there are far better retreats and enjoyments."[17]

Passion Sparks Peace

Regardless of its few shortcomings, Dr. Khatib's QAC initiative exemplifies the role of people's agency for establishing peace in local communities. Although not a particularly renowned peacemaking entity in contemporary India, the QAC opens dialogue in a refreshingly authentic, practical, and local manner.

Dr. Khatib is, for all intents and purposes, an ordinary person: not a full-time nongovernment organization worker or human rights activist or a professionally trained scholar of Islam or even an experienced journalist. She has continued her normal life as a scientist and teacher yet uses her passions and teaching talents to effect extraordinary change in Nagpur. She makes peacebuilding an everyday, routine business that any ordinary individual can participate in by integrating it within the framework of classes. Students who attend her regular, short-term university courses later go on to take university certificate exams in the subject of the QAC. Although Dr. Khatib's QAC initiative has not yet transformed into a public culture of peace, it is far from ineffective. For instance, as of June 2017, according to Dr. Khatib,

> [a total of] 1,067 students have appeared and passed the Nagpur University certificate exam. 166 students have cleared Nasik University exams. At Vidarbha Sahitya Sangh [an RSS-regulated center], 1,106 students have been taught up till now. At the India Peace Centre [a Christian-regulated center], 448 students have been taught so far. All these centers are still running, and, God willing, in future they will continue.

Thus, the running total of QAC alumni as of June 2017 was 2,787, with more being added each year.

In addition, Dr. Khatib's work engages with a remarkably wide audience, allowing Sunnis, Shi'is, Christians, Hindus, Sikhs, Buddhists, hard-core RSS think-tank members, university faculty, men and women, the young and the old to participate in the same QAC initiative. This interfaith bridge between different sects and religions affords all people the same opportunity and capacity for dialogue, scriptural understanding, and peacebuilding. Her work and her initiative have had the greatest impact on the community of Nagpur, which has remained mostly untouched by Hindu–Muslim conflicts. The community heralds Dr. Khatib as a peace ambassador because of her QAC initiative, which has proven capable of quenching ethnic and religious conflicts during an otherwise violence-ridden time.

Dr. Khatib provides inspiration that peacebuilding does not require some extraneous international conglomerate with a host of regulations and limitations of its own. In fact, the QAC does not receive funding or sponsorship from any external sources. Dr. Khatib's passion and dedication to making peace the routine business of individuals instead pave the way for widespread peacebuilding. As an ordinary person who establishes peace through seemingly unremarkable Qur'anic Arabic classes, all the while effecting exceptional change throughout Nagpur, Dr. Khatib provides an extremely interesting instance of people's peace.

Conclusion

People's peace may be a movement distinctive to Nagpur, in the heartland of Hindu India, but it also projects an ethical and visionary approach that exceeds its spatial limits. It represents an attempt to shift the discussion from what is too frequently a state, international agencies, policy approach to one that is less bounded, binary, and reductive. It challenges peacemakers to dig deeper, to think of a conversation in which the speakers are from the grassroots, local-actor level and use multiple idioms. Many of these people may not even be recognized as peacemakers in the pervasive discourse of Western observers. But they advance a certain way of being deeply religious, even monotheistic in their vocabulary, and yet open to good will and collective actions for peacemaking from many stakeholders.

Women work with men, but, as we saw from the example of Dr. Shahina Khatib, they embrace peace as their own mental or rational jihad. Their primary tool is the Qur'an and its proper English translations. The recurrent message is inclusive and multicreedal: all those who are conscious of God, whether non-Muslim or Muslim, can and should ground themselves in a religious ethics that heralds becoming better through interaction with similar yet different people.

Unlike the Gandhian method of nonviolence, the QAC advocates are using knowledge for change as mandated by prophets culminating in Muhammad and clarified in scriptures from the Torah to the Qur'an. Far from an outdated, murky message, theirs is a clarion cry for all to consider—primarily Indians but also those beyond India who engage scripture as much more than a theological exercise divorced from real-life circumstances, seeing it instead as a pragmatic directive to change people's hearts and thus their outlook and actions, their home and the world.[18]

What has been the effect of any of these talks on an Indian audience that includes Muslims, Hindus, and Christians? Do these novel translations as well as modifications of and commentaries about the translations help non-Muslims see Islam as a peaceful religion in a contested place (Nagpur) and at a pivotal time fraught with peril (post-2014, with the success of the BJP in central and state elections)? The QAC's effort is being put forth in India, where Muslims are a sizeable minority yet politically weak and where the prevailing mood has darkened, as it has in so many other countries where nativism and nationalism rely on and project onto all citizens a majoritarian identity, often marked by religion.

In short, although there has not to date been any effort to map the actual results of QAC outreach, one can conclude from its tireless and imaginative labor, not least Dr. Shahina Khatib's, that appealing to a larger, pluralist audience through scripture and multiple modified translations of *meaning* does matter. No translation, of course, can do the work of appealing to different religious groups on its own; such an appeal needs agency and patient persistence. Not merely Asad's translation but also the gatherings in which his key terms are parlayed and the talks they have inspired, such as those given by Dr. Khatib, have been transformative, particularly for non-Muslims.

Does that mean that Islam can be a site for peace? The efforts from Nagpur and especially Dr. Shahina Khatib's labor through the QAC suggest that the grassroots narrative of dialogue, with constructive change, is more promising than the headline stories of Islamic extremism and violence. One can dare to hope that Dr. Khatib's and the QAC's jihad for peace will succeed.

5

Peace, Reconciliation, and Forgiveness

*Early Rabbinic Stories and Their
Implications for People's Peace*

JOEL GEREBOFF

The relationship among notions of peace, reconciliation, and forgiveness are far from clear. The definition of each concept varies from culture to culture, from religion to religion, and within religious traditions. Reconciling previously conflicting parties need not result in peace or even see peace as its goal. Moreover, reconciliation and even perhaps the attainment of peace may not require the offended party's forgiveness of the wrongdoer. Early rabbinic sources, especially a number of stories in the Babylonian Talmud, provide interesting resources for examining these issues. These accounts point to structural and complex emotional factors that frequently occasion conflicts as well as to concerns that successful reconciliations must address. Several rabbinic stories with information about forgiveness and reconciliation from ancient Greece enable us to draw out some implications of these views, which come from cultural, social, and political worlds far different from our own, for the disciplines of peace and conflict-resolution studies and for efforts at achieving reconciliation and peace.

As just mentioned, whether forgiveness is essential for achieving reconciliation or peace is a debated question. The Truth and

Reconciliation Commission in South Africa, for example, explored this matter before proceeding to its actual activities. In a related way, we observe that academic discussions of forgiveness have increased dramatically in the past decade. A search of several research databases shows that entering "forgiveness" as a subject yields 1,250 items in the Atla Religion Database; more than 1,000 in Lexis Nexis, which catalogs law-related publications; and nearly 500 in Philosopher's Index.[1] Many of these publications are products of the past decade. And although smaller numbers of publications appear in databases for criminal justice and political science, it is quite evident that interest in analyzing the character of forgiveness and methods for achieving it has recently risen in significance. Forgiveness serves as a key element in explorations of how to pursue reconciliation and peace on both group and interpersonal levels.

A particularly insightful and valuable analysis of forgiveness from a philosophical and religious angle is that provided by the classics scholar David Konstan. Offering a provocative discussion of the notion of forgiveness in his book *Before Forgiveness*, Konstan observes that "forgiveness is widely perceived as an urgent matter these days, not to say, it is much in vogue." He argues that "the modern concept of interpersonal forgiveness, in the full sense of the term, did not exist in ancient Greece and Rome. Even more startlingly, it is not fully present in the Hebrew Bible, nor in the New Testament or in early Jewish and Christian commentaries on the Holy Scriptures."[2] In the ancient world, offended and offending parties did not strive to overcome conflict or achieve peace by seeking to forgive or be forgiven.

To advance his claim that before the Enlightenment our understanding of forgiveness had not yet been conceptualized, especially in sources from antiquity, Konstan first delineates the key traits of this modern view. According to him, from Kant onward "forgiveness is understood as a dyadic relationship requiring serious transformations on the part of both the offending and the offended parties":

> Forgiveness in the principal modern acceptation is not reducible to the appeasement of anger; rather, it is a bilateral process involving

a confession of wrongdoing, evidence of sincere repentance, and a change of heart or moral perspective on the part of the offender, together with a comparable alteration in the forgiver, by which she or he consents to forego vengeance on the basis precisely of the change in the offender.[3]

Certain actions and emotional transformations are essential for forgiveness in the modern sense. The offending party not only must feel regret but must experience a sense of remorse. Remorse entails the rejection of the offending action in the future and sorrow for the harm done, of having a sense of self-reproach. And the offended party must perceive that the perpetrator has had a true change of heart, and he or she must give up anger, resentment, and a desire for revenge.[4] This complete list of required components is not found, however, in ancient sources as they discuss the reconciliation of interpersonal conflicts.

Classical, Israelite, rabbinic, and early Christian sources depicting conflicts and reconciliation describe offending parties as appeasing the legitimate anger of those offended. In these sources, anger is appropriate only for a superior party to hold toward an inferior. Reconciliation requires the offending, inferior party to acknowledge the superior status of the offended one—that is, to humble himself. The goal is to save the offended party's face by means of the offender lowering his or hers. In some instances, offending parties seek to exonerate themselves, but offering excuses is not seeking forgiveness. In none of the few biblical stories about reconciliation do characters seek forgiveness. In the Hebrew Bible, only God forgives or, more often, pardons. Only God can grant *selicha* and does so only for a generalized rejection of God, not for particular wrongs committed against humans.[5]

Drawing upon writings by Michael Morgan and Louis Newman, Konstan also discusses early rabbinic views relevant to forgiveness.[6] Although these writers focus on dicta in Mishnah and Tosefta, the earliest rabbinic documents date to the period 200–250 CE, containing the views of early sages, the *tannaim*. Konstan concludes his discussion of rabbinic texts extending from the amoraic strata to the Talmud, dating from 200 to 600 CE, with the observation, "Even with regard to Talmudic discussions interpersonal forgiveness is still set in the context of the relationship with the divine. One must again insist on how rare any such discussion of forgiveness is in the corpus."[7] Similarly, early Christian texts do not employ a modern notion of forgiveness. For example, in Matthew forgiveness is not the result of a change of heart on the offender's part; rather, in line with Gary Anderson's views on sin in biblical sources, the offended party decides unilaterally to remit the debt owed him or her because of the wrongdoer's offense.[8] All in all, in the ancient world, restoring relationships ultimately took into account emotions such as anger and shame and required offending parties materially to demonstrate and acknowledge the superior party's power and authority.

Rabbinic Texts on Reconciliation

An analysis of several narratives in the Babylonian Talmud, amoraic sources, makes evident rabbinic views regarding how to overcome offenses. The small number of previous studies of early rabbinic views of forgiveness has almost exclusively commented on the few sayings in early rabbinic documents on this topic, but no one has examined the larger number of narratives that depict conflicts and efforts at reconciliation.[9] More than sayings, stories, even if literary-fictional creations, present far more of the complexity of life situations and indicate the range of factors that are depicted as leading to various outcomes of conflicts. Only some stories end with successful reconciliation, though even they mention neither "peace" nor "forgiveness." Examining these stories provides valuable insights into how Jews have thought about the challenges of overcoming conflicts. To contextualize these amoraic narratives requires a brief review of earlier tannaitic sources.

A small number of sayings related to "reconciliation" appear in the earliest rabbinic documents: Mishnah, Tosefta, and several halakhic midrashim,[10] including m. Yoma 8:9; Avot 4:18, 5:11; B.Q. 8:7; t. B.Q. 8:30, 9:29, 10:14; Sifra Acharei Mot Pereq 8:2 (parallels

m. Yoma 8:9). None of these texts describes forgiveness in the way we now understand the concept. The ultimate goal is far more about attaining forgiveness or atonement from God. None, in fact, delineates exactly what the offender must say, do, or feel. For example, m. Yoma 8:9 asserts:

> A. For transgressions [done] between a person and God, the Day of Atonement atones.
>
> B. For transgressions between one person and another, the Day of Atonement atones only if he appeases [*yeratzeh*] the other.

And m. B.Q. 8:7 stipulates: "Even though a person gives [monetary compensation] to one [whom he has shamed], he is not pardoned [*nimchal*] [by God] until he seeks it [*yevaqesh*] from him [some add: seeks pardon or mercy], as it is written, 'He [Abraham] is a prophet and he will intercede on your behalf, and you shall live'" (Gen 20:7). The text t. B.Q. 10:14 promulgates:

> A. One who steals from a group must return it to the group.
>
> B. More severe is stealing from a group, than stealing from an individual,
>
> C. For one who steals from an individual can appease him [*lefayso*] and return the stolen item to him. One who steals from a group cannot appease them and return the stolen object to them.

Three key words are employed to refer to what the wrongdoer must do in relation to the wronged party: *levaqesh, leratzot, lefayes*. None of these words means "to seek forgiveness."[11] *Levaqesh* generally means to "seek out" or "request," but in the passages quoted earlier what is being sought is not explicitly stated. T. B.Q. 9:29 adds the word *rachamim*, and other rabbinic (not biblical) texts speak of seeking mercy from someone who has been wronged. *Lefayes* is a term derived from the Greek, not attested biblically, and means "to placate" or "to appease." Finally, *leratzot* draws upon a frequently used biblical term, *ratzah*, translated as "to seek to be found acceptable, favorable."[12] In addition, although the offending party does seek out the aggrieved individual or group, the primary goal of the wrongdoer's actions is to achieve atonement or pardon (*mechilah*) from God.[13] Forgiveness and peace are not mentioned in these texts. They do not delineate exactly what the offender (or sinner) ought to say to the wronged party, nor is there any description of either party's emotional dimensions.[14]

Several stories in the Babylonian Talmud tell of interpersonal conflicts and efforts at reconciliation.[15] Since the last decade of the twentieth century, several scholars have offered fresh approaches to the study of Talmudic narratives, demonstrating the rich literary nature of these narratives, their formulation based on the reworking of earlier rabbinic sources, and making their didactic messages clear. Jeffrey Rubenstein especially has shown how these stories often reflect the culture, concerns, and conflicts of Babylonian rabbinic academies of the postamoraic era, roughly the sixth through the eighth centuries CE. The anonymous composers of these narratives express through them their values and equally their anxieties, including a heightened concern for status and appropriate honor and a fear of being shamed.[16] These stories reveal rabbinic views on conflict, forgiveness, reconciliation, and peace.

Three Stories from the Babylonian Talmud

A story in b. Yev. 96a describes R. Yohanan becoming angry when learning that R. Eleazar b. Pedat reported one of Yohanan's teachings without crediting it to him. Two sages, R. Ammi and R. Assi, seek to calm Yohanan by relaying a previous incident in which a dispute between two authorities of equal status became so intense that in their anger they ended up tearing a Torah scroll. Yohanan becomes further enraged by these comments, for they imply that Eleazar is his colleague, not his inferior student. R. Jacob b. Idi then intervenes and successfully placates Yohanan by referring to the biblical text Joshua 11:15, which reports, "As the Lord commanded Moses his servant, so did Moses command Joshua, and so did Joshua, he left nothing undone of all the Lord commanded Moses." Despite the fact that Joshua did not explicitly refer to Moses when giving instruction to the Israelites, they all knew he was conveying Moses's views.

Everyone likewise knows that Eleazar is also conveying Yohanan's teachings. The story concludes with Yohanan critiquing Ammi and Assi for not knowing how to properly pacify (*lefayes*) him as Idi did.

Anger and deference to honor, appeasement, and reconciliation stand at the center of this narrative. In the end, Yohanan is no longer concerned about having lost face and honor. He does not forgive but is merely appeased, his anger pacified. His relationship with Eleazar is restored, but there is no reference to peace.

By contrast, a story in b. B.M. 84a involving insults and disharmony between R. Yohanan and his student Resh Laqish ends with the tragic death of both when Yohanan does not respond positively to efforts to placate him and acknowledge his status.[17] Yohanan offers to transform the former brigand Resh Laqish into a Torah scholar and offers him his sister as a wife if the latter will take up the challenge. Resh Laqish accepts, and all is going well until one day when a discussion takes place about certain objects' susceptibility to uncleanness—a sword, a lance, and a dagger. On this occasion, it appears that Resh Laqish offends Yohanan by offering his own opinion without first following the required etiquette of asking his teacher for permission to do so. Yohanan reacts by snippily insulting Resh Laqish: "A bandit knows his banditry." The student responds not by showing deference but by remarking that he has actually gained little from his time in the academy, for although they do call him "master" (*rav*) there, he had held the same title among his group of thieves. Yohanan becomes distressed mentally, and Resh Laqish becomes physically ill. At this point, Yohanan's sister, the wife of Resh Laqish, enters weeping, acknowledges her brother's authority, and asks him to aid her husband, initially for the sake of her children and then for her own sake. Yohanan does not accept the entreaty, and Resh Laqish dies. The sages realize how much Yohanan misses his former student and seek to find a replacement for him, but Eleazar b. Pedat does not prove satisfactory. Despite efforts by a third party to acknowledge the offended party's authority, that party remains so caught up in his pride and in having been offended that both he and the offending party pass away. Not only is there no peace or forgiveness in the academy, but even reconciliation is not obtained because of Yohanan's hard-heartedness and misplaced concern for honor.

In these two narratives, a third party intervenes to reconcile conflicting parties. In the story of the deposition of Rabban Gamaliel from his role as the head of the academy in b. Ber. 27b–28a, Gamaliel's eventual submission and indication of suffering lead to his partial restoration to his former role.[18] Gamaliel rules over the academy, which is described using militaristic imagery. On one occasion, he humiliates R. Joshua by having the latter stand on his feet while Gamaliel, seated, continues to teach. The sages eventually cannot take this treatment any longer and protest Gamaliel's continual "troubling" of Joshua. They decide to depose Gamaliel. After being appointed as his replacement, R. Elazar b. Azariah opens up the academy to students whom Gamaliel excluded. The story continues by noting that Gamaliel is distressed, realizing that his actions may have, God forbid, "held back Torah from Israel." Gamaliel determines that he must appease (*afayes*) Joshua. After an initial exchange in which Gamaliel further demonstrates his lack of empathy with his students' situation, he declares to Joshua, "I submit to you [*ne'eneti lach*]. Pardon me [*mechol li*]." After this, the sages partially restore Gamaliel to his role as head of the academy but preserve Elazar b. Azariah's honor by having the former hold that position three weeks of the month and the latter for one week. Honor, shame, and resentment, along with what in the end is the critiqued concern for power and control, drive this narrative. The story does not speak of peace or of forgiveness. But the conflict has been resolved. Submission and appeasement allow for reconciliation, respect for honor, and restoration to office.

Forgiveness in Contemporary Conflict-Resolution and Peace Studies

What are the implications of the ancient Greek views and early rabbinic sayings and narratives about interpersonal conflict for contemporary approaches to intergroup reconciliation and peace? These ancient views emerge from worlds far different from our modern one—worlds in which hierarchy and asymmetrical power relations are a given, maintaining power is central, and honor is of great importance. However, based on my selective reading in peace studies and conflict-resolution studies, including Jewish views and information regarding various programs related to the Israeli–Palestinian (Arab) conflict,[19] I note four potential lessons from these much earlier views for our world today. These lessons relate (1) to the very definitions and goals of conflict resolution and peace studies; (2) to the ongoing importance of power, prestige, and existing structures, even according to some views of what constitutes the goal of seeking peace; (3) to the essential role that emotions play in conflict and the need to attend to them in successful efforts at resolving conflicts; and (4) to the location of various current Jewish writings on peace and conflict resolution and to efforts on the ground related to the Israeli–Palestinian conflict.

Website descriptions of various academic programs indicate a range of views regarding the nature and the scope of peace and conflict-resolution studies. Some programs are described as focusing on either peace or conflict resolution. Some combine the two in some way. Other programs deal with peace and social justice. In "Oil and Water? The Philosophical Commitments of International Peace Studies and Conflict Resolution," Elizabeth Dahl offers a rich and insightful analysis of the diverse understandings of these fields and their underlying philosophical assumptions. She "traces their respective philosophical genealogies (including where possible, variations within each) and the concrete implications of these stances in terms of intellectual wagers about power, truth, structure and conflict."[20] Dahl distinguishes among four approaches: mainstream peace studies, mainstream conflict-resolution studies, critical peace studies, and transformative conflict resolution. Her analysis is detailed, but a key point is that each approach, to the degree it is coherent, draws on certain philosophical views about human nature and interpersonal and international relationships. What I find most relevant in her discussion is her clarification that the mainstream approaches in both peace and conflict-resolution studies largely do not seek to alter existing power relationships, nor do they focus on various types of structure, such as economic or political power. Yet they seek to analyze conflicts and, in some cases, to advance peace. In this regard, Dahl references the ongoing influence of Johan Galtung's distinctions between negative and positive peace.[21] For Galtung, negative peace requires merely the cessation of violence. As Dahl makes clear, some practitioners of peace studies subscribe to this view and assume that unequal status and power—what one might call hierarchies or asymmetrical relations—are taken as givens. To achieve negative peace or to operate within the framework of mainstream peace and conflict-resolution studies *does not* require parties to seek forgiveness but only ultimately to concede the existing power relationships and learn to live with them. This approach seeks to "work within the world system" and focus on the parties' interests. Parties must acknowledge and concede these existing power structures and accommodate them. Forgiving offenses is not necessary, but recognizing power is. These significantly limited goals for conflict resolution—or, as some practitioners see it, for pursuing peace—overlap with many of the ideas found in the ancient Greek and Jewish sources. Those texts emerged from societies and eras in which relationships were assumed to be legitimately hierarchical, a concession to reality that current mainstream peace studies also makes.

Konstan's concluding comments to his study underscore the value of examining the foundational texts of "Western civilization" for what they have to say about forgiveness:

> I have sought to show that the notion of interpersonal forgiveness, as it is basically understood today, is not only not universal but also is of relatively recent coinage, and that the ancient societies to which we often look for models for our ethical concepts *seem to have done perfectly well without it.* I do not mean to suggest that they were in any way morally inferior for this absence; my object is simply to have set the record straight about their strategies of reconciliation as a way of understanding their practices in their own terms.[22]

Similarly, whether the rabbinic views about the difficulties and importance of attaining reconciliation and some forms of peace have any salience for our period is, I believe, surely worth pondering.

It strikes me that the rabbinic narratives coincide in many ways with the assumptions and goals of at least mainstream conflict-resolution studies. These stories make no mention of seeking peace. In many ways, in light of the rabbinic literature's larger limited interest in peace as a practical matter, as a normative ideal for living in this world, this omission is not surprising, and *it may well speak to a realism that we all should keep in mind.* Notions of realism are typical of classical international relations approaches and, as Dahl shows, to mainstream conflict resolution and to some views of peace studies. Jacob Neusner, who has sought to identify key categories of thought and organization in early rabbinic texts, observes, "War forms a category formation and peace is a substantive—a word bearing diffuse references. With what consequence? When we come across the word 'war' without further data, we know the content, but 'peace' covers a mass of miscellaneous, free standing facts."[23] These comments underscore that, in practical terms, peace is not an organizing category for rabbinic Judaism, despite the numerous sayings on peace in the full range of rabbinic literature. This is not to say that rabbinic Judaism encourages warfare; indeed, to the contrary, it severely constricts war's legitimacy. Statements about peace in rabbinic texts are more hortatory, sermonic, and exegetical than explicit regarding how to live life on a daily basis.[24] For the here and now, parties to conflicts, be they individuals or groups, may strive for reconciliation and for ensuring all parties' dignity. Hopes for a world at positive peace are the substance of prayers. So long as the realities of shame, honor, anger, and resentment shape human life, so long as these realities define "human nature," however, peace in its fullest sense will have to wait. Thus, as I see it, these ancient texts have much to say about the need for clarity regarding what the goals and definitions of peace and conflict-resolution studies are.

I have already noted a second implication of these ancient sources. They speak of the realities of power and the need to come to terms with them. To be sure, transformative conflict-resolution studies and critical peace studies contest these structures. Social justice requires significant social change and engineering. Although the ancient sources clearly do not advocate such transformations, their insight into the lack of need for receiving an apology or for seeking forgiveness may have relevance to efforts today at pursuing "positive" peace. To the extent that these structures may not always be evident to those in power, efforts at moving forward to more equitable outcomes may not require the admission of guilt and the seeking of forgiveness for past harms. It is sufficient for those who have benefited from such arrangements to acknowledge this and to pursue efforts that result in a more egalitarian set of interpersonal, intergroup, and international relationships. Blaming and requiring forgiveness have their limits for achieving positive outcomes. Do efforts at promoting "people's peace" require assessing guilt and seeking absolution?

A third implication of the ancient sources for conflict-resolution and peace studies is the importance of attending to the role of emotions in the analysis of conflicts and in efforts at promoting peace and resolution. Eran Halperin, professor of social psychology at the interdisciplinary center in Herzliya, Israel, heads the Psychology of Intergroup Conflict and Reconciliation Lab, whose goals are "to understand the roots and functions of emotions in intergroup relations and conflicts and to use our knowledge to cultivate social change in favor of democracy and peace."[25] Although these efforts fall within critical peace studies and transformative conflict resolution, goals not found in the ancient sources, what is important is the central role ascribed to emotions both as causes of conflict and as necessary factors to attend to in efforts at ameliorating conflicts and pursing peace. Halperin lays out his views most recently in his book *Emotions in Conflict: Inhibitors and Facilitators of Peace Making*.[26] Although acknowledging the contribution of cognitive factors such as values and collective memories and of structural-material economic factors, Halperin contends that discrete emotions, such as anger, fear, shame, guilt, despair, and pride as well as the more positive feelings of empathy and compassion, contribute to both the causes of and the solutions to conflicts as well as to the promotion of peace. He observes that much of the scholarship and efforts in peace and conflict studies do not sufficiently, or even at all, attend to the role of emotions in conflicts and peace. The ancient sources examined earlier in this chapter, by contrast, do describe emotions as central to giving rise to conflicts and to overcoming them. Although these ancient views limit their analysis to only certain emotions, and although they seek to restore existing relationships of power, they do take emotions seriously. The rabbinic narratives demonstrate the difficulty of always being successful at obtaining conflict resolution. They underscore the extensive emotional and social dimensions of conflict, emphasizing that parties may be more interested in over-coming their anger from being shamed or dishonored by others. Attending to "saving face" and to other emotional concerns, includ-ing increasing one's empathy for the other party's suffering, may well be critical to minimal efforts at reconciliation as well as to loftier goals of achieving people's peace.[27]

Finally, additional insight into the relevance of the early rabbinic sources discussed in this paper emerges from a brief examination of recent Jewish writings on peace and conflict resolution and on the activities of various Jewish Israeli groups to advance peace and solidarity between Israelis and Palestinians. Howard Kaminsky and Marc Gopin speak about the value of apology and forgiveness in seeking to resolve conflicts and achieve peace.[28] Kaminsky develops a rich presentation of Jewish views on conflict resolution, drawing upon an array of classical, medieval, and modern rabbinic legal and nonlegal writings. Although his work focuses on interpersonal con-flicts, he does note that aspects of what he presents are relevant to intergroup conflicts and resolution efforts.[29] He situates his analy-sis of rabbinic views on conflicts and their resolutions within what he sees as foundational values and concerns. In his view, promoting positive peace is a driving commitment for Jewish life. Although the particular sources on how to resolve conflicts speak only to that spe-cific goal and generally do not include references to peace, he argues that seeking peace is an implicit foundational value in them. This claim is debatable, but his comments on the central role of apology and forgiveness in restoring interpersonal relationships are helpful in explicating my topic here. Kaminsky's approach seeks to identify what became over time rabbinic views on the subjects he covers, and so he focuses on Maimonides's presentation of the laws of repentance (*teshuva*) and forgiveness. According to Maimonides, one who seeks pardon (*mechilah*, also translated as "forgiveness") must appease (*lefayso, leratzot*) the offended individual so that the offended will pardon the offender.[30] Unlike the early rabbinic sayings and stories analyzed earlier in this chapter, according to Maimonides "appeasement" is merely a preliminary step toward the ultimate goal of forgiveness. But what does Maimonides and the broader rabbinic tradition understand as the nature of appeasement? Kaminsky reports that, in fact, the term *lefayes*, "appeasement," is generally left undefined. In his view, rabbinic sources hold the position that "everything is to be determined according to its time and place"—in other words, according to the discretion and good judgment of the party who asks for forgiveness.[31] Although Kaminsky does not treat appeasement as the central factor, he does speak to the emotional nature of conflict and cites views that indicate that appeasement entails the offender humbling himself or herself. Humbling oneself is not identical to professing submission to the offended party, but it does identify the correlated inner psychological dimension of the requirement for appeasement. Particularly relevant to my argument are Kaminsky's comments on the role of apology and forgiveness in current writings and education related to conflict resolution. He notes, "There is a perceptible lack of emphasis on apologies and forgiveness in contemporary conflict resolution."[32]

Marc Gopin has written extensively on the importance of attention to religious views and practices in addressing intergroup conflicts. Regarding the Arab–Israeli situation, he argues for the value of traditional notions of appeasement, apology, forgiveness, and traditional Islamic (Arabic) *sulha* practices. In his view, one must understand each culture's view of forgiveness. Present efforts at promoting "peace" have focused only on "justice" and restitution. Like

Kaminsky, Gopin draws upon Maimonides's views on repentance and forgiveness, and he suggests that appeasement means "to speak kindly" to the offended party.[33] Gopin thus also does not mention the need for the offender to submit to the injured party. But, for Gopin, traditional practices related to forgiveness, including the requirement for appeasement, are essential to achieving peace because they speak to the emotional dimensions of conflict, including honor, humiliation, and the need "to save face."[34]

The importance of attending to religious values is evident as well in the activities of some Israeli Jewish, Palestinian Christian, and Islamic groups that are seeking to address the conflict in Israel–Palestine, with a few groups attending to apology and forgiveness. I focus my comments on the activities of Jewish Israeli groups because they relate directly to the ideas addressed in this paper. A great deal of well-researched scholarship has emerged on the activities of various groups dedicated to promoting a range of goals relevant to achieving some sort of peace between the parties to this conflict.[35] Various nongovernmental grassroots efforts as well as some efforts sponsored by the Israeli government have sought to promote goals that range from increasing all parties' knowledge of each other's religious views, humanizing the other party, and forming interpersonal relations to actively engaging in actions that reduce violations of Palestinians' rights both in Israel and in the Occupied Territories and in some cases to ending the occupation itself. Two groups, the Interfaith Encounter Association (IEA) and Rabbis for Human Rights (RHR), specifically speak about forgiveness.

The IEA bases its efforts on the value of interfaith dialogue and understanding as essential steps in peacebuilding. In its view, religious groups must be part of the solution to the problems.[36] A key component of the IEA's activities is forming encounter groups between Palestinians and Israelis, and a key element of these gatherings is the study of traditional religious texts that present each religion's ethical values. According to its self-description, the IEA "seek[s] to build bridges between Jews, Muslims, Christians and others based on tradition and culture, without any political agenda." It was founded in 2001 and continues many activities today. The group will be sustained by its ability to attract attendees to its programs. Although it is clear that the IEA has had success at increasing interfaith understanding, critics have noted that its failure to address the asymmetric status of Israeli Jewish and Palestinian Arab participants or to address political, social, economic, and cultural assumptions, practices, and structures limits its overall effectiveness at achieving transformations in key dimensions of the Israel–Palestine situation.[37] "Humus and hugs" have achieved only limited outcomes. Nonetheless, the IEA is an example of how attention to religion operates on the grassroots level to promote efforts at peace in the Middle East.

In contrast to the IEA, the RHR, a group formed in 1988, takes a more active role in ameliorating violations of the human rights of Palestinians, including those in the Occupied Territories. In its self-description, the RHR

> is the only rabbinic voice in Israel that is explicitly dedicated to human rights. Representing over 100 Israeli rabbis and rabbinical students from different streams of Judaism, we derive our authority from our Jewish tradition and the Universal Declaration of Human Rights. Rabbis for Human Rights give expression to the traditional Jewish responsibility for the safety and welfare of the stranger, the different and the weak, the convert, the widow and the orphan.[38]

Among the RHR's activities are enabling Palestinian farmers in the Occupied Territories to harvest their crops without interference from Israeli settlers and, through legal intervention, preventing or reversing the taking of Palestinian lands by Israeli settlers or the military. Although the RHR is committed to core Zionist claims of Jewish rights to settlement and to sovereignty, it contests Israeli violations of human rights and seeks to educate Israeli Jews regarding the alignment of human rights with Jewish religious teachings and to address in various ways the situation in the Occupied Territories. On one occasion, the RHR spoke of the importance of forgiveness for achieving peace in Israel–Palestine. For the high holy days in 2011, the RHR published a revised version of the traditional Viddui (confessional prayer) recited on Yom Kippur. Their version "relates to our society today, to the way in which we treat the unemployed and disadvantaged, immigrants, migrant workers, single mothers, the elderly, the exploited women, the Arab citizens of the State and the Palestinians, and those we disagree with politically. The Viddui asks us to take individual responsibility also for the collective sins of our society." Among the sins listed are "not seeing Israeli Arabs as citizens of the state; saying only Jews have rights to land; allowing successive governments to steal or prevent Palestinian access to their lands, demolish homes, pave roads, uproot trees, limit water, torture, abuse and humiliate."[39] Although published online and therefore accessible to both Israeli Jews and Palestinians, this text seems to be directed to Israeli Jews in that the Viddui is meant to be recited or pondered during the period of repentance between Rosh Hashanah and Yom Kippur. This is the only such statement by the RHR that directly speaks to the concern for forgiveness.

Several factors render apologizing and seeking forgiveness difficult in intergroup peacebuilding relationships. First, the parties often dispute who is the offending party, the aggressor. Thus, both parties often feel aggrieved and are reluctant to make the first step and acknowledge their misdeeds. Second, the highly emotional dimensions of conflict, in particular concerns for honor and dignity, contribute to resisting any efforts at peacebuilding. Equally important, some groups may feel pride in thinking of themselves as superior to others. In some ways, as is the case of the ancient sources examined in this paper, these groups may be as much concerned with having the other group acknowledge this superiority as they are with having the other concede its misdeeds. Third, possible legal consequences inhibit people from publicly proclaiming their guilt, for they may then be subject to litigation, perhaps even imprisonment. Fourth, parties resist engaging in peacebuilding when others of their broader group, including those who may exercise power, violence, or social ostracization, object to engaging with "the enemy." The costs for any dialogue can be extremely high. Finally, in situations of asymmetric power, failing to address larger issues of power and injustices not only may prove unproductive but may also be seen as "normalizing" those situations. Apologizing, seeking forgiveness, feeling remorse, and changing behavior are difficult for individuals. And the pursuit of such efforts is even far more challenging within a group or in intergroup situations. Individual members of a group may feel certain emotions, but occasioning regret and remorse in a group as a whole is a formidable task. In the end, as Kaminsky characterizes the situation, one needs to determine, even when it comes to grassroots efforts for people's peace and conflict resolution, whether traditional religious texts and prescriptions on forgiveness "are utopian [or] pragmatic and realistic or [in between these two views] set very high standards and are still idealistic but realistic."[40]

6

Coming Together in Peace

Community and Informality in Cairo

CHAD HAINES

On January 25, 2011, a few political activists made their way to downtown Cairo with the intent of making a protest against the ruling regime of Hosni Mubarak and the recent appointment of his son Gamal as the heir apparent to the dictatorial throne. For several weeks, the activists shared messages across social network sites and hoped that several thousand people might show up, though realistically they expected no more than a few hundred. By early evening of January 25, several hundred thousand Cairenes were lining the streets around Tahrir Square. Many of them stayed, day and night, for eighteen days, while hundreds of thousands returned daily, the numbers increasing each day to an estimated one million people occupying the protest site. On the eighteenth day, with protests spreading across the country and pressures mounting, Mubarak resigned as president of Egypt after thirty years in power.

The extent and nature of the protest testify ultimately to the power of people to effect political change, to foster social justice through direct action, and to imagine new worlds by coming together. Those eighteen days on Tahrir Square are one manifestation of people's peace—people protesting nonviolently, people coming together across social and ideological interests, and people organizing themselves informally to realize their aspirations. Although the protest for January 25 was planned, the numbers that came together were beyond the organizers' imagination. To cope with those numbers, the people themselves organized health centers, security checkpoints, bathroom installations, entertainment, teaching and debate centers, and cleanup of the protest site every evening. No single organization or group had the capacity to handle the hundreds of thousands of people who showed up on the streets; they organized themselves.

As well as an example of dramatic political transformation, the protest is an example of a direct-action people's peace movement, the informal coming together and organizing that are another expression of people's peace, one that peace studies often ignores because academics focus instead on movements, organizations, and ideologies of nonviolence. Although extremely significant, such foci underplay the role of the masses, the people, in realizing peace. Such studies also look at abnormal events, such as the January Revolution in Egypt, as sites where peace is practiced—or not.

Shifting focus to the comings together and informal practices of peace opens new realms of understanding the possibilities for achieving real and sustainable peace in places and times of conflict. It also offers insights into quotidian practices of peace that go unmarked and often even unnoticed yet define the vast majority of our everyday lives. Most of the world does not live in times and places of overt violence, war, and open conflict; we are not called upon to choose between violence and nonviolence, conflict and peace. All of us, however, do live in oppressive systems—within structures of injustice and varying degrees of violence. In coping with and negotiating, confronting and countering those forms of covert violence, we develop and practice a diversity of moral and ethical values: we accept the stranger in our midst, we donate time and money to those less fortunate then ourselves, we learn about different cultures and histories, we share our concerns and listen to others openly. In our everyday lives, we adopt and employ a variety of ethical choices that are expressions of people's peace, our capacity to live in communities, to accept and value social and cultural differences, and to practice empathy and care for those suffering from injustices.

Coming together, informality, and everyday ethics open up a realm of peace studies that significantly recognizes the agency of all people, not merely that of a few social activists, organizers, and iconic figures who transcend their place and time to lead such movements. In abnormal times, we witness unusual acts across the spectrum of human potential—from seemingly inhuman barbarity to extreme acts of self-sacrifice for others. But what about normal times? In our everyday lives, how do we practice peace? How do we confront and resist systemic injustices and violence? What ethical choices do we make to help the world become a better place to live in? What are some of the forces that limit our capacity to act in peace and with justice?

These normal acts cover a range of practices: some of them are everyday acts, whereas some of them are "tactics," as Michel de Certeau suggests,[1] directed as resistance to forces of violence and injustice. While much of world attention focused on the occupation and protests on Tahrir Square, a powerful and iconic moment, the transformative possibilities of people's peace were, in fact, practiced elsewhere after Tahrir Square. With the collapse of the Mubarak regime also came the eclipse of the state and the apparatuses of oppression. For a full year after the occupation of Tahrir Square, Egypt operated with a minimal state. During this time, people's peace thrived. People employed an array of tactics to organize and realize a diversity of community projects, fostering greater equity and social inclusion. With the election of Mohamed Morsi, the ascendance of the Muslim Brotherhood to power in June 2012, and then Morsi's ouster in a violent coup a year later, all those possibilities and the aspirations of the millions who had gathered in Tahrir Square in January 2011 and had enacted new codes of social agency in the year that followed were destroyed by the reassertion of a repressive state. Thousands were arrested, tortured, disappeared, murdered, and otherwise oppressed, and thousands continue to receive such treatment. From the tactics employed during this "people's democratic action," as I call it, people now draw upon other modes of people's peace to negotiate the extreme oppression by the state.

My aim here is to draw attention to the possibilities of transformative action that unfolded during the year after the January 25 Revolution. This focus allows us to reflect on the troubling place of the state in fostering nonpeaceful conditions. In short, the modern liberal state denies peaceful possibilities, curtailing a human future. When the modern liberal state is weakened and eclipsed, the human capacity for peace is powerful.

Transcending the State: Tracing Acts of People's Peace

From my travels and encounters around the world, I can recount countless times when my expectations of difference, distrust, and outright animosity were laid to waste as people rose above and disrupted the borders of differences between self and other that are so entrenched in the modern liberal state, which is predicated on borders, policing, and hierarchies of belonging. In Mali, one of the poorest countries in the world, where I, a rich white American, was sent as a Peace Corps volunteer, the local population's hospitality and giving disrupted my sense of inequality and charity. In Bosnia, a Muslim fly-fishing guide, wounded by Serbian soldiers during the war, expressed his own willingness to accept the marriage of his daughter to a Serb, the hated other. In Belfast, a taxi driver shared his own struggles to marry across religious lines in a city whose streets demarcate boundaries of hatred and invoke memories of victimhood and trauma.[2] Hospitality, acceptance, and inclusion of the other through various ethical, cultural, and personal practices are expressions of people's peace.

Of course, many live in memories of fear and hatred, harbor distrust, and accept the need to produce and reinforce borders of difference that are encoded with violence. But the possibility of transcendence is a powerful assertion of our human capacity to live in peace. Borders of violence exist around the world, with distinct histories and geopolitics that inform the division between one side of the border and the other. The border between Pakistan and India is one such border, born from colonial divisive politics that led to partitioning of political entities, giving rise to one of the largest and bloodiest movements of people in the twentieth century.

At the time of Indian independence from British colonial rule in 1947, borders were drawn between new nation-states and old communities. Prior to the colonial-imposed borders, Lahore was a vibrant cosmopolitan city, steeped in both Muslim and Sikh history, its streets alive with traders from multiple communities and its cultural traditions of Sufi shrines and kite-flying festivals interweaving diverse socioreligious traditions. Lahore was home to leading intellectuals, writers, and activists who gathered in the city's cafés, imagining a new world freed from oppressive colonial rule. However, the borders of Partition were stained with blood; Sikhs and Hindus joined hands in slaughtering Muslims and vice versa as millions of people moved in mass migration to claim citizenship in a new homeland, Hindus and Sikhs fleeing what was now Pakistan, Muslims fleeing what became India. The trauma lives on in the memories of those who survived and in the politics of the two antagonistic states of India and Pakistan, reproduced in popular representations, nationalist histories, and political rhetoric.

Given the memories of senseless violence between neighbors and the manner in which Pakistan and India produce nationalist animosity, popular attitudes became bounded, fostering a distrust rooted in ignorance based on decades of separation. However, under the surface of nationalist animosity lies another reality, a memory of brotherhood, neighborliness, and cosmopolitan ethics.

In 1997, Pakistan offered for the first time since the horrors of Partition a significant number of visas to Indian Sikhs to enter Pakistan on pilgrimage to some of their most holy sites, including the birthplace and burial shrine of Guru Nanak, the founder of Sikhism. As a young graduate student undertaking research in Pakistan that year, I happened to be visiting Lahore and wandering through the Old Anarkali bazaar. Not aware of the context at the time, I was taken aback at witnessing a large group of Sikh men with their colorful turbans and long beards meandering up the street—they were the first Sikhs in such large numbers to have been there in fifty years. I imagined there might be tension between the visiting Sikhs and the Muslim shopkeepers, based on my surface sense of nationalist belonging and memories of trauma. What I witnessed, however, was a deeper memory, rooted in pre-Partition Lahori culture.

As the Sikhs walked through the bazaar, shopkeepers were literally tossing them their wares as gifts, running out and adorning them with shawls and other goods, and inviting them to sit down for tea; brothers were reuniting. The border between India and Pakistan was a violent one, stringently enforced by two antagonistic states. Yet when people transcended those borders and lived their lives outside the dictates of the state, they connected as *bhai*s, brothers. The history did not matter. The religious difference between Muslim and Sikh did not matter. The politics of nation-states did not matter. For the Muslims of Lahore, the stranger, the Indian Sikh foreigner, was a guest, a family member returning home.

Pakistan and India inherited the modern liberal state mapped by the British colonial empire, which institutionalized divisions and constituted hierarchies of social belonging, with state apparatuses defined by military rule. The reproduction of hate and mistrust between Pakistanis and Indians limited each group's capacity to see the other as anything but a hated security threat. Yet at the human level people possess the capacity to transcend the liberal state's artificial and arbitrary divisions.

In 1997, during the final week of Ramadan, the Muslim month of fasting, my father-in-law passed away in India. In a deeply disturbed state, I was able to get a ticket to fly from Lahore to Delhi. At the Lahore airport, the security guard, on seeing my passport full of entry stamps to India, started to question me, pulling all my things out of my carry-on bag. When I informed him that I was going to India because my father-in-law had passed away, he immediately repacked my bag, carried it for me, and walked me through immigration to my gate, informing the staff of my situation; the staff then upgraded my seat to first class and allowed me to board early. I had begun the journey as a suspect because of my previous travels but was transformed into just a human being in the midst of a family crisis. That ability to see the other as a human being rather than whatever is demarcated by a passport or some social identity, be it American or Indian, be it beggar or refugee, is the foundational place from which people's peace sprouts forth.

What we find again and again is how the modern liberal state not only limits our ability to see one another as human beings but also in fact puts in place ideologies of differentiation, violently segregating and separating us and forcing us into normative and formal modes of social interaction. When institutionalized or transformed into a model to implement, people's peace loses its full transformative capacity. It flourishes when we step out of our roles, our identities, our duties and behave with human ethics. It blossoms when a security guard stops behaving like a security guard and treats the suspected other as a human being. In these moments of informality that disrupt imposed borders between self and other, we see the possibilities of a human future.

Informal transcendence of borders of difference is integral to people's peace. So is the ability to come together, to assemble in new kinds of communities.

Practicing People's Peace: From Tahrir Square to the Side Streets of Cairo

The coming together in Tahrir Square was a plurality of people with a plurality of interests, aspirations, and ideologies. They ranged from radical leftists, labor unionists, students, members of mainstream opposition parties, eventually members of the Muslim Brotherhood, and just the curious. Christians and Muslims, rich and poor, young and old, men and women gathered, transcending social divisions and creating a new community and a new future. The gathering was fully inclusive and completely informal; a single group, movement, or organization did not define the protests.

To appreciate fully the significance of the coming together of the Tahrir Square protests, one has first to acknowledge the extent to which the values and practices of coming together were denied under the dictatorial Mubarak regime and the erosion of personal and national dignity. Second, one must appreciate that the eruption on January 25, 2011, did not happen in a vacuum, sparked solely by similar protests in Tunisia. There were years of protests beforehand, though they were small and rooted in certain segments of Egyptian society.

Though the word *tahrir* means "liberation," under Mubarak's police state Tahrir Square, along with the rest of Egypt, was anything but a liberated place. Extensive unemployment and underemployment brought on by the restructuring of Egypt's economy forced by the International Monetary Fund, the World Bank, and the US Agency for International Development had fostered a culture of touts, thugs, and loiterers on the streets leading into Tahrir Square.[3] It was a place of sharp contrasts, colliding worlds where young students at the elite American University in Cairo (located in Tahrir Square until 2008) enjoyed their afternoon meals at McDonald's and Kentucky Fried Chicken, while recent graduates with advanced degrees from Cairo University struggled selling belts and black-market perfumes on the street corners. It was a place of harassment where women, young and old, veiled and unveiled, local and foreign scurried by, attempting to ignore the incessant catcalls and increasing physical abuse. Tahrir Square was a site of oppression that was reproduced across the city and the country. As one protester acknowledged, "For every rich neighborhood in Cairo, there is a slum beside it, thanks to our regime!"[4] More than 40 percent of Egypt's population lives below the poverty level today; inequality was the hallmark of the Mubarak regime.[5] On January 25, 2011, those whose worlds had been in conflict came together in a unique way, transcending their differences, though not erasing them.

The January 25 Revolution was not an unexpected event, though its nature, predominately peaceful, certainly was. A growing number of protests throughout Egypt in the early 2000s laid the foundations for the occupation of Tahrir Square in 2011. Workers went on strike and formed independent unions (counter to the interests of the liberal overseers of Egypt's economic reforms in the World Bank and International Monetary Fund). Judges and lawyers increasingly protested against the ruling regime's manipulation of the judiciary. On a number of occasions, women's groups gathered in central Cairo to demand police action against sexual harassment and the increasing violence against women on the streets. These protests against the absolutism of the state reflected the civil awakening of the Egyptian people. The earlier protests were driven by specific demands from a particular segment or group in society. But all of these interests, concerns, and demands came together on that day in January 2011, imagining a different future.

No revolution can be successful without mass support. One of the unique aspects of Tahrir Square was the formation of an emergent community. There was a spirit of belonging, sharing, and dialoguing that brought diverse people together into a community that transcended its members' particular interests and desires. This sense of community, counter to the spirit of individualism and individual rights of liberal global citizenship, is essential for people's peace to flourish.

Many of the protesters who gathered during those eighteen days in 2011 tell stories of community, of coming together not just as a mass but as individuals. One such story that I recounted elsewhere concerns students from the American University in Cairo, wealthy elites whose families had undoubtedly benefited in some manner from the Mubarak regime's cronyism.[6] They were sitting around the square, passionately discussing the meanings of the protests. One of them started to make tea, boiling water on a special camping stove they had brought. While they were waiting for the water to boil, an older man pushing a tea cart approached. The university student immediately turned off the stove and bought tea for her friends and herself. In remembering that act, she reflected on the meaning, pregnant in that moment of extended protest, of creating new possibilities, of people becoming bound to one another and making the effort to support each other. The poor tea vendor was a part of society, dependent on others to survive and thus deserved the support of others. An everyday act of buying tea became an expression of revolution, of community, of people's peace.

During the attempt by the police early on to stop the protesters from reaching Tahrir Square, the smell of tear gas, the sound of gunfire, and the chants of protesters filled the air of downtown Cairo. "People started to open their houses for the wounded and demonstrators suffocating from the tear gas. People threw vinegar and onions from their balconies to us" to protect against the burning tear gas.[7] One protester, Maha Hindawy, remembers, walking and running after a day of protest, being exhausted and sitting on the curb with her friend when someone offered her a *foul* (baked fava bean) sandwich. "I took it gratefully but then gave it away to other people who were more hungry."[8] This community and belonging were real acts, predicated on an informality that gave rise to a new kind of ethics, an ethical community radically different than the Tahrir Square with its classist divides prior to the revolution.

Although much focus is on the direct protests unfolding in Tahrir Square, the real revolution took place away from the center, where people lived their daily lives in a state of unknowing. The insecurity that the revolution brought was real and palpable. The situation demanded new kinds of social interaction, particularly given that, in one of the more extraordinary aspects of the revolution, the police force vanished from the streets. The police, as the most visible and direct interface between citizens and the state, were understandably the focus of much of the protestors' ire. They were also one of the most corrupt, arbitrary, and violent arms of the state, with little accountability. Yet after several days of protests in Tahrir Square, the police literally disappeared from the streets. The military stepped in as the direct line between the protestors and the apparatuses of government in and around Tahrir Square and patrolled the streets to keep what order they could. But the military did not have the capacity to police an entire city, thus leaving people to protect themselves from potential looters and other criminal elements. Very little looting took place, though, surprisingly, considering that Cairo is a city with more than twenty million people. On their own, youth from the neighborhoods organized watches, rotating patrol units, creating messaging groups in case of emergencies, and checking in on those families and residents who needed assistance. Strangers came together to protect their neighborhoods, creating trust and forging bonds that did not exist prior to the revolution. In such a large and populated city, with no visible police on the streets, little criminal activity was committed. Poor and rich neighborhoods alike organized themselves informally.

In contrast to the absence of theft in most of the city, some looting and robbing occurred in the satellite cities south of Cairo. In order to develop new urban areas for well-to-do Cairenes, Mubarak had granted desert land to his friends and established real-estate developers with intimate connections to the regime. They built malls, corporate centers, and gated communities, pulling wealthy Cairenes out of the inner city of mixed and crowded communities into secure, homogenous residential areas. Even the American University of Cairo bought into the vision, moving its campus from Tahrir Square to the middle of the desert, disconnected from the city and all that it has to offer. Gated communities are inherently singular, with no social diversity except for the workers who serve the wealthy residents. During the revolution, robberies took place in these gated communities because they were not real communities: they were unable to form neighborhood watches, and there was no looking out for one another. Their insularity, lack of diversity, and individuatedness made them vulnerable.

During the eighteen days of the January 25 Revolution in Cairo, people behaved in extraordinary ways to transform their society. They brought down the ruling regime and laid the foundation for a new sense of belonging. For one year, the people of Cairo were given free rein to imagine their future, with minimal interference from the state and its global neoliberal benefactors. The informal activities and projects that people developed were inspiring in that year. Once a new ruling regime was put in place, however, they all ended. The state reasserted its power to define the scope of communal belonging, organizing, and street politics by (re)asserting a narrow nationalist ideology, a concern for security, and a neoliberal ideology of corporatized profiteering.

Reimagining Community and Belonging: Building a Human Future

To trace out further the possibilities of people's peace as lived ethics tactically employed to counter violence, injustice, and oppression, I focus on two developments in postrevolution Egypt: one community's construction of an exit ramp onto the Ring Road on the outskirts of Cairo and the emergence of a vibrant and visible LGBTQ life on the streets of Cairo. Each of these developments reflects different aspects of people's peace. Significantly, each occurred and thrived during a period when the Egyptian state was eclipsed.

More than tactics of social transformation, both developments are linked by their shared condition of precarity. The two populations involved in these developments are marginal, a condition that is ultimately defined and mapped by the capitalist liberal state but also by the society's prevailing normative values. Each community is marked as an outsider, a fringe dweller, whose very presence upsets the image of self. The *ashwaiyyati*, or residents of the informal neighborhoods in Cairo, and queers are deemed threats and so are vulnerable to attack, harassment, and discrimination. The claiming of agency by members of both communities to assert their place within the public arena was confrontational, just as the occupation of Tahrir Square was a confrontation with the state. The mere assertion of the precarious self in public, disrupting the normative to force a greater sense of equality and justice through inclusion, is a powerful expression of people's peace. Because of these groups' precarious status, the assertion took on a particular form in a time when state apparatuses were weak and the fear of reprisal was diminished, thus opening up a space for direct action. These two examples are cases of claiming space and belonging, of claiming a "right to the city,"[9] of making oneself visible in the urban conglomeration.

Cairo is a complex city where layers of history unfold as one moves from one neighborhood to another. One can travel from the tenth century to the twenty-first in a half-hour drive, going from the old bazaar of Khan el-Khalili to the malls of New Cairo. One can also move from the corporate real-estate developments and their gated communities (such as El Rehab) to state-planned neighborhoods (such as Mohandiseen, the well to-do neighborhood built for the engineers of the new nation-state) to informal cities (such as Bulaq ad Daqrur, located across the train tracks from Mohandiseen).

Those living outside the *ashwaiyyat,* the informal neighborhoods, generally perceive these spaces as "no-go" places for a couple of reasons. First, there is really no reason to enter them; they have no attractions, no special markets or services. Second, because they are unknown places, mostly with rural-to-urban migrants from different parts of Egypt, they are perceived as being homes to thieves, drug dealers, and violent extremists. Popular discourses circulated around Cairo depict *ashwaiyyat* and their residents in a negative light, despite the fact that it is estimated that half the population of Cairo resides in these informal neighborhoods.[10]

Ashwaiyyat in Cairo are not patchwork slums with homes built of refuse material, as in so many cities around the world. Rather, they are highly organized developments, brick-and-mortar residential apartments, usually six floors high at most owing to the lack of elevators. They are highly dense, with very narrow alleys between rows of apartment buildings. The neighborhoods are "informal" from a number of perspectives. They were built without state oversight or planning; they are self-regulating on a neighborhood level; and their economies are a blend of employment in formal sectors, shopkeepers and tradesmen, as well as informal vendors and small-scale industries (which feed into the formal manufacturing sector). Although many residents work outside the neighborhoods, many remain inside them.

Within the informal neighborhoods, there are no government offices, no police presence, and no regulatory agencies overseeing the neighborhoods and their development. Thus, in late January 2011, when the police disappeared from the streets of Cairo and when the state itself minimized its presence in the daily life of Cairenes, the residents of the *ashwaiyyat* hardly noticed. Daily life within the neighborhoods continued as always. There was no struggle to create neighborhood watches, for such watch groups already existed as informal relationships between immediate neighbors. There was no concern for a breakdown of state-defined "law and order," for there was no state to begin with.

The eclipse of the state, though, provided other opportunities for the communities to organize and advance their own interests. One example is in the community of Mutamidiya, in the Giza District west of central Cairo. In the 1990s, the Mubarak regime expanded the road network around central Cairo, building a number of link roads and ring roads in an attempt to pull traffic away from the highly congested areas of central Cairo. The Ring Road cuts through a number of *ashwaiyyat*. As one drives along the elevated highway, one can almost literally reach out and touch the buildings. Despite the fact that the Ring Road cuts through a number of neighborhoods, these sections have absolutely no access to the highway itself. Entrance and exit ramps are miles away, feeding into the link roads that connect the outlying satellite cities of Sheikh Zayed and Sixth of October.

Over the years, the people have constructed a number of stairways up to the elevated Ring Road, providing access to transportation as well as informal economic opportunities for tire repair and tea stalls. But those who have motorbikes or cars have had to go miles out of their way through back streets to gain access to the highway—that is, at least until 2011, when some of the immediate neighborhoods along the Ring Road organized, without outside organizations providing any assistance. They collected funds, hired an engineer, and purchased the materials necessary to construct a number of off- and on-ramps from packed dirt.[11]

The state had constructed the Ring Road in part as a mode of dividing communities, limiting access for some while facilitating it for others (the middle- and upper-middle-class residents of the satellite cities and tourists going to the Giza pyramids). When the state was not looking, the communities who were supposed to be divided and disconnected, excluded from the state's development vision of Egypt's future, found a means to include themselves and to participate in facilitating their own daily needs for surviving in the megacity.

Forging inclusion and justice that the liberal state has denied is a form of direct action that reshapes—in the Ring Road case quite literally—the landscape of the city as people claim their right to belong. In a fascinating twist to the story of the on- and off-ramps to the Ring Road, one neighborhood went so far as to invite the governor of Giza to inaugurate the ramps, thus legitimizing them in the eyes of the state, which might otherwise have torn them down.

This mode of people's peace is directed toward the state, though covertly as compared to the Tahrir Square protests. The modern state is, however, not the sole perpetrator of oppression, injustice, and exclusion. The state works through and with ideologies of power and security, national belonging, and social well-being that are naturalized through normative values inculcated and reproduced across society. The residents of the *ashwaiyyat* are marginalized discursively as well as spatially, economically, and politically. They are often represented as not possessing the normative image of an acceptable Cairene. Their informality is perceived as a threat to the state-defined social fabric, and they are depicted as the perpetrators of all that negatively affects Cairo—congestion, crime, and extremism. Their agency is regularly erased, and their demands for inclusion ignored.

Other communities also exist on the margins of the normative Cairene imagining of self. Most notable are members of the LGBTQ communities, regardless of their residence or status, whether they are part of the social elite or among the poor residents of informal cities. Although LGBTQ individuals from the upper classes have the resources to protect and sufficiently closet their activities, many others do not have that luxury. Over the years, Egypt has wavered in its acceptance of homosexuality,[12] allowing a degree of visibility in certain nightclubs and other venues, but then turning around and shutting such places down, arresting accused homosexuals, and often imprisoning and torturing them. The state polices social values, encoding particular conservative values as the norm and providing little scope for alternative visions.[13]

As Shereen El Feki documents in her study of sexuality across the Middle East, homosexuality is quite prevalent in the region. In Cairo, private clubs, home spaces, male prostitutes, and a number of cafés are known to cater to various segments of the homosexual community.[14] The general attitude is this: keep it out of sight, don't be vulgar and obvious, and, *inshallah* (God willing), everything will be okay. At times, though, the police have raided those private spots, creating a much-unwanted visibility and imposing severe punishments on those committing such "antisocial vulgarities" (according to the state-defined heteronormative labeling of homosexuality).

With the eclipse of the state in 2011, homosexuals, like other marginal populations, became bolder, claiming a more visible space for themselves in Cairene society. One of the more dramatic assertions was the claiming of a *shisha* (hookah) café in the Borsa neighborhood of downtown Cairo, just blocks from Tahrir Square.[15] Borsa is a thriving part of the Cairo scene, often referred to as "the Paris" of Cairo. During the evening hours, the maze of back allies come alive with cafés, claiming public space for patrons to smoke *shisha*, drink tea and coffee, play backgammon, party with friends, discuss politics with strangers, and often just sit, watch, and listen to the cacophony. Prior to the revolution, different cafés catered to different clientele: leftists, members of different opposition movements and parties, even members of the Muslim Brotherhood had cafés where they congregated—Islamists sitting across from Marxists, civil society activists near the café where journalists tended to gather. Although traditionally the street cafés of Cairo are predominately male spaces, in Borsa women openly joined the crowds.

Following the revolution, Borsa became a center of discussion and debate, everyone sharing a vision for the future of Egypt. Those whom the state had pushed into the underground, into hiding, were now also able to participate in the discussions. A group of gay friends purchased a café, which became a place for homosexuals to feel at home in the public sphere of Borsa. Over time, they became increasingly bold, even hosting a wedding between two gay partners. Across Cairo, homosexuals felt emboldened, and a number of public weddings were conducted. Though legally unrecognized, these ceremonies were self-performed to celebrate committed relationships.

Gays claimed a space in the new Egypt, taking direct action against social norms. Many leftists and liberal progressives confided to me in interviews that the LGBTQ community had gone too far, however, in pushing the boundaries of acceptability, which in their estimation would undermine the revolutionary spirit. Many people were open to transforming society, but some drew limits on where new norms were to be mapped, and homosexuality continued to lie outside those boundaries. Gays continued to push for their own rights and place within the public purview, though. In Borsa, although many frowned on the gays' café, no one moved to shut it down, at least not until the state returned to its oppressive role as the policer of social norms.

The communities who organized to advance their own interests, be they residents of the informal cities or homosexuals, were part of a larger trend of opening up society, of dialoguing, and, ultimately, of just doing something. The level of activism across the city was astounding as people organized, created new associations and organizations, developed new projects, held seminars and discussion groups, created new art, shared, learned, and debated.

However, all of it came to an end. In June 2012, the Muslim Brotherhood won a majority of the Parliament, and Mohamed Morsi was elected president. Over the next few months, the Brotherhood moved to impose a number of new legislations to "Islamicize" Egyptian society. Then a year later, the military, with a degree of support from progressives, orchestrated a coup against Morsi, and General Abdel Fattah el-Sisi became president. Under Sisi, the social fabric of Cairo returned to the days of Mubarak, though many assert that it is even worse in its oppressiveness. Egypt is once again a police state. In its move to control the street politics, the new regime even shut down all of the cafés in Borsa in spring 2015. The Paris of Cairo does not exist anymore.

The informal communities that had emerged following the revolution and the vibrancy of seeking out dynamic social transformations were halted, at least visibly. Once again, those with a vision that asserted an alternative to that of the state and its imposed social norms—that is, those who had not already been arrested, imprisoned, and tortured—were erased, forced back into hiding.

Conclusion

From the eighteen-day occupation of Tahrir Square to the formation of neighborhood watches to the ethics of care and kindness shown during the occupation to the claiming of belonging to the city by marginal populations, the January 25 Revolution was predicated on multiple tactics of people's peace. The actions taken were informal and organized around principles of coming together, of assembly, and were inspired by claims for the rights of precarious populations.

Coming together to affect social transformation is a powerful symbol. Protest movements—from Gandhi's salt march against British occupation in colonial India to Martin Luther King Jr.'s civil rights marches, from peasants organizing and rising up in early-twentieth-century Russia and China to water protectors protesting against the usurpation of sacred lands on the Standing Rock Reservation in North Dakota—are iconic, filling the pages of history books and providing models for social activists to aspire to. They are the focus of peace studies courses, dominated by lessons on nonviolence and mass mobilization.

Although these iconic moments and their leaders are powerful reminders of our capacity to rise above our normal positions and create change, they also are incomplete stories of rebellion, protest, and revolution. Behind the scenes and usually down the street, a completely different rebellion is taking place. Here, people draw upon a different ethics of coming together than that followed in mass protest. Here, neighborliness, whether real or imagined, forms momentary bonds of commonality. Here, people's shared experiences of precarity drive them to build relationships that are the foundations of social change. Here, people act based on the moment; there is no model or path to follow, no organization dictating how to behave. Rather, people come together based on their own moral values and ethical principles and act on them as situations unfold. They sit back and watch, they learn, they evaluate, and they often change their values and practices. They learn to accept the gays in the café across the way, even if they find their lifestyle inappropriate.

Through informal comings together and assemblies and through informal everyday ethics dialogically employed rather than rigidly imposed, people create a human future. In the case of the January 25 Revolution, the prospects for people's peace in building a new Egyptian society ultimately failed or at least fell short. When the state exerted its control over the public sphere, reclaiming public spaces, the challenges to oppressive and exclusionary social norms receded. In this case, people's peace tactics were not sufficient to transform the state. But this failure does not mean the people lost those values, those aspirations, and those memories of what they could accomplish when given the opportunity. What does arise is the question of our relationship to the modern liberal state. If the liberal state stands so opposed to a human future, perhaps people's peace needs to develop more direct tactics for countering the state.

7

The Iberian Empires

Religious Tolerance in Intolerant Places
and from Unexpected People

STUART B. SCHWARTZ

Freedom of religion and the related idea of religious toleration are broadly held today to be a human right, but the question of freedom of religion has once again in the twenty-first century become a matter of great concern. The rise of various forms of religious fundamentalism and a new surge in the "culture wars" in the United States over the religiosity of the Founding Fathers, God's relationship to democracy, and the public role of religion have made questions of belief core issues of political debate. The ideas of freedom of religion and the related concept of toleration for other religions have for a couple of hundred years been accepted as basic elements of Western society and a key feature—in fact, perhaps an original element—in what we think of as modernity according to the predominant liberal, Western view of the progress of history. Freedom of conscience may be seen as among the first widely recognized of the *human rights*. But with the present surge of fundamentalisms, we are faced with a growing realization that "freedom of religion" and toleration may not have been a conquest to be won once and for all, an endpoint in history, but rather a more political and thus more fleeting victory. Moreover, both freedom of conscience and toleration are concepts that still remain in question in many places, even in ones that have accepted other aspects of the modern world. This comes as a shock to many people and as a challenge to a vision of history that has "naturalized" our Western values as the logical and inevitable result of the historical process.

The way we tell the story of religious toleration has been standardized to a large extent. In western Europe, Christianity spread during the last years of the Roman Empire. The Roman Catholic Church took on the task of maintaining orthodoxy and suppressing heresy. Christianity, as it spread and consolidated, often defined itself in opposition to infidels (Jews and Muslims), who were seen as distinct peoples. There was no possibility of alternative faiths. The church's position was that there was no salvation outside the church (*nulla salus extra ecclesiam*).[1] Almost all authorities believed that order and stability lay in the union of belief between ruler and subjects and in the close collaboration between crown and altar. This was the Europe of the "persecuting society" of the Middle Ages.[2]

The Protestant Reformation in the sixteenth century shattered the unity of the Roman Catholic Church and changed the whole question of "religious tolerance." Now concern was not about traditional "others" or infidels, but about Christian heresies on a scale never before seen. Across Europe, "tens of thousands of towns and villages were split internally. People were 'divided by faith' from their neighbors, friends, and families."[3] From about 1550 to 1650, we enter into the age of religious wars: savagery in the name of God; the Inquisition in Italy, Portugal, and Spain and their colonies; and intolerance throughout most of Europe. Toleration, of course, etymologically meant putting up with something disagreeable, and in a few places it developed as a compromise to end the mutual hostility and violence. Then slowly after 1650 practical and pragmatic adjustments, exhaustion from the violence, and a growing rationality in matters of religion eventually led to the "Enlightenment" of the eighteenth century and flourished into the growth of religious toleration as reason seemed to win out over intolerance and religious extremism. By the nineteenth century, "freedom of conscience" had become a widely accepted and positive idea in the West.[4]

In general, we tell this story as a branch of the history of ideas. The cast of characters are predictable—Erasmus, Spinoza, Hobbes,

Locke, Bayle, Voltaire, to name a few, all of whom were intellectuals who advocated social harmony and charity. It is an inspiring tale but clearly not the whole story. In some places, for example, toleration was born of necessity or perceived economic advantage. The Jews were accepted in Amsterdam in the late sixteenth century because it was good for business; they were readmitted to England in the seventeenth century for that same reason and because of Christian millenarian hopes that their conversion would lead to the Second Coming. In the main, historians have written little about the popular reception of these expressions of tolerance, about why and how they convinced people. Few historians have considered the possibility that these ideas may have been shared by the general population or even may have been generated by them.

In telling this story of the growth of toleration, Europe is always the focus. Not much attention is given to religious pluralism or tolerance in Ming China, the Ottoman Mediterranean, or the Mughal India of Akbar, where religious pluralism and toleration existed to some degree. By the eighteenth century, people such as Voltaire who advocated freedom of conscience and criticized Europe for its absence pointed out that toleration in countries such as China or Siam contributed to good government. Intolerance, said Voltaire, is a "disease peculiar to our climate."[5] But as Anglophone historians tell the story of religious toleration today, it is usually France, England, Holland, the United States, and, to a lesser extent, central Europe that are the protagonists. Spain and Portugal have almost no place at all in this narrative except as the prime examples of a fanaticism that caused these countries and their empires to fall into the status of second- or third-rate powers. The Spanish and Portuguese had based their empires on the conversion of the heathens, and, in the main, their monarchs and theologians considered the exclusive unity of religion as the basis of government and society. Rather smugly, Anglophone historians have told a story of the progressivism of the Anglo-Americans, Germanic peoples, and the French and have explained as part of the "Black legend" the "backwardness" of the Spaniards, Portuguese, and Latin Americans because of their fanaticism and intolerance.

Never mind the Salem witch trials, the English burning of Catholics, and the Geneva persecution of dissidents. Never mind the humanism and humanity of the Spanish missionaries such as Bartolomé de Las Casas. What we have produced is, in effect, a celebratory vision of our own attitudes, a search of the past that sees everything culminating in the adaptation of freedom of conscience, pluralism, and religious toleration as positive aspects of modernity.[6]

But here is the problem. If we examine only state policies and the arguments of learned theologians and political writers, we have looked at only a part of the story. What about the mass of the population or even a dissenting minority? Throughout history, there have been dissenters; but looking for their effect when the records are few or, even worse, when these people were often illiterate or had no way to disseminate their ideas or were punished for doing so severely limits how we can understand their possible influence on the story we wish to trace. It is possible to look for evidence of religious tolerance and freedom of conscience in the unlikely context of Spain and Portugal and their empires by concentrating not on "toleration," by which I mean official policies, but on "tolerance," or attitudes of religious acceptance or indifference based on the lived experience and hopes of common folk as well as on the thoughts and writings of theologians and philosophers.

Let me start with a single but exemplary case. Inocencio de Aldama was a young man from the Spanish Basque country. He had soldiered in the king's armies in Italy but eventually became a vagabond. In 1701, he was denounced to the Inquisition because he had argued that "anyone can save themselves in their own law [religion] whether they be Muslim, infidel, or heretic, and that all religions are branches of the same trunk and they all bear fruit." All of us can be saved in our own religion, he said, "if we profess it responsibly." In the Spain of the Inquisition, such ideas were potentially heretical. The inquisitors tried to convince him of his doctrinal errors. Aldama said he was ready to accept their correction, but on his belief that each person must find his or her own way and that each person has his or her own character and destiny "not even the professors of

Salamanca" could dissuade him. Some inquisitors thought he was a heretic, others that he was mad. Aldama was eventually placed in an asylum.[7] Mad or not, on the issue of the possible validity of other religions, he was not alone. In the records of the Inquisition, I found hundreds of cases of people in Spain, Portugal, and Latin America who said the same thing. For a while, the inquisitors believed that such relativist ideas were found particularly among converts from Islam, but that, in fact, was not the case. Among those who believed that salvation was possible in different faiths were some converts from Judaism or Islam and their descendants, to be sure, but there were also "Old Christians" of impeccable lineage who subscribed to these ideas. Some who dissented from the church's exclusive validity were skeptics and doubted all religion; some were relativists who thought that one faith might be as good as another; some were universalists who believed that all religions were valid; and others believed that only God knew which religion was best. Some of those who considered themselves good Christians believed that the church had simply taken the wrong stance on the use of coercion and that love of one's neighbor required tolerance. How many people held these ideas? That is a difficult epistemological and methodological problem. The cases I discovered were surely a minority and not part of a movement. For the most part, these individuals had simply come to their conclusions by thinking on their own. Many had traveled, and some (but not all) could read and write (although generally they had not attended university); but social class, religious background, travel, and literacy were not the sole determining factors in shaping their attitudes, for they were often denounced by people of the same social and educational background who still adhered to the church's orthodoxy. Individual decisions and conviction, not social characteristics, determined the path of belief that they followed.

One question to ask is if Spain and Portugal were singular places in regard to such a "live and let live" attitude. After all, during the Middle Ages, Christians, Muslims, and Jews had lived together for centuries in an uneasy equilibrium, or *convivencia*, in which a kind toleration was practiced and people came to know each other.[8] The

Christian unification of Spain, the forced conversions, the expulsion of the Jews in 1492 and then of the Moriscos, or converted Muslims, in 1609 had changed all that in terms of state policies, but one can ask if something of the older tradition had not carried on. There were popular sayings that indicated a certain relativism about religions, such as "better a good Moor than a bad Christian" or, even more radical, "each person can be saved in his or her own law." This was a relativism that included not only the traditional three monotheistic faiths but was now also expanded by some to include the Protestants as well and others who felt that Christian charity demanded that, at least, debate and discussion, not repression and force, were the best way to bring dissenters back to the church. There were cases of people who believed that war against the Muslims was also wrong. "Why should the king take the Muslims' homes away when they haven't done anything to deserve this?" questioned one woman. "The God that created the law of the Christians also created the law of the Moors," said another.[9] Such ideas, however, were considered challenges to the church's singular claim to validity, and authorities moved to correct them along with a whole panoply of other doubts— qualms about the saints, the virgin birth, the sinfulness of sex outside of marriage, the existence of hell or of purgatory, the authority of the pope, and other propositions that lived alongside astrology, palmistry, and other "superstitions." In fact, a very large proportion of the Inquisition's activity was directed not against apostasy by Jewish and Muslim converts but at suppression and correction of these doubts and propositions among Catholics.[10]

Where did these ideas come from? The question of salvation, *soteriology*, was central to Christianity. Could a life outside the church be pleasing to God? What about "natural law," that sense of right and wrong that God gave to all humankind? If someone lived by it and did good works, why would he be condemned? Pelagius, a British monk of the fourth century, thought human beings were essentially good and that by good works all could earn salvation. St. Augustine contested that idea and emphasized God's grace as the essential element for salvation, but even though Pelagius was declared a heretic, the question remained long unresolved.[11] Solutions were proposed. One response to the questions raised was the concept of "invincible ignorance," that salvation was possible if a person had never been exposed to the true faith, a concept that became particularly important after Columbus's voyages revealed whole new continents filled with pagan peoples. But some theologians argued that if God had not revealed the true religion to those peoples, it was because they had not merited revelation. The church eventually developed an official position on these issues, but doubts remained.

What is striking in the cases of the many people denounced to the Inquisition for holding that salvation was possible outside the church was that very few mentioned the previous theological debates or even specific texts or sermons as the source of their thinking. What they seemed to depend on instead was a kind of common sense and somewhat practical materialism. "If all the Jews and Moors and pagans are going to Hell, then the Devil would have too much work to do," said one man from Majorca. A French Catholic worker arrested in Spain for doubting that all the French Protestants were condemned could not believe that so many people of quality would be damned. "How was it possible that so many illustrious counts, and dukes, and doctors, and so many Lutheran ladies were all going to Hell?" he asked.[12] A Morisco told the Inquisitors that the differences in religions was God's fault. One of my favorite responses came from a Morisco who said that he believed simultaneously in all three laws—that of Jesus, that of Mohammad, and that of Señor Moses—for if "one of them let him down, he could always fall back on the others."[13] Some of the answers to questioning were even more pragmatic. A converso gave the inquisitors his vision of heaven and hell: "Heaven was when you had alms to give, and hell was when you had to beg for them." When an African slave was caught trying to flee to North Africa and asked if he hoped to save himself by the law of the Moors, he said that "he knew nothing of laws, and wherever they treated him well and gave him what he needed to live, there they had a good law; . . . and as far as going to heaven, he knew nothing, . . . only about having enough to eat and drink."[14] In a similar fashion, a

Morisco, when asked which law, whether of Christianity or of Islam, he had in his heart, answered that "he had no law in his heart for he was too poor to permit himself such luxuries."[15] Such answers should caution us in our tendency to see religious identity and belief as the basis of everything in the early-modern world.

Some in the sixteenth century argued and modern historians have agreed that this attitude of relativism or indifference was particularly characteristic of Spain's converts from Islam or Judaism.[16] After all, they did not want to think their ancestors were burning in hell, so they believed that if their ancestors had lived according to their own religion, they were saved. We know, too, that missionaries in the Americas and China often found native peoples unwilling to accept Christianity because of the same idea that their ancestors were damned. Also, in both the Old Testament and the Qu'ran certain passages (Q2:62; 5:59, 69; 105:6) suggested that God might find other paths acceptable, and in Islam the concept of *fitra*, or the inherent religiosity of all people, led to serious debates about God's intention in creating different faiths. Inquisitors warned the Christian faithful to be on the lookout for such ideas as evidence of backsliding among converts, but a close examination reveals that the idea that all could be saved in their own religion was also to be found among the Old Christians.[17]

Relativism, universalism, and even disbelief existed, and, despite the weight of theology and the policy of an intolerant state, so too did attitudes of acceptance and even respect for other faiths. For example, Christians who returned from long captivity and slavery in North Africa often showed a certain understanding that the Muslims also could be charitable, had their own holy men, and were religious in their own way. André Lopes, a Portuguese musician, refused to attend an auto-da-fé of the Inquisition in the 1620s in Evora because he believed the Jews being punished there were not guilty of any crime.[18] Or take the case of a Spaniard who in 1595 applauded the courage of Jews condemned to die at the stake in Toledo for holding fast to their belief, "like good soldiers, never taking a backward step."[19] Perhaps the most impressive recent research on this issue has been presented by the British scholar Trevor Dadson. His study of the Castilian town of Villarubia de los Ojos has demonstrated that after the town's Moriscos were expelled in 1609, the vast majority of them found ways to stay or return, protected or sheltered by the local lord, high ecclesiastics, or simply their neighbors, a story apparently repeated in other places in Castile and Aragon that undermines the image of Spanish intolerance.[20]

With the conquest and colonization of the Americas, another process was set in motion. America with its teeming populations seemed at first to offer apocalyptic hopes, so many new souls to be converted. Early missionaries to Mexico liked to point out that Hernán Cortés and Martin Luther had been born in the same year (1485) as evidence that God had given the New World to Spain to compensate for what the devil had taken from the church in Europe. Spain and Portugal justified their conquests by the missionary effort and the spread of the true church.[21] But the Americas presented severe challenges to orthodoxy. The state and the church sought to impose policies of exclusion and religious conformity and eventually established three permanent tribunals of the Inquisition in Lima, Mexico City, and Cartagena, but, despite the state and church's vigilance and enforcement, local needs at times resisted these policies. In 1554, for example, the municipal council of Santo Domingo sought to prevent the enforcement of a royal order prohibiting the presence of converts from Islam (that is, Moriscos) by arguing that as artisans and skilled technicians in the sugar mills they were useful members of the community.[22]

In the Americas, heterodox and heretical ideas also flourished. Among these ideas were tolerance, relativism, and syncretism. If all could be saved in their own religion, why not the native peoples as well? Ysabel de Porras, a Spanish widow born in Cuzco, high in the Andes, told her friends in Lima, "Before we Spaniards came here, the Indians who died also went to Heaven."[23] Similar statements were made by others: a carpenter, a pastry chef, and even Fray Miguel de Bolonia, an old Italian Franciscan missionary who, when accused of having said that "all men can be saved by the absolute power of God" and that Spaniards should "take nothing from the Indians without paying," defended himself by saying that he had been trained before the Council of Trent.[24] Syncretism was widespread, not only among Indigenous peoples adopting European customs and religion but in the opposite direction as well. The use of Native and African healers and sorcery by settlers and mestizos implied a belief in alternate ways to contact and influence supernatural powers and at least a tacit acceptance of other ways.

Throughout the Indies, there were even cases of people who questioned the very foundation on which the Spanish and Portuguese had based their conquests: the conversion of heathen peoples to the true faith. In this context, even defenders of the slave trade justified this commerce as the saving of souls from the barbarism and brutality of Africa.

Although humanists and theologians had occasionally raised objections to the slave trade and argued for better treatment and humanity toward the slaves, common folk had also had their doubts. Mateo Salado (or Saladé), a Frenchman who lived many years in Peru, was full of heterodox, semi-Lutheran ideas, was a critic of the pope, liked to read the New Testament for himself, and had developed his own theology. On many matters, his own observation led to his sense of injustice. His dislike of the rich and of the immorality of the ecclesiastical hierarchy as well as his sympathy for the poor made him angry and heretical. On slavery and the slave trade, he said, "Any man who sells blacks and mulattos cannot go to heaven, but is condemned to hell, and the pope who permitted this trade was a drunk." For Salado, the justifications for slavery offered by church and state and the benefits that many derived from the injustice of the slave trade were not enough to silence him. He was tried in 1571 and burned as a heretic.[25] In the 1620s, in the great slaving port of Cartagena de Indias, there lived the carpenter Andrés de Cuevas, a man with a fiercely independent mind, a sometimes blasphemous mouth, anticlerical attitudes, and a sharp sense of social injustice, which in Cartagena was evidenced by slavery. One witness complained that Cuevas had told one of the witness's slaves that he would have been better off as a gentile in Africa. Cuevas was applying a moderated version of the old relativist argument about religion to the situation of the Africans and raising the ancient question of the use of force in conversion. The slave trade was wrong, he argued, and the king was to blame for allowing it to continue. Cuevas the carpenter's questioning of the whole moral and political basis of slavery was a direct affront to both the king's and the church's justification of slavery and the slave trade as well as to the whole theological edifice on which that trade had been built.[26] His position was far more radical than that of the great Jesuit Alonso de Sandoval, who sought in the seventeenth century to alleviate the conditions of the slaves brought to Cartagena, but it grew from the same social milieu.[27] It reveals that antislavery sentiments were by no means limited to theologians; it demonstrates how the ancient idea of the universal validity of other faiths (laws) or cultures could be extended to Africans; and it raises, once again, the intractable question of the direction of influences between learned and popular thinking.

By the eighteenth century, other winds now blowing in the Atlantic world were making the question of religious freedom and toleration important. The Huguenot Pierre Bayle, reacting against the Revocation of the Edict of Nantes in 1685, wrote a brilliant condemnation of religious persecution. John Locke published "Letter concerning Toleration" in 1689, and in 1724 Voltaire published *Letters on England*, in which he approvingly argued, "If only one religion [were] allowed in England, the government would very possibly be arbitrary, if there were only two, the people would cut each other's throats, but since there is such a multitude of faiths, they all live happily and in peace."[28]

A new literature of synthesis was now condemning the practices of intolerance and arguing that freedom of conscience was a liberty that should be guaranteed to all and that such freedom did not necessarily have a negative effect on loyalty to the state or on order in society. Now freedom of religion, rather than being considered a concession, was being presented as a right. Opponents within the Catholic Church called the new proponents of such ideas "Libertines,"

"Deists," "Materialists," "Indifferentists," "Freemasons," and "Atheists," and although the genealogy of such ideas was very old, the prosecution of them was increasingly made among members of the educated middling classes—professionals, merchants, city officials, military men, and the like. In Spain, theological questioning abounded. Between 1780 and 1820, about 6,500 cases were tried by the Inquisition, and about 45 percent (3,026) of them were for "propositions"—that is, doubts about doctrine. The theological problem here was that "free will" was an essential element of Christian doctrine, but "freedom of conscience" would permit doctrinal error, and from "freedom of conscience" the step to other kinds of freedoms of a political, social, or moral nature was dangerously short.

Meanwhile, people continued to think for themselves. People in Spain and Portugal were not unaware of the movement toward toleration in Holland, France, and England. Travelers reported on the social and economic benefits of toleration in other countries, and the growing public press in Spain reported on this issue, paying particular attention to the removal of restrictions against Catholics in England. England and its colonies, in fact, had become for some in the Hispanic world almost a mythical land of liberty. We see this in the case of Antonio de la Abuja in 1711. A Spaniard who had sailed and worked in the Caribbean, Abuja liked to read books, especially the Holy Bible, a copy of which in Spanish (reading the Bible in a vernacular language was prohibited in Spain) he had picked up on a trip to Barbados. When a companion called the English "heretic dogs" and said that all of them were damned, Abuja said, "St. Thomas says, 'Love God above all and your neighbor like yourself.'" Heretics and Muslims were also God's children, he argued. This and other propositions considered unorthodox got him sentenced to return to Spain, but the ship was captured by pirates, and he ended up in Jamaica, where he married and lived as a mariner before being recaptured. This time he told the Inquisitors that the religion of his parents was, of course, the best, but he had lived with the Protestants in Jamaica and found their society amenable. He liked to read the Bible and make up his own mind about religion. In any case, in Jamaica he had not been bothered about his conscience. Not only were there gray areas between religions, but people who lived there accepted some beliefs, doubted others, and, like Abuja, tried to decide God's will for themselves.[29] The kind of tolerance and relativism expressed by Abuja in the early decades of the eighteenth century and by others like him before that created a soil in which the seeds of the philosophes could later flourish. These expressions were exemplary indications of the desire for a "people's peace," a desire to get along with one's neighbors and to live in peace, and they often drew as much on Christian religious principles as they did on rationalism or secularism.

But the story of "freedom of conscience" and religious toleration in Spain and Portugal is not that of the triumphal march of dissident popular opinion and liberal elite sentiments. Religious toleration did not come overnight, and the Inquisition's grip loosened slowly. The state began to separate religious authority from political administration. Madrid celebrated its last public auto-da-fé in 1680, and Lisbon did so in 1683. Punishments for religious offenses now became a more private act conducted within churches before an invited audience of dignitaries. As the power of the state grew, so too did its reluctance to have clerics making political decisions; thus, spiritual matters were increasingly separated from politics, making the state's control clear.[30]

In many ways, it was neither a groundswell of popular opinion nor the telling critiques of liberal opponents that undercut the role of the Inquisition or the official policy of intolerance that it represented, but rather a centralizing regalism that led the way by seeking to redeploy the authority of religion for the Crown's own political ends. But even in the 1790s reformers continued to move cautiously. The reformist Spanish minister and major Enlightenment writer Gaspar Melchor de Jovellanos wrote in 1794 that anti-Inquisition sentiment was still not general and that the best way to control the tribunal was to dismantle it piecemeal.[31]

European thought about freedom of conscience had moved from a simple toleration born of pragmatic convenience in which foreign allies, merchant communities, and minorities were allowed leeway in religion because it was advantageous or profitable in some way. By the close of the eighteenth century, in much of Europe toleration as a philosophical position had become a matter of human rights, freedom, and equality of opportunity that all deserved.

These ideas had supporters in Spain and Portugal and their colonies, and, as argued earlier, there was an ancient dissident tolerant tradition in matters of faith. However, the actual abolition of the Inquisitions in Spain and Portugal, the bastions of the politics of religious exclusivity, came as part of the changing political and intellectual milieu of the period, not as a victory for popular sentiments of tolerance. Napoleon's invasion of Spain led to his abolition of the Inquisition in 1808 because it represented a challenge to civil authority.[32] The Cortes, or assembly, that was convoked in Cadiz in 1810 to organize resistance against the French invasion was dominated by liberals and Jansenists, who set about writing a constitution. To soften opposition from the ecclesiastical establishment, they made Catholicism the religion of the nation, but they also briefly abolished the Inquisition. The monarchy brought it back, though.

The defenders of the traditional order always tended to see ideas about freedom of conscience as extraneous importations. *Liberty* and *equality*, stated a pamphlet published in Seville and then reissued in Mexico in 1810, seemed to be very pleasant words, but they had brought to France nothing but anarchy and, now with Napoleon, the chains of despotism as well. The underlying cause of these horrors was a disregard of religion and the permission of toleration in matters of faith.[33] The following year an anonymous defender of the purity of religion in Venezuela published an extensive critique of what he called "tolerationism," in which he identified the spiritual and civil dangers of allowing false religious doctrines the right to flourish, as "atheists and materialists" such as Rousseau and Voltaire wished to do.[34] But claims that such ideas were only foreign importations ignored the long tradition of popular attitudes of tolerance that the Inquisition's own documentary record demonstrated. Locke, Bayle, Voltaire, and other Enlightenment authors on toleration had provided a systematic argument on freedom of conscience as a concept beneficial to all societies. This concept resonated in Spain and Portugal, as it had elsewhere in Europe, but long before such ideas became a moving intellectual and social force, many common people in the Iberian world and elsewhere had already reached similar conclusions.

In this period of revolutionary political turmoil and foreign invasion, *Inquisition* became a byword and symbol for those who advocated the defense of king, country, and religion, while "toleration" was now a symbol of a liberal vision of a new Spanish nation. These two warring visions of Spain influenced much of that nation's history for the next two centuries. The Inquisition was finally abolished in 1834. In the former Spanish American colonies, the new nations had already done away with the Inquisition during the movements for independence between 1814 and 1825. In Portugal, where during the Napoleonic period the Inquisition had kept a low profile, a liberal revolution in 1821 for constitutional monarchy brought an end to the institution.

The end of the Inquisition, however, did not mean the establishment of religious liberty. Despite the liberal triumph that the end of inquisitions seemed to represent, constitutionalism, freedom of expression, and other aspects of the liberal programs in fact proved easier to obtain than religious freedom in these societies of the Luso-Hispanic world, where the union of religion and politics remained a guiding principal of the political classes and where unity and order overshadowed any attempt at political or social change.[35] Spain and Portugal as well as the new nations of Latin America made Catholicism the exclusive religion of the state. Despite brief attempts earlier in the twentieth century, full freedom of conscience was not enacted in Portugal until the Constitution of 1976 and in Spain in the Constitution of 1978.

So we are left with a conundrum. Given the evidence I have provided of a widespread and long-lived pluralist popular attitude about freedom of religion, a considerable Hispanic Catholic tradition of charity, and theological arguments against the use of force in matters of faith, and given the seeming triumph of liberalism in nineteenth-century Spain and Portugal and their former colonies, why did the right to freedom of conscience come so slowly in the Luso-Hispanic world? Why was it so hard to achieve a "people's peace" in matters of religion?

One line of explanation claims that the society as a whole was basically intolerant and that the Inquisition was simply a "mirror" of public opinion, but this claim diminishes the Inquisition's own records of its repression of dissidence and heterodoxy.[36] Some authors have found fault in the Enlightenment itself and have seen in its projects the origins of many of the social ills of the modern world. Both its successes and its failures have been cast as the forerunners of the worst aspects of modernity, and to its rationalism and its separation of religiosity from public life have been ascribed the origins of genocide, racism, and other social ills. The Enlightenment surely had its shadows. But to apply to that age the standards of our own deforms and obscures its accomplishments. On the issue of religious toleration, it is hard to fault the Enlightenment, and in much of northern Europe the extension of freedom of conscience was very much a central feature of its influence.

One possible explanation of the slow pace of the movement toward religious freedom in the Luso-Hispanic world is provided by the Spanish scholar Javier Fernández Sebastián, who argues that the Enlightenment in this cultural zone was so profoundly Catholic and deeply influenced by dogma that the close association of religion with monarchy and the nation itself in early-modern times was rarely questioned by Hispanic reformers and liberals, who, although open to political, economic, and even social changes such as freedom of speech or of the press, found freedom of religion difficult to accept. But this explanation has also been questioned because in the eighteenth century there was no lack of advocates of toleration in the Luso-Hispanic world who looked admiringly at the progress of England, Austria, France, and the United States, nor was there a lack of theologians who disagreed with coercion in matters of faith. Nevertheless, their inability to overcome the view in favor of religious exclusivity remains a historiographical challenge.[37]

Finally, I want to make three points about this peculiar tale of the roots of tolerance and a people's peace in a political context of intolerance. First, Spain and Portugal and their empires, dedicated as they were to religious unity and policies of intolerance, can serve as the limiting cases. If we can find evidence in these countries of attitudes of popular tolerance and even of admiration or respect for people of other faiths, then the possibility that such ideas may have existed elsewhere is high. Historians of Europe are increasingly revealing that "popular tolerance" is a phenomenon that existed in much of Europe, but that the story of violence, confessionalization (that is, the forming of religious identities), and religious conflict has been so dominant that historians have given the contrary evidence little attention. That situation has changed greatly in the past two decades.[38]

Second, once we get below the level of doctrine and state policy, there is much evidence of pragmatism, accommodation, and toler- ance—often born, to be sure, of convenience and self-interest but resulting in tolerance all the same.[39] In Poland, Hungary, and the Balkans, such arrangements were common, but even in France, Eng- land, and Italy such attitudes could be found. There were places in France, for example, where Protestants and Catholics shared the same church bells or even the same churches and where Protestants and Catholics interacted, intermarried, and coexisted. The so-called peace of religion grew not only out of political needs and pragmatic considerations but also from a sense of community and a desire for order and stability.[40] Christian charity, incredulity, indifference, doubt, and a simple sense of justice also made their contribution alongside practical considerations. In England, there was a strong current of doubt and dissent often contradictory to state-sponsored intolerance. Many people saw the crux of their faith by living the Golden Rule. After the Restoration in the seventeenth century, min- isters of the Church of England complained that in the countryside many people were "rustic Pelagians," not caring what church their neighbors attended so long as they lived a good life and kept their pigs out of their neighbors' gardens. We know about these attitudes because churchmen complained of them constantly as evidence of the irreligion of the times.

Third, the common people usually have a place in the histories of toleration or freedom of religion only as an audience. It has been assumed that the intellectuals' ideas eventually circulated down and affected popular thought. But almost all of the arguments made by the thinkers of toleration appear at least in embryo in the discourse of common people as well—not as developed or as consistent to be sure, but there all the same. We should at least question the argument that the ideas of change always flowed from the elite to popular culture. On this point, history and sociology overlap in the study of tolerance. The great thinkers codified and synthesized, but they were not alone in their views on tolerance.[41] That fact has increasingly captured the attention of a new generation of scholars, whose studies have redefined and broadened our understanding of the history of religious toleration. Much of that work has not emphasized elites and governmental policies, but rather the quotidian practices of peoples in religiously diverse communities. In one of the best examples of that scholarship, Benjamin Kaplan reminds us that the long-told story of toleration as a triumph of reason and the product of secularization is partial at best and in many ways a celebratory myth underlining Western values such as individualism, equality, and privacy. His work emphasizes that religion in general need not be associated only with intolerant forms of religion and that non-Western societies could find their own paths to religious accommodation.[42]

So if the story of religious accommodation shifts to everyday practices and to the actions and thoughts of common people, what should we make of historical characters such as Cuevas and Abuja who appear in these pages? What did they represent? Every society has its oddballs and cranks, so we must wonder if they were just marginal dissidents representing nothing but their own marginality and individuality. The usual kind of quantitative social analysis does not seem to answer these questions. Social characteristics—profession, age, place of origin, gender, class, civil status, geographical mobility—do not seem do distinguish the "tolerants" from the population as a whole or even from those who denounced them. Moreover, a quantitative method that measures these characteristics is more appropriate when searching for normative behavior, and those who expressed religious tolerance were clearly not the norm. They seem to be people who were thinking for themselves and, based on their own experience and understanding of a variety of intellectual and religious traditions, had reached a similar conclusion. I think that, given the constraints and penalties faced by dissidents in the Iberian monarchies and their empires on these issues, Abuja and Cuevas and people like them probably represent the tip of an iceberg. But even if they do not, and even if they were not like their neighbors, it is still important to include them in the story of religious thought. We celebrate and study Erasmus, Luther, and Spinoza not because they are like everyone else, but because they are not and because their individuality ultimately had an effect on the course of history. Can we grant the same privilege to obscure men and women? After all, the cumulative or collective effect of their arguments and individual decisions about their acceptance of religious diversity, their vision of a society without persecution, and their desire to create a "people's peace" that would allow freedom of religion eventually won out or at least provided a context for the policies of toleration.

The story of "freedom of conscience" and toleration still needs to be written. The old narrative about the triumph of reason and the secularization of society crafted by great intellectuals is clearly incomplete, and the rise of new fundamentalisms and religiosities now make us less sure of the permanence of the purported achievement of the Enlightenment or its long-term history. The recent incidences of a fusion of religious intolerance and nationalism in India, Myanmar, Israel, western Europe, the United States, and the Islamic Middle East have raised questions about the inherent unity of toleration and modernity and societies' ability to maintain practices of tolerance during moments of ethnic and political tensions. In recent years, this human right has remained unreachable by some communities, and even in the areas where it has triumphed, its future is still contested. The case of the Iberian world, in which a long tradition of popular expressions of religious tolerance existed despite a regime of intolerance but in which the struggle to achieve freedom of conscience was long and difficult, underlines both the modern possibilities and hopes of a people's peace built on religious tolerance and the political, ethnic, and historical obstacles that always threaten it.

PART TWO

People in Action

8

"US out of El Salvador!"

The Maryknoll Sisters and the Transnational Struggle for Human Rights

AMANDA IZZO

It might seem counterintuitive to argue that Christian foreign mission, historically a vector of European and American global domination that is often assigned particular responsibility for the cultural violence of imperialism, has also served as a catalyst for human rights mobilizations. Yet over the second half of the twentieth century, religious organizations with missionary roots have established a pivotal presence in transnational activist networks. One such group, the Maryknoll Sisters of St. Dominic, offers a telling example of the complex history of religious participation in the global human rights movement, especially in its mobilization of activist resources in the wake of an international incident in 1980 in which security forces in El Salvador executed two Maryknoll sisters and two fellow US Catholic missioners.

The enduring power of the well-publicized story of the deaths of the four women—lay missioner Jean Donovan, Ursuline sister Dorothy Kazel, and Maryknoll sisters Ita Ford and Maura Clarke—defies

Originally published in slightly different form as chapter 7 in Amanda L. Izzo, *Liberal Christianity and Women's Global Activism: The YWCA of the USA and the Maryknoll Sisters* (New Brunswick, NJ: Rutgers Univ. Press, 2018). Copyright © Amanda L. Izzo. Reprinted by permission of Rutgers University Press.

present-day tendencies in the US popular memory toward rose-tinted recollections of Ronald Reagan's presidency. While the fervor with which his administration heated up the Cold War with its array of clandestine and brazen military interventions is often forgotten, the women provided and continue to provide rare visibility of the appalling casualties of counterinsurgency campaigns. The narrative surrounding the churchwomen's murders stretches from the discovery of their bodies in 1980 to the present day. And although their execution was a singular event, one that has captured an extraordinary degree of public attention in the United States, its significance should not be gauged only by the ways in which it has peppered news headlines of the past thirty-five years. Rather, the decades-long quest to hold the women's killers accountable provides a compelling case study in people's peacemaking, a process that radiated out from the community level of interpersonal relations to mass protest directed at the US state and then ultimately to engagement with international law.

The Maryknoll search for peace was propelled by the order's visionary but pragmatic faith in action. Its success at putting belief into practice in an effort to stem state-sponsored violence in El Salvador by stanching US aid gave it a critical role in an often overlooked US antiwar movement in the 1980s. The story of the churchwomen's deaths provided a symbolic touchstone that joined secular liberal-leftist protest movements to the peace and justice ministry of the Catholic Church that emerged after the sweeping reforms of the Second Vatican Council (1962–65). The Maryknoll effort to marshal the power of the story was more than symbolic, though. The order's dedication to achieving justice in El Salvador—not only for those whom they embraced as martyrs but also for Salvadorans suffering from the gross human rights violations of a US-funded proxy war—garnered it significant leverage in the realm of advocacy. Quietly but determinedly, the organization invested the mobilization with a belief that "effective love can form us into one people and overcome the barriers which separate us." Its message was both Catholic and catholic: born of the conciliar reimagining of the corporeality of Jesus in the lives of the poor and appealing to a universal ethics of cooperative care. The sisters faced off against "political structures which . . . destroy the image of God in the human person."[1]

Interpreting the Maryknoll efforts as a quest for a people's peace requires consideration of the diversity of strategies employed by the order to bring justice in the churchwomen's case. The order's involvement with the case transpired at three distinct levels of engagement. The first was that of the faith-driven, interpersonal encounters of religious mission, which for the order had been significantly affected by the social movements and church reforms of the 1960s and 1970s. The second level developed from the sisters' central location in a network of grassroots activists and nongovernmental organizations (NGOs) in the 1980s whose protest and lobby compelled the US government to act. Finally, the realm of international law enabled the sisters and their supporters to open up new judicial avenues for the redress of human rights abuses. The multiple levels at which their advocacy work unfolded offer models for understanding how the pursuit of a people's peace can be consequential. Each form of engagement had an impact on its own, whether the provision of emergency services in mission or inside access to US congressional figures. Ultimately, however, it was the synergy among these disparate approaches that made the movement both durable and politically effective. By welding personal faith to collective protest to move the machinery of the state, the Maryknoll Sisters and their advocates were crucial actors in directing grassroots protest toward policy change and human rights accountability. Though the Maryknoll women mobilized from a position of privilege in social movement networks, they contributed to the bottom-up construction of a people's peace in their struggle to reshape US–Central America relations.

It is worth emphasizing the degree to which activism around the churchwomen's deaths made progress toward peace, but it is also critical to recognize the profound limitations of the mobilization. Present-day unrest—as reflected in continuing on-the-ground struggle in El Salvador, human rights violations directed against Latin American immigrants in the United States, and the ongoing toll of unilateral militarism in US foreign policy—supports Latin American studies scholar Christine Wade's contention that the conclusion of the Salvadoran Civil War "appears to be a questionable model for peacebuilding, as it represents the very real challenges of an incomplete peace."[2] Foremost, this is a story of peace efforts that affected people and political life in the United States. It would be a distortion to dismiss the churchwomen's case as having no effect on the course of the civil war, but it is undeniable that the efforts recounted here did woefully little to ameliorate conflict in El Salvador.

Nevertheless, there is value in viewing activities that originated in the United States as bearing on the creation of people's peace, particularly as a case study in the attempts of social movement actors in the Global North to parlay their privileged standing and transnational solidarities into international political leverage that countervailed their own governments' repressive interventions in struggles in the Global South.[3] First, an examination of the Maryknoll Sisters' multiple forms of influence suggests that aspirations for and mobilizations toward a people's peace can radiate beyond grassroots action at local sites of conflict. People's peacemaking may be distinct from the mechanisms of conflict resolution waged at the governmental and intergovernmental levels, yet, as the churchwomen's case demonstrates, transnational advocacy networks can enlist these mechanisms to pursue the grass root's interests.

Second, the markedly incomplete nature of the justice that was eventually achieved in this case suggests that a people's peace is not an endpoint but rather a set of practices that must always remain in motion. In contrast to the illusions of finality that characterize nation-states' official treaty making, visions of a people's peace emerge through forms of contestation and solidarity building that require ongoing effort to be renewed and kept alive. Understanding a people's peace as a process rather than a product, an aspiration that inspires action rather than a concrete and static outcome, allows us to grasp

the significance of the Maryknoll Sisters' mobilization while still recognizing the degree to which Salvadoran society remains torn by the
aftermath of US imperialist militarism and the rise of neoliberalism.

■   ■   ■

Shifting from the imperial ambitions of the foreign-mission movement of the early twentieth century to the social justice wing of the
Catholic Church of the 1970s, the Maryknoll Sisters traveled a dramatic arc in theological and political commitments over the twentieth
century. The group was founded in 1920 as the US Catholic Church's
first foreign-mission order of women religious. It developed alongside
but in many ways independently from a companion order of male
clerics and religious brothers, the Maryknoll Fathers and Brothers.
The missiological origins of both Maryknoll orders were strongly
rooted in ideologies prevalent in the age of empire. Sisters established educational and medical facilities in places they designated
mission territories, which included communities of racial minorities in the United States. They aimed to convert "pagans in heathen
lands and . . . Asiatics in Christian countries" to the Catholic faith,
stoke devotionalism, and spread the ostensibly salubrious influence
of Western culture.[4] Proselytization and religious instruction figured
centrally in their work, but the social services they provided perhaps
better account for their success in establishing a long-term mission
presence in East Asia, East Africa, and Latin America.

During the 1960s, shifts outside the Catholic Church, in particular the waning Cold War consensus in the United States and the efflo-
rescence of leftist global social movements, were integral to changes
in the Maryknoll personnel's social consciousness and political allegiances. At the same time, reforms within the church initiated by
the Second Vatican Council supplied sisters with new intellectual
and institutional tools for interpreting the inequalities and unrest
that they encountered firsthand in mission.[5] This expansive spirit
prompted many Maryknoll women to question traditional conceptions of mission and to pursue the social justice–oriented ministries
newly sanctioned by the Vatican. Even as the membership of this
and other religious orders dropped precipitously after the council,

the Maryknoll Sisters emerged from this period of upheaval with a powerful, renewed sense of purpose.[6]

The success of the Sandinista uprising in Nicaragua in 1979 was an invigorating experience for a number of Maryknoll sisters, a high point of synergy between the liberation theology that had transformed Latin American peoples' movements and the on-the-ground work of foreign mission. Maryknoll women looked optimistically to the Sandinista regime as proof of the revolutionary power of Christianity to create structural change. But if the Nicaraguan revolution seemed to demonstrate the great potential of liberation-inspired reform, the El Salvador conflict revealed the profound dangers such commitments entailed. A handful of Maryknoll sisters worked in El Salvador in the late 1970s when the country's archbishop, Óscar Romero, invited members of missionary religious orders to replace the dozens of Salvadoran church workers who had been killed or disappeared in the undeclared civil war that had claimed the lives of nearly one thousand people by mid-1980. Drawing the devotion of campesinos, 73 percent of whom tuned in to his Sunday radio sermons, Romero became the paragon of liberation theology in action. His homilies detailed a military state of violent repression that the press ignored. His call for missionary assistance in continuing the church's work was a plea for the international community to declaim atrocities and to eliminate the military aid fueling this violence. With the vision of working alongside the revered archbishop, Maryknoll sisters Carla Piette, Ita Ford, and Maura Clarke answered the request for volunteers and made arrangements to transfer to El Salvador in 1980.[7]

They were not able to arrive in time to meet Romero. After broadcasting a sermon that called for soldiers to lay down arms, Romero was assassinated by a sniper while saying mass on March 24, 1980. Each of the sisters had considerable experience in Latin American conflict regions; however, Ford and Piette's time in Chile during the coup of 1973 and Clarke's time in the Nicaragua of the Somoza dictatorships did not prepare them for the unvarnished repression that marked day-to-day life in El Salvador. The Catholic ministry's basic efforts, the provision of social services and pastoral outreach to the poor, marked church personnel as enemies of the state. For the first few months following their arrival in the spring, Ford and Piette pondered how to navigate this chaotic undertaking as they stayed with Maryknoll colleagues in La Libertad. There, they worked with a group of missioners sponsored by the Diocese of Cleveland, Ohio, a team that included Jean Donovan and Dorothy Kazel. In the summer, Ford and Piette made their way to Chalatenango, the capital of a department that was overwhelmed by refugees as campesinos fled the violence-riddled countryside. Working with a parish priest, the two sisters distributed food and medicine as well as comfort and care to a traumatized population. Father Paul Schindler later reflected on some of the presumptions that guided the decision to rely on these sisters instead of on local priests to carry out the fraught tasks of refugee work. He believed that their presence as "blond, blue-eyed women" would mitigate the danger: privileges of gender, race, and nationality would shield them from being treated as disposable subversives.[8]

The sisters envisioned their task as solidarity with the disenfranchised in a struggle for survival. The Maryknoll ministry in El Salvador was rooted in the "preferential option for the poor," a field of pastoral outreach premised on an understanding of Jesus as the savior to the oppressed classes in society—the poor, the sick, foreigners, and the exiled.[9] Women religious had historically trained to perfect themselves as individuals in order to cultivate the indwelling of God. But the influence of liberation theology, which earned the institutional support of many in the Catholic hierarchy in the late 1960s, inspired many Maryknoll women to orient their understanding of divine immanence toward the presence of Jesus in the lives of the marginalized people who shared his experiences of persecution. Sister Madeline Dorsey, one of the Maryknoll women stationed at La Libertad, recounted her role in these plain terms: "Accompanying the people, being with them . . . right now all we can do is to be with these people, to share with them, because they are hurting very badly."[10] Ita Ford similarly described the challenge of her vocation: "Am I willing to suffer with the people here, the suffering of the powerlessness? Can I say to my neighbors, 'I have no solution to this situation . . . ; but I will walk with you, search with you, be with you?'"[11] The Catholic Church's on-the-ground activity marked the most basic level at which the Maryknoll Sisters and similar religious communities put faith into action in search of a people's peace. By providing emergency services and standing witness to forces of dehumanization, church workers sought to ameliorate the everyday trauma of structural violence.

Tragedy struck early among the new arrivals. A car accident in which Carla Piette lost her life in August 1980 left Ita Ford deeply shaken, having narrowly survived the wreck that took her closest friend. Maura Clarke then arrived to take Piette's place. Meanwhile, army commander Ricardo Peña Arbaiza, whose office sat opposite the dormitory where Clarke and Ford lived, made his contempt for the Catholic Church's work in El Salvador increasingly clear. By fall, soldiers "had virtually taken control of the church building," their presence a constant warning to church officials and potential parishioners.[12] In the last week of November, a note was posted over the door to Ita Ford's room that read, "Every person who enters this house dies. We know that you are communists. . . . We know that the military takes no action against you, but we will execute you. . . . Death to Communism."[13]

The threat was carried out. No single explanation has satisfactorily accounted for the motivation behind the kidnapping and murder of Clarke, Donovan, Ford, and Kazel on December 2 as they returned from the San Salvador Airport. Four national guardsmen, who carried out the crime in plainclothes, were ultimately convicted as the direct perpetrators. As the case unfolded over the years, some of the men said nothing about why they intercepted the women at a roadblock, drove them to a remote field, assaulted them, shot them point blank with high-powered rifles, and left their bodies at the side of the road. A few of those involved explained that the women attracted attention because they were spotted at the airport with packages assumed to be weapons and subversive literature—items later inventoried as a handbag and a box of books.[14] The guardsmen claimed to be on high alert because sympathizers to the leftist cause

were pouring into Salvador for the funeral of several guerrilla movement leaders, whose kidnapping-murder had made international
news. Other perpetrators insisted that the guardsmen's sergeant,
Luis Colindres Aleman, told them to carry out the act because he
had orders to do so.[15]

The day after the murders, a campesino reported to a town official the discovery of bodies alongside an isolated path, and the official arranged a secret burial of the victims. That would have been
the end of the story for most Salvadorans. But word of the discovery
reached the rest of the mission team as well as US ambassador Robert White. With an international contingent of journalists, they all
traveled to the gravesite to identify the bodies. A haunting Associated
Press photograph that appeared in newspapers on December 5 alerted
many in the United States to the story: dirt-flecked corpses that had
been lifted out of a common grave, their disfigurement obscured by
branches that had been placed over them by their colleagues, who
knelt in prayer nearby.[16]

The stories of the four women soon became shorthand for the
ongoing human suffering wrought by the global Cold War. To a
significant extent, this interpretive framework took hold in public forums because the Maryknoll Sisters actively labored to bring
these connections to light. Although small-scale ministry among the
marginalized had drawn the sisters to El Salvador—the first level
of peacemaking—Maryknoll women sought to elicit meaning from
the deaths by advocating in the United States for urgently needed
structural change. In the wake of the events, the order mobilized
grassroots supporters, utilized the resources of human rights NGOs,
and pressed federal authorities in Washington to take action. This
vigorous domestic campaign constituted the second element of the
Maryknoll pursuit of a people's peace. The sisters helped activate a
peace movement by integrating the symbolic power of their narrative of martyrdom into direct-action protest and civic lobby. Yok-
ing institutional acumen to convictions of faith, the order assumed
a prominent place in a coalition that attempted to reshape US policy
according to principles of peace and transparency.

The missioners' insider/outsider status proved a social movement asset for raising awareness and demanding accountability in El Salvador. They were insiders in mission communities, witnesses of day-to-day violence and deprivations. But they were also outsiders, US citizens with privileged standing who could not be dismissed as easily as quotidian political enemies. Evidence quickly surfaced indicating that the Salvadoran armed forces had killed the missioners.[17] They were the enforcers of an autocratic regime that meted out a startling amount of extrajudicial violence using the full-throttle material and military support provided by the US government. To bring this connection to light, Maryknoll leadership first responded to the deaths with a press release that interpreted the events as a call for justice. A joint announcement from the Maryknoll Sisters and Fathers explained the commitments that had brought the women to El Salvador. "Solidarity with the poor is not an option but a sign of the Kingdom [of God] that must be made explicit in our day," it stated, underscoring that dedication to the poor stood at the center of the women's identity as Christians. The pledge to live by a "Gospel imperative" demanded not only charitable solicitude but also the active pursuit of "justice . . . for those who suffer hunger, who are naked and homeless, . . . and those who are persecuted." This imperative was inseparable from the surrounding political context. Though the churchwomen's deaths were unconscionable, the statement continued, it was urgent that the congregation's loss "not overshadow the murders of nearly 9000 less known people in that country." The Gospel principles of peace included rejection of violence "in the hands of an assassin"—that is, the actions of the individuals who had killed the churchwomen—as well as rejection of violence "in structures"—that is, the policies and practices that enabled the US-propped regime to carry out the killings. The press release implored the public to take action. "As Christian missioners and citizens of the US, whose ties with El Salvador have now been sealed in blood," it read, stressing the transnational allegiances of foreign mission, "we ask you to join with us in urging President Reagan that he does not permit our Government to send to the Salvadorian Government any military aid to be used by security forces which would only serve to further the violence against their own people."[18]

Because the order had formally incorporated advocacy into its institutional infrastructure, Maryknoll leadership handily marshaled organizational resources to elaborate the political implications of its faith commitments. Prompted by the intensification of unrest in mission territories, the Maryknoll Sisters had created the Office of Social Concerns in 1974 as a means of sharing information and coordinating lobbying efforts with a blossoming network of human rights NGOs. Utilizing global media access, this activist network was often treated as a trusted source of information about conflict regions.[19] In addition to sharing information and participating in NGO networks, the office encouraged individual Maryknoll personnel to raise awareness in the United States of the "interdependence and inter-complicity of events which . . . nurture injustice throughout the world." The task was one of "reverse mission," designed to make Americans aware of their own role in fostering violence in the developing world. Reasoning that "only a sister who has lived among the people for a number of years can present the reality of a people, a country, and a culture with the knowledge and empathy that is warranted," the office asserted that the sisters were uniquely able "to speak of the needs of the peoples of the Third World and of minority groups in the U.S." amid the postassassination flurry of interest in the Maryknoll orders. From these initiatives, many everyday Americans heard firsthand accounts of the impact of structural violence from sisters and human rights activists speaking at local churches, press interviews, and public talks.[20]

The sisters' symbolic importance should not be underestimated in accounting for the peace mobilization.[21] Describing the religious coalition that gave life to the US–Central America solidarity movement, Sharon Erickson Nepstad emphasizes that social movement stories "engage people . . . when they dramatically portray a situation with moral clarity,"[22] and even though the politicization of women religious drew criticism in the postconciliar years, the perceived altruistic integrity of the Catholic nuns evoked an undeniable moral clarity that held the Maryknoll Sisters in good stead. The killing of women associated with the pure intentions of chastity and religious service stirred an indignation in the United States that had not been aroused by the abstract awareness of mass death in a foreign country. The unfathomable violence that already had claimed thousands of lives became legible to the American public only when it was written on to the bodies of pious white women. For those who might not have otherwise been drawn to the political questions at hand, the modern narrative of martyrdom had an electrifying effect. The women became sanctified in the sacrifice to their faith, and this added a mystical valence to their antiwar, pro-poor cause. The cult of martyrdom worked in concert with a legacy of colonialism that was embedded in the representations and retellings of the women's deaths. Such cultural operations of power shaped the ways in which the women's story moved audiences in North America to action. Like women missionaries of an older era, the churchwomen garnered a particular sympathy and visibility as assumed agents of maternalistic goodwill.[23] With news portrayals that lauded the women as admirable and full of promise, their fate uniquely registered as a senseless tragedy, while the experiences of Salvadorans retreated into the background.

Coverage emphasizing the loss of the American women as special or exceptional was indeed the product of the devaluation of lives in the Global South, but for many US voters it also turned the mirror to the US presence in Latin America. As the sisters bore witness to the Salvadoran struggle, they rallied grassroots action in the United States. In the wake of the deaths, Catholics in particular turned out for a "variety of protest activities," which a *Washington Post* reporter called "unmatched by few—if any—reactions to past issues, including the controversy over abortion." Within weeks, spontaneous demonstrations had proliferated, each publicizing the links between state-sponsored violence in Latin America and US military aid. From the banner hung outside of the San Francisco cathedral that read "US Dollars Kill US Nuns" to countless memorial masses and statements of protest, a mobilization stretching from the pews to the bishops lined up to denounce military intervention in Central America.[24] Even as Reagan's inaugural parade coasted on the good feelings wrought by the announced release of the Iran hostages, it passed by counter-demonstrators' placards demanding "US Out of El Salvador."[25]

The churchwomen's cause was aided by impressions of a lack of moral credibility from the incoming Reagan administration in its efforts to address the case. The spectacle proved an inconvenient obstacle to the administration's aggressive repudiation of Jimmy Carter's human rights policy goals in favor of generous support of anti-Communist governments and armed opposition movements, a priority articulated even as the sisters' deaths remained front-page news. The first attempts to manage public opinion on the matter played out disastrously. Jeane Kirkpatrick, designated ambassador to the United Nations, fired an early volley, discrediting the sisters in an effort to justify the escalation of counterinsurgency campaigns. In a news interview, she attributed the killings of the missioners to the actions of a far-right fringe group and further indicated that the women bore responsibility for what had happened to them, having lent their services to a leftist movement. Their religious vocation, Kirkpatrick suggested, was a cover for something more sinister: "I don't think the government [of El Salvador] was responsible. The nuns were not just nuns; the nuns were political activists . . . on behalf of the Frente [the revolutionary coalition] and somebody who is using violence to oppose the Frente killed them."[26] The misleading comments raised eyebrows; touching biographical accounts of the women and their families that spread through news outlets in response to Kirkpatrick's claims belied the unfounded allegations of revolutionary subversion. Secretary of State Alexander Haig took a tack similar to Kirkpatrick's as the El Salvador crisis dominated policy debates during his first months on the job. He, too, insinuated that the sisters had reaped the consequences of their involvement in armed resistance. Anthony Lewis of the *New York Times* expressed the revulsion felt by those moved by the sisters' tragedy: Haig, "talking about the vicious killing, suggested they were responsible in some measure for their fate." When Haig was challenged on his view, Lewis continued, "he tried to slither away, joking and expressing amazement and blaming the press."[27]

A story assessing the first months of the Reagan presidency reported that El Salvador, "which two months ago looked like a good place to 'draw the line' against communist expansion," produced "the first notable backlash," with mail "running 10 to 1 against the administration's new emphasis on military aid and advisers" to the country.[28] The difficulties of the churchwomen's case rendered Central America the preeminent foreign-policy issue of the early presidency. The fight to raise awareness of the Salvadoran state's violence and the degree to which this violence depended on the US government's support brought to the surface much of the American Left's unfinished business: the betrayals of Vietnam, the unsustainability of military-industrial culture, the endurance of empire, and the victimization of people of color, women, and the poor. The coalition of liberal, leftist, and religious groups that was called the "Latin America solidarity movement" had a wealth of conflicts to address, but El Salvador and Nicaragua figured most prominently. The Committee in Solidarity with the People of El Salvador would become the largest of the solidarity groups focused specifically on that country, and at the peak of the movement in the mid-1980s there were two thousand local groups working under a score of national organizations on solidarity issues.[29] The bumper sticker "El Salvador Is Spanish for Vietnam" made its appearance after the churchwomen's deaths. Feminists, antinuclear activists, and antiwar protesters participated in major actions. A news story about a protest that brought twenty-five thousand to the Pentagon in May 1981 focused on the motley crew of protesters, with a "flea market atmosphere, something for everyone," but the accompanying photo highlighted the central issue for the demonstration's organizers: the banner leading the march read, "Make Jobs Not War, US out of El Salvador!"[30]

The Maryknoll Sisters drew sustained support from a Catholic voting bloc, which garnered it direct access to Congress. With telegrams and sermons, newspaper ads and mail campaigns, the order's Catholic supporters hounded elected officials to respond to the outcry. Politicians running in the elections of 1982 marveled that "Catholic church activism is getting extraordinary."[31] Several influential figures affiliated themselves with the cause. The *New York Times* profiled the politicized religious commitments of Massachusetts Democrat Thomas (Tip) O'Neill, Speaker of the House and "caustic" critic of Central America policy, as indicative of the influence of Catholic activism on Washington. O'Neill, in turn, named Maryknoll women, including his aunt Eunice Tolan, as his "main sources of information about Central America."[32] Bob Woodward later deemed the influence "profound and almost mystical"; O'Neill became "a missionary in his opposition" to counterinsurgency campaigns, believing that the "nuns and priests spoke the truth" in a political context full of obfuscation and self-interest.[33] Over the early 1980s, like-minded politicians called sisters to testify before the House and Senate on aid questions. Before one such body, Melinda Roper, the Maryknoll Sisters' president, underscored the interconnections between the group's religious commitments and the impact of American foreign affairs: "The deaths of the four women cannot be separated from the general pattern of the persecution of the Church . . . and from the deaths of thousands of innocent Salvadorans," nor could they be "separated from U.S. policy toward that government."[34]

Upon pressure from voters and using information shared by religious lobbies, Congress pursued questions of human rights as Reagan and his advisers made their case for steep increases in aid to El Salvador. The churchwomen's supporters scored an important legislative victory in September 1981, making that aid contingent on a biannual certification that the regime was instituting human rights advances. Progress in the churchwomen's case stood at the forefront of the issues that the US Congress required the Salvadoran government to address.[35] Though the certification measure fell far short of the goals of protestors, who sought nothing less than a fundamental dismantling of military support, it threw a significant hurdle before Reagan's Cold War agenda. The requirement meant publicity about the churchwomen's case every six months from 1981 to 1984, when the guardsmen were finally convicted for the murder. According to the United Nations Truth Commission findings in 1992, threats of aid reduction also contributed, however inadequately, to a decline in indiscriminate death-squad activity.[36] In the estimation of Helene O'Sullivan, who directed the Maryknoll Sisters' Office of Social Concerns during this period, the struggle produced a true grassroots movement. "We had a lot of frustration," she stated, citing the obstructive tactics used by the Department of State, which withheld information and downplayed the documentation provided by the order throughout the murder investigation. "Yet we had a staggering amount of support," she continued. "Just staggering. We couldn't have done it without the support of the American people." Civic protest, she argued, effected tangible change. Every six months, Reagan insisted on military aid increases to El Salvador, but for the most part during his first term, O'Sullivan pointed out, his demands were rebuffed.[37]

Though opposition to Salvador aid obstructed Reagan's Central America agenda, the escalation of his counterinsurgency campaigns could not be thwarted. Advisers in the executive branch harangued, wheedled, and—when other methods failed—stole and lied to deliver military might to the Right in Central America.[38] Though Reagan did not receive the increases in aid to El Salvador that he continually sought, he was able to divert an enormous amount of resources to accelerate the military offensive against revolutionary forces. David Duell Passage, US ambassador to El Salvador in the mid-1980s, called the country "the most important foreign issue to the United States." During his tenure, the number of embassy staff was exceeded only by the staff in Cairo and New Delhi, and El Salvador received "the third largest disbursement of U.S. foreign aid." The amount of aid supplied to the Salvadoran military over the 1980s is remarkable: in 1981, it totaled $5.9 million; it reached $206.6 million in 1984; and between 1984 and 1986 (after the criminal conviction of the churchwomen's killers), combined economic and military disbursements to the El Salvadoran regime totaled nearly $2 billion. "It was generally agreed," Latin American studies scholar Diana Villiers Negroponte concludes, "that without the funding, the Salvadoran government could not have survived one day."[39]

The divergence between the US government's path to closure and that pursued by the sisters and their advocates widened as the criminal investigation came to an end in 1984. After intense pressure from the US Department of State, the Salvadoran courts convicted four low-ranking National Guard members of aggravated homicide, sentencing each to thirty years imprisonment.[40] It was the first case in which members of the Salvadoran armed forces were convicted of murder in a civilian court.[41] From that point forward, El Salvador issues became less pressing in US foreign-policy debates. Contra aid in Nicaragua thereafter became the Latin American battleground for both Congress and US antiwar protestors.[42]

The court convictions and El Salvador's diminished visibility in US public discourse masked the glaring fact that accountability had not been achieved: not for Maryknoll, not for the churchwomen's families, and especially not for the thousands of Salvadoran victims of the ongoing civil war. For the human rights organizations that had lent their resources to the Maryknoll cause, the inadequacy of the criminal investigation remained the pivotal issue for revealing the depth of US and Salvadoran state involvement in acts of terror against civilians. Rank-and-file patrolmen were held responsible for the crime, but the authorities who had connections to the killings and who continued to inflict egregious human rights violations in the name of counterinsurgency had not faced even minimal investigation. The United States continued to supply those authorities with the resources necessary for sustaining the civil war, including the training of Salvadoran military units responsible for some of the most shocking massacres of the conflict.[43]

Accordingly, though the churchwomen's case by the mid-1980s had ceased to be a flashpoint for direct action or congressional debate, core participants in the movement were not content to let the campaign for justice peter out. Branching outward from their initial efforts at interpersonal care and their subsequent role in an antimilitarist campaign, the Maryknoll Sisters added a powerful and significant third level of engagement to their efforts at a people's peace. They employed the US civil courts—a perhaps unexpected venue—as an institutional space for shaping and extending human rights policy. After the federal government washed its hands of the problem, a team of human rights organizations, including the Maryknoll Sisters' Office of Social Concerns, pressed for an official inquiry to be extended into the Salvadoran military command. The Maryknoll women explained the tenacity of the legal campaign in terms of a faith-driven mission to achieve "true justice" through the prosecution of the "intellectual authors" of the crime.[44] Madeline Dorsey, who had worked alongside the slain women, reflected on the determination to utilize tort law as a means of securing justice for all those who suffered during the civil war: "We see so many connections with the victims and the causes of violence, and you hope the truth this time will come blasting out. I guess the hope is that the truth will be revealed and there will be an end to impunity."[45]

As peace accords brought an end to the civil war in 1992, the United Nations Truth Commission report supplied evidence indicating that the guardsmen had killed the women under orders. That trail led to two top-ranked generals: José Guillermo García, minister of defense, and Carlos Eugenio Vides Casanova, the head of the National Guard. To considerable surprise, it was discovered that by that point the generals had gained US residency and retired to Florida. Armed with this knowledge, Ita Ford's brother, William (Bill) Ford, filed a lawsuit under the provisions of the Torture Victim Protection Act (TVPA) of 1991, legislation that asserted an extraterritorial jurisdiction for the US courts in matters of human rights. With that entrée into international law, the United States became the only country in the world where nonnationals could bring suit against other nonnationals for human rights abuses. For Bill Ford, as for the Maryknoll Sisters, much more was at stake than securing damages for his sister's and the other churchwomen's deaths. Helene O'Sullivan recalled the motivation behind what would become a thirty-year mobilization: "When we started that case . . . ten thousand people had been killed by death squads. Not one iota of attention to ten thousand deaths." "By the time we finally brought it [the case] to trial," she continued, "seventy-six thousand people were dead . . . , just taken away. Men taken away, women taken away in the dead of night. . . . We pursued the case of our sisters to stop the death squads."[46]

Ford lost his case in 2000, and appeals were unsuccessful. The case hinged on the principle of command responsibility, and jurors concluded that the chaos of the civil war meant that commanders could not control the actions of their troops. Ford was not disheartened, however: "We probably tried to prove too much. We were trying to prove everything that happened in Salvador for forty years." He hoped this case would encourage "more and more Salvadorans in the U.S. who were abused by this machine [to] come forward because now we have . . . a way of pursuing these things." This soon came to pass. His prosecution effort made it possible for another human rights legal group, the Center for Justice and Accountability, to sue the two generals on behalf of three Salvadoran refugees whose evidence of the experience of torture demonstrated command responsibility more successfully.[47] *Ford et al. v. Garcia and Vides Casanova* opened a conversation. The success of the subsequent case, *Romagoza Arce et al. v. Garcia and Vides Casanova*, established a precedent that assigned responsibility for abuses to commanders who allowed them to flourish. With the *Romagoza* case in 2006, which levied $54 million in damages for the plaintiffs, the extension of liability established a new point of leverage in US human rights law, fulfilling the TVPA's intent to provide, in the words of scholars Robert Drinan and Teresa Kuo, "some concrete relief for dealing with violations of fundamental human rights."[48]

Ultimately, the *Romagoza* case and post–September 11 antiterrorism legislation set into motion deportation proceedings for both García and Vides Casanova, the latter of whom had twice received a Legion of Merit award from a US president for advancing human rights reforms in the Salvadoran military. The cases advanced in immigration court in February 2014, with the deportation orders upheld after appeal. The decisions were, according to the *New York Times*, "an unusually expansive and scalding" acknowledgment from the US government that its allies committed atrocities.[49] The court concluded that the generals' "lack of initiative" in investigating the case "sent a message to troops . . . that extrajudicial killings— even high profile murders of American church personnel—could be committed with impunity." The judge in Vides Casanova's deportation case waved away a defense that the armed forces' actions had been supported, even rewarded, by the United States. The "jurisdiction of the court," James Grim wrote, "does not extend to a review of foreign policy decisions." Vides Casanova's argument that "his actions were consistent with U.S. policy" was not relevant to the case.[50] Vides Casanova and García were removed to El Salvador in 2015 and 2016, respectively.[51]

An uncollectible multimillion-dollar judgment for three individuals and the deportation of two elderly generals are scant reparation for the massive destruction caused by war. The conclusions of Truth Commission documents and immigration court cases did not elicit from the US government any sort of repudiation of Reagan-era Central America policy. If we can consider this sequence of events to be a version of a people's peace, then it is one of distressingly limited scope. The profound struggle that continues to rend Salvadoran society cannot be overlooked, and neither can the endurance or even intensification of the US security apparatus's unchecked support for human rights abuses.

Nevertheless, to dismiss such results as insignificant would be to overlook the profound spiritual commitments, dogged persistence, and considerable organizing savvy that anchored the Maryknoll-led quest for accountability. Although insufficient, this movement's small victories secured some measure of justice—a necessary step in the pursuit of peace. If the impact of the mobilization was not enough to address the scale of conflict and violence either in El Salvador or in other regions torn by US militarism, the long-term determination to intervene on the levels of interpersonal relationships, US national policy making, and international law reflects the yearnings and persistence that make peace possible. As the churchwomen's story remains in the news some thirty-five years after the events unfolded, it is a reminder that a people's peace is less a destination and more a process that is always in the making.

9

Human Rights City Initiatives as a People's Peace Process

JACKIE SMITH

Much peace research focuses on government-led, top-down interventions aimed at ending violent conflict. Less attention is devoted to the ways civil society groups help prevent conflicts from escalating into violence by promoting values and practices that foster social justice and peace. The Human Rights City initiative is an example of how popular groups are organizing to advance policies and support values and practices that nurture human rights and peace. Since the 1990s, activists around the world have been developing this model for addressing economic inequality, discrimination, and other root causes of conflict. The work of residents of Pittsburgh (including me) to advance human rights in that city enabled it to become the fifth Human Rights City in the United States in 2011, and the work of Human Rights Cities to advance dignity and justice for all residents serves as a model for building a people's peace that can reduce violence and foster justice in communities.

This consideration of "people's peace" processes begins with a critique of some of the prevailing approaches in the peace research literature that have limited the literature's ability to advance understandings of peace and knowledge of how to reduce violence. These dominant approaches start with the implicit assumption that peace agreements must operate within the existing, highly militarized interstate order. In doing so, these approaches privilege top-down methods of peacebuilding, where the national state is central to peace processes. Furthermore, they reinforce existing centers and margins, reproduce "market epistemologies,"[1] and neglect the world-historical context in which states and societies are embedded.

In contrast to conventional, state-centric approaches, world-historical perspectives situate the modern state in the context of the capitalist world system, which is based on competition for resources that reproduces inequality, exploitation, and violence.[2] Such inequities and violence—as well as the wars and "state failures" they generate—are reproduced by an interstate system in which states have no choice but to compete in an increasingly globalized economy. Yet virtually all postwar peacebuilding agreements require that states emerging from wars enact economic policies aimed at (re)integrating that state into the world economy—such as trade liberalization, privatization, and reduced government regulation and spending—despite the association between these policies and the underlying causes of violent conflict.[3] In short, there is a strong case to be made that the structural violence produced by the capitalist world system is a major contributor to militarized conflicts and other forms of physical violence in the modern world.[4] Thus, to be effective, peacebuilding strategies—whether local or global—cannot avoid the need to transform the structures of the capitalist world system.

A second critique of existing literature is its tendency to privilege states and other elite actors as the main protagonists in peace processes, despite the fact that most analyses of peacebuilding conclude that civil society actors play vital roles in the processes of postwar peacebuilding. Among the tasks civil society actors perform are intermediation and facilitation between citizens and the state, advocacy for marginalized groups, monitoring for accountability, socialization for a culture of peace, and the fostering of social cohesion.[5] Clearly, these functions are at the core of building peace in any society, and they are common features of what this volume's contributors are calling "people's peace." It should go without saying, however, that in most postwar contexts civil society actors are left weakened and relatively powerless to engage in these tasks that are so essential to achieving a de-escalation of violence and a return to some semblance of peace. This is particularly so in cases where war and militarized conflict have produced physical dislocations and devastation as well as heightened social polarization. Moreover, even where conflicting parties are not engaged in violence, institutional arrangements are not likely to be very supportive of and may even hinder civil society's performance of these critical tasks.[6] Thus, peace researchers and practitioners should devote far more attention to a wide range of *people's peace processes*—that is, the ongoing work of social movements that contributes to these kinds of peacebuilding-related activities *in nonwar contexts* in all parts of the world, not just the Global South.[7] The aim of this work should be not only to document people's peace processes and make them part of the larger framework of discussions about peacebuilding but also to identify the practices and policies needed to support civil society actors in their critical peacebuilding functions of helping people realize their own "emancipation from a world economic system based in inequality and violence."[8] Support for people's peace projects and the civil society peacebuilders who advance them will inevitably run counter to the interests of privileged political actors.

The Human Rights Cities Movement

An important example of a people's peace project is the Human Rights Cities movement, which includes a variety of local initiatives aimed at achieving people's "right to the city"—that is, implementing international human rights norms in local contexts. Such initiatives have been proliferating around the world since the 1990s. The Peoples Decade for Human Rights Education (PDHRE) launched the formal "Human Rights Cities" initiative in the wake of the World Conference on Human Rights in Vienna in 1993. The initiative aims to mobilize people in communities to "pursue a community-wide dialogue and launch actions to improve the life and security of women, men and children based on human rights norms and standards."[9] The process of becoming a Human Rights City (HRC) can vary, and some communities start with a city council resolution designating the city an HRC. In other contexts, organizers work to build broad community alliances to support human rights principles before seeking a formal HRC designation. The key point is the intention of using human rights as a framework for community governance and the active engagement of popular groups in support of this aim.

In 1997, Rosario, Argentina, became the first HRC, motivated by residents' desires to prevent another military dictatorship and to reduce overall violence and social exclusion. Since then, activists around the world have been developing this model for transforming policy making and raising public consciousness.[10] PDHRE has spread the idea of HRCs through a variety of mechanisms, including World Social Forums, where tens of thousands of social justice organizers have gathered on an annual or biannual basis since 2001.[11] There are currently more than two dozen HRCs around the world, with growing numbers in the United States.[12]

Recognizing that prevailing social policies have done little to effectively address social problems such as poverty and social exclusion, HRC advocates contend that this initiative helps mobilize civil society actors in support of a policy agenda that promotes peace and social justice. The Human Rights City initiative

> encourages local communities to take charge of their own future by understanding their needs and the causes of the various forms of deprivation. . . . Where local government is ineffective, corrupt, or non-existent and few opportunities are available to mobilize beyond the family and clan, a human rights cities initiative is a vehicle for raising awareness and transforming that awareness into action for social change.[13]

Beyond providing a model for local organizing, the HRC initiative is also valuable for its ability to connect local communities with a global movement and to offer a rich body of international human rights law that validates and reinforces local claims. The value of such an international connection cannot be underestimated for its role in motivating community engagement, providing guidance and models for local action, and gaining attention from policy makers and other elites in the community. The PDHRE's examination of the impacts of HRC organizing in cities around the world led to the conclusion that

> those who have participated in the creation of Human Rights Cities have acquired a skill set and confidence for questioning those power relations that make deprivation of human rights possible. They use the legal and administrative systems to their advantage and address problems of urban poverty as participants in change rather than [as] victims of fatality or recipients of charity. . . . The idea that social and economic injustice is "the way the world is" yields to awareness that people can change their condition by civic engagement for societal development based on human rights.[14]

By remedying the significant failures of top-down and state-centered approaches to peacebuilding, this people's peace approach supports fundamental changes in local communities that are necessary for a durable and just peace.

Pittsburgh's Human Rights City Alliance

Pittsburgh officially became the fifth HRC in the United States in April 2011, when high school students working in the local American Friends Service Committee's Racial Justice through Human Rights Program proposed the initiative to the Pittsburgh City Council. Following the passage of the Human Rights City Proclamation, however, there was no organized follow-up by activists to implement the proclamation until they came together to plan a rally for International Human Rights Day in 2013. Organizers recognized an opportunity in the recent election of a mayor who had been a city councilman when the HRC proclamation was passed.

The core leadership of the Human Rights City Alliance in its early phase comprised several faculty members and graduate students at the University of Pittsburgh (including me); members of the American Friends Service Committee, whose youth group made Pittsburgh an HRC; and a handful of activists from some of the main social and racial justice groups in the city.[15] We recognized early on, following social movements in other places, that work for human rights needs to begin with a focus on those who are least able to enjoy their rights.[16] Yet these very same people have the most difficulty attending meetings and otherwise participating in the work of the HRC Alliance and other activist groups. Knowing that racial, generational, and other differences and tensions have long complicated efforts to build movements in the United States, we sought to learn from past experiences and to be intentional about our aim of building a multiracial and multiclass alliance for human rights. We thus spent our first year learning about issues most critical to low-income and African American residents and developing relationships with leading organizers on these issues. We sought guidance from leaders in those communities and worked to sensitize more privileged residents to the ways that prevailing institutions and practices deny many people their basic human rights and dignity. We built a steering committee for the HRC Alliance with the intention of having a majority leadership from historically oppressed groups.

Expanding the Political Imagination

By calling on people to imagine how our city could look if it were organized around the goal of promoting universal human rights, we realized that we were inviting them to imagine a very different place. Alliance participants quickly recognized that we needed to change the mindsets of politicians and the public, who are accustomed to thinking of local politics as mainly about parties and elections and policies aimed at attracting businesses to the city while avoiding tax increases. People could very quickly see (if they didn't already) that the privileging of economic growth in public policy meant that human rights would always be neglected. As David Harvey observes,

> We live in a society in which the inalienable rights to private property and the profit rate trump any other conception of inalienable

rights you can think of. This is so because our society is dominated by the accumulation of capital through market exchange. . . . We must imagine a more inclusive, even if continuously fractious, city based not only upon a different ordering of rights but upon different political-economic practices.[17]

In addition, the human rights lens clarified for us how economic growth systematically undermines the ability of some groups in the city—in Pittsburgh, this means African Americans and immigrants—to enjoy even the most basic rights.[18] From here, we invited residents to consider not just different policies but also new practices and institutions that could better accomplish the aims of our Human Rights City.

With this invitation, HRC initiatives are invoking creative social and political leadership from people and communities. One observer highlighted this sort of translation work in Washington, DC:

DC is working towards empowering residents, empowering the community in the Shaw and the District to know and claim their rights. It is this work that begins to make DC a human rights city, as organizing working-class and low-income communities of color and helping them build the power necessary to claim and protect their own rights is [*sic*] at the core of what human rights mean.[19]

What is also worth noting is that helping people know and embrace the full range of their human rights reinforces their understanding of the indivisibility of economic and civil/political rights, thereby reducing the likelihood that the initiative will be co-opted by defenders of the status quo. It also leads to critical reflection on the overarching principles and values around which we build our society. Such reflection opens space for considering and imagining radically different alternatives. For example, Sacajawea Hall, a climate-justice organizer who is part of the Jackson, Mississippi, HRC initiative, articulates the idea of a "people-centered human rights," which encompasses a system-level antiviolence emphasis that is essential to building a culture of peace:

A people's centered [*sic*] human rights framework grows out of what oppressed people define for ourselves based on our struggles and goes beyond the limits of international legal text, it confronts white supremacy, settler-colonial capitalism, patriarchy and other systems of oppression that deny us our human agency and dignity. *This framework is grounded in the understanding that we can only realize our full human rights when we change social relationships, structures and institutions.* . . . We have to put forth our people-centered human rights framework, link it with the emerging Rights of Mother Earth Framework and the concept of "buen vivir" (roughly translated as "living well together") and reclaim our agency, social space, and the right to live in harmony with each other and our provider and sustainer, Mother Earth.[20]

Here we see the emphasis on redefining the basic relations of society in ways that confront and challenge a current order that is based in the violence of colonialism, patriarchy, and racism. By naming the violence of this social order and creating spaces where residents can reflect on and work to reshape social relations, projects like the HRCs can address systemic, structural violence and enable true peacebuilding to occur. Moreover, we are seeing in contemporary social movements an effort to connect human rights with environmental justice or, rather, to enable people to confront and transform the violent nature of humans' relationship with the earth. The ideas of *buen vivir* and Rights for Mother Earth are clearly integral to the realization of human rights, yet they are also fundamentally incompatible with the existing world system.

By creating spaces where residents can share their visions and discuss concrete strategies, HRCs invite participants to expand their political imaginations. In doing so, they challenge the prevailing political culture, which relies on passive and uncritical citizenship, organized within the electoral framework of elite-controlled political parties and the goals they define. Of course, the prevailing mindsets and socialization in the dominant political culture also make it difficult for many people to imagine social change happening outside the formal, top-down government policy framework. This same culture also complicates the work of mobilizing and sustaining large numbers of volunteers for the long, hard work aimed at transforming the basic structures of society from the bottom up.[21]

The key point here is that peacebuilding requires work to disrupt and transform our current political and economic system to one based on principles of cooperation, inclusion, and human rights. Much of the work of peacebuilding, then, must focus on changing people's consciousness and their understanding of community priorities, values, and governance. HRCs work to change the script of politics to make human rights a priority, and HRC leaders are effectively working to "translate" principles from the global arena for local audiences. This translation has enabled our group and other HRC initiatives to mobilize people from a diverse array of backgrounds around a collective project, which helps overcome the demographic segregation and issue silos that plague conventional organizing. As Sally Engle Merry observes,

> Human rights translators work . . . within the constraints of existing discursive fields whose complex and multivocal messages are open to various, and uncontrollable, interpretations. Human rights intermediaries put global human rights ideas into familiar symbolic terms and use stories of local indignities and violations to give life and power to global movements. They hold a double consciousness, combining both transnational human rights concepts and local ways of thinking about grievances.[22]

The realization of the principles and ideals in international human rights law is not an automatic process or one that can be dictated from above. It requires intentional interventions of processes by people to engage diverse local populations in the shared work of building a just and peaceful society.

It is also important to note how countries involved in either internal *or external* wars—including the United States—often insulate themselves from discussions about international law and norms. In the United States, American exceptionalism can also limit the resonance of human rights as an organizing framework. For instance, Amy Finnegan, Adam Saltsman, and Shelley White interviewed organizers in more than forty activist groups in Boston about their views of human rights as an organizing framework. They found that only a third of these groups was actively using human rights frames in their organizing.[23] In our work in Pittsburgh, we are also finding that human rights is not immediately resonant in many segments of the activist community. Yet human rights language does have resonance, and it has proved effective at illuminating intersections among different struggles and nurturing local solidarities. Its international orientation encourages people to consider how their concerns transcend local and national politics and to see common identities with people engaged in similar struggles elsewhere. Perhaps for this reason, respondents to the Boston study noted that many of their groups' staffs relied on a human rights framework in their thinking, and a third of the groups whose organizers the authors interviewed were beginning to move toward greater use of human rights language. Most of the respondents felt human rights are an effective tool for local organizing, despite the unique political and cultural constraints in the United States.[24] Thus, the work of human rights translators is clearly a critical element of people's peace processes, particularly in settings where politics and violent conflict actively obstruct the values of social inclusion, peace, and justice.

The HRC model, therefore, has been useful for creating links between a local community and global movements and ideals. For instance, HRCs have helped translate global human rights principles into local settings in their work to promote awareness of the Universal Declaration of Human Rights of 1948 and other human rights treaties. For some participants in the United States, the gap they confront between the declaration's principles and the experiences of people in their community is jarring.[25] Projects that include the monitoring of international human rights treaties such as the Convention on the Elimination of Racial Discrimination (CERD)[26] and the introduction of local legislation to implement global treaties, such as the Cities for CEDAW (Committee on the Elimination of All Forms of Discrimination against Women) initiative,[27] are common elements of HRCs. And annual celebrations of International Human Rights Day—December 10—reinforce people's understandings of the history and universality of human rights.

Because using human rights as a framework for governance entails a paradigm change, we are finding in the Pittsburgh HRC initiative that a big part of our work involves disrupting dominant ways of thinking and acting. At this early phase of our work, we spend a great deal of effort working with community leaders to encourage them to consider how a human rights framework might advance their group's goals. We are also working to raise greater awareness about the ways different groups—such as African Americans, immigrants, LGBTQ residents—are denied many basic rights. In our outreach, we are working against an often competitive nonprofit culture that leads many organizers to be suspicious of our motives. We are essentially working to change culture as much as policy; our work must take place at many levels—from policy arenas to schools and neighborhoods to interpersonal and interorganizational relations.

My participatory research on HRCs has helped illuminate the basic tasks that HRCs do. In table 1, I outline some of these tasks and illustrate how HRCs implement them. These functions mirror those that have been associated with civil society's peacebuilding roles. For instance, HRCs empower residents to monitor public policies and practices and to press for change where policies do not meet human rights standards, with projects such as the annual Human Rights Report Card in Washington, DC. HRCs work to foster a human rights culture to challenge a mainstream culture based in consumerism, individualism, and economic growth. And they create public spaces where diverse residents can come together to engage in dialogue, learn about each other's experiences, and build commitment to shared principles and projects. By simply calling residents together to envision and build an HRC, organizers mobilize residents around a shared public vision, thereby strengthening local democracy and creating an essential foundation for lasting peace.

Table 1. Human Rights Cities and the Functions of Peacebuilding

Functions	Actual HRC Projects (in Pittsburgh and Elsewhere)
Advocacy for Marginalized Groups	
Mobilizing and legitimating demands for social inclusion	Monitoring local-level compliance with international treaties such as CERD[a]
	Pressing for local adoption of international treaties such as CEDAW and CRC[a]
	Building and strengthening community relationships and diverse alliances that support human rights
	Drafting and enacting a Human Rights City Action Plan
Holding public officials accountable to human rights values	Referencing human rights criteria in appeals to policy makers on a variety of issues
	Writing "Welcome to our Human Rights City" open letters to new public officials
	Relating local demands to national and international human rights norms and laws, regardless of their formal ratification status
	Appealing to HRC status to advocate for and justify pro–human rights initiatives
Socialization for a Culture of Peace	
Expanding the public space where the "common good" can be discussed, imagined, and defined by diverse groups of residents	Creating spaces for public deliberation
	Holding public events on Human Rights Day and identifying changes needed to realize human rights
Fostering mutual understandings and sensitivities to inequalities and power dynamics	Organizing events that enable dialogues about human rights and their implications for policy
	Helping residents understand the intersections of various issues and demands; reframing diverse aims in terms of human rights
Building engaged citizenry and participatory models of governance versus passive citizenship and leadership by "experts"	Building a community task force to research public policies and recommend strategies for improving human rights outcomes

Table 1. Human Rights Cities and the Functions of Peacebuilding *(Cont.)*

Functions	Actual HRC Projects (in Pittsburgh and Elsewhere)
	Engaging residents in monitoring human rights practices
	Inviting and facilitating actions to hold public officials accountable to human rights
Fostering Social Cohesion	
Encouraging popular engagement in shared projects to envision and build a better society	Building networks among diverse community leaders
	Defining a shared project for community coalitions
Public consciousness raising and human rights education	Building a "human rights culture" or "making human rights a way of life" in the community
	Providing human rights training for youth and adults, community leaders, public officials, and police
	Advocating a human rights curriculum for schools
	Sponsoring human rights cultural work—e.g., film festivals, essay contests, music groups

[a] CERD = Convention on the Elimination of Racial Discrimination; CEDAW = Convention on the Elimination of All Forms of Discrimination against Women; CRC = Convention on the Rights of the Child.

The work of the Pittsburgh HRC Alliance advances peacebuilding functions in our community, specifically by advocating for marginalized groups, fostering social cohesion, and advancing socialization for a culture of peace.

Advocacy for Marginalized Groups and Fostering Social Cohesion

Capitalism relies on its ability to exploit differences and inequalities among groups of people in order to maximize profits for the owners of capital. Thus, the globalized capitalist system has generated institutions that reproduce and expand inequalities and reinforce divisions and hierarchies in society, inhibiting communication and cooperation across differences. As a result, we are finding in our HRC work that even decisions about when, where, and how we hold our meetings are very political and that working to be inclusive of diverse groups—especially those most affected by rights violations—takes conscious planning and investment of resources to be successful. But we also have found that by creating spaces where people who do not ordinarily come together can meet, our alliance is fulfilling an important need in our race- and class-divided city. Indeed, democracy depends on public deliberation among *all* members of a community, and such deliberation has been inhibited by prevailing practices and institutions as well as by pervasive inequalities. So the work we are doing strengthens both democracy and social cohesion. Moreover, by helping residents gain awareness of global human rights law and movements, we translate lessons from international peacebuilding into local settings. Our one-on-one work with community leaders and volunteers also contributes to building the relationships that nurture the values and practices of a democratic culture.

The most important public actions the HRC Alliance organizes are public forums where participants can learn about human rights as well as about other residents' diverse experiences and perceptions of human rights. For example, we set up International Human Rights Day rallies and organized a panel to honor International Mother Earth Day.[28] These events were designed to bring the voices of the most marginalized groups to the fore so that all of us could reflect collectively on the challenges and opportunities for advancing dignity and justice for everyone. We also have worked to ensure that youth voices are heard in these spaces, aiming both to nurture young leaders and to help older folks appreciate the needs and challenges faced by our city's youth. It is clear in these meetings that more-privileged participants are challenged by hearing the firsthand accounts of people being denied their rights because of their race, class, gender, citizenship status, or ability. But our work to facilitate ongoing conversations and relationships among different organizations, leaders, and constituencies has helped sustain and build participation and support for the HRC initiative. This work has benefitted from residents' previous efforts to fight racial injustice and division, which include an annual Summit against Racism, where we organize panels, identify allies, and build networks to support the HRC initiative and its racial justice component in particular (see our 2015 and 2016 reports[29]).

Our most recent work around Human Rights Day led us to the innovation of holding Human Rights Days of Action rather than organizing just a single event to mark this day.[30] This change enabled us to reach out to a wider range of groups and encourage them to link their own work to a human rights framework. In turn, we helped publicize their human-rights-related events to a larger audience. In this way, we were able to expand the numbers of people working to frame their demands in terms of human rights as well as to enhance people's awareness of the intersectionalities among movements.

In addition to holding public forums, we have also worked to support mobilizations against police brutality and racial discrimination. In the fall of 2014, Pittsburgh's mayor appointed a new police chief, whom we welcomed to the city in October with an open letter.[31] The key point of the letter was to make sure our new chief was aware of Pittsburgh's status as a Human Rights City. Moreover, we wanted to offer community support for human-rights-oriented policing practices, and members of our group engaged in research to learn more about the recommendations from other cities and from the United Nations in this regard. Later that fall, we joined the local Amnesty International chapter during its annual Human Rights Day letter-writing action to issue a letter to the police chief raising specific human rights demands that had been identified by local groups working specifically on police accountability.[32]

In addition to these activities, we spent much of the first year of our HRC Alliance learning about the work being done in the community and speaking with community groups and leaders about their policy priorities and visions. This work informed our Human Rights City Action Plan,[33] which we made public at our International Human Rights Day rally in 2014. The Action Plan identifies some demands and changes essential to moving us closer to being a true Human Rights City, such as ensuring universal health care, eliminating racial disparities, and instituting living-wage laws. It is intended as a blueprint to guide policy makers and local organizers, and it has inspired the creation of new task forces of volunteers working to implement specific components of the plan. As we continue to build, we are working to deepen connections between human rights organizers and area universities, and in the summer of 2015 we organized a workshop to bring together activists and scholars from within and beyond Pittsburgh to examine the lessons and possibilities of Human Rights Cities.[34]

These actions illustrate how the HRC Alliance has supported the work of diverse organizations and leaders and built understanding and trust among groups that do not ordinarily work together. Such understanding and trust as well as the networks of relationships behind them are critical to nurturing shared identities and social cohesion. Moreover, in this work it has become even clearer to me that peacebuilding requires conscious efforts to mobilize people in ways that counter the competitive and exclusionary nature of the prevailing social order and institutions. Because our people-centered human rights framework privileges voices of those marginalized by the existing institutions, it helps sensitize participants to power dynamics and exclusion, enabling group trust and cohesion to develop. The *process of organizing* toward a "human rights city"—more than organizing for any single event or action—unifies participants around a shared project and set of principles that builds and deepens social relationships.

This is not to say that the process has been easy. We remain a rather small network of committed organizers, and our work still consists largely of learning about the human-rights-related work and concerns of diverse community residents, meeting with different community leaders to build relationships, and supporting collaborative projects among area organizations. It requires patient and persistent efforts to demonstrate how uniting around human rights can strengthen the overall work for social justice in our city. We are often seen as pushing yet another issue and advancing the interests of our "organization," and so we also find ourselves working to transform prevailing activist mindsets. We frequently must stress that we are not attempting to be a new and distinct organization but rather an alliance of like-minded groups that can support cooperative and coordinated efforts toward a shared vision for social change.

Socialization for a Culture of Peace

Our work to transform Pittsburgh into a Human Rights City has helped residents appreciate that human rights cannot simply be legislated. As HRC organizers have stressed, the goal is to make human rights a "way of life" for people in our region. This goal requires multiple kinds of activities in multiple places of social life. It encourages a transformation of values and priorities and people's understanding of "the political" beyond conventional boundaries.

One initiative taken in Pittsburgh in this regard has been the support for recognizing Indigenous Peoples Day on October 12. The idea for this day first arose in 1977 at the International Conference on Discrimination against Indigenous Populations in the Americas.[35] In 2014, Seattle, also a Human Rights City, adopted a resolution renaming October 12 Indigenous Peoples Day there, explicitly linking the decision to that city's status as an HRC. One of our alliance members attended a rally organized by Seattle activists honoring Indigenous Peoples Day in October 2014, and he brought ideas from that rally to a meeting where we were planning that year's Human Rights Days activities. We drafted a text to submit to the Pittsburgh City Council based on Seattle's resolution and that incorporated a demand by local activists for "the teaching of Indigenous peoples' history as recommended by Indigenous communities in our public schools." The city council passed a Will of the Council "recognizing the 12th of October as 'Indigenous Peoples' Day'" on the eve of Human Rights Day in 2014.[36]

Work on this initiative conveys the importance of questioning the celebratory accounts of Christopher Columbus's encounter with the Americas and the subsequent European settlement of the place Native peoples call Turtle Island. Pittsburgh does not have a large population of Indigenous peoples, given its history; thus, the voices of those displaced from this region are largely absent from this area's public discourse and consciousness. But the work of Indigenous social movements that have been calling for Indigenous Peoples Day and reflections on this issue by human rights organizers convinced us of the importance of "truth telling" about this country's imperialist, colonial, and genocidal history as a key first step in our work to nurture a human rights culture as we build a city that observes and protects human rights for all residents. As we know from studies of postwar societies, truth telling is essential to promoting healing and to realizing a culture of human rights. Thus, the transformation of consciousness and culture we are seeking with the HRC initiative requires that we tell new stories about our past so that we can imagine a different future that advances dignity and justice for everyone. Toward that end, we are building a task force that is planning activities to collaborate with area Indigenous people's organizations to raise public consciousness as we honor the first officially recognized Indigenous Peoples Day in Pittsburgh.

The alliance's ongoing aims are to continue to create spaces and support dialogues as well as to do cultural work that encourages residents to incorporate human rights into their everyday lives and thinking. With the help of our local Raging Grannies and some more youthful artists, our Human Rights Day rally in 2014 was punctuated with human rights caroling, and activists shared lyrics that we hoped would inspire more thinking and creative actions around human rights. We have also worked with labor groups to encourage a broader human rights framing of labor activism, and this effort is further supported by the rise of a movement of fast-food workers for a $15 minimum hourly wage and the right to unionize. We have worked to support the city's annual May Day March for Immigrant Rights, led annually by local labor and immigrant rights organizations. In 2017, we helped lead work to sustain this multi-organization collaboration in support of immigrant rights beyond a single march by organizing a teach-in on the connections among the detention and deportation of immigrants, the larger prison-industrial complex, and the mass incarceration of African Americans and other people of color. In any case, by fostering more thinking and public discussion about human rights, this initiative contributes to a "culture of peace"—that is, a respect for human rights and dignity, a commitment to community and to cooperative and peaceful approaches to addressing social conflicts, and greater awareness of those in the community (and beyond) who are excluded from the full enjoyment of human rights.

Conclusion

Attention to people's peace highlights the social processes through which values and practices that support peaceful social relations are generated and reproduced. Conventional, top-down approaches neglect these basic relations of society because they begin with the interests and perspectives of elites, who have little interest in addressing the structural sources of violence, even if they recognize them. The HRC initiative engages people in thinking about and working to realize bottom-up changes in institutions, practices, and culture that prioritize support and protection for human rights. This work makes visible the claims of excluded groups and forces attention to the underlying causes of inequality and discrimination by creating spaces where people can identify values relevant to peace that are present in their communities. It also helps communities come together to prioritize and defend such values, despite their marginalization by prevailing political and economic discourses. In Pittsburgh and other HRCs, this work has created organizing processes aimed at incorporating human rights into public policy and the institutions of society. The orientation around advancing *universal* human rights—both economic, social, and cultural rights as well as civil and political rights—encourages attention to those groups in society that have been least able to enjoy such rights.

Significantly, this work runs counter to the prevailing social and political order. Analysts of globalization have demonstrated how neoliberal economic policies have undermined equality, democracy, and environmental sustainability everywhere—including the United States and other wealthy countries. Because democracy is typically understood as an essential tool for building peaceful communities, peace researchers must address the links between the organization of the global economy and its effects on the root causes of violence. Such work is not likely to be the project of elites but rather of the people most affected by violence. It is to those groups that we must look for leadership in finding solutions to the pervasive and persistent violence in contemporary society.

The Human Rights City initiative offers an alternative, bottom-up approach for mobilizing people and groups around a unified framework that can challenge prevailing market-based paradigms and policies that reproduce structural violence. We have found in Pittsburgh that the initiative has appealed to diverse groups and that it has been especially helpful in fostering new dialogue and learning among people who have had difficulty coming together. As it does this, it encourages critical reflection and discussion of the operation of power and inequality in our community and offers a space where we can actively confront questions about structural racism and how it is manifested in everyday practices and attitudes.

I will end with a few observations about the role of people's peace projects such as HRC initiatives in peacebuilding and recommendations for how policy makers and analysts might better support this bottom-up peacebuilding work.

• Conventional peacebuilding models privilege states and actors that can threaten to disrupt "peace" with violence. Because people's peace initiatives are not seen as a threat, they are often left out of peace negotiations despite their centrality to constructing a durable peace founded on principles, practices, and a culture consistent with the values of peace and human rights. We must advocate for the inclusion of these initiatives in formal peace processes and ensure that peace agreements provide ample resources to support these kinds of peacebuilding initiatives in the aftermath of violent conflict.

• Dominant institutions tend to reproduce what Sabine Lang calls "institutional advocacy," which avoids conflict and contributes to the marginalization of less-powerful groups. Conventional peacebuilding approaches focus on a few large, often well-funded players that are seen as organized voices of publics. In doing so, these approaches neglect the voices of those most affected by structural violence and "hollow out the foundations of civil society."[37] The work of people's peace initiatives calls for attention to building strong civil societies through public engagement and voice. Supporting groups that work to incubate engaged publics and to prioritize the values of human rights and peace is essential to advancing a people's peace.

• Movement-building projects such as the HRC initiative explored here are essential to the work of building a culture of peace. These projects tend to involve coalitions of different groups with few independent resources or staff; thus, they often rely on the leadership of a few motivated individuals and volunteers. Yet their work to foster dialogue and understanding across diverse groups and to build social cohesion and unity around shared projects is critical to promoting peace. Efforts to better support such people's peace initiatives are needed.

• Strengthening international human rights can reinforce local human rights initiatives and related people's peace processes. At the same time, people's peace processes contribute to the strengthening of international human rights law in what Mary Kaldor calls a "double-boomerang."[38] Thus, we see how global peace processes can be enhanced by more attention to and support for local human rights work and the local implementation of international human rights principles, such as the initiative described in this chapter, in order to help actualize global rights norms in local settings.

10

Is Ferguson the Same as Gaza?

Diaspora Grassroots Activism and Intersectional Alliances

ATALIA OMER

American Jewish Palestine-solidarity activists embody and practice a form of people's peace in various ways, connecting and threading together seemingly disparate sites of injustice and conflict zones: from Ferguson, Missouri, where racism against African Americans is pronounced, to Gaza, an embodiment of Palestinian resilience and resistance despite decades of Israeli occupation. First, they articulate their activist agenda in terms of peacebuilding, aspiring for a just peace in Palestine/Israel that will redress past injustices and transform the logic that enables the Israeli occupation of Palestinians. Second, American Jewish critics of Israeli policies and of Zionism more broadly also constructively develop a post-Zionist religiosity that is deeply multivocal, challenging the Jewish establishment from below while also prefiguring a new paradigm for Jewish American collective identification. Third, Jewish Palestine-solidarity activism often intersects with other justice issues, such as racism, homophobia, militarism, and neoliberalism. American Jewish critics of Israeli policies and Zionism who partake actively in Palestine-solidarity work thus exemplify people's peace, being part of a broader global Palestine-solidarity social movement that can also be explained in those terms as well as a grassroots social movement that aims to transform and redefine American Judaism. Finally, the Palestine-solidarity practice of a people's peace can also help us grapple with the limits of intersectionality analysis and conceptions of coresistance as peacebuilding mechanisms.

Many observers have identified the changing landscape of American Jewish communities, especially along intergenerational lines.[1] A Pew Research Center survey released in 2013 also furnishes data that substantiate this observation.[2] The analysis in this chapter is based on my systematic assessment of participant-observation work and interviews with American Jewish Palestine-solidarity activists as well as on their public and online presence. Many of my interviewees are highly active in community organizing on intersecting social justice issues and interpret their activism in terms of their Jewish commitment to an ethical life and to social justice. This commitment is complexly related to their universalist interpretation of the lessons that ought to be learned from the Shoah. Although the movement includes older Jews, especially those with a long tenure in human rights and antimilitarism activism, many of those who serve as the impetus of Jewish Palestine solidarity are millennials, and so the narrative of the Shoah plays very different roles in their social and political memories.

The changing landscape of American Judaism also manifests in an interrelated reframing of the centrality of Israel and the logic of Zionism to Jewish life in the diasporas. That for so many American Jews social justice, an ethical life, and the universal lessons of the Shoah are pivotal for what it means to be Jewish increasingly stands in opposition to the images depicting Palestinian experiences. As one young activist commented to me, "I understood myself as standing in a long tradition of Jews who participated in justice work and felt compelled to be in solidarity with the underdog because for most of their history Jews were the underdog. When I went to Palestine for the first time, . . . I saw . . . the underdogs . . . were not Israeli Jews." Another young woman reinforced this sentiment: "When I went to the West Bank . . . , I found myself identifying with Rachel Corrie, the American peace activist who . . . was . . . killed by an Israeli bulldozer about to demolish a Palestinian home." These two quotations represent the reexamination of Jewish attachments, loyalties, and solidarities in light of ethical scrutiny and the unlearning of narratives about Jewish identity and its teleological connection to Zion. They also capture the persistence of using the narrative and experiences of "white" or Ashkenazi European Israelis as the norm and of silencing the experiences of marginality among Mizrahi, Ethiopian, and other nonhegemonic Jewish communities.

This essay analyzes the growing movement of American Jewish critics of Israeli policies and their processes of challenging and subverting the reigning Zionist paradigms and modes of policing the boundaries of Jewish identity in US contexts. In addition, this movement participates in intersectional global grassroots Palestine-solidarity and social justice activism. The multivocality of this movement is integral to its capacity in promulgating and emboldening people's peace initiatives and processes. It manifests in (1) employing human rights discourse in intersectional activism with other grassroots organizing on social justice issues; (2) drawing on prophetic sources in interfaith activism with Christian liberal and progressive churches in campaigning for divestment from companies benefiting from the occupation as well as in articulating the indispensability of anti-Islamophobic campaigns to cultivating the conditions for peacebuilding through discursive change; and (3) reclaiming alternative interpretations of Jewish histories, texts, and contexts in challenging the Jewish establishment and in prefiguring Jewish spaces and imaginations through ethical outrage and protest.

Human Rights

Analogical Categories of Analysis

The largest and most networked organization of American Jewish critics of Israeli occupation is Jewish Voice for Peace (JVP), whose membership increases with every new crisis in Israel and Palestine.[3] In fact, JVP is the largest group within the spheres of Palestine-solidarity activism. JVP and smaller organizations, such as If Not Now (INN) and Open Hillel (OH), not only define themselves as oriented toward the pursuit of peace but also actively challenge the paradigms of internal Jewish debate and the meanings of Jewish attachment to Israel. Thus, in addition to fighting the Israeli occupation of Palestinians and acknowledging their own complicity in that occupation as Americans and Jews, they also refigure American Jewish identity from the ground up. OH emerged in 2010 on American campuses as a protest against the stifling of debate within the Jewish community. OH activists understood censorship and the refusal to feature critics of Israel in public events as a paternalistic approach to young Jews' supposed inability to be confronted by counterarguments and complexity. Many of these youth are not necessarily subversive; they simply reject the Jewish establishment's control over a Jewish narrative.[4]

The Center for Jewish Nonviolence (CJNV) commits the Jewish people's movement against the Israeli occupation to nonviolent direct action.[5] I joined the CJNV's Jewish Palestine-solidarity delegation to the West Bank in 2017, marking fifty years of the occupation of the West Bank, the Gaza Strip, East Jerusalem, and the Golan Heights. Four years into the CJNV's founding, participation grew exponentially from the previous year's action in Hebron.[6] CJNV's delegation included 140 mostly American diaspora Jews who went to the Occupied Territories of 1967 determined to put their bodies and (mostly white) privilege on the line and in solidarity with Palestinian partners.[7] Working with All That's Left,[8] an on-the-ground Jewish diasporic collective, as well as with Israeli and Palestinian partners, the CJNV is part of a historic coalition that established the Standing Rock Sioux's inspired Sumud Freedom Camp on the site of the demolished Palestinian village of Sarura in the Southern Hills of Hebron. Some activists associated with the Sumud Freedom Camp also engaged independently in another INN action of nonviolent civil disobedience as its members formed a human wall in an attempt to prevent the violent Flag Parade of Israeli Jews, an infamous parade through the Muslim Quarter of the Old City of Jerusalem to mark the "reunification" or occupation of East Jerusalem on Jerusalem Day. Some of the activists associated with INN and the CJNV have reached a high level of indignation and have resolved to be the generation to end the occupation. INN's hashtag #WeWillBeTheGeneration, generated following the explicit display of white supremacy in Charlottesville, Virginia, on August 12, 2017, captures the movement's analysis of the interconnections between white supremacy in the United States and Israel and the relevance of antisemitism[9] to the analysis of American racism and thus embold-ens intersectional coresistance. The apparent threat to Jews' inclu-sion in American whiteness that the election of Donald Trump in 2016 signaled only deepened Jewish activists' intersectional analysis. Accordingly, their struggle against antisemitism is interlaced with, not distinct from, fights against all other bigotries and economic injustice.[10] These conceptual interconnections are indeed quite famil-iar to the tradition of the Jewish Left,[11] but they are augmented from the ground up through acts of intercommunal solidarity in the face of hate crimes in the age of Trump.[12]

Lacking the same economic capital that is concentrated in the hands of a mostly older generation funding the massive infrastruc-ture of American Jewish socialization and lobbying, Jewish Palestine solidarity increasingly builds cultural and social capital through its intersections with other causes and human rights discourse. The Pew findings that the majority of American Jews consider social justice and living ethically as most essential about being Jewish thus become a relevant dimension of the analysis, even though more than 40 per-cent also indicate their attachment to Israel as significant. The nature of this attachment is clearly changing, a change shaped in part by the growing disapproval of Israeli policies, racism, and exclusion-ary practices. Many of my interviewees cited a sense of estrange-ment from Israeli society. One told me about her shock in realizing that explicitly racist remarks about "Arabs" and "Ethiopians" were uttered casually, with no sense of shame. Israel did not cohere with her own values and commitments.

Intersectional Palestine-Solidarity Framing

Jewish Palestine-solidarity activism overlaps and intersects with the global Palestine-solidarity movement without being reduced by it.

The global Palestine-solidarity movement constitutes a form of people's peace: it operates at a grassroots and counterhegemonic level and assimilates various sites of marginalization and struggle. To this extent, "people's peace" indicates an activism involving an analysis of power and demands of justice that prioritize communities and individuals who occupy various margins. Emblematic of this form of people's peace is the World Social Forum (WSF), which took the banner of Palestine solidarity at its gathering in Porto Alegre, Brazil, in 2012, referring to the gathering as "WSF–Free Palestine" (WSF-FP).[13] Foregrounding the Palestine struggle in this context illumines the metaphoric force of Palestine as a trope for human rights activity across the globe. The liberation of Palestine is neither an Islamist cause nor a narrow nationalist one, but rather a cause framed by the language of human rights. Palestine, therefore, is a progressive cause of global civil society.

Highly consistent with the WSF-FP, Palestine-solidarity activism in the United States often explicitly involves intersectional analyses that lead, or at least aspire to lead, to coalitional practices of coresistance and protest by all those marginalized against globally interconnected structures of injustice and domination.[14] First, intersectionality exposes the actual, demonstrable connections between Israel's security machinery and the militarization of US police.[15] Many reports point to the direct contacts and training sessions that have led to what one commentator termed the "Israelification" of the American police in its racial profiling, discrimination, and harassment of racialized minorities, especially Muslims.[16] Other interconnections highlight immigration and xenophobia with respect to Latinos/as. The direct role Israeli security plays in erecting a proposed wall on the Arizona border with Mexico has deepened Chicano solidarity with Palestinians. On March 30, 2012, at the nineteenth annual national conference of the Movimiento Estudiantil Chicano de Aztlan, the movement endorsed the call for boycott, divestment, and sanctions (BDS) against the Israeli occupation. In a joint press release with Students for Justice in Palestine (Arizona State University Chapter)—one that suggests cross-movement activism—the Movimiento

Estudiantil Chicano de Aztlan endorsed the BDS campaign as consistent with Cesar Chavez's legacy to support "ongoing civil rights and anti-colonial struggles for Latin@s and Palestinians."[17]

The recognition of parallels and connections between the Mexican American experiences and the Palestinian colonization has sharpened since this endorsement.[18] These connections are embodied in the (apartheid/security and border) walls and specifically reinforced by the news that in March 2013 the Israeli company Elbit Systems was awarded its second contract with the US Department of Homeland Security to provide surveillance systems and drones for patrolling the Arizona border. Israeli security apparatuses have likewise facilitated the expansion of systems of digital surveillance at the border.[19]

Examining the deadly exchanges between US and Israeli mechanisms of state violence,[20] as JVP and other Palestine-solidarity organizations have done, opens up a global analysis of the operation of white supremacy and interlocking structures of violence. During and after the presidential campaign of 2015, we witnessed the mainstreaming of white supremacy, antisemitism, Islamophobia, homophobia, sexism, and xenophobia in the United States as well as complicity and hesitation on the part of Israel[21] to confront such threats so long as white supremacy also endorsed Zionism.[22] The JVP's National Members Meeting was convened four months after Trump's inauguration in 2017 and explicated the need to struggle concurrently against white supremacy in the United States and in Israel.[23] One route of resistance and transformation is the foregrounding of Jews of Color and Sephardi/Mizrahi (JOCSM), whose perspectives from the margins offer resources for refiguring Jewish narratives.[24] The JOCSM Caucus (affiliated with JVP) challenges the universalizing of the white Jewish experience but also demands that white Jews recognize their privilege and the experiences and historical memories of African American, Latinex, or other racialized minorities (Jews and non-Jews).[25] This challenge highlights pathways for deepening intersectional social activism and resources for reimagining Jewishness outside the Ashkenazi-European hegemonic frame. Interventions by

JOCSM, which became more pronounced as an outcome of social movements' demands,[26] facilitate processes of decolonizing and deorientalizing Jewishness and Jewish tradition.

Solidarity and the formation of cross-movement activism, therefore, go beyond any "hard data" that produce a rationale for such activism against transnational militarism. Solidarity resides also on the level of storytelling and cultural narratives about suffering, subjugation, displacement, discrimination, and colonization. Solidarity, in other words, is also about identifying cultural and other affinities, elucidated by shared stories about marginality. The struggle for and in solidarity with Palestinians offers both a trope and a context for intersectionality in theory and an opportunity for forming productive cross-movement strategies of protest and activism. Transformative peacebuilding, however, requires more than equating or analogizing Ferguson and Gaza and more than recognizing common negative narratives of pain and marginality. To understand the limits of intersectionality, we must first gain further comprehension of the intersectional lens.

Global Palestine Solidarity: The Intersectional Moment in Context

The framing of Palestine as a leftist revolutionary symbol is not a new phenomenon but instead has its roots in a long history of interconnectivity with anticolonial and anti-imperialist agendas in the Global South.[27] Palestine began to intersect globally with the political Left after the War of 1967, known within the Israeli narrative as the Six Days War and within the Palestinian historical account as the Naksa (Setback). Specifically, Helga Tawil-Souri explains, the Palestinian Liberation Organization (PLO) resonated with other nationalist and anti-imperialist struggles in the Global South or the "Third World." In this earlier phase of "Third Worldism" (the 1970s and 1980s), Palestine symbolized the colonial moment, and its nationalist discourse spoke for all national liberationist efforts. A "global civil society" and the emergence of the Global South replaced Third Worldism and reframed the meaning of Palestine, putting a stronger premium on the legacies of slavery, colonialism, and economic exploitation as well as on the ideologies that authorize such modes of domination (i.e., racism, orientalism, capitalism, neoliberalism). The two stages in co-opting Palestine are clearly interrelated but also distinct. Importantly, the framing of Palestine as a human rights cause (not an Islamist one) is key to understanding the broad support it has garnered through the BDS campaigns and other solidarity activism initiated in response to a call from a host of Palestinian civil society organizations, targeting companies that benefit from the Israeli occupation of Palestinians.[28]

Jewish Palestine-solidarity activism on one level focuses on this broader landscape: activists understand their activism as an obligation because of their complicity with injustice, both as Americans and as Jews. Without exception, the (Ashkenazi) Jewish activists I interviewed underscored their "white privilege" as a factor central to their engagement in or support of Palestine-solidarity work. Of course, white privilege is not something all Jews enjoy, and one of the increasingly recognized limits of this argument relates to the aforementioned internal marginalization of Arab Jews and black Jews (Ethiopians and African Americans, especially) as well as of Sephardi religiosity. The use of the category "white privilege," therefore, anticipates the limits of intersectionality as employed by the interconnected solidarity movements. The movements' dependency on analogies invites a conflation of terms and a unitary, totalizing narrative about the forces against which the disparate justice fronts are struggling. Zionism, in other words, is read reductively through and equated with the legacy of American racism, Western Christian (settler) colonialism, and other related ills. This lens precludes the possibility of a hermeneutical reimagining of Israeli Jewishness and Zion, a process necessary for genuine peacebuilding, which Palestine solidarity as a manifestation of people's peace seeks to bring about.

From Ferguson to Gaza and Back Again

The title of this chapter refers to two locations: Gaza, Palestine, and Ferguson, Missouri, two places threaded together in a narrative of a global social justice movement. They were joined on August 9, 2014, when eighteen-year-old Michael Brown was shot by a white policeman in what many understood as yet another instance of police brutality against and disregard for black lives. Brown's shooting sparked outrage not because it was an unusual event, but because such killings have become routine in what Michelle Alexander terms "the New Jim Crow" regime of disproportionate incarceration rates of African Americans and systemic obstacles against living with dignity and mobility.[29] The hashtag #BlackLivesMatter, which formed in July 2013 in the aftermath of the acquittal of George Zimmerman, who killed an African American teenage boy named Trayvon Martin, accelerated as a movement with the killing of Brown and a host of other black men and boys that same year (for example, Eric Garner in New York City and Tamir Rice in Baltimore), not to mention black women's and girls' deaths and disappearances, which are even more inaudible and ungrievable.

"We wish to express our support and solidarity with the people of Ferguson who have taken their struggle to the street, facing a militarized police occupation," read a statement of solidarity with the plight of African Americans signed by Palestinians in Palestine and various diasporas around the world only days after the attainment of a cease-fire that concluded the most recent chapter of assault on Gaza by Israel.[30] Cyberspace was filled with images of Palestinians holding signs that expressed solidarity with the people of Ferguson and commiseration over the hypermilitarized police brutality in response to the protests in Ferguson as well as with tweets sharing practical advice about how to handle US-manufactured tear gas.[31] The striking similarities between images from the Israeli occupation and the confrontations with the Ferguson police reinforced the underpinning logic of intersectionality as operationalized by the solidarity movement. The connections and parallels between Ferguson and Palestine tightened with the endorsement of BDS campaigns by Dream Defenders, a movement related to #BlackLivesMatter. These connections further deepened with a decision to send a delegation to Palestine in January 2015, organized by the Institute for Middle East

Understanding. In a video of a solidarity demonstration in Nazareth, one delegate said, "We come to a land that has been stolen by
greed and destroyed by hate. We come here and we learn laws that
have been co-signed in ink but written in blood of the innocent and
we stand next to people who continue to courageously struggle and
resist the occupation. From Ferguson to Palestine the struggle for
freedom continues."[32] The "laws that have been co-signed in ink but
written in blood of the innocent" are the laws that enslaved, colo-
nized, and disposed communities around the world, connecting the
narratives of Ferguson, Standing Rock, and Sarura.

Another related example of this analogical mode is a statement
cosigned in August 2015 by more than one thousand black activists,
including prominent intellectuals, leaders, and political prisoners,
such as Cornel West, Boots Riley, Mumia Abu-Jamal, and Angela
Davis, as well as by thirty-eight organizations, including Dream
Defenders, Hands Up United, and the Malcolm X Grassroots Movement. Concluding a year that started in Ferguson and marking what
the drafters called a "high profile growth for Black–Palestinian solidarity," the statement underscores black solidarity with the Palestinian struggle: "Out of the terror directed against us—from numerous
attacks on Black life to Israel's brutal war on Gaza and chokehold
on the West Bank—strengthened resilience and joint struggle have
emerged between our movements." Although the statement recognizes (without describing) the idiosyncrasy of Israeli "apartheid" and
variations of settler colonialism, it nonetheless insists on "see[ing]
connections between the situation of Palestinians and [the situation of] Black people [in the United States]."[33] Further amplifying
this insistence was a video released on October 14, 2015, featuring
more than sixty leading black and Palestinian artists and activists
who affirmed black–Palestinian solidarity. The group's Facebook
page describes black–Palestinian solidarity: "We choose to join one
another in resistance not because our struggles are the same, but
because we each struggle against the formidable forces of structural
racism and the carceral and lethal technologies deployed to maintain
them." The solidarity captured in the video and in other statements,

therefore, "intends to . . . assert our humanity" as well as to highlight global interlocking structures of oppression and violence.[34]

This manifestation of black–Palestinian solidarity is the outcome of decades of black activism connected with Third Worldism and anticolonial struggles that signified the liberation of Palestine as its cause. It also stands on the shoulders of a substantial black intellectual tradition from W. E. B. Du Bois and James Baldwin to Angela Davis and Cornel West, who have critically analyzed race relations in the United States, identifying its transnational and global interconnectivity with multiple forms of oppression. Du Bois's visits to the Warsaw Ghetto shortly after the conclusion of World War II solidified his analysis of the black experience in the United States and helped him to see American segregation in the Jim Crow era along a conceptual continuum with the total destruction of Jews in Europe.[35] Baldwin wrote about the moral choice that American (European Ashkenazi) Jews made to participate in and benefit from American whiteness, explaining that this acquiescence to American racism explains black antisemitism.[36] Davis and West have been emboldened by the global analysis of the interconnection among sites of oppression. West, for instance, echoing Du Bois, calls Gaza "the hood on steroids" and underscores the drive to identify the interlocking systems of domination, locally and globally. The concept of the "hood" also resonates with the interrelated concept of "ghetto," which, like "concentration camp," used by West to describe Gaza, is a word loaded with shifting meanings that entail spatial segregation and dehumanizing mechanisms authorized by a racial logic embedded in multiple narratives.[37] West's pronouncement touches upon key elements in the complicated terrain of black–Palestinian solidarity as it features within a global intersectional social justice movement.

Davis, the African American feminist scholar, exposed early on the interconnections among Israel and the prison-industrial complex in the United States.[38] She and other black feminists, such as Beverly Guy-Sheftall, have participated in Palestine solidarity for decades, underscoring antiracist feminisms as pivotal for imagining intersectional social justice struggles. The current intersectional moment threading together antiracist movements is different from the civil rights era because it intersects gender as well as other markers: "The assumption that Black freedom was freedom for the Black man created a certain kind of border around the Black struggle which can no longer exist." For Davis, bringing in feminist methodologies and concerns with gender recovers the critique of capitalism at the heart of intersectionality theory and connects it to racism, colonialism, gender nonconformity, and postcolonialities. Feminism, therefore, unlocks "a range of connections among discourses, and institutions, and identities, and ideologies that we often tend to consider separately," while also cultivating epistemologies from the margins and recognizing "connections that are not always apparent." For this reason, Davis connects Palestine liberation to all sites of injustice, facilitating solidarity and affinity among "what appear to be separate" while also operating to untangle what appear to be naturally interconnected.[39]

Black–Palestinian solidarity was further augmented with the release of a political platform for the Movement for Black Lives (MBL) in 2016. The platform is embedded in and informed by radical antiracist feminism, clearly identifying with the special protections for and vulnerabilities of cis and gender-nonconforming people and black women and how their marginality relates to a broader socioeconomic and political analysis. The MBL's platform discusses Israel's genocidal and apartheid-like practices under a broader heading, bringing attention to a divestment from militarism and prisons as mechanisms for black liberation: "The US justifies and advances the global war on terror via its alliances with Israel and is complicit in the genocide taking place against the Palestinian people." Its complicity, the platform continues, manifests in "requir[ing] Israel to use 75 percent of all the military aid it receives to buy US-made arms," with the implication that US taxpayers' wealth is transferred yearly to gun manufacturers, which then lobby for increased militarism.[40] Thus, funds are diverted away from social policies, and US citizens are complicit in Israeli apartheid policies. The platform, therefore, clearly connects militarization, neoliberalism, and the Palestinian predicament with African Americans suffering the consequences of militarism, neoliberalism, and the deep legacy of uprootedness, racism, and genocidal experiences in the United States. Classifying Israeli actions and policies against Palestinians as genocidal is contested in both scholarship and popular perceptions,[41] but this comparative category has been a source of African American affinity with Jews as well as with Palestinians.

When the MBL calls the Palestinian predicament "genocidal," it conveys its own standing in a black intellectual tradition engaging in decolonizing (and therefore deorientalizing) grievability, to recall Judith Butler's important intervention in examining what makes for (or whose life is considered) a grievable life. Butler refers to those people who, for whatever reason, are excluded from the definition of "the human" and stresses that at stake is "an insurrection at the level of ontology, a critical opening up of the questions, What is real? Whose lives are real? How might reality be remade?" The lives of the excluded are considered unreal, a designation that is in and of itself a form of violence. Unreal lives, accordingly, "cannot be mourned because they are always already lost or, rather, never 'were,' and they must be killed, since they seem to live on, stubbornly, in this state of deadness."[42] Butler highlights the example of the ungrievability of Palestinian deaths. The ungrievability of black lives, of course, led to the hashtag #BlackLivesMatter, underscoring the requirement to insurrect on the level of ontology in ways that connect multiple communal experiences of ungrievability, augmenting Palestine's metaphoric resonances.

JVP and INN (as well as several other Jewish organizations, such as Jews for Racial and Economic Justice) distinguished themselves in their embrace of the MBL's platform, which received indignant condemnation across the Jewish spectrum in the United States, objecting to the platform's use of the word *genocide*.[43] JVP in particular offered its support through the closely linked JOCSM Caucus, and in the opening session of its National Members Meeting of 2017 it admitted the need to grapple with white (Ashkenazi) supremacy within the organization itself. Alliance with the MBL emboldened, therefore, the intramovement's process of unlearning, decolonization, and deorientalization of Jewishness. This process gained further push with the explicit manifestation of antisemitism in the Trump era, one that demanded an intersectional analysis of white supremacy.

To elucidate Palestine as a human rights issue, Jewish solidarity activists confront the reigning discursive formations that enable the silencing of Palestinian narratives and the marginalizing of JOCSM, attesting to white supremacy within Jewish communal spaces in Israel and in the United States. In addition, Jewish Palestine-solidarity activists participate in a broader discursive effort to challenge patterns of pinkwashing the occupation that rely upon deep-seated orientalism and the logic of sexual politics in the West.[44] A critical engagement with Palestinian human rights and the realities of the occupation often involves, for American Jews, politicization on multiple issues, including gender and militarism, and an intensive focus on unlearning and decolonizing their "common sense."[45] Beyond engaging in this deconstructive critique of interlocking systems and ideologies of oppression, they also participate in constructive hermeneutical work that illumines self and communal transformation beyond (yet pivotal for) the specific movement's objectives.

Intra- and Intertradition Hermeneutical Work

Discursive Reframing

A major aspect of Palestine-solidarity work inevitably takes place on the level of denaturalizing, renarrating, and critiquing the dominant discourse. Foregrounding JOCSM's perspectives and experiences within the movement and connecting to the narratives of Mizrahi and Ethiopian marginality in Israel has proved an effective deconstructive mechanism. Unfortunately, the language of human rights is insufficient for the processes of denaturalizing and renarrating. Both need a degree of positive hermeneutical work in identifying and historicizing how particular religiocultural meanings, symbols, and narratives participate in authorizing hegemonic structures. In particular, renarration requires creative hermeneutical work within a tradition to excavate and innovate through a relational approach to justice. As mentioned, Jewish activists, such as those in JVP, participate in diverse Palestine-solidarity organizations. However, they also occupy a distinctive role, primarily by challenging discursive formations that contribute to skewed and silencing narrations of Palestinians' predicament and histories. For instance, JVP's campus report "Stifling Dissent" exposes the intentional silencing of debates on American university campuses, a silencing that is grounded in the equation of any critique of Israeli policies with antisemitism.[46] JVP's various other campaigns, including #DeadlyExchange and the Network against Islamophobia, are aimed at undoing the force of the discourse, necessary for reimagining identities and political meanings.

Jewish participation in intersectional work amounts, therefore, to discursively sensitive and self-scrutinizing intertradition and interidentity in contrast to conventional understandings and outcomes of "interfaith" work that often functions more to conserve respective (often male-elite) interpretations of tradition rather than to innovate and interrogate the tradition relationally. The case of Jewish Palestine solidarity demonstrates that intertraditional work within the context of a social movement can result in introspective scrutiny and a reimagining of tradition. The first area of JVP's intersectional "interfaith" work is aimed at challenging Islamo/Arabophobia.

Islamophobia and Arabophobia: Tackling Orientalism

Jewish Palestine-solidarity activists have been especially instrumental in exposing and denaturalizing the connections between Islamo/Arabophobia at home and the enduring strength of the narrative authorizing Israeli atrocities and suppressing an entire population for decades. One level of activism involves, for example, exposing the direct connections between anti-Arab and anti-Muslim propaganda as it relates to the "war on terrorism," on the one hand, and Zionist and Israeli networks, interest groups, and organizations, on the other. JVP's Network against Islamophobia provides documentation of links between US Islamo/Arabophobia and Israeli politics and resources on Islamophobia. It likewise challenges the American

Jewish institutional framework for its support of Islamophobia.[47] It highlights the deep interconnections between antisemitism and Islamophobia, thereby destabilizing the presumption that Islamophobia or anti-Islam is associated with pro-Israel sentiments and thus with a rejection of antisemitism (per the already established point concerning the conflation of antisemitism and any critique of Israeli policies).[48]

The Network against Islamophobia, therefore, expands the discursive level of the solidarity struggle to trace the historicity of the construction by Israel and its supporters of the Muslim as the "enemy," identifying patterns of money flows from the Israel lobby to Islamophobic campaigns and challenging the bad-versus-good Muslim binary.[49]

Activists explain the links between Islamo/Arabophobia in the United States and the support of or complicity with the Israeli occupation of Palestinians in terms of orientalism. Jews' participation in this counterdiscursive work is pivotal because of their embodied destabilizing of the Israel litmus test. Because their own position as critics of Israeli policies renders them "self-hating" or "bad" Jews, the discursive challenge also necessitates imagining different ways of being Jewish outside the Zionist paradigm as it intersects with orientalism. One level in which this reimagining has unfolded is in JVP's grappling with and confronting the meanings of antisemitism in holistic, collaborative, and intersectional ways. This engagement with the meanings of antisemitism emerged out of the movement's dynamics and demands by partners to gain further clarity on how to identify antisemitism and how to think about it in a nuanced way that takes into account JOCSM, Palestinian, Christian, and Muslim perspectives.[50] Furthermore, the Trump era has also revealed that antisemitism is hardwired into American white supremacy and anti-black racism. This clarifies the interconnectedness of the hatreds: antisemitism and Islamophobia.[51] Another level on which this reimagining takes place is grassroots interfaith coresistance. In addition to working against Islamophobia and anti-Arab discriminatory practices, extensive intertraditional hermeneutical work takes place with churches and Christian denominations coming to terms with how the legacy of Christian anti-Judaism has shaped post-Holocaust myopic attitudes concerning Israeli practices.

Intertraditional Work: The Case of Divestment

Jewish American Palestine-solidarity activists participate actively in various Christian churches and denominations' efforts to consider divestment from companies invested in or profiting from the Israeli occupation of Palestinians or both.[52] Notably, the Presbyterian Church USA voted narrowly in favor of selective divestment from the occupation in June 2013. This vote signaled a sustained study of the Israeli–Palestinian conflict and the logic and scope of Israeli occupation as well as an effort to grapple with classical Christian antisemitism. The deliberations were substantive and resulted in a congregational study guide titled *Zionism Unsettled*, which culminated the work of the Israel/Palestine Mission Network and the Presbyterian Peace Fellowship and Mission Responsibility through Investment and which also generated controversy among the Jewish establishments affected by the divestment.[53] The text engaged the Christian legacy of antisemitism and the complicity of post-Holocaust theology with Israeli militarism, specifically citing Martin Buber's criticism of Zionism as a perversion of Judaism. Marc Ellis, the Jewish ethicist and theologian, and Rabbi Brant Rosen, formerly of a Reconstructionist synagogue in Evanston, Illinois, and currently the leader of a new non-Zionist Jewish community in Chicago, are included in the narrative. Ellis offers contemporary articulations of Jewish non-Orthodox resistance to Zionism, and both he and Rabbi Rosen are cited in *Zionism Unsettled* to encourage the push for divestment. Ellis refers to the historical moment of Constantine's conversion to Christianity and the subsequent complicity of Christianity in the cultivation of empire as a paradigm applicable to Zionism's perversion of Judaism. Rosen focuses on the prophetic threads within Jewish resources to reassert the humanistic and universalist lessons, messages, and teachings of Judaism and to de-Zionize the Jewish tradition. Both readings constitute an effort to resist chauvinistic and exclusivist interpretations that foreground national narratives and modes of authorizing violence. This hermeneutical focus on the prophetic legacy and on Jewish histories of resisting, committing to the underdog, and *being* the underdog becomes the primary currency that critical Jews employ in conversing with "faith-based" interlocutors.

To exemplify this kind of intertraditional work, I return to the case of the Presbyterian Church's decision to divest selectively from companies benefitting from the Israeli occupation. Actively engaged in week-long deliberations at the General Assembly meeting of the Presbyterian Church USA in Detroit in the summer of 2013, activists from the JVP encouraged delegates to overcome their fears of challenging Israeli policies. Wearing T-shirts that read "Another Jew Supporting Divestment," they engaged in vigils and discussions of Christian histories of anti-Judaism and what these legacies mean to commitments to justice in the post-Holocaust era. Susannah Nachenberg, an organizer with the JVP who focuses on interfaith engagements, wrote a blog post about her dismay at how the Jewish establishment and lobby handled the Presbyterian vote: "I . . . want to voice my disturbance of the institutional Jewish community's response . . . who opposed divestment by saying it would ruin Jewish–Christian relations, and even offered a meeting with Prime Minister Netanyahu if the church voted no on divestment."[54] Another Jewish activist who supported the divestment deliberation told me that the contrast between the deep relationships formed between Jewish activists and Presbyterian commissioners over the course of the week-long assembly and the last-minute appearance of Jewish challengers to divestment, with their rhetorical pronouncements and manipulative lure of a meeting with the Israeli prime minister, in effect made a difference in the minds of the commissioners, who found the Jewish establishment's threats quite disingenuous.

Nachenberg, for her part, underscores that "the divestment overture embodied a central tenet of Judaism: justice." She challenges the presumption that all Jews speak with one voice and that supporting the Israeli occupation of Palestinians is a Jewish imperative (through the invocation of security arguments that share elective affinities with messianic commitments to the Greater Eretz Yisrael).[55] The process of reaching a decision at the level of the institution of the church—a decision articulated in terms of peace and justice—entailed hours, days, months, and years of research, consultation, deliberation, and the kind of grassroots interfaith work that Nachenberg and other Jewish activists engage in. Notably, Nachenberg stresses, the decision to divest was articulated in a constructive tone that sought "positive investment, an affirmation of Israel's right to exist, support for a two-state solution and a commitment to interfaith partnership." She describes a moment when "our group of Jews and Presbyterians joined hands to pray. We started to sing, 'peace, salaam, shalom.' The mood was solemn but hopeful. Some commissioners joined us, while anti-divestment Jews watched from afar." A Presbyterian seminary student offered a prayer for considerations of justice to guide the pending decision. "I felt," Nachenberg concludes, "the amazing power of interfaith partnership."[56] A similar dynamic of discursive hermeneutical intertradition work also unfolded in the months leading to the Mennonite Church USA's passing of a divestment resolution in July 2017.[57] Following a first failed attempt in 2015, the eventual success resulted from relationship building with JVP rabbis and activists, who illuminated the diversity of the Jewish landscape and undertook trips to the West Bank and on-the-ground engagements with peace activists.[58] This discursive intertradition work facilitates both unlearning a hegemony of Jewish suffering and processing the Christian legacy of antisemitism's role in turning a blind eye to injustice committed against Palestinians. However, without also owning up to the interrelated legacies of colonialism and orientalism, certifying Christian BDS activism as antisemitic and presenting Zionism as mere perversion of Judaism flirt with antisemitic tropes. This issue, together with the deployment of LGBTQI rights and other modes of "washing" the occupation, highlights the complex discursivity that people's peacebuilding must navigate.

An Intersectional Approach to Intertraditional Hermeneutics

I have underscored how the kind of interfaith engagement that transpired in the Presbyterian Church USA General Assembly demonstrates a highly historical and contextual assessment of religion's intersections with social and political formations. Social movement discursive activism enables grappling with what Marc Ellis calls "the interfaith ecumenical deal" that "silence on the Christian side brings no criticism of anti-Semitism from the Jewish side."[59] Confronting a post-Holocaust ecumenical pact is not the only area of hermeneutical work, however. Christian actors in particular also expose how Christian Zionism has animated the "pro-Israel" attitudes of mainstream Evangelical Christians in the United States. Although the commissioners officially participate in the deliberation of the Presbyterian Church USA, they are not endowed with a particular authority. Likewise, Jewish activists are community organizers and grassroots actors. My discussion of this grassroots interfaith work, therefore, suggests an analytic shift from presuming that justice is the purview and initiative of religious elites and institutions only. The focus on how religiosity participates in constructing and deconstructing the meanings of belonging and citizenship broadens the scope of what qualifies as a religious action. It challenges what the sociologist of religion Paul Lichterman calls the "default model," which has conventionally defined certain actions as "religious," otherizing them as not coeval or, if coeval, then somehow not authentic.[60] Coevality can be productively examined in the context of broad-based community organizing in global urban centers and in the democratic grassroots' cultivation of countersocial and countercultural capital and norms within this context, as is accomplished in Jeffrey Stout's book *Blessed Are the Organized*.[61]

Such attentiveness to broad-based community organizing can open up theoretical spaces for examining grassroots innovations and "poaching" (to invoke Michel de Certeau's and Henry Jenkins's analysis of how "poaching" constitutes a form of resistance and innovation even while employing dominant and dominating idioms).[62] The case of Jewish Palestine solidarity also illumines how a social movement can provide a space for religious interrogation and innovation that is, in turn, instrumental for the broader solidarity movement insofar as Jews participate not only in denaturalizing the orientalist discourse about Palestine but also in innovating through prefiguring post-Zionist Jewishness.

An Intersectional Approach to Intratraditional Hermeneutics

Fueled mostly by young Jewish people, the engine of change is not economic but ethical, which leads to a robust self-scrutiny of their Jewishness. They resist the injustices endured by Palestinians because they *are* Jewish and thus also challenge the dominant Zionist narration of Jewishness. To this degree, their work is prefigurative and transformative: prefiguring an alternative vision of American Jewishness and transforming and diminishing the Jewish establishment's hold on socialization and representation.

Many of my interviewees commented that they feel both increasingly alienated from uncritical Jewish supporters of Israel and a sense of community with their fellow activists. One of the specified foci of JVP is "Jewish community transformation": "JVP is confronting Jewish institutions that are maintaining the status quo and building alternative Jewish communities that act on values of justice," its website reads.[63] Under this transformative activism, JVP has cultivated its rabbinical council and reinterpreted rituals and liturgies, relating them to the Palestinians' perspectives and experiences.[64] The most striking example of prefigurative work relates to the establishment of Tzedek Chicago in the late summer of 2015 in a temporary space provided by a Lutheran church. The synagogue, as explicated in its online statement of values, foregrounds its prophetic orientation:

> We draw our inspiration from Torah's central story of liberation, from the voices of prophets who courageously spoke truth to power, from the chutzpah of ancient rabbis who responded to the reality of exile with a vision of healing and rightlessness and from countless generations of rebels, radicals, revolutionaries and rabble

rousers—Jewish and non-Jewish alike—who challenged the status quo in order to create a better, fairer and more equitable world.[65]

Tzedek Chicago's orienting values, according to its website, include promoting Judaism beyond borders, underscoring "a universalist Jewish identity," and rejecting "the view that any one people, ethnic group or nation is entitled to any part of our world more than any other." This commitment is consistent with many of the members' involvement in Palestine-solidarity work and is intricately connected to a second orienting value of a Judaism of solidarity: "our tradition's sacred imperative to take a stand against the corrupt use of power." The value of solidarity also resonates with "the Jewish historical legacy as a persecuted people," which "bequeaths to us a responsibility to reject the ways of oppression and stand with the most vulnerable members of our society."[66] Hence, the first call to action articulated in the pilot gathering of the synagogue a few weeks prior to its inaugural Rosh Hashanah services was a call to fast in solidarity with the hunger strikers in Chicago who were protesting the threatened closing of Dyett High School, the only open-enrollment public school in Chicago's historic Bronzeville neighborhood.[67] This cultivation or recovery of a Judaism of solidarity informs intersectional activist efforts and is related to a Judaism of nonviolence. "We openly disavow those aspects of our religion—and all religions—that promote violence, intolerance and xenophobia," reads the description of Tzedek's orientation.[68] Indeed, its pilot Shabbat service confronted head on the most violent passages from Deuteronomy, which describe the conquest of the land of Canaan. This biblical story manifests today in the form of the Israeli occupation of Palestine and the ideologies sustaining it, according to Ashley Bohrer, a PhD student at DePaul University and an activist with the JVP who gave the day's Dvar Torah (sermon) on Deuteronomy 7:12–11:25: "If we cannot confront this part of our tradition, if we cannot do the hard work of undermining the conquest mentality that has made us, we are not only agents of violence, we have lost an essential component of Judaism." Bohrer's constructive grappling with the dark, violent passages of the Torah embodies Tzedek's value orientations and commitments. She concluded her Dvar Torah with an affirmation of Tzedek's intersectional angle: "We live, here in Chicago, on stolen land of the Potowami. Just as Chicagoans we must confront this history of genocide, and on the first Yartzeith of Michael Brown's murder, we as Americans must confront the living history of structural racism, so too as Jews we must recognize in our traditions the living history of the conquest."[69]

In light of this intentional prefigurative community, it becomes clear that Jewish Palestine solidarity participates in a broader ethical and multiperspectival interrogation of tradition. On the eve of Yom Kippur, one Tzedek member spoke about the marginalization of Sephardi and Mizrahi traditions and narratives within the Jewish community in the United States.[70] The prefigurative community, therefore, is not only postnational but also deeply democratic and pluralistic in its processes of self-interrogation and the construction of grassroots norms. Jewish Palestine-solidarity activists, such as Bohrer, whose activism takes place explicitly within Jewish spaces, read texts and liturgies relationally from the perspective of Palestinians (or Canaanites). At the same time, they are committed to interrogating and renewing their tradition. But what also distinguishes Jewish Palestine activists' critique from the long intellectual tradition of Jewish critics of Zionism (from an ethical rather than a theological perspective) is precisely its social movement and grassroots dimensions. The grassroots dimensions are likewise highly intersectional and thus cross-fertilize with other justice struggles, which hints at the complexities undergirding the question posed in the title of this chapter. At stake are not only the identification of analogies between different kinds of marginality and oppression (a negative mode of critique of recovery) but also the identification of constructive hermeneutical resources for grassroots norms' renarration (a positive and hermeneutical mode of engagement).

Contemporary internal debates and contestations that unfold within the American Jewish community exemplify a discursive intra- and interreligion scrutiny. One can identify the role of hermeneutics in articulating an ethical outrage, forming the dramaturgy of pro-test (as in erecting a public Sukkah during the holiday of Sukkot), deconstructing Zionist teleology, and reshaping the Jewish American community from the bottom up along non-Zionist commitments. Religion and the practice of peace, therefore, are highly complex endeavors that are misleadingly assigned to (mostly male) religious leaders, thus overlooking both the complex ways in which religion intersects with social and political identities and motivations as well as the lived practices and processes of innovation and change. At the end of the day, Jewish Palestine-solidarity activists engage in a grass-roots transformation of American Jewish communities, another area that constitutes a people's peace. However, this transformation's nor-mative work and reembrace of diasporism also points to the limits of intersectionality within this activist space.

The Limits of Intersectionality

When asked about an "optimal solution" to the Palestine–Israel conflict, my Jewish interviewees responded almost exactly the way non-Jewish Palestine-solidarity activists responded. In both activist sectors, the optimal reconfiguration of Israel and Palestine cohered with the slogan "one person, one vote," reflecting the human rights discourse while offering little attention to how narratives of identity would need to be reinterpreted substantively by Jews inside and out-side Israel. In other words, as I have written elsewhere,[71] the human rights lens falls short of offering resources for reimagining concep-tions of identity, a crucial process in efforts to interrogate justice dis-courses and imagine peacebuilding processes beyond decolonization and deorientalization. Specifically, most interviewees underscored that it was for Israelis and Palestinians to determine the shapes and forms of however many nation-states will end up there. Accordingly, they stressed their commitment to the abstract principles of equality and democracy.

For all of the immense sophistication in which Jewish Pales-tine solidarity operates, overlapping and occasionally certifying the broader Palestine-solidarity movement, its vision of the contours of

an optimal peace employs a thin secularism reflective of the intersectionality activists' own uneasiness with religion. This inclination
is not unique to Jewish Palestine solidarity but rather is a common
denominator enabled through intersectionality's overemphasis on
structures across spheres of Palestine-solidarity activism. Despite
the importance of solidarity activism, we note that the thin and
generic imagining of the future of Israel/Palestine is symptomatic
of the degree to which solidarity with Palestinians offers a space
and a context primarily for renegotiating (even opposing) American
Jewish identity outside a Zionist teleology. Hence, Jewish Palestine
solidarity is not concerned with reimagining hermeneutically Jewish
approaches to power beyond the prophetic motifs and the reliance on
secularist conceptions of statehood and citizenship. Peacebuilding,
however, requires more than just deconstructive resources. Thus,
when Efrat Yerday, an Israeli Ethiopian activist who partook in the
JVP's National Members Meeting in 2017, spoke on a panel with
MBL's activists about police brutality against Ethiopians in Israel,
she connected Israel's black Jews to broader US-based conceptions of
race dynamics, stressing that for activists in both the United States
and Israel the enemy is white supremacy in all its structural, cultural, and symbolic manifestations.[72] Yet when Yerday spoke about
Ethiopian Zionism outside of Euro-Zionism, her remarks were not
acknowledged as relevant to the movement or to the panel's broader
theme, which underscored the need to dismantle Zionism as a pre-
condition for justice discourse. Constructive hermeneutical work recognizes the need to account for Jewish meanings attributed to the
land as important peacebuilding transformative mechanisms on the
ground if the movement's aim is peacebuilding as a transformation
of narratives, structures, and political identities. Zion cannot simply
be theorized out of existence, nor can it be simply metaphoricized
as a spiritual destination, which "non-Zionist" and "anti-Zionist"
non-Israeli Jewish critics interject through their renarration of Jewishness, as in Tzedek Chicago's explicit values and JVP's Statement
on Zionism.[73] Such metaphoricization and spiritualization diminish
the capacity to articulate robustly Jewish alternative imaginations

for non-hegemonic Jewish inhabitation of the Middle East. Hence, to reiterate, the relation of Jews to the land of Palestine cannot be reduced to or read exclusively through the frame of settler colonialism, even if this category of analysis is critically relevant.

The overemphasis on global structures of oppression refers to intersectionality's tendency to succumb to unsituated critiques of power.[74] One of the limits of intersectionality as a feminist methodology and critical political and scholarly approach is its silence on religion (especially religious women's agency), on the presumption of baseline consensus about the good, and on the meanings of non-oppression, freedom, agency, and human flourishing.[75] Any attempt to recapture the public imagination beyond dismantling oppressive structures and ideologies exposes the limits of an intersectional analysis that overlooks positive subjectivities and difference outside the experiences and conditions of oppression.[76] Recapturing the imagination requires, in other words, more than a structural critique of power. It necessitates hermeneutical work that is firmly grounded, Jakeet Singh explains, in identity "as a site of oppression but also as a source of values, normativity, ethical aspirations, and political projects."[77] Such foundation recalls standpoint feminist theory's initial mainstreaming within intersectional theorizing and its contribution to difference as both positive and negative.[78] However, the later emphasis on the critique of structures of domination and oppression signaled a shift from standpoint feminist engagement with differences through intersectionality to a focus on the "intersecting axes of domination, subordination, disadvantage, division."[79] As a result, the structural moment denotes an unsituated focus on power, a departure from standpoint feminist insights about identities as sites of moral imagination. Zionism may be, by definition, exclusionary and supremacist. However, cancelling it with appeals to Jewish diasporism as most authentically Jewish precludes the possibility of cultivating alternative modes of imagining the relations between Jewish identity and space in the region, which is a pivotal resource for peacebuilding on the ground.

To conclude, reading Jewish Palestine-solidarity activism as a people's peacebuilding force illuminates its multivocality, strength, and limitations. The work of such activism shows the need to strengthen an intersectional approach to solidarity work with intra- and inter-tradition hermeneutical grassroots renegotiation and the rearticulation of norms. However, this approach is not without its limitations. The JVP and other Jewish Palestine-solidarity groups constitute a people's movement that challenges and seeks to transform what it means to be Jewish and American by examining both the norms operative within the Jewish community and its institutions as well as the broader intersectionality of these norms with the discourses of orientalism, militarism, neoliberalism, and so forth. The JVP's activism also involves a hermeneutical reimagining of Jewish texts, rituals, and community that cultivates an ethos of diasporism, reversing the ethos of Zionist teleology. The rededication to work against injustice through a process of reframing Zionist interpretations captures the process of refiguring Jewish American identity to cohere with human rights sensibilities. Allying with the MBL, which particularly distinguished JVP and INN in the aftermath of aggressive reaction to the MBL's political platform in 2016, allows Jewish organizing to embrace the experiences of the JOCSM insofar as the latter are not white and offer resources for reimagining Jewishness outside of Euro-Ashkenazi supremacy. Yet analyses that assimilate (Euro-)Zionism onto a global critique of white supremacy and settler colonialism and JOCSM onto antiracism and anticoloniality remain uncomfortable with Yerday's allusions to Ethiopian Jews' longing to return to Zion as integral to their religiocultural imagination. Can one read the Ethiopian experience only through the lens of Ferguson and Palestine? Yerday says "no," and this "no" spells the limits of intersectionality as an unsituated critique of power. Ferguson is not Gaza when one shifts from diagnosis and deconstructive facets of the analysis of violence to peacebuilding and conflict transformation.

11

Peacemaking at the Intersection of the Local and Global in Bali

LESLIE DWYER

In the context of postgenocidal Bali, Indonesia, multiple generations have worked, often in quite different ways, to address legacies of mass violence. For a younger generation seeking to build bridges between the children and grandchildren of perpetrators and victims, languages of reconciliation, conflict transformation, and transitional justice have provided compelling frames for reworking histories of violence. For an older generation, especially women who lived through the violence and now serve as family and community ritual experts, peace and healing are more likely to be found in the domain of Hindu–Balinese religion, where women communicate with murdered ancestors through trance and ceremonial offerings, reimagining social relationships and the karmic nature of justice. At the same time, national and international organizations continue to press for globalized transitional justice models, including fact-finding projects, state accountability, and a truth-and-reconciliation commission. Drawing on long-term, engaged ethnographic research in Indonesia, I explore the tensions and possibilities that emerge from this landscape, asking how a "people's peace" may be forged through and across entangled visions of social and political repair and how "local" peacemaking efforts are rarely bounded by local imaginations.

Local/Global Tension Points

"It's already the era of *demokrasi*, you know," Pak Ketut says, nodding his head in firm approval, stretching out each syllable of the Indonesianized English as if savoring a potent taste. As he speaks, he glances over his shoulder at the framed photograph that hangs on his living-room wall, showing a much younger version of himself beginning a term as representative to Bali's provincial legislature. The grainy black-and-white image is stained and faded behind its frame's polished glass, but as my colleague Degung and I follow Pak Ketut's gaze, we can see how a young man's bones, sharp and angular, are still shadowed in an old man's face. "You are both educated people," he continues, his eyes now focused on us with rigid intensity. "You know what that means. That means we have to forgive each other, to move on from the past to build the future. Maybe we cannot forget, but for our children's sake, we must have reconciliation. It's people like us, people who are educated, who must lead others toward reconciliation. Without reconciliation, our nation cannot survive."

But education—at least the scholarly literature on violence, memory, and postconflict social life in which Degung and I have been immersed—has not been enough to prepare us for this conversation. For we are here in this living room, a mere hundred-meter walk from Degung's ancestral home in Bali's capital city, Denpasar, talking to one of the last people to have seen Degung's father alive. Pak Ketut has spent the past hour reminiscing about Degung's father, describing him as an intense young man who brought his vocation as a teacher to the village, sharing his knowledge of Sanskrit philosophy, his modern views on labor and Hindu ritual, and his fascination with Marhaenism, the mystically tinged populism that Indonesia's first president, the charismatic Sukarno, devised as a syncretic blend of anticolonial nationalism, religion, and communism. And Pak Ketut has just told us how in December 1965, as the Indonesian military's drive to eliminate the Indonesian Communist Party (Partai Komunis Indonesia, PKI) and Sukarno's leftist supporters intensified, he was called, as a local leader of the anti-Communist Indonesian

Nationalist Party (Partai Nasionalis Indonesia, PNI), to deliver those named on a list of alleged Communists to the district military command. He tells us he had no choice; not obeying orders would have endangered his own survival and that of his family. He tells us he was gentle in his unwanted duty, cradling Degung's father's head in his lap and speaking to him softly in the respectful high Balinese owed to one of high caste as he lay bleeding in the back of an army pickup truck. Pak Ketut tells us he did not yell as loudly as the others or feel the same brutal joy singing through his veins when Degung's father was paraded through the streets of Denpasar and made a public spectacle of the "Communist threat" to the nation. He tells us that he regrets all that happened but that he, too, was a victim of the state, which used the PNI to carry out its dirty work but then later banned the party to consolidate its control. As Pak Ketut tells us these things, his gnarled hands shake, knocking his coffee cup to the floor in a thick slosh of liquid. But as he glances again at his uniformed self on the wall—proof that he had once been someone important in the days before "democracy" and "reconciliation" shook the certainty of long-honed hierarchies—he seems to regain his composure. "Besides," he tells us, his voice now confident, "if I had wanted to kill people, do you think I would have left any of your family alive?" he says to Degung.

As we leave Pak Ketut's house, we are quiet, lost in our own thoughts. I am turning the term *reconciliation* over in my mind, wondering how this word, so fraught with possibilities and pitfalls, might be made to resonate with what has just occurred. What could reconciliation be said to mean in such a context, between two people who have lived side by side for almost four decades, praying at the same village temple, shopping at the same market, passing each other on the streets without speaking but without enacting overt violence against each other? Is reconciliation this establishment of civil social intercourse between those who lived through terror and now, across divides of experience and power, call themselves "victims"—this sharing of sweetened coffee over an all too bitterly familiar story of violence and its rationalization? Or is it precisely this civility, this sharing of terms grown global in their reach, of conduct that smooths down the sharp edges of memory, that empties reconciliation of its potential to focus political will and ignite social change? Degung's thoughts are more painful, shuttling wrenchingly back and forth between past and present, between the allure of imagining a democratic future and the pull of memories of what even now cannot be imagined. How, he wonders, can victims of violence in the name of the nation reconcile not only with those who carried out atrocities but also with the call to take up a citizenship so long denied and so long despised? Why does it seem so much easier for so-called perpetrators, many of whom held onto power in the aftermath of violence, to "speak and be healed," when so many others speak and still hurt or stay silent in the labyrinths of memory? What kind of call to speech does reconciliation encode, and what kind of subject does it demand? And what does it mean when perpetrators make claims to the status of "victims," when "being a victim" has a status, when suffering takes on a moral height from which "forgiveness" must be bestowed? But Degung thinks mostly about why this meeting, so long considered, has left him feeling so little, stilled by a drumming of ideas grown alien and inexact as they emerge from the mouth of a man who says he had spared him.

■　■　■

Since 1999, I have been working as an anthropologist on a long-term ethnographic project on the aftermath of mass violence in Bali, Indonesia. This work has focused on the state-sponsored violence of 1965–66 in which some 500,000 to 1.5 million Indonesians, including an estimated 100,000 Balinese (5–8 percent of the island's population at the time), lost their lives and hundreds of thousands of others experienced long-term social marginalization and the strict curtailment of their civil rights. In my position as an anthropologist, my orientation to this work has been resolutely local in the priority I place on the experiences, narratives, and peacemaking efforts of survivors, whose hopes and concerns have often stood in tension with national and international frameworks. Yet identifying the local, identifying the "people's peace" that animates survivors' imaginations of what justice and reconciliation could be, has never been straightforward. Not only is the local crisscrossed by particular—and even competing—discourses of peace, it has also been highly permeable to divergent interests and interpretations that move through the globalized cultural, political, and economic space that is Bali.

Indeed, working on issues of mass violence, peacemaking, and postconflict transitional justice in Bali, Indonesia, has quite often been a *dis*locating endeavor. Sometimes this dislocation has been intentional, as when I and my research partner, Degung Santikarma, entered spaces such as the living room of our neighbor Pak Ketut, where the ordinary routines of life and learning cracked under the weight of terror's banality, ideologies of politeness and progress tainting "peace" with a bittersweet tang. At other times, dislocation seemed inevitable when, after days of interviewing Balinese survivors of mass violence, we ventured out to the island's tourist oases. There the mass graves of 1965–66 rest under hotels, villas, and minimarkets, while the subjectivities of the Balinese themselves—branded as "peaceful, spiritual, and harmonious"—are sold to the island's 9.5 million or more yearly visitors. And every once in a while, dislocation took the form of an unexpected bridge compressing distance, as when I was ten thousand miles away from Bali at a conference in Washington, DC, and an acquaintance from a well-known think tank told me that "transitional justice is a dead issue." Courteously, I asked her to explain. "There's no empirical proof that it *works*," she said. "There's no real evidence as to its *outcomes*. I mean, transitional justice is expensive—truth commissions, tribunals, reparations, all those things are huge drains on postconflict economies. There's a growing consensus that it just doesn't make sense to be looking backward." All I could think was just how similar her perspective was to what I had heard from my Balinese neighbor, equally convinced that the absence of overt present violence was enough of a charter to "move on" from the past.

Such scenes of dislocation are, I think, worth considering seriously, given that recent years have seen the fields of peacebuilding and transitional justice place increasing emphasis on the importance of local perspectives. Anthropologies of peacebuilding and transitional justice have called attention to the frequent slippages, contradictions, and misfits between the lived experience of survivors of mass violence and the models for social repair that circulate globally, including transitional justice's tool kit of tribunals, truth commissions, and reparations.[1] Highlighting the complex and often contested contexts in which peace or reconciliation or justice emerge as practices and ideals, locally oriented ethnographers have critiqued modular, one-size-fits-all interventions in conflict and postconflict societies and have supported grassroots mechanisms for effecting reconciliation.[2] In addition to using ethnographic approaches, scholars and practitioners have also generated tools, such as the Everyday Peace Indicators project, that help avoid the imposition of top-down models for peace work.[3] Scholars committed to the perspectives of survivors of conflict have also begun to challenge the "postconflict optic"[4] that, in the aftermath of mass violence, brackets complexities and takes for granted liberal peacebuilding models that pose democracy, free trade, and securitized rule of law as panaceas for conflict.[5] Yet although there has been tremendous power in these critiques, they have also led to new sets of questions about the relationship of peace work to neoliberal economic and governance regimes as well as to ongoing economic and political inequalities that belie the notion of a bounded local. Critiques of universalist models for peacebuilding also tend to bracket the far-ranging narrative spaces through which claims to peace and justice—or their death—circulate, movements that highlight both structural divisions hardened by particular visions of transition and the narrative quality of transitional justice itself as a story told about suffering and temporality and as a set of technologies for producing and marginalizing certain kinds of voice. And, perhaps most importantly, valorizing the local as a unified field makes it sometimes difficult to ask and answer questions about whom peace work "works" for and how its benefits are so often differentially distributed.

Regarding these questions, it is perhaps not surprising that an aging Balinese perpetrator of violence and an up-and-coming

Washington expert would find common cause in a strategic disengagement with the violent past. In both contexts, similar visions of progress are privileged, one imagining an idealized national unity unmarred by the scars of suffering or the risks of accountability, the other suspicious that postconflict justice, when all is said and done, might offer a negative return on investment. Both visions evoke a fantasy of pastlessness, a future of weightless flow in which memory slows down forward motion and the barriers to (someone's) development dissolve. Indeed, these justifications for transitioning quickly past justice—indicators, efficiency, capital, progress, even democracy—resonate so closely that they seem almost to dissolve old global/local binaries: our common cause demanding that we all just get back to shopping or, in the Bali case, to being commodifiably photogenic, unforgettable while forgetting.

Bali out of Bounds

Bali serves as an instructive case for thinking about these relationships between the local and the global in peace work for several reasons. First, of course, is the island's fame as a space of encounter between Balinese and travelers from across the globe, who bring with them fantasies of a paradisiacal retreat from the ordinary world as well as images of Bali and Balineseness that become the basis for transactions in the image marketplaces of tourism. This context gives rise to a particular political economy of violent memory that shapes possibilities for peace, leading many Balinese to believe that speaking of past and present suffering is economically irrational, given tourist demands of the Balinese.[6] In addition, Bali—and Indonesia more broadly—is noteworthy for the gaps that have persisted between calls for peace and justice by activists and the situation at both national and community levels. Despite Indonesia's internationally lauded transition to democracy in the aftermath of Suharto's thirty-two-year regime (1966–98), the country has earned the dubious distinction of becoming one of the only nations in the world to authorize first, in 2004, a truth commission inspired by international models and later, in 2006, to see the commission scrapped by the nation's Constitutional Court.

In 2012, a report by Indonesia's National Human Rights Commission, which concluded that state-sponsored gross human rights violations, including the killing of up to 1.5 million alleged Communists, had occurred in 1965–66, was dismissed by the Attorney General's Office as insufficient grounds for investigation.[7] More recently, in January 2015, *The Look of Silence* (titled *Senyap* in Indonesia), a film about efforts to find justice in the aftermath of the 1965–66 massacres by award-winning documentarian Joshua Oppenheimer, was banned by Indonesia's Film Censorship Institute on troubling grounds, including the claim that the film violates local social norms of "politeness," "encourages viewers to be sympathetic . . . to the teachings of communism," and "creates social and political tensions which weaken national resilience."[8] Perhaps unsurprisingly, a number of commentators have concluded that transitional justice has "failed" or been "derailed" in Indonesia.[9] At the community level as well, efforts to promote peace, justice, and reconciliation have been enmeshed in a complex politics in which local and global are deeply entwined. Yet in Bali creative efforts to promote—and ultimately to reimagine—peace have much to teach us, shedding light not simply on "the local" as a site of difference from global presumptions but also on the structural barriers that block transitions from becoming real transformations as well as on the politicized narratives through which both constraints and new futures emerge.

To illustrate this, I turn to the story of the 1965 Park, inaugurated in 2005, forty years after the anti-Communist massacres and seven years after Suharto stepped down from power. In Bali's capital city, Denpasar, a group of youth inaugurated the first built space commemorating the civilian casualties of 1965–66, a small square of stone and grass set in the courtyard of an extended family home.[10] During the park's first years, the children and grandchildren of perpetrators and victims of violence drew heavily upon familiar tropes of truth telling and witness to articulate their peacebuilding aims. At a time when Indonesia's public culture still remained closed against calls to account for the casualties of state-sponsored violence, the park was to be a place for people to share their stories openly, a

catalyst for bridging differences, and a site to make public memories of harm and betrayal that had been constrained over decades
of censorship and fear. It was to be a new Indonesia writ small, one
privileging democratic freedoms of speech, spanning the divisions
created by violence, and creating a shared narrative of new social
forms. It was also to be a resolutely modern space that would, in the
words of one of the park collective's members, challenge "the ritual-
ization of worldly problems," posing a liberal valorization of voice
and experience against the long-standing Balinese practice of divert-
ing the resolution of conflict into ritual entreaties to the Hindu–Balinese deities or the realm of *karmapala*, where justice is assured in the
fullness of time without risking potentially dangerous face-to-face
confrontation.[11] Through local dialogues on reconciliation, fact-finding projects documenting the testimonies of Balinese survivors, and
an exhibition of photographs of the dead—a call to public memory
that echoed global testimonial representations of the disappeared
of mass violence—the park collective positioned itself firmly within
globalized peacebuilding and transitional justice discourses of truth
and dialogue as essential nation-building projects. As part of their
work to make suppressed stories of the past compelling to a younger
generation, the park collective's members also engaged in a creative
project to recover old poems and prose written by former political
prisoners and to set these words to blues, rock, and punk music.[12]

In constructing the 1965 Park, these Balinese youth looked outward as well as inward, drawing on what they had seen or heard of
projects to memorialize the past elsewhere. Many of these youth had
as schoolchildren viewed images at the New Order's monumental
Museum of the Indonesian Communist Party's Treachery in Jakarta,
which concretized an official history of the military's triumph over
an alleged leftist threat in celebratory statuary and gruesome diora-
mas. All of them had heard the public calls to commemorate with
a monument the victims of the Bali bombings in 2002, those 202
mainly foreign tourists who had perished in a terrorist attack that
the then governor of Bali had termed "the worst tragedy the island
had ever experienced." The 1965 Park was to be, they explained,

a kind of countermonument to these suspect framings of the past that, in their eyes, concealed far more than they revealed in their stone surfaces. Where the Jakarta museum wrote a teleology of a triumphant nation, the 1965 Park would remember those denied not only citizenship but also their humanity and would thus challenge the state's claims to represent its people. And where the Bali bomb memorial called for the mourning of an innocent island of peace and social harmony senselessly attacked by Islamist outsiders, the 1965 Park would draw aside the curtain of Bali's exoticism, exposing internal histories of terror and betrayal that challenged the touristic commodification of silence about violence. And in contrast to both the Museum of the Indonesian Communist Party's Treachery and the Bali bombing monument, the 1965 Park would be designed not as an authoritative text to be passively read but as a space that, once empty, could now be filled by a community's active engagements with its experiences and with each other.

The 1965 Park youth also positioned themselves in relation to both local and globalizing ideas about youth as a social category and political force in their attempts to turn their memorial park into a community movement for peace. Their (varied) command of foreign languages—many of them had studied English, and several, thanks to an uncle who had escaped the violence by moving to Europe, spoke French—allowed them to access foreign media, which, in addition to rendering them fluent in transnational ideas of youth as "agents of change," gave them a sense of themselves as more worldly and progressive than their parents. Their understandings of justice thus became inflected with globalizing meanings at the same time as they themselves became a symbol of a new, self-ascribed status as competent to navigate the public domain of community leader-ship in ways traditional Balinese concepts of the lifecycle would nor-mally not recognize until they had households of their own. Indeed, the 1965 Park youth often consciously positioned themselves against what they saw as the restrictions of tradition, deliberately opening their meetings and events to youth from a range of class, caste, and ethnic backgrounds.

For this reason and others, the project to commemorate and consolidate a community through explicit reference to a violent past soon proved to be far more complex than these youth had first envisioned. In the aftermath of violence, when suspicion and surveillance had been embedded in social life, circumscribing a community defined by shared origins in and orientations to the past faced multiple challenges. What emerged from the 1965 Park project was not a collective social memory standing outside of and in resistant opposition to state history. Nor was it a brave "breaking of the silence," a straightforward speaking of and to power that could coalesce political will. The park instead provoked claims and counterclaims over suffering and its representation, over memory and its multiple forms, and over the possibilities and limits of "community" after atrocities that were at once mass in their scope and intimate in their impacts.

One of the most powerful questions the 1965 Park provoked was what it means to mark off a social and political category of "victim" of violence. Since the fall of Suharto and the slow emergence of stories of state-sponsored terror and repression into Indonesian public culture, those who had been targeted as "Communists" or labeled as having an "unclean political environment" through their familial or associational ties to alleged leftists have had the opportunity to recast their identities as "victims," or *korban*. This new marker of identification empowered many Indonesians, who used it to claim rights that had been unjustly abrogated, to form social links among those who had been alienated from full national or local social belonging, or to find shared languages to describe experiences that exceeded the bounds of commonplace speech. The description of the 1965 Park as "a shared space for victims to share their experiences" was also comfortably resonant with powerful globalizing assumptions about the prerequisites for social repair, which stress an inherent connection between speaking of the past and personal or communal healing. What soon became clear, however, was that this idea of a shared articulation of experience in fact reflected and intensified tensions among the youth as well as between the youth and their elders.

Once the 1965 Park had been planted with lush grass, and the low, concrete wall surrounding it was set with stones arranged to shape the repeated date "1965, 1965, 1965," its planners held an open discussion to lay out their aims. Their enthusiasm was palpable but not universally shared. Several weeks after the discussion, I spoke with one young man I call Madé here (not his real name), who had sat in silence as his peers had spoken of the need for victims to tell their stories. He told of how their words had brought his memories back to when he was a young boy, fascinated by a glimpse of his grandfather's sword, hidden in the recesses of a cabinet. Madé had not thought much about it until the park's inauguration, when he felt called to take up the name "victim." He had gone then to his grandparents and heard their reluctantly told story of how his grandfather had joined an anti-Communist militia and helped to slaughter residents of the village in, he claimed, an attempt to ensure the safety of his immediate family. "What kind of victims are we? And how can I tell this story to those who lost their family members?" asked Madé, sharing a deeply painful sense that the 1965 Park's narratives could not easily ascribe him a political position as supportive of "truth telling" yet torn by his love for and desire to understand his grandfather, whose experiences and choices felt alien and troubling from the perspective of the present. And Madé's story was not the only such one to emerge.

As the 1965 Park project got further under way, tensions over how to make sense, identity, and political practice out of the past often translated into divisions along generational lines, sparking questions about what it means to claim the past as one's own. For the children and grandchildren of survivors of the violence who were active in the park's creation, the violence of 1965 was "their history" as well as their elders', despite the fact that most of them were born after the massacres. Many of these younger people described how their planning discussions allowed them to assert an origin point for certain aspects of their selves, helping to restructure personal biographies that were often marked by struggles for social acceptance, foreclosed educational or economic opportunities, and confusion about the secrets that seemed to saturate their family histories. This socially mediated recognition of having been shaped by the state's designation of them as *anak PKI*, or "children of the Indonesian Communist Party," worked against state aims of fragmenting potentially resistant solidarities. Where the state had attempted to alienate survivors of violence from each other by monitoring public speech and recruiting citizens through fear and indoctrination to self-surveil their communities, the staking of an identity in a shared relationship to the past raised the possibility of directing widespread social suffering into focused political energy.

Yet by claiming 1965 as "their history," as a kind of cultural property in which they held equal shares, paid for in the currency of pain, these young people often ironically ended up acting in ways resonant with state practices. They sometimes grew frustrated with those elders they saw as reluctant to tell them about what they had experienced in linear, expository form, and they used a language of "rights" and "responsibilities" to attempt to elicit—or sometimes force—oral histories. These calls to narrate and witness were often received uncomfortably by those who had felt terror firsthand and who had over the decades found nonverbal ways of expressing their memories—including, especially, through ritual—that posed less risk of arousing the state's wrath. These survivors were not, as their children assumed, simply silent, muted by power and awaiting the release of their words. They had long used languages of karmic justice to whisper of the misfortunes of killers or the corruption of the judiciary or had communicated through ritual trance or divinations with those who had been executed to discover who had reincarnated in their families' children. Yet such ceremonial work of remembering was often discounted by the young activists, for whom religious practices resonated politically with state attempts to control Balinese subjectivities by asserting an apolitical cultural traditionalism.

These generationally contested understandings of the social life of history also marked off gendered divisions, when the younger people cast older women who showed ambivalence about openly sharing their memories as ignorant of politics or trapped by a misplaced maternal protectiveness supposedly inherent to a traditional feminine self. That there were stories these women did not desire to tell was difficult for the park's planners to accept and difficult for these women to communicate when they felt there was no public, shared language in which to speak about the sexual assaults many of them had suffered at the hands of local militias. Women who had lived through "examinations" for bodily signs of communism—searches by military or militia personnel for a fantasized hammer-and-sickle tattoo on the vagina or lower abdomen, which were often followed by rape—did indeed say they wished to protect their children and grandchildren from the knowledge of their abuse, less out of a feminine shame or self-blame than out of a concern that this information would spark retaliatory violence in the neighborhood among young people who did not yet have the maturity to manage their anger or to socially map the neighborhood and its sites of potential tensions. But they also explained that newly popular discourses of transitional justice, which called on Indonesians to decry state violations of human rights and to resolve legacies of conflict among neighbors, seemed to offer them little space for their own stories. The gendered violence of 1965 was enabled by military propaganda that demonized women's political participation as a transgression against sexual order, but it was also deeply embedded in structural inequalities that have continued to shape Balinese gender relations, marginalizing women from formal political participation and offering them unequal access to inheritance, rights within marriage, and custody of their children. To the extent that their stories refused a conciliatory stance with such inequalities and exposed the cultural underpinnings of violence, they were much harder to read as heroic local "resistance" or compromise-based "peacebuilding."

Ironically, even when older women showed support for the youth's efforts, providing coffee and food for their meetings and taking breaks from their daily activities to sit and listen to their discussions, they were generally still assumed to be there primarily in a maternal, caretaking role rather than demonstrating a real engagement with the park's aims. The few suggestions for the park I heard older women make, including the idea that a Balinese *pelinggih*, or ancestral shrine, be erected in the corner so that spirits of those killed in the massacres could return to visit their families, were immediately dismissed as insufficiently "political"—despite the fact that for these women the domain of reincarnation and deification of the dead was one of the major sites where they contested the New Order state's attempts to erase alleged Communists from national memory. The naturalized exclusion of older women from an arena marked "political" became especially apparent when a plainclothes agent from the local military intelligence unit visited the park, asking the young planners questions about upcoming events and who would be attending them. The young people insisted that they were not afraid of such surveillance; they had nothing to hide; besides, it was now a new era in Indonesia, when they knew their rights and were prepared to defend them. What they worried about, they said, was the possibility of a traumatic impact on the older women who had lived through the violence, whom they saw as needing to be sheltered from awareness of the park's potential repercussions. "If they knew, they wouldn't be able to handle it," worried one young man, his genuinely heartfelt concern seeming to overshadow his awareness of just how much these women had already "handled." Indeed, the discourse of victimhood these young people were operating within seemed to offer two gendered polar positions for postconflict subjects: the heroic victim, who finds a political identity in the resistant articulation of experience, and the tragic victim, whose inability to utter the past leaves her trapped in a voiceless, vulnerable state of "trauma."

The tensions between the youth and the older men of the family took a strikingly different form, with men's opposition to the park explained by both youth and elders in much more antagonistic terms. For those men who had spent decades struggling to downplay their political marginalization as former "Communists" within village economic and political structures, their sons' attempts to cast the date "1965" in concrete in the space of their home's courtyard seemed foolhardy at best and treacherous at worst. Like the older women, they doubted their children's ability to navigate the fraught local landscape of memory and to avoid resurrecting issues that could be used against them, as their Communist links had been manipulated in the years after 1965 to force them to labor on public-works projects and to deprive them of tracts of family land. Those men who had been barred from the vast civil service because of their political stigmatization and who had later found a modicum of success in the private tourism sector were especially ambivalent about the benefits of articulating the violent past. They knew quite well that Balinese tourism is driven by images of a harmonious, aesthetically appealing "culture," not by memories of mass killings and protests against human rights abuses.[13]

To the older men, the park seemed to challenge the choices they had made to keep their families safe and seemed to be moved by a naive, thrill-seeking resistance—a *lomba keberaian*, or "bravery competition," as one man disdainfully put it—that drew recklessly on the energy of youth to claim erroneously to speak on behalf of a community. For their part, the young park planners saw their elders as ensnared in the past and bounded by the circumscribed space of the village, unaware of the cosmopolitan currents now flowing through Indonesia to bring new options for addressing political matters. "They don't even know the word *rekonsiliasi* [reconciliation]," one youth complained before launching into a parody of an imaginary Balinese peasant trying to pronounce the unfamiliar Indonesianized English term. Inasmuch as the youth perceived transitional justice ideas to have originated in a modern, elite, educated international space, they could draw upon their self-positioning as conceptual gatekeepers to ascribe to themselves a privileged status in hierarchies of progress and sophistication, challenging not only ideas about how to grapple with the past but also ideas about the role and power of youth in the present.

Soon these tensions grew even more heated as some supporters of the 1965 Park started to see the older men's opposition not simply as an old-fashioned conservatism but as a potential sign of complicity with power. One of the park's supporters commented, "I think it is very possible that those who disagree with the park are trying to hide their own involvement in 1965," referring to the long-standing rumors that moved surreptitiously through the neighborhood concerning who might have informed on their relatives to maneuver themselves into a position of local power or to deflect threats to their own lives. "You know, we can use the 1965 Park as a kind of 'diagnostic tool' [*alat diagnostik*] to discover the truth of the past," he claimed. "Those who are against it, we should ask if they have something to hide." What the park's presence had diagnosed, he continued, was a particularly pathological effect of violence. "Our real enemy is not the state," he said. "It is our own families."

Yet as the years passed, the 1965 Park continued to change. Those who had founded it and those who had been drawn to its promise of new possibilities for peace slowly transitioned away from ambitions of consensus toward a deep recognition of the multiple and fragmentary legacies of violence, the shards of conflict buried deep within Balinese selves and society. For those involved in the project, it also became increasingly clear that the outpouring of witness to the past that the project first provoked had done little to change the fundamental inequalities that had violently ripped the fabric of Balinese society. In the aftermath of Suharto's repressive regime, Bali's vast disparities of wealth only intensified as Indonesia's new "political stability"—what peace studies scholars might identify as a resolutely "negative peace"[14]—allowed global capital to move ever more confidently across Bali's landscapes. While elites were profiting from unrestrained tourist development, a majority of Balinese were experiencing a rise in land prices faster than that in Dubai, chronic water shortages as supplies were diverted to serve the island's foreign-tourist enclaves, the poisoning of groundwater and coral reefs from unmanaged waste, and limited job opportunities whose room for advancement rarely extended higher than housekeeper, waiter, or tour guide. Widening its lens on what it might mean to make peace, members of the park collective began explicitly to address ongoing inequalities, sponsoring dialogues, performances, and art exhibitions on issues such as HIV/AIDS and lesbian, gay, and transgender rights; discrimination against religious minorities; the failures of public education; and the role of cooperatives in combating poverty.

Since 2013, members of the park collective have been at the forefront of the Resist Reclamation (Tolak Reklamasi) movement, vigorously protesting a state-sponsored plan to allow a developer to fill in 838 hectares of the Benoa Bay in South Bali to create a series of artificial islands that would host lavish tourism facilities, including a casino, a marine park, a theme park, a Formula One racetrack, a golf course, and five-star hotels.[15] Here the challenges have been not only to identify and resist the continuities that have marked Bali's transition but to intervene in narrative domains that set limits on social change. Decried as "antidevelopment," "backward," and, in an expression of just how much the past still haunts Indonesia's present and future, "children of communism," the youth of the park collective demonstrate in their struggles the centrality of narrative praxis—the shifting of what can and cannot be said about justice and the direction of transition—to any people's peace.

For the youth of the 1965 Park, hegemonic frames of peace and justice were of immense value as a starting point for engagement with the violence of the past and its continuing effects on the present. Yet the new social critiques articulated by the park collective have arguably been even more powerful. By reworking peacebuilding's globalized master narratives of liberal peace, political stability, and nationalist, civil selves, the park collective challenges us to rethink our own questions and answers about peace. For whom should peace work work? For state builders and investors? For foreign tourists, seeking to purchase Balinese narratives of peace and harmony? For those who still struggle to find ways to live side by side with memories of violence and disparate ways of dealing with them, or for those who see the peace as too fragile to accommodate a critical diversity of voices? And what future are we imagining when we evoke a "people's peace"? A democratic ideal of plural voices or an engagement with the structures of inequality that deflect critique in the name of progress? A dream of unrestrained development, made possible by peace and stability? Or a transformational justice that can accommodate divergent pasts and futures?

12

People's Peace at Stake

An Assamese Experience

YASMIN SAIKIA

How did a culture of people's peace in Assam become a site for people's violence? What is the role of religious politics in disrupting peace? How can opposing communities overcome their distrust and renew the commitment to people's peace? The success of people's peace in Assam, India, was, until recently, a socially lived experience ebbing and flowing along with the rhythms of riverine life. Everyone was a part of it and contributed to maintaining it. Today, this peace is contested by exclusivist politics controlled by the Bharatiya Janata Party (BJP, Indian People's Party). The Assam case is complex and intriguing because people's peace is a cultural way of being Assamese, but in seeking to become identifiably Assamese, the people are undoing that peace. To understand the paradoxical and intertwined relationship between peace, community, culture, and politics, we must accept the inherent ambiguity. As a culture, people's peace along the riverbanks of the Brahmaputra has historically included new communities, which are always in the making. Along the Brahmaputra, a people's history took shape. This local history, a cultural artifact, became threatened with the rise of Hindutva religious politics. Yet because this politics is bound to a political chronology, there is hope that it will be temporary. In suitable conditions, the process of re-creating people's peace will be renewed.

From the perspective of the Assamese culture, people's peace is underscored by the spirit of coexistence, enabled by the river Brahmaputra, which promotes *xamonnoy*, a union of people and ecology that produces a *xanmiholi*, or blended culture.[1] *Xanmiholi* defines economic, social, and cultural organization. Interactions with others in this context are flexible and changeable, sustained by the alchemy of interdependence. The different people constitute an extended family, or *poriyal* in the Assamese language.[2] People's peace in this sense is a lived experience internally making the Assamese, a story outside the officially produced history. Today, many political organizations and agents are actively engaged in undoing the local family of the Assamese, and the people's shared social understanding is coming apart with religious and political violence.

In Assam, the politics of disruption of peace emerged soon after India became independent in 1947. The haphazard demarcation of India and Pakistan in 1947, based on the Redcliff Line, created a border in the east running along the Kushiara and Brahmaputra Rivers, literally a porous border. The annual flooding of the rivers regularly displaces communities, which in turn creates a competition for arable land and resources. In independent India, the government focused on resettling the Hindu communities living along the southeast end of the Kushiara to more stable places, but the Muslim peasants living along on the southwest end of the Brahmaputra were not relocated.[3] Rather, the rhetoric identifying the "Bengali Muslim infiltrator" was given credence, and their movement from the sandbanks, known as *charlsor* and *sapori*, to higher grounds during floods was deemed a "Bangladeshi invasion." Removing the "infiltrators" was seen as a way forward for the Assamese. Beginning in the 1960s, another tool, language, became the divider: Assamese speakers targeted Bangla speakers with violence. The language movement resurfaced in the early 1970s, and in the late 1970s it transformed into a people's movement for cultural, economic, and political justice for the Assamese. The historical local culture of living side by side in peace with others was undone in these eruptions.

If these complicated issues of history, ecology, and ethnicity were not enough, the religious politics of the Rashtriya Swayamsevak Sangha (RSS, National Volunteer Organization) and the BJP is creating upheaval in local community relationships. The BJP further allies itself with the plains tribes, making Assam more divisive. The party encourages the Assamese to find "peace" by identifying and isolating the "enemy within" and by targeting the predominantly poor Bengali Muslim communities. They are referred to as "outsiders," "foreigners," "Bangladeshis," "vultures," and "termites," among other things, so that a discourse of "them" against "us," human and nonhuman, is constructed along ethnic and religious lines.

Juxtaposed against this exclusivist sphere of peace for "us" there is the traditional Assamese *xanmiholi* culture. I advocate for both the limits and possibilities of this kind of people's peace because, being a lived experience, it is unorganized and unconscious and thus vulnerable to politics. The BJP's ability to undermine the people's peace in Assam reveals *xanmiholi*'s fragility and precariousness. A vigilant public that recognizes the claptrap of modern national politics of religious identity and creatively continues to represent an inclusive ethos is required to sustain *xanmiholi* and people's peace. They have to recognize and learn to question the fiction of politics that undermines peace.

In this article, I first briefly outline the history of blending and fusing that generated *xamonnoy* and created the living culture of *xanmiholi*, which I present as the people's history of peace. Accepting Assam's *xanmiholi* is integral for producing interdependence and connection between neighbors and friends. Next, I focus on the 1970s "Assam Agitation" and highlight specific events and individuals that created an enemy within Assam and leading the way for undoing the culture of people's peace. The lines have been hardened with the more recent intrusion of Hindutva ideology promoted by the BJP government bent on undoing people's peace. In the concluding section, I discuss how the ongoing work of peace, particularly after the announcement of the National Registration of Citizens (NRC) and Citizens Amendment Bill (CAB), create new challenges to the meaning of people's peace as a public endeavor in Assam. I conclude that the renewal of people's peace in Assam rests on the commitment to an inclusive politics privileging humanity that must be valued and maintained for Assam's future.

Xanmiholi: Blending People for Peace

Assam is a small, landlocked state in northeastern India constituted by two river valleys—the Brahmaputra and the Barak. According to a recently concluded NRC (which I discuss further later), Assam has 32 million residents: 61 percent Hindus, 34 percent Muslims, and 4 percent Christians, Buddhists, and other undefined religious groups. In the Brahmaputra Valley in eastern Assam, Assamese speakers dominate, whereas in the Barak Valley and parts of western Assam Bangla is the native language of the majority. Assam shares an international border with Bangladesh on the south and with the Kingdom of Bhutan on the north, and it is connected to the Indian mainland by a slender "chicken's neck," the Siliguri Corridor in northwestern Bengal. Assam, Arunachal Pradesh, Manipur, Meghalaya, Mizoram, Nagaland, Sikkim, and Tripura constitute the current northeastern region of India.

Historical Assam was dotted with independent kingdoms that included several of the current northeastern states and served as a connecting corridor between the Mughal Empire of India and the kingdoms in Southeast Asia. The dominant Ahom kingdom of Assam was not strictly demarcated but was an expansive territory sustained by the Brahmaputra, and the riverine agricultural economy continuously assimilated new people. The Ahom kings' subjects did not have a specific name for themselves. This is expressed in the local chronicles of Assam called *buranji*s, where the people are simply referred to as the *kun-how*, or the "we" community.[4] At the crossroads, the *kun-how* people mingled and merged, exchanged and shared with different neighboring groups, including Indians, Tais, and others, creating a distinctive *xanmiholi*, or blended society and culture. Ecology, people, polity, and culture were symbiotically connected. Each informed the others, and the processes of construction and reconstruction of both space and people were continuous.

In 1827, the British acquired Assam from Burma through the Treaty of Yandabo, and in 1874 Assam became a designated province within British India. British Assam was a vast province that included the entire Brahmaputra Valley, east and west, as well as large tracts of the current-day states of the northeastern region, including Sylhet, which was demarcated from East Bengal (after 1947, Sylhet was transferred to East Pakistan). Because Sylhet was predominantly Muslim, its inclusion in Assam during the colonial period increased the Muslim population there from 11 percent to 28 percent.[5] The British ruled the plains of the Assam Province and through a topographical demarcation called the "inner line" left the hill communities to manage their own affairs. The British demarcation reduced the communication between the hills and plains people, and colonial policy restricted Assam's relationships with mainland India and Southeast Asia. From a porous crossroads, Assam was transformed into a "frontier."[6] Within the frontier, the colonial government adopted two polices—taming the "hostile tribes" and making the valley-dwelling communities productive for revenue generation. It called the revenue-paying subjects of the Brahmaputra Valley "Assamese." The shared language of the agrarian communities, also called Assamese, became the marker of the community.[7] Along with the "lazy and barbaric hill tribes," the Assamese were considered "degenerate" and "stupid,"[8] and the colonial administration sought out East Bengali cultivators to migrate to Assam to increase crop production.[9] The immigrant communities were encouraged to bring "wasteland" and sand banks under cultivation to increase food and cash-crop production, while the colonial investment was made in tea, coal, and oil production to facilitate capital worth for the empire. In these sectors, the colonials imported laborers from other parts of India, creating distinct communities of displaced people in Assam. At the same time, based on a "line system," in 1920 the colonials geographically divided the Assamese and the plains tribes' communities from the new group of Bengali Muslim settlers. The Bengali settlers were not allowed to occupy submontane land, which was highland; they were confined to the lower-level riverbanks and wasteland, which made their lives precarious owing to seasonal floods, and they were isolated from the Assamese Muslims. The main thrust of immigrant settlement occurred during the partition of Bengal, 1905–11, and again a decade before independence, 1937–46, to support the "grow more food" scheme as the colonial commercial ventures in tea cultivation, oil, and gas drilling were expanded in Assam.

The settlement of new immigrants enlarged the Assamese community. The local people received the settlers as another group of "new Assamese," although in colonial terminology they continued to be immigrant Bengalis. The local concept of *xanmiholi* enabled the inclusion of the newly arrived, and the shared condition of agricultural occupation made everyone more or less alike. All were poor peasants. A brief review of the cultural history of Assam based on *xanmiholi* is important to establish the local ethos privileging human interaction and blending. *Xanmiholi* was everywhere in early-twentieth-century Assam: in material and affective culture facilitated by *xamonnoy* (union) and in the feelings of *morom* (affection) and *sneh* (familial affection) between the different communities of people.[10]

In Assam's history, the spirit of *xanmiholi* is evident in lived experiences. In historic buildings, we see its imprint quite visibly. Muslim masons combined Islamic building techniques and aesthetic sensibilities with Hindu and Buddhist forms and styles. Likewise, in royal coinage and inscriptions, Tai, Sanskrit, and Assamese mingled with Persian and Arabic scripts. In the everyday culture—folk music, dance, community festivals, and even religious rituals—the emphasis was on borrowing and mixing various traditions. The primary community festival of the Assamese is Bihu, a harvest celebration, which is a perfect example of *xanmiholi*. During Bihu, the Southeast Asian practice of the Songkran water festival and ancestor worship are mixed with the Hindu practice of cow veneration. Islamic choral chants of *jari* and *husori* along with a variety of sticky rice–based dishes popular among the plains tribes add to the community festivities. The mixing of cultures is also evident in Assamese Islamic practices. Assamese *zikr*s, or remembrances that takes the form of religious chants, combine Islamic religious stories with Hindu Vaishnava poetry, Bhatiyali music (sung by Bengali boatmen), and non-Hindu veneration of ancestors. Before 1946, the space of interaction between the people and cultures of different communities constituting the Assamese thus created a living, humanistic coexistence—the foundation of a people's history and people's peace in Assam.

There are many terms for "peace" in Assamese. Peace is commonly referred to as *xanti*, derived from the Sanskrit term *shanti*. *Xanti* is an inner tranquility and peacefulness of the mind. Individual *xanti* and community *xanti* are interlinked because an ordered mind depends on peacefulness in a community. *Xanti* in this sense is both personal and social.[11] Because this kind of peace requires inner striving by each individual, it is detached from the political order and contributes to the community's sense of peacefulness.

Another concept of peace in Assam, *xampriti*, emphasizes the maintenance of social and political order through fellow feeling. This term, too, originates in the Sanskrit word *sampriti*, denoting attachment. Although accounting for differences between multiple groups that constitute the Assamese collective, *xampriti* emphasizes the development of interactive and interdependent relationships through cooperation and collective behavior for amity and communal harmony. *Xampriti* is different from *xanti* in the sense that it addresses social concerns. For *xampriti* to thrive in a political community, *bisxakh*, "trust," between people, as well as *nyay*, "justice," and *xanman*, "respect," are vital. Together they ensure equality, enabling people to foster peaceful living. Also, *xamonnoy*, "union," sustains *xampriti* because the collective is foregrounded—"community before self," which is an Asian ethical value, as Fred Dallmayr argues.[12] Likewise, the emphasis on maintaining social order through *xampriti* resonates with such Western concepts as Thomas Hobbes's "social contract" and Immanuel Kant's "program" of peace based on good reasoning, negotiation, and dialogue, establishing just governance for proper social functioning.

Xanti and *xampriti* are paired concepts used to describe peace in Assam. Neither *xanti* nor *xampriti* has a religious origin. They do not flow from a divine order or God, but, rather, individuals and community are expected to engage in keeping peace through mutual understanding of love, respect, and a concern for justice. It is simply a way of being with others in peace. In today's terms, one can say it is a form of "local cosmopolitanism" that connects with and includes diverse others while preserving the local within it.

The Assamese cultural approach to peace is not without problems. Because the guardianship is in the hands of the people, the constant awareness of a socially engaged community respectful of traditions and practices is crucial. How does one cultivate and maintain this awareness in the face of politics that encourages religious intolerance and distrust between the different communities? Are the history and culture of *xanmiholi* sufficient to overcome divisive politics? These questions are not new ones.

The erosion and undermining of the local concepts of peace happened at the time of the anticolonial nationalist movement. Elsewhere in India, Gandhian principles of nonviolence (*ahimsa*) and direct action (*satyagraha*) against British colonial rule were accepted for engaging in anticolonial politics. But whereas Indian nonviolence was a good political tool and a very good story for the Western media, it was destructive of Assam's internal culture of peace, which calls for continuous and sustained work between multiple individuals and collective groups at an everyday level to maintain *xampriti*. The political method of nonviolence as event eclipsed this culture. It took away the labor of living in peace with different others as a conscious and regular effort. Gandhian nonviolence was a political tool, not a cultural way of being.

In independent India, the ballot box and elections became the most important tools for the new democracy. Democracy, as the West sang its praises, became the mantra for peace. "Democratic countries do not fight wars against each other" became the easy tune. In India, democracy and electoral politics as both concept and

method created the pathway for "majority" politics and new problems. Today in Assam, a state with a diverse population and multiple "minority" groups, the BJP politics supporting the ascendency
of the "majority" Hindu community is generating new problems of
unpeacefulness. The BJP hopes that with the support of the Hindu
Assamese community, a "vernacularization process" of its Hindutva
ideology will replace secular *xanmiholi* and will knit Assam within
the projected Hindu *rashtra* (Hindu nation).[13] The BJP government's
religious nationalism is leading the way for a *Hindu people's peace*
at the cost of committing violence against "threatening Others" and
undoing the lived culture of people's peace.[14]

Eroding *Xanmiholi* with Hindutva: The "Assam Agitation"

India's independence from British colonialism did not herald the
benefits of full citizenship to the people of Assam. Because Assam
was considered a frontier, no investment in it was made, and Nehru-
vian development projects did not reach the place and better people's
lives. Instead of addressing the problems of economic underdevelop-
ment and Delhi's othering of the Assamese as "tribal" backward people, the local Congress Party government in Assam, as led by each
successive chief minister (Gopinath Bordoloi, 1947–50; Bishnu Ram
Medhi, 1950–57; Bimala Prasad Chaliha, 1957–70), deflected public
questions by creating the discourse of an "enemy within." Assamese
energy was directed against the immigrant Bengalis as their enemy.

In 1948, the new "land for language" formula became the motivating factor for the Muslim Bengalis to adopt Assamese as their
mother tongue.[15] This formula increased the Assamese-speaking
population from 31 percent in 1931 to 56.7 percent in the 1951 census. The Hindu Bengalis, however, resisted the Assamese language,
compelling the government to recognize Bangla as the second official language in the Barak Valley.[16] The Assamese, therefore, viewed
the Hindu Bengali middle class, the beneficiaries of government jobs
and education, as a problem. The Assamese-versus-Bengalis controversy took the shape of language riots in 1960.[17] The All-Assam Students Union (AASU) and the Assam Sahitya Sabha (Assam Literary

Society) believed that by declaring Assamese the state's official language, they could overcome the Bengali problem. In the language
riots that ensued, many Assamese and Bengalis died. Yet in the midst
of the violence, invoking the spirit of *xanmiholi*, Bhupen Hazarika,
the poet-bard of Assam, and his Bengali friend Hemango Biswas
organized music concerts and took their message of Assamese-Ben-
gali amity to the people.[18] The song "Haradhon–Rongmon katha"
(A Story of Haradhon and Rongmon), depicting the loss suffered by
two peasants, an Assamese and a Bengali, was a rallying message
against violence, and Hazarika's song "Manuhe-manuhar baabe"
(We Humans Must Be for One Another) rekindled people's peace.

Politics took a different turn in the 1970s. As police officer
Premkanta Mahanta proudly claims in his memoir *Rajbhaganar
para kalthokalaike* (From the Breakage of the State to a Mere Trivi-
ality, 1994), he and the deputy inspector general of the Border Police
Force, Hiranya Kumar Bhattacharyya (later removed from service
and then joining the BJP), were instrumental in alerting the AASU
student leaders that the Muslim, not the Hindu, Bengalis were the
problem for the Assamese.[19] The state chief minister, Golap Borbora,
a member of the Janata Party (the Congress Party's rival), empowered Bhattacharyya to "detect foreigners [read: illegal immigrants
from Bangladesh]," a directive that Mahanta and Bhattacharyya
used to influence the student leaders.[20] The Muslim Bengali cultivators, previously recognized as "new Assamese," were now recast as
"Bangladeshi land grabbers" and "infiltrators." Invoking the memory of the 1937 elections when Sir Mohammad Saadullah, a Muslim
Assamese, became the premier of Assam with the support of Bengali
voters, the Assamese directed their concern against the new land-
owning Muslim Bengalis, who were seen as dabbling in politics and
making inroads. The "settler characteristics of the Assamese," in
Sanjiv Goswami's description, worked against the Muslim Bengalis.[21] Driving the Muslim Bengalis out of Assam became the focus
in regaining Assamese power and undermine Delhi's tutelage. The
plains tribes' support for this Assamese cause "clearly shows that
from the very beginning it had a pro-Hindu slant."[22] The culture

of *xamonnoy* was cast aside, and the flag of subnational Assamese politics was raised.

On June 8, 1979, the AASU called for a total *bandh* (closure) of Assam to protest the inclusion of Bengali "illegal" voters in the by-election of the Mongoldoi constituency seat. The by-election and the issue of illegal voters are considered the origin of the Assam Agitation of 1979–85, which became the undoing of Assam's culture of people's peace. On October 9, 1979, the AASU held a rally with a hundred thousand supporters. Along with the demand for economic, cultural, and social justice, the "removal of all outsiders" (*bohiragoto kheda*) was the resounding slogan in the public sphere. The Assamese congratulated themselves on their newfound voice, claiming Assam exclusively for themselves, although no one quite knew what an "Assamese" was.[23]

Hidden behind the obvious question about "outsiders" and illegal voters was an Assamese political agenda to control political power by marginalizing other ethnic groups (including the plains tribes, who later revolted against the Assamese). To the Muslim Bengalis, their designation as "Bangladeshi" came as a surprise.[24] They had thought of themselves as officially Assamese, had assimilated and become part of the cultivating riverine communities contributing to both economy and culture of Assam, and were recognized by the Assam Sahitya Sabha as a "new Assamese" community. Being deemed "illegal voters" in the by-election and labeled "infiltrators" was dehumanizing.[25]

The Assam government's anti–Congress Party politics and assumption that illegal voters were the root of the problem were strengthened by S. L. Shakdher, India's chief election commissioner, who in 1978 warned against "foreign nationals" and their possible impact on the electoral outcome.[26] Statistics and numbers created a narrative of "invasion." The religion of the "intruders," Islam, became *the* problem, a shift from language to religion as the enemy. What led to the shift? Should it be linked to the influence of Hindutva and the work of the RSS in Assam? Sanjiv Goswami, an active member of the RSS and the BJP, hints at the answer.[27]

The presence of the RSS and the Akhil Bharatiya Jana Sangha (All India People's Party; the BJP was not formed until 1980) in the political arena before 1979 was not public knowledge in Assamese circles.[28] But the two parties had been there from 1946, and the RSS's current publicity secretary, Shankar Das, claims, "In 1980, the RSS made it clear that Hindu migrants would be given the refugee status, but the Muslims would be regarded as foreigners."[29] Various Marwari businessmen, all of whom were RSS supporters, bankrolled temple building and religious activities in Assam. The Marwaris were settlers from Rajasthan who had come to Assam during colonial expansion and had established themselves in trade. As early as 1930, with Marwari financial support, non-Assamese Hindus rioted against the Bengali Muslims in the oil-drilling town of Digboi. Again in 1946, on the eve of India's independence, with the help of the Marwaris, the RSS staged massive riots in Digboi over the issue of cow slaughter by some Muslim Bengalis. In 1947, the RSS had only one unit (*shakha*) in Assam, but the organization has grown exponentially there since then. Currently, there are 903 *shakha*s in 730 places that support 118 *milan* (gathering places) and 47 *mandali* (political religious circles) with 42 local *pracharaks* (propagandists) in four branches spread throughout the state.[30] Another external interest group actively sowing seeds of conflict between the Assamese and the Muslim Bengalis in the late 1970s and early 1980s was the West Bengal–based Ram Krishna Mission, which expanded its reach through schools in rural and outlying areas in Assam.[31]

Assamese Hindu bureaucrats also contributed to the public anxiety concerning the "Muslim immigrant" based on their selective reading of C. S. Mullen's exposition of the immigrant problem published in 1931.[32] Mullen, perhaps knowingly, left out of his narrative the colonial economic ventures that had created the so-called immigrant problem. It was the colonial settlement policy that had increased the Muslim population in the Brahmaputra Valley from 659,111 in 1911 to 911,179 in 1921 and then to 1,314,700 in 1931, which was 23 percent of the total population of 5.6 million.[33] The Bengali peasant was thus a crucial element in the population growth and expansion of the colonial economy. The "line system" demarcation policy of 1920, mentioned earlier, and the agricultural extension policy of September 1928, called the "colonization scheme," were approved to bring new wasteland areas under cultivation.[34] Large numbers of Bengali immigrants were encouraged to cultivate wastelands in the areas of Barpeta and Nowgong as well as in the sandbank *charlsor* and *sapori* areas, "where the demand of land from the local people was negligible,"[35] but the scheme produced new anxiety and suspicion among separated neighbors.

After the partition of India in 1947, the Bengali Hindus were resettled, which made the Muslims the dominant group along the Assam–Bangladesh border.[36] In 1950, the government implemented the Immigration Expulsion Act to deal with the rising Muslim population on the Assam border. Riots ensued, and more than 53,000 Muslim families fled to East Pakistan. But even after the Nehru–Liaqat Treaty was signed on April 8, 1950, Muslims did not return immediately to Assam.[37] Hence, when an NRC was undertaken in 1951, thousands of people were left unrecorded; when they returned home, they were considered "outsiders." Their association with East Pakistan was part of the problem. They symbolically carried the enemy identity—Pakistani. During the riots of the 1960s and early 1970s in Assam, although the Muslim Bengalis, unlike the Hindu Bengalis, were not targeted because they were Assamese speakers, they too were targeted as "outsiders." By the late 1970s, the scenario changed further; the Assamese and the plains tribes were encouraged to rally against the Muslim Bengalis as "illegal."[38] The problems for the Muslim Bengalis settled in the low-lying riverine sandbanks was compounded by massive floods and land erosion, which forced them to migrate and settle in vacant higher land. The impermanency of "home," poverty, and illiteracy worsened their situation. And they had no advocates for their case.[39]

The Assamese press, in particular *Alok* (Light), an RSS mouthpiece, was active in spreading the story of the Bengali Muslim "invasion."[40] Myron Weiner's book *Sons of the Soil: Migration and Ethnic Conflict in India* (1978) was translated, serialized, and published in the weekly newspaper *Nagorik* (Citizens), which raised public fear.[41] Several newspapers and weekly magazines were launched in support of the agitation against the "illegal" Bengalis. The people's history of Assam was suppressed, and a new history of fear and invasion was rewritten.

The AASU's call to the Assamese to "come out of your homes and drive the foreigners away" directly involved the people. The Bangladeshi body became the body of some *other* that the Assamese were determined to purge. The otherness of the Bengali Muslims, derogatorily referred to as *miyah* (derived from the place-name "Mymensingh," where they had originally migrated from), was emphasized; a good Assamese was expected to hate the *"miyah* immigrant."[42] Thus, the Assamese veered away from the path of *xampriti* and politicked for an exclusive and divisive identity.

The six years of agitation from 1979 to 1985 were marked by public demonstrations; boycotts of schools, colleges, and public offices; road blockades; protests and marches; indefinite fasting; suspension of government work; and so on. Everyday life became political, and religious divisions in the public sphere destroyed the Assamese community's secular spirit. These actions were a way of showing support for the AASU movement, as Nandana Dutta argues.[43]

On February 18, 1983, several thousand people (the official number is 2,191, but unofficial reports say more than 10,000) were killed in Nellie and adjoining villages in central Assam, only forty-five miles from the capital city, Guwahati, because they were suspected of being Bangladeshi. Anti-Muslim sentiments were brewing there among the Lalung and Tiwa tribal communities for a while, and in the charged political environment these sentiments became the trigger to kill, brutalize, and terrorize the Muslims under the guise of anti-Bangladeshi campaign. Some consider the killings in Nellie the "most shocking incident" of this period and compare it with the Jallianwala Bagh massacre in Punjab in 1919 during the British colonial rule.[44] The victims in Nellie were poor Muslim peasants. No one took responsibility for the violence, no culprits were punished, and the single-member Tiwari Commission that investigated the violence never released its report. The macabre violence in Nellie was erased from official memory, and the Assamese people distanced themselves by blaming the plains tribe communities for it. In making the deaths of the vulnerable and marginalized "forgettable," the Assamese shortchanged their culture and the ethos of *xanmiholi* and became exclusivist, undoing the socially agreed people's peace by which they had lived in earlier times.

The central government in Delhi offered a solution to what was perceived as the Bengali Muslim immigrant issue by passing the Illegal Immigration Detection by Tribunal Act (IMDT) in 1983, putting the onus on the local government to detect and deport the "illegal immigrants." This law encouraged neighbors to spy on neighbors and to falsely accuse them of being "Bangladeshi." On August 15, 1985, the central government signed the Assam Accord with the student leaders of the AASU. This accord was followed by the Citizenship Amendment Act of 1986, by which the date March 24, 1971, was fixed as the cut-off for recognizing citizenship: those who had entered Assam after this date were deemed "illegal."[45] But this date contradicted the date accepted in the rest of India, July 19, 1948, as the official date for establishing Indian citizenship. The "citizenship exception" in the case of Assam produced new tensions and divisions between people according to religion. It was a new twist in destroying people's peace.

The religious divide widened during the 2016 elections in Assam. The erstwhile regional political party, the Assam Gana Parishad (AGP, Assam Peoples Association, which was formed during the agitation), and the Bodoland People's Front (BFP) allied with the BJP in the elections. The discourse of change (*poriborton*) promised to safeguard "land, boundary, and community" (*mati, bheti aru jati*) and deliver justice to the Assamese. The BJP hopes to transform the blended Assamese into an exclusive Assamese Hindu community. Hemanta Biswa Sharma, a minister for the BJP government in Assam, has identified the Muslim Bengalis as the "enemy" and has asked the Assamese to recognize this inimical relationship because, "after all, the country was divided in the name of religion."[46]

To give substance to this religious division, the BJP government completed a new NRC, which, they hope, will enable them to oust the "illegal Muslim settlers" from Assam. Various organizations— such as the Assam Public Works, which had spearheaded the detection of "foreigners"—demand this outcome. In the new NRC list completed in July 2018, 4 million, or 12 percent of the 32 million people in Assam, were left out.[47] These noncitizens do not have the fifteen documents of proof that are needed for claiming citizenship. Although the BJP government has not made the list public, the rhetoric of referring to Muslims as "illegal" circulates in public discourse. Interestingly, a vast number of these illegal noncitizens in Assam are non-Muslims, such as the Matuas, Gorkhas, and several semi-Hindu communities.[48] In order to "take care" of these floating populations and make them BJP supporters for current and future elections, including in 2019, the government wants to legalize the currently illegal Hindu settlers under the new Citizenship Amendment Act of 2016. Hindus, the BJP claims, came to Assam as refugees fleeing persecution from Muslims.[49] The BJP president, Amit Shah, openly dehumanizes Muslim Bengalis, referring to them as "termites" and targeting them for deportation.[50] One of his stand-out lines on the campaign trail during the recent elections of 2019 was his dehumanizing attack on so-called Bangladeshi immigrants: "The illegal immigrants are like termites. They are eating the grain that should go to the poor, they are taking our jobs," he said.[51] The BJP government's policy is to delete the people's history of *xanmiholi*.[52] But some Assamese are aware of this pernicious development and the BJP's machinations and are slowly banding together to reclaim the Assamese people's capacity to re-create a political humanity for people's peace.

Resisting the Destruction of a People's Peace

Grassroots organizations and individuals concerned about human rights are exposing the abuse against noncitizens in Assam. They assert that the citizenship issue cannot be communalized against the Muslims. The current AASU leaders are actively resisting the communalization. Assamese academics, such as Hiren Gohain, Udayon

Misra, Sanjib Baruah, and Sanjay Hazarika, suggest seeking a solution "within humanitarian parameters" for the noncitizens. One of the areas of redress is to provide legal assistance to the so-called D-voters, or "doubtful citizens," many of whom are currently imprisoned in six detention camps within state prisons (see map 1). Even though Hindus compose the larger number of noncitizens, according to the NRC, the majority of D-voters locked away in detention centers are Muslims—teachers, doctors, journalists, cultivators, menial workers, and simply the unemployed. They are Bengali as well as Assamese. The Justice Forum, founded by a group of local lawyers and social workers, is creating public awareness of the plight of D-voters and is petitioning their cases for citizenship. I attended a public meeting of this forum organized by the Delhi Action Committee for Assam, the Socialist Party (India), and Khudai Khidmatgar (Servants of God) in Delhi on April 3, 2017, at the Gandhi Peace Foundation. Speakers passionately decried human rights abuses and the politics of communal marginalization. In Guwahati, too, similar discussions were being organized, as newspapers reported.[53] The All-Assam Minorities Students' Union, the Communist Party of India (Marxist), the Forum for Social Harmony, the Association for Protection of Citizenship Rights, and the Krishak Mukti Sangram Samiti (Peasant Rights and Liberation Association, an influential grassroots group led by a firebrand activist named Akhil Gogoi) are involved. The Assam Sangmilita Mahasangha (Assam Combined Peoples Federation), a conglomeration of thirty organizations, is resisting the BJP government's move to communalize citizenship and to grant "Hindus refugees" citizenship rights while denying the same to Muslims.[54] Public meetings are being held by these different organizations. Under the banner of Janagosthiya Joutha Sangrami Mancha (Indigenous People's Platform), a public meeting was organized to bring to light the inhumane condition of the D-voters and demand abolition of the camps. On behalf of the transgender community, one of the most marginalized groups in Assam, the All-Assam Transgender Association, led by Swati Bidhan Baruah, a transgender activist and lawyer, is raising awareness of the NRC's negative impact

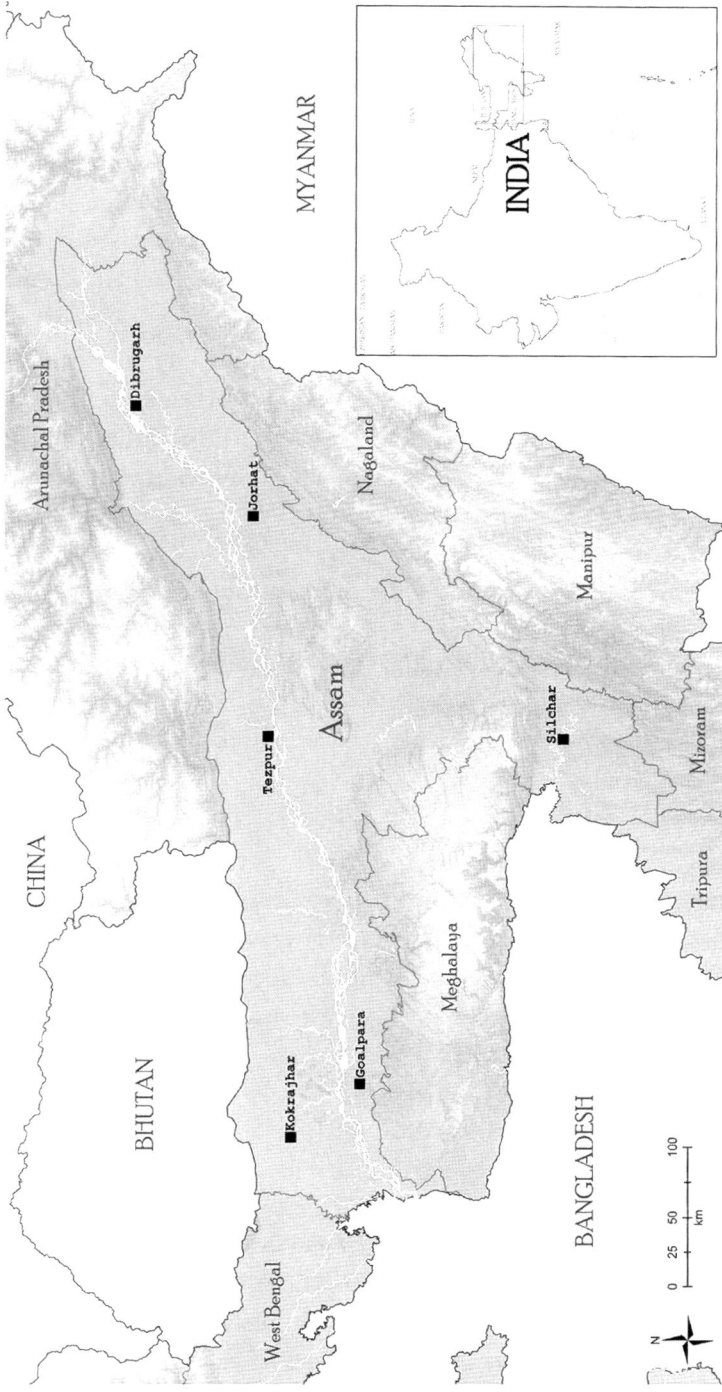

1. Detention centers in Assam, India, 2019. Photograph by Matthew Toro. Arizona State University Library Map and Geo-spatial Hub.

on transgender people.[55] In art and media, voices of protest against the human division in Assam are also emerging. Aklantika Saikia's song "Matal" (Intoxicated) subtly questions the government's deception of dividing the people along religious lines and undoing Assam's blended history. At the heart of the people's effort is this question: How can people's peace be protected? Can the culture of *xampriti* sustain people's peace in these uncertain times?

The BJP and its supporters in Assam are not eager for the resurgence of people's unity. The Assam Public Works is demanding more scrutiny of Muslim Bengalis and their citizenship under the new NRC. Further, the BJP is using tribal communities to drive a religious wedge between the Muslims and Hindus. The SHIVA Foundation, Friends of Tribal Society, Vanavasi Kaylan Ashram, the Patriotic People's Front of Assam, and Geeta Ashram, among other organizations—all RSS/BJP affiliates—are preparing the plains tribes for "self-defense" against Muslims. The Marwari trading group's interest in this political tussle is crucially important.[56] As BJP supporters, the Marwaris are motivated to "capture" land and resources.

Is there a way out of the problems created by the political maneuverings? It may not be enough to blame only the BJP because various sections of the Assamese also harbor divisive ethnic identity and are complicit in undoing *xampriti* and peace. A renewed understanding of Assam's history is important. Recognizing the colonial motivation of bringing Muslim Bengalis to Assam as agricultural workers, followed by the haphazard partitioning of 1947 that divided people's fields and homes along the Redcliffe Line; the environmental disasters caused by floods, earthquakes, and changing the course of the Brahmaputra River; the Bangladesh war in 1971 and the entry of refugees into Assam; and other related issues of local history must be considered. The fact is that the Muslim Bengalis did not move illegally to Assam: British colonial policy encouraged many communities to relocate, and in postpartition India the new map moved people's homes and lands. These people are colonial and postcolonial refugees. In addition, environmental factors, such as land erosion owing to floods, have made them into climate refugees.[57]

Humanistic intervention is urgent. Assam has to reclaim and safeguard its people's history of mixing and blending. It has to make a choice between the internal *xanmiholi* and the BJP's spreading of the poison of religious intolerance. Historically, Assam has been best served through relational arrangements between the different ethnic, religious, class, and regional communities. *Xanmiholi* is Assam's lifeline of being Assamese, now and in the future.

Let me end with a personal story that emphasizes the factor of choice that is before the Assamese to reclaim people's peace. In 1950, my mother's hometown, Jorhat, in the heartland of eastern Assam, was torn apart by communal riots. Defying the curfew orders, Robin Sharma, an Assamese Brahmin who was a close family friend, took my mother's family into his home. No one in his Brahmin neighborhood questioned why a Muslim family was staying with a Brahmin family. "We were like one family; Assamese people were like that then," my mother explains about the internal harmony between the communities despite the violence raging outside. In contrast, my brother-in-law's family, who also lived in Jorhat, had to leave their home because their Marwari tenants were becoming restive. The Marwaris, a transplant community, had no understanding with their Assamese Muslim neighbors; they were strangers to one another.

An epistemic break from the *xanmiholi* past is integral for the BJP's mission to write a new narrative for Assam. The Assamese have to make a conscious decision to reimagine through humanistic and peaceful means the solutions to both their economic and their political problems and thus to reclaim their cultural dignity. People's peace, not divisive politics, must lead the way to serve the greater good of the community.

Conclusion

Looking Ahead, People and Peace in the Future

CHAD HAINES AND YASMIN SAIKIA

Transcending Hate

For several years, we have been traveling to postconflict places. In each place, we have experienced firsthand the beauty and the power of resilient human life. The violence of war and conflict cannot overshadow the spectacular reality of the everyday even in conflict zones. People live their daily lives, going about their business, doing what they have to do to preserve and care for the living, while also planning and investing in a better future for themselves and their community. Our experiences in North and South Cyprus, Northern Ireland, Iraq, Bosnia, Serbia, Croatia, Catalonia, India, and Pakistan have reinforced and renewed our respect for the efforts that ordinary people make to live in peace. Again and again, in these and other places people have told us that they do not feel hatred toward their erstwhile enemies. The wars are not forgotten, many live in the nightmares of their traumas, and some cannot let go of their hatred, but many seek the normalcy and comfort of living with their neighbors in amity now and in the future. Humanity survives beyond violence, which is one of the most endearing and heartening messages that people have shared with us, reinforcing the potential of people's peace, even in the most extraordinary of times following conflict. We want to share three particular stories for explaining this understanding: the first from Bosnia, the second from Northern Ireland, and the third from the border of India and Pakistan.

We met Amir in Bosnia. He was a soldier in the Bosnian army. Toward the end of the war, in the hills of Bihac in northern Bosnia, Amir was badly injured by Serbian snipers. He took three gunshots to his stomach. When he returned home after being discharged from the army, he had little to go by financially and emotionally, and psychologically he was a wreck. After three years of struggling with his precarious mental condition, his wife left him and remarried. Amir had to support his two young children on a very small pension and an uncertain future. Yet, despite having very little, he refused to give up. We met Amir in a chance encounter.

In the tourist office in Bihac, we saw an advertisement for fly fishing, and Amir offered to be our guide. While wading through the gentle rapids of the Una River, eyeing a number of rainbow trout in a small pool, carefully casting his fly in the midst of them, Amir recounted his war experiences. He told of the long nights in the forests during the war, often alone, waiting, wondering what or who he might encounter around the next bend. "One day in broad daylight, I was shot, shot three times in the stomach, and I thought I will die, but I made it back to my unit," he said. Over the next few days, as we waded along the river fishing trout, he told us more about his life and the long and slow process of healing from the gunshot wounds and the less-visible emotional wounds of the war. He also shared with us his own hopes and desires to be a prize-winning fly-fishing guide. We have no doubt he will achieve it someday. We also discussed his two children, who are now grown-up young professionals in Sarajevo. It was at this moment that our conversation took the most interesting turn with an unusual and stunning comment from Amir that has stayed with us since then.

He said he had sent his children to study and work in Sarajevo because there were opportunities for them there. For Amir, it is also the only cosmopolitan place in Bosnia. He wanted his children to have this experience and enjoy the opportunity and possibility of meeting new and different people. Emboldened by the confidence he was showing toward us in discussing his children, we asked how he might react if his daughter or son met and settled down with a Serbian partner. Amir did not hesitate for a second to answer our question: "The war is over; there is no reason to continue hating the Serbians now. I'd welcome a Serbian person to my house." We were taken aback. The Bosnian people had suffered great loss in the war. The reminders of the war are everywhere on Sarajevo's pockmarked, bullet-ridden buildings. The war cemetery at the edge of the city is a poignant reminder of the thousands who died in the violence. Most Bosnian Muslims have lived with their traumas since the war, their bloody memories and fears of violence. Schools in many mixed communities are segregated even today; Muslims attend classes in the morning, while Christian Serbs attend the same school in the afternoon. There is little interaction between the communities. The Srebrenica cemetery recalls the thousands who were killed; many bodies still remain to be found and given a proper burial. The Dayton Peace Accords, signed on December 14, 1995, brought a cessation to violence, certainly a positive development, but they did not bring peace. Even twenty years after the imposed "peace," the reality on the ground in Bosnia continues to be uncertain. However, Amir was not uncertain of his feelings toward the Serbs. For him, the only clear path was one of forging personal relationships with his former enemy, to the point that he could easily accept a Serbian daughter- or son-in-law. We also learned from him the possibility of having a humane response to hatred and transcending one's own traumas to see in the other a friend, a neighbor, and even a family member.

In Belfast, Tony opened another door to people's peace for us. He took us on a tour of the "divided" city of Belfast. The divide is real even now. The Protestant loyalists and Catholic nationalists live segregated lives in their neighborhoods, blocking each other off with tall walls, barbed wire, and community gates that are locked at night to control movement and ensure safety. The Catholic and Protestant streets are painted in different colors to mark the separation, and people from one community do not cross into the other community's streets knowingly. Schools for Protestant and Catholic children are separate. Catholic and Protestant taxis ferry children to their respective schools; they have different health-care centers and libraries; even convenience stores and salons are separate for the two communities. Colorful and vivid murals painted on the walls of people's homes, public places, and street corners tell the story of the bloody violence between the two warring communities, reminding the denizens of the divided city not to forget. We walked the streets where people killed each other without mercy, stopped at Falls Road, Shankill Road, and the separating World Famous Peace Wall. Everywhere we saw the open wounds of violence from not so long ago. At the end of the day, we sat down with Tony to discuss what this division means to him.

He told us the story of his family's involvement in the violence, but he was not a part of it, he said. His family was upset because he refused to take sides with them. They wanted him to hate the other side because, to them, it was "the enemy destroying us." Tony could not. He instead eloped with his girlfriend, who was from the "other community," and they got married in Northern Cyprus. Tony and his wife chose to get married in Northern Cyprus because, he said, "the people there are like us, unrecognized and isolated by others." They returned to Belfast after their wedding and settled on the "secular" side of the town, the area near the Queen's University of Belfast, because both sides of the family refused to accept their marriage. Tony is Catholic, and his wife is Protestant. Their families' denial of their relationship have made Tony and his wife even more committed to transcend the hatred between the communities, and they raise their children with "religious values incorporated from both sides, with a secular outlook toward life."

Finally, we have a story from the border of India and Pakistan. We frequently travel to both India and Pakistan to do research, but it is not an easy journey. In Delhi, it is almost taboo to speak about journeying to Pakistan. There is a great deal of anxiety and uneasiness also in Pakistan about going to India. Because the Delhi–Lahore flight is not reliable and operates infrequently, only once a week, we have for the past few years opted to cross the border on foot through the Wagha border corridor that connects India and Pakistan-Punjab. Our first crossing was rather uncertain. On arriving at Amritsar airport, we gingerly approached the taxi stand to hire a cab to take us to the border. The desk clerk casually took our request and booked us a cab; without asking a single question, the taxi driver took our luggage, and we set off to the border. The ride to the border from the airport took an hour, enough time to chat with the driver, Deepak. Deepak immediately told us that he wants to go to Lahore, too. He has pined to go there because he knows "so many good people in Pakistan." Some of them are his regular clients, he said. He then went on to relate a story about one of his Pakistani clients who had overstayed by a day in India and was refused an exit permit. So Deepak took him to a nearby hotel to stay the night, with the promise to fetch him the next morning. But the next day, when his passenger again could not cross the border, Deepak took him to the police station to discuss a solution. At the station, the police superintendent scolded Deepak for taking the law in his hands and threatened him with arrest and prison time. Deepak said, "I told the officer, 'You are a big man, a government officer, and I am a poor man. But we are both called upon at this moment to show humanity to the stranger who is stuck in a foreign country without family or friend. You can punish me if you want, but let this man go back to Pakistan, where he belongs. He has overstayed only one day. Is this world ours to own that we decide who gets to stay here how long? It is God's land, and He decides our time here.'" The chagrined officer had no way out. He wrote up a permit letting the Pakistani man cross the Indian border and return to Pakistan. As we were approaching the border, Deepak asked about our return trip and offered to pick us up to take us to the airport, which we readily agreed to. He had one request, though. "In Lahore, they make the best desserts, would you bring me some? A very small amount would do." We assured him we would but were curious why he wanted some dessert from Lahore when he can find something similar in Amritsar. Deepak's response was profound: "I want to eat something sweet from Pakistan because when I ingest their sweet, it will become part of me. It will improve my humanity.

Both the countries need to let their people experience their humanity." Deepak since then has become our regular driver to Wagha from Amritsar Airport and back from Lahore. We look forward to the lessons of improving people's peace in the region that we learn from him and from others who join him in our cross-border trips.

The acceptance expressed by Amir, Tony, Deepak, and several others we have met in our journeys perfectly encapsulates our understanding of "people" when it comes to expressions and actions of peace. What is envisioned in these conversations is a fluid idea of the shifting terrain of affinity, which at the most basic level is our shared humanity. The expectation of an idyllic world in which we all recognize our humanness in one another is nice, but it is also naive. We see in one another differences, and we act based on those perceived differences. Those differences are fluid and socially constructed, and borders between them do not have to be imagined as black and white or as a threat. A verse in the Qur'an states, "O mankind, indeed We have created you from male and female and made you peoples and tribes that you may know one another" (49:13). Difference is to be celebrated, not erased or imagined as a threat to one's own self-identity.

Amir, after being aggressively and violently invaded by the Christian Serbian other, after being wounded by a Serbian sniper, after knowing the horrors of the war, no longer sees the Serb as the enemy he needs to take up arms against. The war is over. The Serbian other has shifted from enemy to neighbor, from threat to potential son- or daughter-in-law. Alignments change as human relationships are created and a new affinity toward the other as an integral part of family emerges, as we heard from Tony. Admittedly, Tony's and Amir's willingness to transcend the violence of their pasts is unique. Few Bosnians or Irish are so open to acceptance of the other. Indeed, across Bosnia and Northern Ireland, the wars have remained painful memories etched on the landscape, a lived memory. Despite the imposed "peace" between warring factions arising from the Dayton Accords and the Good Friday Accord, communities remain divided. Deepak, who makes a living by transporting passengers across the divide between India and Pakistan, reminds us, though, that for true peace to take root, it is not laws and rules but new visions of the other that must be created, circulated, and internalized. Not an easy task in this particular case, given the constant reminders in media and politics of the enmity between India and Pakistan. But around the world one witnesses many examples of transcendence, of people celebrating difference, of people coming together to counter violent outbreaks, real and possible. In these sites, one witnesses a sustained peace that no states, no militaries, no armed peacekeepers, no accords can create.

People's peace is not a single type, nor is it a model to be implemented. It is a lived value that becomes articulated through a diversity of actions and practices. One aspect of people's peace is its fluidity. The movement from enmity to neighborliness or even to intimate and familial relationship is not constant. There are forces disrupting this possibility, challenging the transcendence. New demands are made when new neighbors move in, new groups of immigrants and refugees seek assistance, new issues arise that require unique affinity groups to emerge. This fluidity of coming together is fundamental to people's peace.

A second aspect of people's peace that all three stories highlight is that the value of people's peace begins with a personal recognition of the possibility. It is a value that an individual has to struggle to come to terms with and to realize. The value of acceptance comes with reconciliation, of accepting neighborliness. Belonging is not part of an ideological discourse. It does not advance the agenda of one group over another. Although such values may exist in the large social sphere, internalizing them and acting on them are personal choices. The choice is not to align or define oneself with a group, a movement, or an organization that has clearly delineated and policed values of self and other.

Significantly, people's peace is distinct from grassroots movements. They often share ideas and values, but movements are predicated on advancing a particular cause. Enactors of people's peace are sometimes consciously addressing a problem with their ethical values, but people's peace is often just what people do in their everyday lives. It is not a movement; rather, it is just lived practices of getting along with one another, negotiating differences, seeing in the other something of value rather than hate and fear, and in some cases just falling in love.

As a self-expression, Amir's, Tony's, and Deepak's value of acceptance of the other as another human deserving respect and care cannot be framed into a model to be implemented by some organization or institution. Thus, a third aspect of people's peace is that it is not embedded formally in an organization. At times, it can become a structured movement, but only if it remains fluid and transcends being bounded to a particular ideology can it be realized. People's peace is what people do, not what they are taught or paid to do by some government or nongovernment organization. It requires an awareness and the capacity to accept the potential in us as humans living in a shared world. Certainly, it is not easy, but it is not impossible.

Challenges of People's Peace

People's peace is not singular, not bounded, nor is it fixed. It is often disruptive to prevailing ideologies and senses of communal belonging and, as such, is often ignored in peace studies as well as by policy makers seeking a quick fix to eruptions of violence and by implementers in the field whose funds are provided by outside donors looking for quantifiable results.

As we learned from the diverse contributors to this volume, people's peace takes on a diversity of flavors and colors, is deeply rooted in local cultural values and expressions, and is shaped by particular geopolitical contexts. Although it is clear what people's peace is *not*, it is not always evident what it *is*. As the contributors to this volume reflected on the issues, a variety of themes took shape. Out of these themes, several challenges emerged in how we map and place people's peace within the broader rubric of peace studies. One of those challenges is recognizing the diversity of visions and aspirations for the future. Whose future ultimately are we moving toward? The second challenge many of us grapple with is the idea of people's peace as a social movement compared to people's peace as a personal ethics toward the other in our midst. Is people's peace a movement or an ethical value? The third challenge we recognize is the interplay between local cultures and global cultures and movements. This tension is deepened when we recognize that some structures of violence and oppression are local and national, whereas others are global and often interconnected. How do people connect their issues and concerns, through their own language and idioms, to other local peace efforts, transcend the local, and relate to and question the national struggles for global peace?

However one maps people's peace, it is ultimately a choice between violent and nonviolent responses to oppression, as David Cortright argues in his chapter, as well as a choice between the kind of future we are thriving for, as problematized by Leslie Dwyer in her chapter. People's peace can follow diverse and sometimes diverging paths, but it ultimately accepts the multiplicity of future possibilities. It is not just a struggle for inclusion and plurality but also processes of acceptance of the other that simultaneously disrupt and transform structures of inequality and exclusion. Herein lies one of the challenges of mapping people's peace: imagining the future for whom and on what terms.

One answer to that question is to move away from envisioning the future as a fixed set of values, structures, and institutions and to rather imagine a future that is culturally relevant to our conditions and supportive of interpersonal relationships defined by values of difference and ethics of inclusion. The example of the Mvskoke provides one avenue of this inclusive future, the creation of a confederation of communities living in balance with one another, as Don Fixico details in his chapter. Inclusion is a fluid process built upon trust, shared values, and peace. Amanda Izzo makes a similar discovery, on a smaller scale, in her study of the struggle by victims of horrific violence for accountability by perpetrators. For Izzo, people's peace is not a destination but rather a process, a "making."

In his fictional biography of St. Francis of Assisi, Nikos Kazantzakis has the saint wondering about the existence of God. As Francis is wandering through the woods with a small group of followers, enjoying the sound of the birds and the fragrances and colors of the flora, he announces, "Who knows, perhaps God is simply the search for God."[1] Perhaps people's peace does not exist; perhaps people's peace is the search for peace. The British public intellectual Ziauddin Sardar comes to a similar insight in *Desperately Seeking Paradise*. For him, "paradise is not a place of arrival but a way of travelling. Just as we cannot stop living, we cannot stop searching for our paradise. But the search is for a continual kind of becoming."[2] Naguib Mahfouz, a Nobel Prize winner for literature, writes in his provocative book *The Journey of Ibn Fattouma* that the destination of peace is a horizon, a journey toward something, not a fixed place of arrival.[3]

But that search, that becoming, is not an individual journey; it is one we have to undertake as a community. It is not a selfish path toward personal enlightenment, pursuing and consuming this method and that, trying to find our own inner peace. Rather, it is an acceptance of our relationship and responsibility toward one another.

Focusing on rabbinic texts, Joel Gereboff highlights an approach to people's peace based on interpersonal ethics that are multiple and suggests that, ultimately, it is the acceptance of multiplicity that comes to define future possibilities. He reminds us that as human beings we also have feelings of resentment and anger, that we are driven by ideas of honor and shame, all of which shape our relationships with others. When such emotions define our relationships, people's peace is not possible to realize.

The expressions of personal emotions and individual ethics of belonging are not universal. They are local, culturally informed, expressed within particular contexts that have to be fully appreciated. Particular expressions and actions are too often taken out of context, allowing us to misread and misinterpret what is happening. The call for appreciating local idioms of expression is highlighted in several of the chapters, including Bruce Lawrence's study of local, woman-led Qur'anic exegesis in India. Peace activists and peacemakers often ignore the fact that people speak a different "peace language," and in doing so they attempt to impose universalizing ideologies as their vision of peace. Lisa Sowle Cahill and Leslie Dwyer similarly draw our attention to the diversity of registrars of peace, each with distinct narratives and diverging solutions to fostering peace. The inclusion of these local registrars is essential for sustainable people's peace.

However, the structures of violence, oppression, and injustice are not just local, but also global. How do local actors challenge systems of oppression that are beyond the local? This is the third challenge of people's peace. One solution, as Atalia Omar considers, is the need for "intersectionality," for transcending the local to connecting and networking with other local actors. Built within intersectionality is a transformative process of reinvisioning discourses of self and other. Too easily we naturalize hegemonic discourses toward others that are rooted in racist, bigoted, and sexist histories. We need to trace out how orientalism, nationalism, imperialism, liberalism, and neoliberalism operate discursively and to reforge human relationships freed from ideologies of distinction and difference. Again, people's peace is not about erasing difference and reducing us to some base human value, but rather about reimagining difference as something to celebrate.

Intersectionality often implies there is some mode of social movement, a collective consciousness and assembly struggling for social justice and transformation. This becomes the third challenge of people's peace: Is it a grassroots movement, or is it a set of interpersonal values and ethics of social transformation? The contributions to this volume take diverging paths in their search for answers to this question. For Jackie Smith as well as for Cahill, organizing around an issue and cause is essential for affecting change. Fostering a common cause, unity, and cohesion and building inclusive collaborations are strategic for creating people's peace. Chad Haines acknowledges the significant role of organized movements but draws our attention to the place of informality and fluidity in our coming together. Organizations too often take on an identity of their own, struggling to define their cause and their membership rather than struggling for change. Assembling, coming together, and establishing affinity are all ways of rethinking how people organize to transform their society. However, not all assembling around a cause can produce people's peace. The opposite may result, as Yasmin Saikia shows. The very site on which people's peace was made in Assam in the early twentieth century has become now the site for identity politics and divisiveness. People's peace is undone by negative politics. The state's apparatus is threatened by the elusive nature of people's peace and needs to "control" it, which can unravel the precarious peace achieved by the people. Constant vigilance and willingness to stand up for that peace can assert its realization even in difficult times.

As Stuart Schwartz reminds us, it is not just by looking toward the future but also by drawing upon our past that we can discover the possibilities of people's peace. In his study of the Iberian Peninsula during the European medieval period, he shows that, despite oppressive regimes, there were significant struggles for "freedom of conscience," tolerance, and peace that individuals claimed, lived, and died for. The past is thus not merely a lesson but part of the need to reimagine a new narrative that leads us out of the cul-de-sac of Western liberal thinking, where particular values are universalized, erasing other possibilities.

Although not all the contributors and imagineers of people's peace agree, in many ways Western liberalism is the proverbial elephant in the room. Liberalism provides us keywords and notions such as *tolerance, equality, inclusion*, and *democracy*—all integral concepts to forging peace on all levels. But as Wendy Brown reminds us in her study of aversion, tolerance as a concept is often employed as a mechanism of control over others and a means of judging and policing others we deem to be intolerant.[4] Liberalism is tainted by its intimate history with slavery, colonialism, and genocide, all conducted as a means of converting others to a particular ideology or, worse, to advance Western imperial interests.[5] The attempt to place a particular ideology as a universal value and global principle of interstate relations contradicts the inherent ideas of people's peace as expressions of local cultures, values, and struggles. This tension between liberalism and people's peace requires more concerted dialogues to move us toward a deeper understanding and appreciation of diverse struggles and expressions for peace around the world.

Prospects for a Human Future

There is no single definition of people's peace, no simple model to implement, no given set of values and practices to teach. Indeed, the lack of definition and the inability to place it inside a box are the power of people's peace. It is not an idea to be imposed but a process of valuing and fostering the lived practices of peace already in existence. People's peace is about recognizing that diverse cultures and societies possess their own practices of peace, about giving voice to those undocumented values, and about fostering ways they can flourish when they are disrupted.

Today's world is wrought with intensive violence, wars, militant movements, and state-sanctioned oppressions; perhaps people's peace seems like a naive venture, at best a call to document the fading local practices of communal cohesion, tolerance, and justice. Yet, as elaborated in the ideas and case studies in this volume and countless others, we find that very real struggles for peace emanate from lived practices. Further and more significantly, although war and violence dominate our headlines and seem increasingly to be the definers of our world, the reality is that the vast majority of us do live in peace. For many of us, the luxury of economic well-being and political stability provides a structure of peaceful living. Even then, however, the increasing rhetoric of violence, new modes of state-sanctioned oppression, and vigilante groups policing our borders and streets disrupt our peaceful lives. For many around the world, though, structures of stability and well-being are not their reality. Yet despite the violent realities, the vast majority of people continue to live their everyday lives peacefully. Where there are structures of peace, people still have the potential of living violently, and where the structures of peace have collapsed, people have the potential of living peacefully. These are the spaces where people's peace is significant.

Local values and practices of peace are often disrupted through a variety of violent means, sometimes overt; more often than not, though, violence is perpetrated not through the gun barrel but through discriminatory practices predicated on inherent differences between self and other that ignite hate and insecurity. The other in our midst, the stranger next door, becomes one of the greatest challenges for people's peace. People's peace is not about erasing differences or fashioning the other to be like one's self; rather, it is about seeing in the other something of value, about celebrating and valuing difference rather than perceiving it as a threat.

Nationalist rhetoric advocating hardened borders between self and other is one of the greatest challenges to peace. As our identities become aligned with imagined affinities that transcend our local and construct a semblance of commonality, our perception of those who are different changes. We are no longer capable of seeing others as neighbors but fear them as strangers. Our lived ethical values shift, naturalizing both covert and overt forms of violence against the other.

Today, the intensification of migration, in particular forced migration, sets in motion a variety of responses, rooted in different ideological locations. We react with nationalistic fear, demanding a closure of our borders, more secure walls to keep the other out. But we have another option: we can act against such nationalistic policies; we can react humanistically by creating spaces of sanctuary for those less fortunate. The latter option calls upon human values, often rooted in religious ideas, to see in the other an equal. It is here that we see people's peace in action, but as a direct counternarrative to narrow nationalism and conditions that create unpeacefulness. Strangers accept and care for the other next door. Human response does not need a specific set of guidelines or policies. It needs a capacity to believe in others' humanity, as Martha Nussbaum suggests.[6] As refugees are settled in poorer neighborhoods in urban centers in the United States, for example, we find people providing necessary things to help them settle: transportation to grocery stores and for doctors' visits, impromptu and informal language practice, and invitations to share in holiday meals. Although many of these acts are formalized through local nongovernmental organizations, they also happen informally, between neighbors or with strangers down the street. Herein lies the power of people's peace.

The future is one of increasing diversity and increasing experiences of violence and trauma. Many of us will participate in that violence as we internalize ideologies of fear and hate. But the vast majority of us will continue to see in the other our own humanness and humanity. We all may not act on this perception in direct ways, but the fact that we do not act violently, do not shut others out and deny them opportunities, speaks volumes to our capacity to encode and practice the values of people's peace. The refugee, the displaced, the traumatized other are our biggest challenges. Today, there are more than sixty-five million refugees in the world. Their trauma, their experiences, their capacity to create new lives and our willingness to provide them the space to recover their humanity are tests for the power of people's peace. For scholars, it is here where we see our own future, tracing out those voices, those experiences, those possibilities as our next project. It is the refugee who demands our greatest attention, for the refugee reflects back on us our own capacity for being human. In upholding that responsibility, we forge a future, a human future, that is ours to make and cherish. This is not a new or original idea. In history, time and again people have shown this capacity, have tended to their local practices of peace with the other, "kept their own paths, absorbed by what they encountered there and largely oblivious to events [and rhetoric] at the state level, despite efforts to attract their attention," as Laura Edwards has argued in her study of the American South in the postrevolutionary era.[7] The content and future of such a peace today and in the future are not about governance, but about relationships and practices that may vary from locality to locality. At their center is the human that connects us to this peace.

Notes
■
Bibliography
■
Contributors
■
Index

Notes

Editors' Introduction

1. "Twenty-one approaches to peace have been developed in the twentieth century," according to Chadwick F. Alger ("Peace Studies at the Crossroads: Where Else?" *Peace Chronicle* 12, no. 6 [1987]: 117). The crossroads metaphor that he uses suggests the possibility of coalescing peace studies, peace actions, and peace research for exploring sustainable peace as well as of bringing together grassroots-level workers with international and global organizations, leaders, and businesses.

2. Roger W. Wescott, "Reflections on the Etymology of Some Words for 'Peace,'" *International Journal on World Peace* 7, no. 3 (1990): 95.

3. Mohandas K. Gandhi, *Hind Swaraj and Other Writings*, ed. Anthony J. Parel (Cambridge: Cambridge Univ. Press, 1997).

4. Jacques Derrida, *Margins of Philosophy*, trans. Alan Bass (Chicago: Univ. of Chicago Press, 1982).

5. Jonas Hanway (1712–86), the founder of the Marine Society, an active charity that regulated and disciplined the work and benefits received by seamen, served as the governor of the Foundling Hospital and established the Magdalen Hospital to improve the system of parochial birth registration in London.

6. Michel Foucault, *Discipline and Punish: The Birth of the Prison*, trans. Alan Sheridan (1977; reprint, New York: Vintage, 1995).

7. For an extended reading on the Christian views of peace, see Thomas Hippler, "Images of Peace," *New Centennial Review* 13, no. 1 (2013): 45–70.

8. Annemarie van Heerikhuzen, "How God Disappeared from Europe: Visions of a United Europe from Erasmus to Kant," *European Legacy: Towards a New Paradigm* 13, no. 4 (2007–8): 401–11.

9. For further reading on Spinoza, see Necati Polat, "Peace as War," *Alternatives: Global, Local, Political* 35, no. 4 (2010): 317–45.

10. Gordon L. Anderson, "The Elusive Definition of Peace," *International Journal on World Peace* 2, no. 3 (1985): 101.

11. In an essay published in 1969, Galtung developed the ideas of "negative" and "positive" peace, which he elaborated in subsequent publications. See Johan Galtung, "Violence, Peace, and Peace Research," *Journal of Peace Research* 6, no. 3 (1969): 167–91.

12. Felix Berenskoetter, "'Friends, There Are No Friends': An Intimate Reframing of the International," *Millennium: Journal of International Studies* 35, no. 3 (2007): 647–76; Ahmed Achrati, "Deconstruction, Ethics, and Islam," *Arabica* 53, no. 4 (2006): 472–509.

13. Mohammed Abu-Nimer, John Esposito, Abdul Aziz Sachedina, Fred Dallmayr, and Emmanuel Levinas, among others, are important for understanding the Jewish concept of shalom and the Islamic pillars of *zakat* and Ramadan for peace in Jewish and Muslim communities.

14. See Oliver Richmond, *A Post-liberal Peace* (London: Routledge, 2011).

15. For an extended reading on these terms and their impact on individuals and community, see Takeshi Ishida, "Beyond the Traditional Concepts of Peace in Different Cultures," *Journal of Peace Research* 6, no. 2 (1969): 133–45.

16. Hu Weixi, "On Confucian Communitarianism," *Frontiers of Philosophy in China* 2, no. 4 (2007): 475–87; Chenyang Li, "The Confucian Ideal of Harmony," *Philosophy East and West* 56, no. 4 (2006): 583–603.

17. See Maulana Wahiduddin Khan, "War and Peace in Islam," *New Age Islam*, Sept. 22, 2014, at http://www.newageislam.com/islamic-society/maulana-wahiduddin -khan/war-and-peace-in-islam/d/99197.

18. See Steve Coll, *Ghost Wars: The Secret History of the CIA, Afghanistan, and Bin Laden, from the Soviet Invasion to September 10, 2001* (New York: Penguin Books, 2004).

19. Michael Howard, *The Invention of Peace: Reflections on War and International Order* (New Haven, CT: Yale Univ. Press, 2001).

20. Matthew Evangelista, ed., *Peace Studies: Critical Concepts in Political Science*, 4 vols. (London: Routledge, 2005).

21. David Cortright, *Peace Works: The Citizens Role in Ending the Cold War* (Boulder, CO: Westview Press, 1993).

22. Peter Van den Dungen and Lawrence S. Wittner, "Peace History: An Introduction," *Journal of Peace Research* 40, no. 4 (2003): 363; Alger, "Peace Studies at the Crossroads."

23. Halvard Buhaug, Jack S. Levy, and Henrik Urdal, "50 Years of Peace Research: An Introduction to the *Journal of Peace Research*," *Journal of Peace Research* anniversary special issue 51, no. 2 (2014): 139–44.

24. Van den Dungen and Wittner, "Peace History"; Alger, "Peace Studies at the Crossroads"; Johan Galtung, "Twenty-Five Years of Peace Research: Ten Challenges and Some Responses," *Journal of Peace Research* 22, no. 2 (1985): 141–58;

L. Gunnar Johnson, *Conflicting Concepts of Peace in Contemporary Peace Studies*, Sage Occasional Paper no. 4, International Studies series (Beverley Hills, CA: Sage, 1976).

25. Johnson, *Conflicting Concepts of Peace*, 19.

26. Galtung, "Twenty-Five Years of Peace Research," 151–52.

27. Here we are referring in particular to works such as Emmanuel Levinas, *Otherwise Than Being or Beyond Essence*, trans. Alphonso Lingis (Pittsburgh, PA: Duquesne Univ. Press, 2011); Jacques Derrida, *Of Hospitality: Anne Dufourman-telle Invites Jacques Derrida to Respond*, trans. Rachel Bowlby (Stanford, CA: Stanford Univ. Press, 2000); and Mona Siddiqui, *Hospitality and Islam: Welcoming in God's Name* (New Haven, CT: Yale Univ. Press, 2015).

28. Oliver Richmond, *Peace in International Relations* (London: Routledge, 2008), 109.

29. David Roberts, "Beyond the Metropolis? Popular Peace and Post-conflict Peacebuilding," *Review of International Studies* 37, no. 5 (2011): 2537.

30. Roberts, "Beyond the Metropolis?" 2553.

31. Hannah Arendt asks, "What is the end of peace?" She argues that peace, as a value, is total and absolute, an end to itself (in *On Violence* [New York: Harcourt, Brace and World, 1970], 51). We, however, believe that peace is not an end in itself and that it enables the realization of social justice, a world without war, human rights, ecological stability, and other much-needed values.

1. Inspiring Peace

1. Theology is "faith seeking understanding" (Anselm of Canterbury, eleventh century); that is, theology is critical and systematic reflection on the meaning of religious experience and its primary expressions, especially scripture. Theology as an academic discipline may be distinguished from religion as the first-order experience, both individually and communally, of God.

2. I have been a theological consultant to the Catholic Peacebuilding Network, sponsored by the Kroc Institute at the University of Notre Dame and Catholic Relief Services. Their three target areas are the Great Lakes region of Africa; Mindanao, the Philippines; and Bogotá, Colombia. As a board member of the international theological journal *Concilium*, I participated in the conference "Religion and Identity in Post-conflict Societies," held in Sarajevo in 2014 on the twenty-fifth anniversary of the fall of the Berlin Wall. I am also a member of the Kroc Institute's project Contending Modernities: Catholic, Muslim, Secular.

3. Jon Sobrino, SJ, *Christ the Liberator* (Maryknoll, NY: Orbis, 2001), 107, 168.

4. For background, see "Friar Ivo Markovic/Bosnia," Tanenbaum Peacemakers in Action Network, n.d., https://tanenbaum.org/peacemakers-in-action-network

/meet-the-peacemakers/friar-ivo-markovic/, accessed Sept. 1, 2017, and Solange Lefebvre, "Reconciliation through Creativity: Story-Telling and Music," in *Reconciliation: Empowering Grace*, ed. Jacques Haers, SJ, Felix Wilfred, Kristien Justaert, and Yves De Maeseneer (London: SCM Press, 2013), 13–23.

5. For background on Myla Leguro and her work, see Nathan Schneider, "Peace from the Ground Up: An Interview with Myla Leguro," The Immanent Frame: Secularism, Religion and the Public Square, Oct. 12, 2010, at http://blogs.ssrc.org/tif/2010/10/12/leguro/, and Myla Leguro, "The Many Dimensions of Catholic Peacebuilding: Mindanao Experience," paper presented at Fifth Annual Catholic Peacebuilding Network Conference, Univ. of Notre Dame, Apr. 2008, at http://cpn.nd.edu/announcements-media-and-past-events/annual-conferences/5th-annual-cpn-conference-at-the-university-of-notre-dame-april-2008/background-papers-about-catholic-peacebuilding/.

6. Schneider, "Peace from the Ground Up."

7. Quoted in Lefebvre, "Reconciliation through Creativity," 21.

8. Quoted in Lefebvre, "Reconciliation through Creativity," 20.

9. R. Scott Appleby, *The Ambivalence of the Sacred: Religion, Violence, and Reconciliation* (Lanham, MD: Rowman and Littlefield, 2000), 281, 282, 307, italics in original.

10. Reinhold Niebuhr, *Moral Man and Immoral Society: A Study in Ethics and Politics* (1932; reprint, New York: Scribner's, 1960), xi–xii.

11. Sobrino, *Christ the Liberator*, 157.

12. Daniel Franklin Pilario, "Restorative Justice amidst Continuing Violence," in *Reconciliation*, ed. Haers et al., 72–73.

13. See John Paul Lederach, *Building Peace: Sustainable Reconciliation in Divided Societies* (Washington, DC: United States Institute of Peace, 1997). Though a Mennonite, Lederach is a staunch and key member of the Catholic Peacebuilding Network.

14. Appleby, *Ambivalence of the Sacred*, 238–39.

15. Appleby, *Ambivalence of the Sacred*, 241.

16. Leguro, "The Many Dimensions of Catholic Peacebuilding," 1.

17. "Friar Ivo Markovic/Bosnia."

18. W. Sibley Towner, "Clones of God: Genesis 1:26–28 and the Image of God in the Hebrew Bible," *Interpretation* 59, no. 4 (2005): 349; Douglas John Hall, *Imaging God: Dominion as Stewardship* (Grand Rapids, MI: Eerdmans, 1986), 107.

19. For a discussion of the history and current interpretation of the image of God, see Towner, "Clones of God," and Janell Johnson, "Between Text and Sermon: Genesis 1:26–28," *Interpretation* 59, no. 2 (2005): 176–78.

20. Towner, "Clones of God," 350.

21. See Appleby, *Ambivalence of the Sacred*, 249–52.

22. One excellent diagnosis is given in James Waller, *Becoming Evil: How Ordinary People Commit Genocide and Mass Killing* (Oxford: Oxford Univ. Press, 2002). See also Stephen J. Pope, *Human Evolution and Christian Ethics* (Cambridge: Cambridge Univ. Press, 2007).

23. Augustine of Hippo, *The City of God*, trans. Marcus Dods (New York: Random House, 1950), book 1, preface, 3.

24. Atalia Omer and Jason A. Springs, *Religious Nationalism: A Reference Handbook* (Oxford: ABC-CLIO, 2013), 17–20.

25. Wendy Kroeker, presentation at the Mindanao Peacebuilding Institute, published in Mindanao Peacebuilding Institute (MPI), *Annual Training Report: MPI 2014 Annual Peacebuilding Training* (Mindanao, Philippines: MPI, Oct. 2, 2014), 15, italics in original, at http://mpiasia.net/2014-annual-peacebuilding-training-report .html.

26. Pilario, "Restorative Justice," 70.

27. For more thorough discussions, see Lisa Sowle Cahill, *Global Justice, Christology, and Christian Ethics* (Cambridge: Cambridge Univ. Press, 2013), 204–46, and Peter Schmiechen, *Saving Power: Theories of Atonement and Forms of the Church* (Grand Rapids, MI: Eerdmans, 2005).

28. "Friar Ivo Markovic/Bosnia."

29. St. Columbans Mission Society, "The Life and Death of Father Fausto Tentorio," Nov. 16, 2011, at http://www.columban.org.au/e-news/e-news-vol.-4-no.-10 /the-life-and-death-of-father-fausto-tentorio.

30. Giacomo Galeazzi, "Philippines: Communist Rebel Nuns Accused of Being Enemies of the Army," *Vatican Insider*, La Stampa, Apr. 10, 2015, at http://vatican insider.lastampa.it/en/world-news/detail/articolo/filippine-philippines-filipinas-suore -nun-monja-15315/.

31. Leguro, "Many Dimensions of Catholic Peacebuilding," 3.

32. Nell Bolton and Myla Leguro, *Local Solutions to Land Conflict in Mindanao: Policy Lessons from Catholic Relief Services* (Baltimore: Catholic Relief Services, Oct. 2015), at https://www.crs.org/sites/default/files/tools-research/local -solutions-to-land-conflict-in-mindanao.pdf.

33. Gorazd Andrejc, "Small Steps: Youth Interfaith Work in Post-conflict Bosnia-Herzegovina," *Perspectives*, Winter 2014–15, 10–13, at http://www.academic.edu /9550196/Small_Steps_Youth_Interfaith_Work_in_Post-Conflict_Bosnia-Herzegovina.

34. Andrejc, "Small Steps," 13.

35. Renée LaReau, "Meet Myla, M.A. '10," Alumni Profiles, Kroc Institute, June 6, 2011, at https://kroc.nd.edu/profiles/myla-leguro-2010/?section=ma.

2. The Power of Peace

1. Quoted in Joan V. Bondurant, *Conquest of Violence: The Gandhian Philosophy of Conflict*, rev. ed. (Princeton, NJ: Princeton Univ. Press, 1988), 23.

2. Mohandas K. Gandhi, "Working of Non-violence," *Harijan*, Feb. 6, 1939, in *The Collected Works of Mahatma Gandhi*, 75 vols. (New Delhi: Publications Division, Ministry of Information and Broadcasting, Government of India, 1999), 68:388.

3. Jawaharlal Nehru, *Toward Freedom: The Autobiography of Jawaharlal Nehru* (New York: John Day, 1941), 80.

4. Interview with Cesar Chavez, in *In the Footsteps of Gandhi: Conversations with Spiritual Social Activists*, ed. Catherine Ingram (Berkeley, CA: Parallax, 1990), 119.

5. Martin Ceadel, *Thinking about Peace and War* (New York: Oxford Univ. Press, 1987), 157.

6. Michael Walzer, *Just and Unjust Wars: A Moral Argument with Historical Illustrations*, 2nd ed. (New York: Basic Books, 1977), 333.

7. Martin Luther King Jr., "Letter from a Birmingham Jail," in *A Testament of Hope: The Essential Writings and Speeches of Martin Luther King, Jr.*, ed. James M. Washington (San Francisco: Harper San Francisco, 1991), 290.

8. Gene Sharp, *The Politics of Nonviolent Action*, 3 vols. (Boston: Porter Sargent, 1973).

9. Gene Sharp, *From Dictatorship to Democracy* (Cambridge, MA: Albert Einstein Foundation, 1994).

10. Barbara Deming, "On Revolution and Equilibrium," in *Revolution and Equilibrium* (New York: Grossman, 1971), 199.

11. Quoted in Judith M. Brown, *Gandhi: Prisoner of Hope* (New Haven, CT: Yale Univ. Press, 1989), 375.

12. Walter Wink, *Engaging the Powers: Discernment and Resistance* (Minneapolis, MN: Fortress, 1992), 252.

13. Václav Havel, "The Power of the Powerless," in *Without Force or Lies: Voices from the Revolution of Central Europe in 1989–90*, ed. William M. Brinton and Alan Rinzler (San Francisco: Mercury House, 1990), 99, 123.

14. Jonathan Schell, *The Unconquerable World: Power, Nonviolence, and the Will of the People* (New York: Metropolitan Books, 2003), 201, 205–6.

15. Erica Chenoweth and Maria J. Stephan, *Why Civil Resistance Works: The Strategic Logic of Nonviolent Conflict* (New York: Columbia Univ. Press, 2011).

16. Maria J. Stephan and Erica Chenoweth, "Why Civil Resistance Works: The Strategic Logic of Nonviolent Conflict," *International Security* 33, no. 1 (2008): 7–44.

17. Adrian Karatnycky and Peter Ackerman, "How Freedom Is Won: From Civil Resistance to Durable Democracy," *International Journal of Not-for-Profit*

Law 7, no. 3 (2005), 51, at http://www.icnl.org/research/journal/vol7iss3/special_3 .htm#_ednref1.

18. Chenoweth and Stephan, *Why Civil Resistance Works*, 201–19.

19. Chenoweth and Stephan, *Why Civil Resistance Works*, 39, 30.

20. Schell, *The Unconquerable World*, 236, 240.

21. Stephan and Chenoweth, "Why Civil Resistance Works," 21.

22. Erica Chenoweth and Maria J. Stephan, "How the World Is Proving Martin Luther King Jr. Right about Nonviolence," *Monkey Cage, Washington Post* blog, Jan. 18, 2016, at https://www.washingtonpost.com/news/monkey-cage/wp/2016/01/18 /how-the-world-is-proving-mlk-right-about-nonviolence/?utm_term=.f7a9f7b3f811.

23. Erica Chenoweth and Kurt Schock, "Do Contemporaneous Armed Challenges Affect the Outcomes of Mass Nonviolent Campaigns?" *Mobilization: An International Quarterly* 20, no. 4 (2015): 427–51.

24. Omar Wasow, "Do Protest Tactics Matter? Evidence from the 1960s Black Insurgency," Feb. 2, 2017, at http://www.omarwasow.com/Protests_on_Voting.pdf.

25. Quoted in Susan Ferris and Ricardo Sandoval, *The Fight in the Fields: Cesar Chavez and the Farmworkers Movement*, ed. Diana Hembree (New York: Harcourt Brace, 1997), 114.

26. Deming, "On Revolution and Equilibrium," 211.

27. Reinhold Niebuhr, *Moral Man and Immoral Society: A Study in Ethics and Politics* (1932; reprint, New York: Scribner's, 1960), 250.

28. Maciej Bartkowski and Mohja Kahf, "The Syrian Resistance: A Tale of Two Struggles," *openDemocracy*, Sept. 23, 2013, at https://www.opendemocracy .net/civilresistance/maciej-bartkowski-mohja-kahf/syrian-resistance-tale-of-two -struggles.

29. Human Rights Watch, "Syria: Events of 2016," in *Human Rights Watch World Report 2017* (New York: Human Rights Watch, 2017), at https://www.hrw .org/world-report/2017/country-chapters/syria.

30. See Sharp's famous list of 198 methods of nonviolent action in Gene Sharp, *Waging Nonviolent Struggle: 20th Century Practice and 21st Century Potential* (Boston: Extending Horizons Books and Porter Sargent, 2005), 51–64. See also Peter Ackerman and Christopher Kruegler, *Strategic Nonviolent Conflict: The Dynamics of People Power in the Twentieth Century* (Westport, CT: Praeger, 1994).

3. The Spiritual Balance of Peace in the Red Stick War, 1813–1814

1. Joel W. Martin, *Sacred Revolt: The Muskogees' Struggle for a New World* (Boston: Beacon Press, 1991), 18.

2. Michael D. Green, *The Politics of Indian Removal: Creek Government and Society in Crisis* (Lincoln: Univ. of Nebraska Press, 1982), 18.

3. John R. Swanton, *Early History of the Creek Indians and Their Neighbors*, Bureau of American Ethnology Bulletin no. 73 (Washington, DC: US Government Printing Office, 1922), and *The Social History and Usages of the Creek Confederacy*, Forty-Second Annual Report of the Bureau of American Ethnology (Washington, DC: US Government Printing Office, 1928).

4. Jean Chaudhuri and Joyotpaul Chaudhuri, *A Sacred Path: The Way of the Muscogee Creeks* (Los Angeles: American Indian Studies Center, Univ. of California at Los Angeles, 2001), 21.

5. The story of the twins is recounted in Chaudhuri and Chaudhuri, *A Sacred Path*, 30–39.

6. David Lewis Jr. and Ann T. Jordan, *Creek Indian Medicine Ways: The Enduring Power of Mvskoke Religion* (Albuquerque: Univ. of New Mexico Press, 2002), 44–45.

7. Quoted in Green, *The Politics of Indian Removal*, 29.

8. J. Leitch Wright Jr., *Creeks and Seminoles: Destruction and Regeneration of the Muscogulge People* (Lincoln: Univ. of Nebraska Press, 1986), 15.

9. Steven C. Hahn, *The Invention of the Creek Nation, 1670–1763* (Lincoln: Univ. of Nebraska Press, 2004), 12–13. For the early historical development of the Mvskoke Creek Confederacy, see Robbie Ethridge, *Creek Country: The Creek Indians and Their World* (Chapel Hill: Univ. of North Carolina Press, 2003), 22–31.

10. Green, *The Politics of Indian Removal*, 14.

11. Donald L. Fixico, *The American Indian Mind in a Linear World: American Indian Studies and Traditional Knowledge* (New York: Routledge, 2003), 11.

12. Homi Bhabha, *The Location of Culture* (London: Routledge, 1994), 53–56.

13. Lewis and Jordan, *Creek Indian Medicine Ways*, 7–8.

14. David H. Corkran, *The Creek Frontier, 1540–1783* (Norman: Univ. of Oklahoma Press, 1967), 145–46.

15. Corkran, *The Creek Frontier*, 150–59.

16. Claudio Saunt, *A New Order of Things: Property, Power, and the Transformation of the Creek Indians, 1733–1816* (Cambridge: Cambridge Univ. Press, 1999), 255.

17. Green, *The Politics of Indian Removal*, 32.

18. A short biography of Alexander McGillivray can be found in Michael D. Green, "Alexander McGillivray," in *American Indian Leaders: Studies in Diversity*, ed. R. David Edmunds (Lincoln: Univ. of Nebraska Press, 1980), 41–64.

19. Green, *The Politics of Indian Removal*, 36.

20. Joshua Piker, *Okfuskee: A Creek Indian Town in Colonial America* (Cambridge, MA: Harvard Univ. Press, 2004), 201.

21. Robert V. Remini, *Andrew Jackson and His Indian Wars* (New York: Viking Penguin, 2001), 62.

22. "It was considered at first, a war upon the whites; it became at length, and mainly, a war, almost of extermination against the Indians [Mvskokes]" (H. S. Halbert and T. H. Ball, *The Creek War of 1813 and 1815* [1895; reprint, Tuscaloosa: Univ. of Alabama Press, 1995], 22).

23. Wright, *Creeks and Seminoles*, 172.

24. Martin, *Sacred Revolt*, 151–53.

25. Martin, *Sacred Revolt*, 155.

26. Andrew Frank, *Creeks and Southerners: Biculturalism on the Early American Frontier* (Lincoln: Univ. of Nebraska Press, 2005), 130.

27. Halbert and Ball, *The Creek War*, 31.

28. Wright, *Creeks and Seminoles*, 167.

29. Martin, *Sacred Revolt*, 157–58.

30. Kathryn E. Holland Braund, "Red Sticks," in *Tohopeka: Rethinking the Creek War and the War of 1812*, ed. Kathryn E. Holland Braund (Tuscaloosa: Univ. of Alabama Press, 2012), 96.

31. Gregory A. Waselkov, *A Conquering Spirit: Fort Mims and the Redstick War of 1813–1814* (Tuscaloosa: Univ. of Alabama Press, 2006), 116–36.

32. George C. Eggleston, *Red Eagle and the Wars with the Creek Indians of Alabama* (New York: Dodd, Mead, 1878), 219–25.

33. Lewis and Jordan, *Creek Indian Medicine Ways*, 9.

34. Quoted in Remini, *Andrew Jackson and His Indian Wars*, 63.

35. Jackson wrote to his wife, "In fact when I reflect that he as to his relations is so much like myself I feel an unusual sympathy for him," because Jackson had lost both his parents and brother at an early age, and no relatives wanted to raise him (Andrew Jackson to Rachel Jackson, Dec. 29, 1813, in *The Papers of Andrew Jackson*, vol. 2: *1804–1813*, ed. Harold D. Moser and Sharon MacPherson [Knoxville: Univ. of Tennessee Press, 1980], 515–16).

36. A miscommunication among Jackson's commanders led to attacks on several Hillabee towns that had agreed to peace; they felt betrayed and then fought fiercely against Jackson. See Remini, *Andrew Jackson and His Indian Wars*, 67–68.

37. Piker, *Okfuskee*, 201.

38. Roy S. Dickens Jr., *Archaeological Investigations at Horseshoe Bend National Military Park, Alabama* (Moundville: Alabama Archaeological Society, 1979), 10.

39. Ove Jensen, "Horseshoe Bend: A Living Memorial," in *Tohopeka*, ed. Holland Braund, 147.

40. Martin, *Sacred Revolt*, 43; Remini, *Andrew Jackson and His Indian Wars*, 78.

41. Remini, *Andrew Jackson and His Indian Wars*, 78.

42. "Treaty with the Creeks, 1814," Aug. 9, 1814, in *Indian Treaties, 1778–1883*, comp. and ed. Harold D. Moser and Sharon MacPherson (New York: Interland, 1972), 107–10.

43. "Treaty with the Creeks, 1814."

44. Martin, *Sacred Revolt*, 2.

4. Exegeting Peace from Nagpur

1. The name "Shahina Khatib" is also spelt, often in her own messages, "Shahina Khateeb." By either spelling, she has had an extraordinary journey, from a background with degrees in mathematics and physics to a career as Arabic scholar and peace advocate through Qur'anic commentary/exposition. She has been as tireless in responding to my queries as she has been in all her efforts on behalf of the QAC.

2. One of the participants in the People's Peace Conference at Arizona State University in April 2014 was Professor Stuart B. Schwartz. I am indebted to Dr. Schwartz for highlighting the ethos of common people in his insightful monograph *All Can Be Saved: Religious Tolerance and Salvation in the Iberian Atlantic World* (New Haven, CT: Yale Univ. Press, 2008). Moriscos are among his primary subjects. Though they were afflicted by Iberian Catholics, they maintained that each person, whether Christian or Muslim, could be saved according to his or her own law (Q5:48). For the echo of that Qur'anic passage in an early-nineteenth-century satirical poem, which appeared in both Castilian and Galician, note this refrain, repressed by the Inquisition but enduring as part of a common people's ethos:

> The law of Jesus Christ is a law of charity and love.
> We should take its counsel and not betray it.
> We should live well and have compassion for our neighbor,
> For God it is who illumines us and guides our hearts.
> The people live in the law that they inherited from their grandparents,
> The Moor in his, the Galician in his, each judges his is best. (quoted in
>   Schwartz, *All Can Be Saved* 64–65, 240)

3. Quotes from Dr. Khatib come from our conversations, her talks, and email messages she sent to me.

4. This passage comes from the address that preceded our workshop in Nagpur on September 8, 2014. Despite the esteemed scholar's claims that the Qur'an is easy to understand and to translate, the verse he quotes signals reliance on one prior translator over others. Only Muhammad Asad renders *dhikr* as "bear in mind" or "take to heart"; all other major translators, except for Abul-A'la Maududi, use the familiar translation "remembrance" or "to understand and remember." Maududi does say "easy as a reminder," but one can deduce that the rendition here closely

follows Asad rather than Maududi by the sequel rhetorical query: "Who is now willing to take it to heart?" That phrase echoes what occurs only in Asad: "Who then is willing to take it to heart?" For the QAC's reliance on Asad, see my analysis in the remainder of the chapter. The evident contrast is with the multilingual (Urdu, Hindi, English) translation by Abdul Ghafoor's revered father, Abdul Karim Parekh. Parekh renders Q54:22 into English as "And in truth WE have made the Qur'an easy to understand (and remember); but is there any that will receive admonition?" (Tashreehul Qur'an, para, 27, 748–51, at http://www.explore-quran.com/).

5. On finding the right passages, I am reminded of the conversation between the pastor and Lila in the novel *Lila* (New York: Farrar, Strauss and Giroux, 2014) by Pulitzer Prize–winning author Marilynne Robinson. There the pastor exclaims: "It's amazing how I always think about the parts [of the Bible] I like best. And there are a lot of them. But there *is* all the rest of it" (132, emphasis in original). And that's the challenge posed to Abdul Ghafoor Parekh and Dr. Khatib, as it is for all who engage scripture, whether Jews, Christians, Muslims, Hindus, Buddhists, or Sikhs: how to lift up the parts that accent a common humanity while not ignoring those other parts that stress division, hierarchy, strife, and violence—in short, *all* the rest of it or at least too much of the rest of it to rely solely on scripture as one's ultimate authority.

6. For a fuller examination of Muhammad Asad and his distinctive approach to Qur'an translation, see my recent book on strategies for translating the Qur'an into English: Bruce B. Lawrence, *The Koran in English: A Biography* (Princeton, NJ: Princeton Univ. Press, 2017), esp. 65–73, 104, 127, 135–37, and 145–46.

7. Imam Mohamad Bashar Arafat visited the QAC in Nagpur in 2010. He is the founder and president of the Civilizations Exchange and Cooperation Foundation as well as of Better Understanding for a Better World. Based in Baltimore, Maryland, both organizations are described in detail online at http://www.cecf-net.org/, where one can also find an impassioned rejection of the ISIS attacks in France in 2016 as "criminal and inhumane acts, in defiance of all the schools of Islamic Law, that pervert the teachings of the Qur'an and Shariah Law to serve their own immoral, political and criminal ideology."

8. Abdullah Yusuf Ali, *The Holy Qur'an: Text, Translation and Commentary* (Lahore: n.p., 1934). This work has appeared in multiple editions since its first publication in 1934, including later ones with Arabic text, ones reprinted without commentary, and ones with changes to the title (e.g., *The Meaning of the Holy Qur'an* [1977]).

9. Dr. Khatib then added that "an extensive workshop was arranged on this topic," but it did not—for it could not—resolve the question of how precisely to render this injurious word.

10. Because Muhammad Asad, a translator of the Qur'an often cited by Dr. Khatib, is the first and most consistent advocate of the translation of *taqwa* as "God

consciousness," one might deduce that in the italicized sentence she is simply following Asad's translation in *The Message of the Qur'an: The Full Account of the Revealed Arabic Text Accompanied by Transliteration*, explained by Muhammed Asad, transliterated by Ahmed Moustafa (1980; reprint, Britton, UK: Book Foundation, 2003), but that deduction needs to be qualified. Above all, it needs to be modified at a practical, everyday level. Although the source of Dr. Khatib's inspiration and word choice is indeed Asad, his rendition has been modified and republished in not one but two Indian editions. Both are by Adam Eisabhai. The first, *The Spirit of the Qur'an* ([2006] 2013), provides a hardback Indian edition of Muhammad Asad's work (966 pages), while *The Message of the Qur'an* (2010) offers a paperback Indian edition.

Even more interesting than these two Indian editions of Asad's classic is their publisher: the first book comes from Alhuda Publications in Daryaganj, New Delhi, while the second comes from Parekh Publications in Lakadganj, Nagpur, and it is, of course, Parekh Publications—both Abdul Karim the father and Abdul Ghafoor the son—with whom Dr. Khatib is deeply involved in her labor on behalf of the QAC and IPC.

11. Asad, *The Message of the Qur'an*, 8 n. 2.

12. Q33:35, translated in Ali, *The Holy Qur'an* (1938 ed.).

13. Asad, *The Message of the Qur'an*, xi. Asad's choice also has antecedents within the community of Muslim Qur'an translators, including Muhammad Ali and Marmaduke Pickthall, as well as among successors both Muslim (notably Sayyid Abul-A'la Maududi and Sayyid Qutb) and non-Muslim (Alan Jones and Thomas Cleary). For further discussion of the charged nature of translating *muslimun* as "those who submit" and *Islam* as "submission" within the orb of Qur'anic translators, see Lawrence, *The Koran in English*, 129, 221–22 n. 9.

14. Abdel Haleem (as also Wahiduddin Khan) seems to have taken his cue from Asad and provides more inclusive language: "For men and women who are devoted to God—believing men and women, obedient men and women, truthful men and women, steadfast men and women, humble men and women, charitable men and women, fasting men and women, chaste men and women, men and women who remember God often—God has prepared forgiveness and a rich reward" (Muhammad Abdel Haleem, trans., *The Qur'an: A New Translation* [Oxford: Oxford Univ. Press, 2004], 269). For those aficionados who want to follow the trajectory of using "Allah" or "God" for this verse, Sayyid Qutb and A. J. Arberry follow the "God" option, whereas others, such as Pickthall, Maududi, and, of course, Khan/Hilali, maintain the "Allah" option, not just for this verse but throughout their endeavors to render Arabic into English in expressing the meaning of the Holy Qur'an; see islamawakened.com.

15. Adam Eisabhai has Indianized Asad's translation. That local appropriation has led to the expansion of Asad's vision into a new context. It has become and remains a resource for the pursuit of peace from the ground up, utilized and modified by activists such as Dr. Khatib.

16. The first "Allah" reference (Q6:43) comes back to the key word *taqwa* or *ittaqi*, again with the accent on "consciousness" and "consciousness/awareness" of God/Allah that derives from and circles back to Asad's work *The Message of the Qur'an.*

17. These are but two samples from the many essays, articles, speeches, interventions on the website Explore al Quran (www.explore-quran.com). At the site, there are sixty subsets under the heading "Articles," with many of the web pages having several items within each of them. Among the guest authors are Asghar Ali Engineer and Maulana Wahiduddin Khan.

18. I am indebted to Professor Yasmin Saikia not only for organizing the People's Peace Conference at Arizona State University in April 2015 but also for providing invaluable feedback to the initial draft of this essay, which allowed me to expand its scope, tighten its argument, and clarify its applicability for peacemaking.

5. Peace, Reconciliation, and Forgiveness

1. Searches conducted on June 22, 2017.

2. David Konstan, *Before Forgiveness: The Origins of a Moral Idea* (Cambridge: Cambridge Univ. Press, 2010), 170, précis. For this book, in addition to using his own studies, Konstan drew upon papers in David Konstan and Charles Griswold, eds., *Ancient Forgiveness: Classical, Judaic, and Christian* (Cambridge: Cambridge Univ. Press, 2012). Michael Morgan's essay in that volume, "Mercy, Repentance, and Forgiveness in Ancient Judaism" (137–57), contributed extensively to Konstan's comments on biblical and rabbinic thinking.

3. Konstan, *Before Forgiveness*, 21.

4. Konstan's delineation of the traits of forgiveness overlaps extensively with those proposed by my colleague Jeffrie G. Murphy in, for example, "Forgiveness and Resentment," in Jeffrie G. Murphy and Jean Hampton, *Forgiveness and Mercy* (Cambridge: Cambridge Univ. Press, 1988), 14–34.

5. Konstan, *Before Forgiveness*, 105. In *How Repentance Became Biblical: Judaism, Christianity, and the Interpretation of Scripture* (New York: Oxford Univ. Press, 2016), David Lambert similarly demonstrates that many biblical texts previously interpreted to indicate that ancient Israelites required an interior experience of repentance by offending persons in actuality refer to actions that materially demonstrate the Israelites' diminished status and suffering to provoke mercy or pity on the part of the thereby-acknowledged-superior offended party.

6. See note 2.

7. Konstan, *Before Forgiveness*, 112.

8. See Gary A. Anderson, *Sin: A History* (New Haven, CT: Yale Univ. Press, 2009), and *Charity: The Place of the Poor in Biblical Tradition* (New Haven, CT: Yale Univ. Press, 2013).

9. Others in addition to Morgan ("Mercy, Repentance, and Forgiveness in Ancient Judaism") have published on the issue of repentance in Judaism. See Louis Newman, *Repentance: The Meaning and Practice of Teshuvah* (Woodstock, VT: Jewish Lights Press, 2010), and "Balancing Justice and Mercy: Reflections on Forgiveness in Judaism," *Journal of Religious Ethics* 41 (2013): 435–56; Tzvi Marx, "Theological Preparation for Reconciliation in Judaism," in *Religion, Conflict, and Reconciliation: Multifaith Ideals and Realities*, ed. Jerald D. Gort, Henry Jansen, and Hendrik M. Vroom (Amsterdam: Rodopi, 2002), 93–103; Yishai Kiel, "Penitential Theology in East Late Antiquity: Talmudic, Zoroastrian, and East Christian Reflections," *Journal for the Study of Judaism in the Persian, Hellenistic, and Roman Period* 45 (2014): 551–83; and Scott Hoffman, "The Evolution of the Concept of Repentance in Biblical, Second Temple, and Rabbinic Sources," PhD diss., New York Univ., 2012. Owing to the relative priority of the divine–human relationship in rabbinic texts, these studies focus predominantly on Judaic views of it rather than on interpersonal ones.

10. Morgan discusses a number of these texts in "Mercy, Repentance, and Forgiveness in Ancient Judaism."

11. See Francis Brown, S. R. Driver, and Charles Briggs, *Hebrew and English Lexicon of the Old Testament* (Boston: Houghton Mifflin, 1907); Marcus Jastrow, *A Dictionary of the Targumim, the Talmud Babli and Yerushalmi, and the Midrashic Literature* (New York: Judaica Press, 1971); and Michael Sokoloff, *A Dictionary of Jewish Babylonian Aramaic of the Talmudic and Geonic Periods* (Ramat Gan, Israel: Bar Ilan Univ. Press, 2002).

12. In "How Does Almsgiving Purge Sins?" in *Hebrew in the Second Temple Period*, ed. Steven Fassberg, Moshe Bar Asher, and Ruth A. Clements (Leiden: Brill, 2013), Gary Anderson argues that a secondary meaning of the term *ratzah* is "to repay" and connects this meaning to the notion that sins are debts (5).

13. Both Konstan (*Before Forgiveness*) and Morgan ("Mercy, Repentance, and Forgiveness in Ancient Judaism") underscore this point in their discussions of several of these tannaitic sources. The term *mechilah* is not found in the Bible, appears once in the Dead Sea Scrolls, and then is common in rabbinic sources. It is best translated as "pardon," not as "forgiveness." See also Mitchell First, "What Is the Origin of the Word *Mechilah*?" *Hakirah: The Flatbush Journal of Jewish Law and Thought* 18 (2014): 147–58.

14. Talmudic texts (y. Yoma 8:9 45c; y. B.Q. 8:10; b. Yoma 87a, b) flesh out some of these passages, in some cases providing prescriptions of the required actions on the part of the offending party, and also speak of the challenges of achieving reconciliation. According to the passage in y. Yoma, "It is necessary to appease one whom one has injured [even] at his grave and to say, 'I have sinned [*sarchit*] against you.'" None of these texts speaks of forgiveness, yet they do seek restoration of previous relationships.

15. Additional stories in the Palestinian and Babylonian Talmuds on these themes include: y. Demai 1:3 22a, y. Ta. 3:1 67c, b. Hul. 7a, y. Peah 8:9 21b, y. Sheq. 5:4 49b, y. Kil. 9:4 32b, y. Ket. 12:5 35a, b. M.Q. 16b, y. B.B. 2:3 13b, y. Sanh 2:1 19d, y. Hor. 3:1 4a, y. Sanh. 2:6, b. Ber. 51b, b. Yoma 87a, b, b. Naz. 49b, b. Qid. 52b, b. Git. 56a, b. B.M. 59a, b. B.Q. 117a, b. Hor. 13b, and b. Men. 93b. Richard Kalmin has analyzed numerous stories in the Babylonian Talmud describing conflicts among sages, but only some of these stories move to the stage of seeking reconciliation. See, for example, Richard Kalmin, *Sages, Stories, Authors, and Editors in Rabbinic Babylonia* (Atlanta, GA: Scholars Press, 1994), and *The Sages in Jewish Society in Late Antiquity* (London: Routledge, 1999).

16. The study of rabbinic stories has expanded immensely in the past fifteen years. I provide an analysis of some of the key scholars and trends in Joel Gereboff, "Talmudic Stories about Angry and Annoyed Rabbis," in *A Legacy of Learning: Essays in Honor of Jacob Neusner*, ed. Alan J. Avery-Peck, Bruce Chilton, William Scott Green, and Gary G. Porton (Leiden: Brill, 2014), 82–109. In his book *The Culture of the Babylonian Talmud* (Baltimore: Johns Hopkins Univ. Press, 2003), Jeffrey Rubenstein elaborates on the importance of shame, violent metaphors, and anger in stories in the Babylonian Talmud. See also Michael Satlow, "From Salve to Weapon: Torah Study, Masculinity, and the Babylonian Talmud," in *Religious Men and Masculine Identities in the Middle Ages*, ed. P. H. Cullum and Katherine Lewis (Woodbridge, UK: Boydell and Brewer, 2013), 16–27.

17. I draw here upon comments in Daniel Boyarin, *Carnal Israel: Reading Sex in Talmudic Culture* (Berkeley: Univ. of California Press, 1993), 212–25, and Admiel Kosman, "R. Johanan and Resh Lakish: The Image of God in the Study Hall: 'Masculinity' versus 'Femininity,'" *European Judaism* 43 (2010): 128–45.

18. I utilize analyses in Devora Steinmetz, "Must the Patriarch Know *Uqtzin*? The Nasi as Scholar in the Babylonian Aggada," *AJS Review* 23 (1998): 163–89; Jeffrey Rubenstein, *Stories of the Babylonian Talmud* (Baltimore: Johns Hopkins Univ. Press, 2010), 77–90; Robert Goldenberg, "The Deposition of Rabban Gamaliel II: An Examination of the Sources," *Journal of Jewish Studies* 23 (1972): 167–90; Ronit Nikolsky and Tal Ilan, "Mihatam lihacha, 'From There to Here' (b. Sanh. 5a): Rabbinic Traditions between Palestine and Babylonia: An Introduction,"

in *Rabbinic Traditions between Palestine and Babylonia*, ed. Ronit Nikolsky and Tal Ilan (Leiden: Brill, 2014), 1–21; and Avraham Walfish, "Halakhic Confrontation Dramatized: A Study of Mishnah Rosh Hashanah 2:8–9," *Hebrew Union College Annual* 79 (2008): 1–41.

19. My ongoing research does not focus on peace studies, but this paper has led me to learn about the scope and trends of this field by examining many websites that describe academic peace and conflict-resolution studies and by reading several articles on the history of these disciplines.

20. Elizabeth S. Dahl, "Oil and Water: The Philosophical Commitments of International Peace Studies and Conflict Resolution," *International Studies Review* 14, no. 2 (2012): 240. See also Landon Edward Hancock, "Peace Studies and Conflict Resolution: Similarities, Differences, and Blurred Boundaries," International Studies Association website blog, Jan. 8, 2014, at http://www.isanet.org/ISA/Sections/PEACE/News/ID/228/Peace-Studies-and-Conflict-Resolution-Similarities-Differences-and-Blurred-Boundaries.

21. For example, see Johan Galtung, *Peace by Peaceful Means: Peace and Conflict, Development and Civilization* (Thousand Oaks, CA: Sage, 1996), and *Peace: Research, Education, Action*, Essays in Peace Research no. 1 (Copenhagen: Ejlers, 1975).

22. Konstan, *Before Forgiveness*, 171, emphasis added.

23. Jacob Neusner, "War in the Halakhah, Peace in the Aggadah," *Review of Rabbinic Judaism* 14 (2011): 134–35. The word *shalom*, generally translated as "peace," has a far more diverse range of meaning, including "security," "integrity," "well-being," and "equity." See "Peace," *Encyclopedia Judaica*, 2d ed. (Detroit: Macmillan, 2007), 15:700–703. Neusner also collects numerous individual episodic comments about the importance of peace in *War and Peace in Rabbinic Judaism* (Lanham, MD: Univ. Press of America, 2011). There are several longer discussions in rabbinic texts about the great value of peace as well: Sifre Numbers 42, Sifre Deut. 199, Lev. Rab. 9:9, and Pereq Hashalom. They, however, speak in general terms, not in directly actionable ones. The connection between peace and the messianic age appears in M. Ed. 8:7. Also, for the notion that in rabbinic views peace is generally a messianic goal, see Catherine Hezser, "Seduced by the Enemy or Wise Strategy? The Presentation of Non-violence and Accommodation with Foreign Powers in Ancient Jewish Literary Sources," in *Between Cooperation and Hostility: Multiple Identities in Ancient Judaism and the Interaction with Foreign Powers*, ed. Rainer Albertz and Jakob Wohrle (Göttingen, Germany: Vandenhoeck and Ruprecht, 2013), 221–50. The connection between reconciling conflicting parties and peace finds expression in a tradition in ARN A 12:3, which describes Aaron as bringing formerly conflicting parties to overcome their anger, express regret, and hug and kiss each other.

24. Recent works on peace and war include Robert Eisen, *The Peace and Violence of Judaism from the Bible to Zionism* (New York: Oxford Univ. Press, 2011),

and essays in Yigal Levin and Amnon Shapira, eds., *War and Peace in Jewish Tradition: From the Biblical World to the Present* (London: Routledge, 2011). Two recent volumes, making a case for the importance of pursuing peace, underscore that striving for peace has not been a central goal of current Jewish efforts, nor was it a self-evident priority throughout the history of Judaism: Alick Isaacs, *A Prophetic Peace: Judaism, Religion, and Politics* (Bloomington: Indiana Univ. Press, 2011), and Amy Eilberg, *From Enemy to Friend: Jewish Wisdom and the Pursuit of Peace* (Maryknoll, NY: Orbis Books, 2014).

25. See the Psychology of Intergroup Conflict and Reconciliation Lab homepage at http://portal.idc.ac.il/en/main/research/picr/pages/default.aspx.

26. Eric Halperin, *Emotions in Conflict: Inhibitors and Facilitators of Peace Making* (New York: Routledge, 2015).

27. Marc Gopin, who has published extensively on Jewish and other religious views on peacemaking, observes, "Face is a critical category in conflict analysis. Saving face is a key generator of conflict in many situations, for a variety of reasons, including the inability to back down from the action–reaction spiral of aggressive behavior due the fear of losing face" ("Judaism and Peacebuilding," in *Religion and Peace Building*, ed. Howard Coward and Gordon Smith [Albany: State Univ. of New York Press, 2004], 116).

28. Howard Kaminsky, *Fundamentals of Jewish Conflict Resolution: Traditional Jewish Perspectives on Resolving Interpersonal Conflicts* (Brighton, MA: Academic Studies Press, 2017); Marc Gopin, *Between Eden and Armageddon: The Future of World Religion, Violence, and Peacemaking* (New York: Oxford Univ. Press, 2002), *Holy War, Holy Peace: How Religion Can Bring Peace to the Middle East* (New York: Oxford Univ. Press, 2002), and "Judaism and Peacebuilding."

29. Kaminsky, *Fundamentals of Jewish Conflict Resolution*, 36.

30. Maimonides, *Hilkhot Teshuva* 2:9.

31. Kaminsky, *Fundamentals of Jewish Conflict Resolution*, 330–31.

32. Kaminsky, *Fundamentals of Jewish Conflict Resolution*, 403.

33. Gopin, *Holy War*, 127.

34. Gopin, *Between Eden and Armageddon*, 181–88.

35. Among these works are Marvan Darweish, "Israeli Peace and Solidarity Organization," in *Conflict, Transformation, and the Palestinians: The Dynamics of Peace and Justice under Occupation*, ed. Alpaslan Ozerdem (New York: Routledge, 2016), 229–46; Ifaz Maoz, "Peace Building in Violent Conflicts: Israeli–Palestinian Post-Oslo People to People Activities," *International Journal of Politics, Culture, and Society* 17 (2004): 563–74; Rabah Halbi, *Israeli and Palestinian Identities in Dialogue: The School of Peace Approach* (New Brunswick, NJ: Rutgers Univ. Press, 2004); Maxine Kaufman Lacusta and Ursula Franklin, *Israeli Nonviolent Resistance to the Israeli Occupation* (Reading, UK: Garnet, 2011); Tamar Hermann, *The Israeli*

Peace Movement: A Shattered Dream (New York: Cambridge Univ. Press, 2009); and Charles P. Henderson, "Organizations Working toward a Just and Lasting Peace in the Middle East," *Crosscurrents* 58 (2008): 227–443. Yvonne Margareta Wang provides a detailed analysis of eight Palestinian and Israel–Jewish religious organizations involved in peacebuilding in "How Can Religion Contribute to Peace in the Holy Land? A Study of Religious Peace Work in Jerusalem," PhD diss., Oslo Univ., 2011, at https://www.duo.uio.no/bitstream/handle/10852/37783/1/dravhandling -wang.pdf, a short version of which appeared as "Strategic Engagement and Religious Peace-Building," *Approaching Religion* 4 (2014): 71–82.

36. Information on the IEA was gleaned from sources cited in the previous note and from its website at https://interfaith-encounter.org/.

37. Mohammed Abu-Nimer has presented in a number of his publications detailed descriptions and critiques of the IEA and other solidarity-oriented group efforts. Among these publications are Mohammed Abu-Nimer, *Dialogue, Conflict Resolution, and Change: Arab–Jewish Encounters in Israel* (Albany: State Univ. of New York Press, 1999), and Mohammed Abu-Nimer, Amal Khoury, and Emily Welty, *Unity in Diversity: Interfaith Dialogue in the Middle East* (Washington, DC: United States Institute of Peace Press, 2007). Additional comments on the IEA appear in Wang, "How Can Religion Contribute to Peace in the Holy Land?," and in Frida Kerner Furman, "Religion and Peacebuilding: Grassroots Efforts by Israelis and Palestinians," *Journal of Religion Conflict and Peace* 4 (2011), at http:// www.religionconflictpeace.org/volume-4-issue-2-spring-2011/religion-and-peace building-grassroots-efforts-israelis-and-palestinians.

38. For this description, see the RHR's website at https://rhr.org.il/eng. Information on the RHR is also taken from Wang, "How Can Religion Contribute to Peace in the Holy Land?," and Atalia Omer, *When Peace Is Not Enough: How the Israeli Peace Camp Thinks about Religion, Nationalism, and Justice* (Chicago: Univ. of Chicago Press, 2013).

39. RHR, "We Ask Forgiveness," Sept. 30, 2011, at https://rhr.org.il/eng/2011 /09/we-ask-forgiveness/.

40. Kaminsky, *Fundamentals of Jewish Conflict Resolution*, 456–57.

6. Coming Together in Peace

1. Michel de Certeau, *The Practice of Everyday Life*, trans. Steven F. Randall (Berkeley: Univ. of California Press, 1984).

2. See the conclusion of this volume for further elaboration of these ordinary people imagining a human future.

3. Quoted in Ray Bush and Habib Ayeb, introduction to *Marginality and Exclusion in Egypt*, ed. Ray Bush and Habib Ayeb (Cairo: American Univ. in Cairo Press, 2012), 3–13.

4. Maha Hindawy, "My Egyptian Revolution," in *Voices of the Arab Spring: Personal Stories from the Arab Revolutions*, ed. Asaad Alsaleh (New York: Columbia Univ. Press, 2015), 76.

5. For the deep impacts and violent displacements of the World Bank–imposed restructuring regime implemented under the Mubarak administration, though with roots to the rule of Anwar Sadat (1970–81), see Rabab el-Mahdi, "Against Marginalization: Workers, Youth, and Class in the 25 January Revolution," in *Marginality and Exclusion in Egypt*, ed. Bush and Ayeb, 133–47, and Roberto Roccu, "David Harvey in Tahrir Square: The Dispossessed, the Discontented, and the Egyptian Revolution," *Third World Quarterly* 34, no. 3 (2013): 423–40.

6. Chad Haines, "Dialogical Din and Everyday Acts of Peace: An Islamic Perspective," in *Women and Peace in the Islamic World: Gender, Agency, and Influence*, ed. Yasmin Saikia and Chad Haines (London: I. B. Tauris, 2014), 58.

7. Sara Hany, "It is Just . . . the Beginning," in *Voices of the Arab Spring*, ed. Alsaleh, 68.

8. Hindawy, "My Egyptian Revolution," 77.

9. David Harvey, *Rebel Cities: From the Right to the City to the Urban Revolution* (London: Verso Books, 2012).

10. Asef Bayat and Eric Denis, "Who Is Afraid of Ashwaiyyat? Urban Change and Politics in Egypt," *Environment and Urbanization* 12 (2000): 185–99; also see the various contributions in Diane Singerman, ed., *Cairo Contested: Governance, Urban Space, and Global Modernity* (Cairo: American Univ. in Cairo Press, 2009).

11. I am indebted to Omar Nagati for educating me about this development. Nagati is the founding director of CLUSTER: the Cairo Lab for Urban Studies, Training, and Environmental Research. I met and interviewed him during my research visit in Cairo in May 2013. CLUSTER published several books on various aspects of Cairo's development following the January 25 Revolution, including Omar Nagati and Beth Stryker, eds., *Archiving the City in Flux: Cairo's Shifting Urban Landscape since the January 25th Revolution* (2013), and Beth Stryker, Omar Nagati, and Magda Mostafa, eds., *Learning from Cairo: Global Perspectives and Future Visions* (2013), the proceedings of a conference.

12. I use the term *homosexual* because the issue I am discussing is cis gay men who more often than not self-identify either as "gay" or as "homosexual," generally even using these English words. Although there is some gender bending in the community and perceived differences between those who penetrate versus those who are penetrated in the sexual act, most still identify as male. There are a transsexual community and a very significant lesbian community as well, but the greatest attention is given to male homosexuality.

13. Michael Warner, *The Trouble with Normal: Sex, Politics, and the Ethics of Queer Life* (Cambridge, MA: Harvard Univ. Press, 1999).

14. Shereen El Feki, *Sex and the Citadel: Intimate Life in a Changing Arab World* (New York: Pantheon Books, 2013), in particular chapter 6, "Dare to Be Different."

15. Information on the changing place of homosexuals following the revolution comes from several interviews I conducted in Cairo in May 2013.

7. The Iberian Empires

1. I have developed these arguments more fully in Stuart B. Schwartz, *All Can Be Saved: Religious Tolerance and Salvation in the Iberian Atlantic World* (New Haven, CT: Yale Univ. Press, 2008). Much of this chapter is drawn from that book, but I have added material in a number of places, updated the citations, and tried to address issues about the slow adaptation of religious tolerance in the Iberian world despite evidence of a desire for it. On the question of salvation outside the Catholic Church, see Francis A. Sullivan, *Salvation outside the Church* (New York: Paulist Press, 1922), 22–28; Louis Capéran, *Le probleme du salut des infidels*, 2 vols. (Toulouse: Grand Séminaire, 1934), and Bernard Sesboúe, *Hors de l'Église pas de salut* (Paris: Desclée de Brouwer, 2004).

2. See Perez Zagorin, *How the Idea of Religious Toleration Came to the West* (Princeton, NJ: Princeton Univ. Press, 2003), and John Christian Laursen and Cary J. Nederman's edited volumes on toleration, such as *Beyond the Persecuting Society: Religious Toleration before the Enlightenment* (Philadelphia: Univ. of Pennsylvania Press, 1997). See, too, the classic by Joseph Lecler, *Histoire de la tolerance au siècle de la Réforme*, 2 vols. (Paris: Aubier, 1955); an English-language edition appeared in 1960.

3. Benjamin J. Kaplan, *Divided by Faith: Religious Conflict and the Practice of Toleration in Early Modern Europe* (Cambridge, MA: Harvard Univ. Press, 2007), 3.

4. Jonathan Israel, *Radical Enlightenment: Philosophy and the Making of Modernity, 1650–1750* (Oxford: Oxford Univ. Press, 2001); O. P. Grell and Roy Porter, eds., *Toleration in Enlightenment Europe* (Cambridge: Cambridge Univ. Press, 2000). See the important revision of this history in Kaplan, *Divided by Faith*.

5. Quoted in Rolando Minutii, "Toleration in China and Siam in Late Seventeenth Century Travel Literature," in *Paradoxes of Religious Toleration in Early Modern Political Thought*, ed. John Christian Laurensen and María José Villaverde (Lanham, MD: Lexington Books, 2012), 109.

6. Henry Kamen is one of the few historians in the twentieth century who questioned the exclusion of Spain from the history of toleration. See his essays "Toleration and Dissent in Sixteenth-Century Spain: The Alternative Tradition," *Sixteenth-Century Journal* 19 (1988): 3–23, and "Inquisition, Tolerance, and Liberty in Eighteenth-Century Spain," in *Toleration in Enlightenment Europe*, ed. Grell and Porter, 250–58. Juan Pablo Domínguez has taken up the question of toleration in

early-modern Spain in "Los progresos de la tolerancia religiosa en el mundo vista desde la España del siglo XVIII," *Hispanic Research Journal* 15 (2014): 120–36, and "Tolerancia religiosa en la España afrancesada," *Historia y Política* 31 (2014): 195–223.

7. The trial of Inocencio de Aldama is recorded in Inquisición (Murcia) 2845, Archivo Historico Nacional (AHN), Madrid. See the summary in J. Blázquez Miguel, *La Inquisición en Albacete* (Albacete, Spain: Instituto de Estudios Albacetences, CSIC-CECEL, 1985). I have provided a fuller discussion of the case and its source in Schwartz, *All Can Be Saved*, 89–91.

8. On the great debate over *convivencia*, useful starting places for the Anglophone reader are Maria Rosa Menocal, *Ornament of the World* (Boston: Little Brown, 2002), and David Nierenberg, *Communities of Violence* (Princeton, NJ: Princeton Univ. Press, 1996). The literature on the ethnic and religious relations and conflicts in medieval Spain is enormous.

9. These statements come from an inquisitorial investigation in Soria in the 1480s: "Libro de declaraciones de testigos sobre delitos en que entiende el Santo Oficio dela Inquisición de Soria y otras partes," Patronato Real, Inquisición, 28–73, fs. 937–1,121, Archivo General de Simancas (AGS), Simancas, Spain; all translations are mine unless otherwise noted. The investigation has been the subject of two studies. See María Monsalvo Antón, "Herejía conversa y contestación religiosa a fines de la edad media: Las denuncias a la inquisición en el obispado de Osma," *Studia Historica* 2, no. 3 (1984): 109–39, which emphasizes the converso background of those accused. For a contrary view, see John Edwards, "Religious Faith and Doubt in Late Medieval Spain: Soria circa 1450–1500," *Past and Present* 120 (1988): 3–25.

10. Schwartz, *All Can Be Saved*, chap. 1, "Propositions," 17–42. See also Juan Antonio Alejandre and María J. Torquemada, *Palabra de hereje: La Inquisición de Sevilla ante el delito de proposiciones* (Seville: Univ. of Seville, 1998).

11. See Dante, *Divine Comedy: Paradise*, canto 8.

12. "Relación de las causas de la fe que se han despachado en la Inquisiciónm de Mallorca desde diez de octubre de 88 hasta ultimo de diciembre principio de noventa," in *El Tribunal de la Inquisición en Mallorca: Relación de causas de fe*, ed. Lorenç Pérez, Leonard Muntaner, and Mateu Colom (Palma de Mallorca, Spain: Miquel Font, 1986), 109–10; Schwartz, *All Can Be Saved*, 85–86.

13. Inq. (Murcia) 2022, AHN, Madrid.

14. J. M. García Fuentes, *La Inquisición de Granada en el siglo xvi* (Granada, Spain: Universidad de Granada, 1981), 239; A. Martín Casares, "Cristianos, musulmanes, y animistas en Granada: Identidades religiosas y sincretismo cultural," in *Negros, mulatos, zambaigos*, ed. Berta Ares and A. Stella (Seville: Escuela de Estudios Hispano-Americanos, 2000), 207–21. Denying the existence of heaven or hell

306 | NOTES TO PAGES 145-47

was considered to be atheism. See Julio Caro Baroja, *De la superstición al ateísmo* (Madrid: Taurus, 1974). On the argument that prior to the seventeenth century atheism was not intellectually possible, see David Wooten, "Lucien Febvre and the Problem of Unbelief in the Early Modern Period," *Journal of Modern History* 60 (1988): 695–730.

15. Quoted in D. Bramon, *Contra moros y judíos* (Barcelona: Península, 1986), 194.

16. Inquisitors in sixteenth-century Spain warned that this proposition was to be found particularly among converts from Islam.

17. See Yohanan Friedmann, *Tolerance and Coercion in Islam* (Cambridge: Cambridge Univ. Press, 2003), 87–89; Susan Stroumsa, *Freethinkers in Medieval Islam: Ibn al-Rawandi, Abu Bark at-Razi, and Their Impact on Islamic Thought* (Leiden: Brill, 1999); and Mercedes García-Arenal, *Inquisición y Moriscos: Los procesos del Tribunal de Cuenca* (Madrid: Siglo XXI, 1978), 108–9. In a sweeping review of recent work on Moriscos in early-modern Spain, García-Arenal has mistakenly suggested that *All Can Be Saved* missed the association that inquisitors made between Moriscos and the idea of salvation in all faiths. See Mercedes García-Arenal, "Religious Dissent and Minorities: The Morisco Age," *Journal of Modern History* 88 (2009): 888–920; cf. Schwartz, *All Can Be Saved*, 66–67.

18. Inq. Evora, maço 64, n. 608, Arquivo Nacional da Torre do Tombo, Lisbon.

19. Inq. (Murcia), leg. 2022, n. 25, AHN, Madrid. The accused, Pedro de Ludena, received only a fine because the inquisitors found him to be a man of "little understanding"—that is, ignorant in matters of theology.

20. Trevor Dadson, *Tolerance and Coexistence in Early Modern Spain: Old Christians and Moriscos in the Campo de Calatrava* (Woodbridge, UK: Tamesis, 2014). A more extensive version of this book, with accompanying documentation, was published in Spanish as *Los Moriscos de Villarubia de los Ojos (siglos XV–XVIII): Historia de una minoria asimilada, expulsada y reintegrada* (Madrid: Iberoamericana-Vervuert, 2007).

21. See Adriano Prosperi, "America e Apocalisse: Note sulla 'conquista spirituale' del Nuovo Mondo," in *America e Apocalisse e altri saggi* (Pisa, Italy: Istituti Editoriali e Poligrafichi Internazionale, 1999), 15–65.

22. Santo Domingo 49, ramo xiv, n. 95, Archivo General de Indias, Seville, published in Genaro Rodríguez Morel, *Cartas de la Real Audiencia de Santo Domingo (1530–1546)* (Santo Domingo, Dominican Republic: Archivo General de la Nación, 2007), 431–41.

23. Inq. (Lima) lib. 1028, f. 464–464v, AHN, Madrid.

24. Inq. V. 187, exp. 2, Archivo General de la Nación, Mexico City; Inq. Lib. 1064, fl.33, AHN, Madrid.

25. For Mateo Salado/Saladé's story, see José Toribio Medina, *Historia del Tribunal del Santo Oficio de la Inquisición de Lima*, 2 vols. (Santiago de Chile: Gutenberg, 1887), 1:52–55.

26. The details provided here in the case of Cuevas have been drawn from the summary included in the *relaciónes de causas*, 1610–37, in *Cincuenta años de Inquisición en el tribunal de Cartagena de Indias, 1610–1660*, ed. Anna Maria Splendiani, José Enriquiez Sánchez Bohorquez, and Emma Cecilia Luque de Salazar ([Santafé de Bogotá]: Centro Editorial Javeriano, Instituto Colombiano de Cultura Hispánica, 1997), 275–79.

27. Alonso de Sandoval, *Un tratado sobre la esclavitud*, ed. Enriqueta Vila Vilar (Madrid: Alianza, 1987).

28. Quoted in Roy Porter, *The Creation of the Modern World* (New York: Norton, 2000), 108.

29. Inq. 5349, n. 4, "Relación de Causa, 1710–15." See the fuller analysis of this case in Schwartz, *All Can Be Saved*, 227–30.

30. The historian Francisco Bethencourt notes that the three Portuguese tribunals tried 7,024 cases between 1675 and 1750 or about 100 a year; but between 1751 and 1767 it heard only 743 cases for an average per year of half the previous level. See the chapter "A Inquisição" in Francisco Bethencourt, *História religiosa de Portugal*, 3 vols. (Lisbon: Circulo dos Leitores, 1998–2000), 2:95–131.

31. Richard Heer, *The Eighteenth-Century Revolution in Spain* (Princeton, NJ: Princeton Univ. Press, 1958), 408.

32. Francisco Bethencourt, *História das Inquisições* (Lisbon: Circulo de Leitores, 1994), 341–59, provides a useful summary of the abolition of the tribunals.

33. *Manifesto da las variaciones de Europa, y de las vilezas y usurpaciones francezas* (Mexico City: Mariano Ontiveros, 1810), 6–8. There are numerous loyalist tracts like this one. See, for example, "Breve discurso sobre la tolerancia," III-C-29, fls. 4v.–10v, Real Biblioteca del Monasterio del Escorial, San Lorenzo de El Escorial, Spain.

34. See *Apologia de la intolerancia religiosa* (Caracas, Venezuela: Juan Baillio, 1811).

35. Javier Fernández Sebastián, "Toleration and Freedom of Expression in the Hispanic World between Enlightenment and Liberalism," *Past and Present* 211 (2011): 159–97.

36. José Pedro Paiva and Giuseppe Marcocci, *História da Inquisição Portuguesa, 1536–1821* (Lisbon: Esfera dos Livros, 2013).

37. Fernández Sebastián, "Toleration and Freedom," 159–63. Juan Pablo Domínguez questions this position in "Los progresos de la tolerancia." Domínguez also points out the deeply Christian tradition of advocacy for tolerance. See his essay

"Reformismo Cristiano y tolerancia en España a finales del siglo xviii," *Hispania Sacra* 65, extra no. 2 (2013): 113–72.

38. Aside from Kaplan, *Divided by Faith*, other good examples of this tendency are Keith Luria, *Sacred Boundaries: Religious Coexistence and Conflict in Early-Modern France* (Washington, DC: Catholic Univ. of America Press, 2005); Alexandra Walsham, *Charitable Hatred: Tolerance and Intolerance in England, 1500–1700* (Manchester, UK: Manchester Univ. Press, 2006); and Thomas M. Saffey, ed., *A Companion to Multiconfessionalism in the Early Modern World* (Leiden: Brill, 2011).

39. It is sometimes argued that expressions of toleration were usually self-interested and practical but that expressions of orthodox intolerance were always based on religious conviction and belief. Orthodox intolerance, however, also brought advantages or benefits to individuals or social groups who were able to use their "orthodoxy" to justify the advantages that intolerance brought them. In Lima in the 1630s during a great Inquisition campaign, for example, all of the Old Christian merchants were members of the merchant guild (*consulado*), and their principal competitors who were not in the guild were denounced as "New Christian" and therefore suspected of backsliding to Judaism. See Harry Cross, "Commerce and Orthodoxy: A Spanish Response to Portuguese Commercial Penetration in the Viceroyalty of Peru," *The Americas* 35, no. 2 (1978): 151–67.

40. See Olivier Christin, *La paix de religion: L'autonomisation de la raison politique au xvi siècle* (Paris: Seuil, 1997).

41. Lecler, *Histoire de la tolerance au siècle de la Réforme*.

42. Kaplan, *Divided by Faith*, 354–58. On this point, see also Joachim Whaley, *Religious Toleration and Social Change in Hamburg, 1529–1819* (Cambridge: Cambridge Univ. Press, 1985); Chris Benecke, *Beyond Toleration: The Religious Origins of American Pluralism* (Oxford: Oxford Univ. Press, 2006); Evan Haefeli, *New Netherland and the Dutch Origins of Religious Liberty* (Philadelphia: Univ. of Pennsylvania Press, 2012); and Luria, *Sacred Boundaries*.

8. "US out of El Salvador!"

1. "Joint Statement by Sr. Melinda Roper and Fr. James Noonan," Feb. 1981, Maryknoll and Church: Immediate Responses, El Salvador Martyrs, Maryknoll Sisters Archives (MSA), Maryknoll Mission Archives, Maryknoll, NY.

2. Christine J. Wade, "El Salvador: Contradictions of Neoliberalism and Building Sustainable Peace," *International Journal of Peace Studies* 13, no. 2 (2008): 15–16.

3. Margaret Keck and Kathryn Sikkink, *Activists beyond Borders: Advocacy Networks in International Politics* (Ithaca, NY: Cornell Univ. Press, 1998), 13.

4. Constitution of the Foreign Mission Sisters of St. Dominic, 1931, chap. 1, no. 2, MSA.

5. On these developments more generally, see Helen Rose Ebaugh, "Vatican II and the Revitalization Movement," in *Religion and the Social Order: Vatican II and U.S. Catholicism*, ed. Helen Rose Ebaugh (Greenwich, CT: JAI Press, 1991), 3–19.

6. Penny Lernoux, *Hearts on Fire: The Story of the Maryknoll Sisters* (Maryknoll, NY: Orbis, 1993), 166–73. In 1965, when membership reached its height, Maryknoll counted 1,661 sisters; in 1979, around 900 belonged to the order ("Personnel, 1932–1994," Reports, Internal, MSA).

7. The timeline of events presented in the text uses Judy Noone, *The Same Fate as the Poor*, rev. ed. (Maryknoll, NY: Orbis Books, 1995), for general background.

8. Father Paul Schindler, interviewed in Gail Pellett, dir., *Justice and the Generals* (Brooklyn, NY: First Run/Icarus Films, 2002), VHS.

9. For an overview of liberation theology themes, see Alfred T. Hennelly, introduction to *Liberation Theology: A Documentary History*, ed. Alfred T. Hennelly (Maryknoll, NY: Orbis Books, 1990), xv–xxi.

10. Quoted in Loren Jenkins, "Maryknollers Reconsider Role in El Salvador after Action by Priest," *Washington Post*, May 14, 1981, A15.

11. Quoted in Noone, *Same Fate as the Poor*, 82.

12. Lawyers Committee for International Human Rights, *Justice in El Salvador: A Case Study* (New York: Lawyers Committee for International Human Rights, 1982), 21–23, in Bureau File 163-49105, Undefined FBI File on the American Churchwomen Killed in El Salvador, December 1980, sec. 10, Federal Bureau of Investigation Library, Library of Congress, Washington, DC, accessed through Gale World Scholar: Latin America and the Caribbean (hereafter FBI–Churchwomen).

13. Quoted in Amembassy [*sic*] San Salvador, "Threats against U.S. Citizen Nuns Working in Chalatenango," Dec. 11, 1980, US Department of State El Salvador Declassification Project, at http://foia.state.gov/Search/Collections.aspx (click on project title).

14. Margarito Perez Nieto, statement, Dec. 22, 1981, in sec. 7, FBI–Churchwomen.

15. Larry Rohter, "4 Salvadorans Say They Killed U.S. Nuns on Orders of Military," *New York Times*, Apr. 3, 1998, at http://www.nytimes.com/1998/04/03/world/4-salvadorans-say-they-killed-us-nuns-on-orders-of-military.html; Robert Varenik interviewed in Pellett, *Justice and the Generals*.

16. "Bodies of 4 American Women Are Found in El Salvador," *New York Times*, Dec. 5, 1980, A3.

17. Harold Tyler, "The Churchwomen Murders: A Report to the Secretary of State," Dec. 2, 1983, 21–47, in sec. 10, FBI–Churchwomen.

18. "Joint Statement by Sr. Melinda Roper and Fr. James Noonan," Feb. 1981.

19. Svenja Blanke, "Civic Foreign Policy: Human Rights, Faith-Based Groups, and U.S.–Salvadoran Relations in the 1970s," *The Americas* 61, no. 2 (2004):

241–43; Roger Peace, *A Call to Conscience: The Anti–Contra War Campaign* (Amherst: Univ. of Massachusetts Press, 2012), 60–61.

20. Office of Social Concerns to Sisters, Oct. 1981, Office of Social Concerns: Correspondence and Reports, MSA. See also Timothy Byrnes, *Reverse Mission: Transnational Religious Communities and the Making of U.S. Foreign Policy* (Washington, DC: Georgetown Univ. Press, 2011), 90–92; Sharon Erickson Nepstad, *Convictions of the Soul: Religion, Culture, and Agency in the Central America Solidarity Movement* (New York: Oxford Univ. Press, 2004), 100–103.

21. Susan Fitzpatrick Behrens assesses the symbolic resonance of these events in "From Symbols of the Sacred to Symbols of Subversion to Simply Obscure: Maryknoll Women Religious in Guatemala, 1953–1967," *The Americas* 61, no. 2 (2004): 205–16.

22. Erickson Nepstad, *Convictions of the Soul*, 105.

23. Dana Robert, "The Influence of American Missionary Women on the World Back Home," *Religion and American Culture* 12, no. 1 (2002): 66.

24. Colman McCarthy, "The Maryknoll Order," *Washington Post*, Apr. 19, 1981, G1; Marjorie Hyer, "Four Murders Trigger US Catholic Protests," *Washington Post*, Dec. 10, 1980, A38.

25. William LeoGrande, *Our Own Backyard: The United States in Central America, 1977–1992* (Chapel Hill: Univ. of North Carolina Press, 1998), 9.

26. Quoted in "Reagan-Appointed Democrat Speaks Her Mind on World, Domestic Politics," *Tampa Tribune*, Dec. 25, 1980, A23.

27. Anthony Lewis, "Abroad at Home; Showing His Colors," *New York Times*, Mar. 29, 1981, E21.

28. Edward Walsh, "Reagan Gets First Public Opinion Backlash—on Salvador Policy," *Washington Post*, Mar. 27, 1981, A9.

29. Peace, *A Call to Conscience*, 53–80; Van Gosse, "'El Salvador Is Spanish for Vietnam': The Politics of Solidarity and the New Immigrant Left, 1955–1993," in *The Immigrant Left in the United States*, ed. Paul Buhle and Dan Georgakas (Albany: State Univ. of New York Press, 1996), figures taken from 318, 327.

30. Mike Sager, "25,000 Demonstrators March on the Pentagon," *Washington Post*, May 4, 1981, C1.

31. Margot Hornblower, "Rumbles of War Give Hill the Jitters," *Washington Post*, Mar. 8, 1982, A1.

32. Philip Taubman, "The Speaker and His Sources on Latin America," *New York Times*, Sept. 12, 1984, B10.

33. Bob Woodward, *Veil: The Secret Wars of the CIA, 1981–1987* (New York: Simon and Schuster, 1987), 225. Representative David Bonior, Michigan Democrat and leader in the fight against Contra aid, similarly attributed his "interest in Central

America" to his early education from "nuns interested in Haiti and Nicaragua" (quoted in Peace, *A Call to Conscience*, 93).

34. "Testimony of Melinda Roper before the Foreign Relations Committee of the US Senate," Apr. 9, 1981, El Salvador: Martyrs, Responses US–El Salvador Policy, MSA.

35. Bill Peterson, "Reagan Plea Rejected, Senate Votes Terms for Salvadoran Aid," *Washington Post*, Sept. 25, 1981, A5. Other cases affecting US citizens were bundled into certification reports, the most prominent of which was the assassination of two civilian labor advisers in the lobby of the San Salvador Sheraton Hotel.

36. United Nations Commission on the Truth for El Salvador, *From Madness to Hope: The 12-Year War in El Salvador* (New York: United Nations, 1993), 31–33.

37. Helene O'Sullivan, telephone interview by the author, Feb. 12, 2014. See also William Chapman, "Plea to Restore Aid to Salvador Does Not Persuade Congress," *Washington Post*, June 12, 1982, A6; Margot Hornblower, "Panel Votes Most of El Salvador Aid," *Washington Post*, May 12, 1983, A1; and "House Votes to Extend Curbs on Military Aid to Salvador," *Washington Post*, Oct. 1, 1983, A19. At some points, Congress proved less of an obstruction to the White House, but, notably, House Democrats successfully overturned a Reagan pocket veto of certification requirements. See Ronald Kessler, "Pocket Veto by Reagan Overturned," *Washington Post*, Aug. 30, 1984, A1.

38. LeoGrande, *Our Own Backyard*, 281–82.

39. David Duell Passage, testimony, in "Carlos Eugenio Vides Casanova Removal Proceedings," US Department of Justice, Executive Office for Immigration Review, Dec. 17, 2012, at 71, Center for Justice and Accountability, at http://cja.org/downloads/Vides%20Casanova%20Removal%20Proceedings.pdf; Diana Villiers Negroponte, *Seeking Peace in El Salvador: The Struggle to Reconstruct a Nation at the End of the Cold War* (New York: Palgrave Macmillan, 2011), 26.

40. "5 Salvadorans Are Found Guilty in Slaying of U.S. Churchwomen," *New York Times*, May 25, 1984, A1.

41. United Nations Commission on the Truth for El Salvador, *From Madness to Hope*, 65. The men lost an appeal of their case under postwar political amnesty statutes because the killings were ruled to be nonpolitical and thus not protected by reconciliation measures. Three of the men, including Colindres Aleman, have since been paroled for good behavior.

42. See Theresa Keeley, "Reagan's Real Catholics vs. Tip O'Neill's Maryknoll Nuns: Gender, Intra-Catholic Conflict, and the Contras," *Diplomatic History* 40, no. 3 (2016): 530–58.

43. United Nations Commission on the Truth for El Salvador, *From Madness to Hope*, 45–54, 114–21.

44. Quoted in Robert McCartney, "5 Salvadorans Get 30 Years for Killing Missionaries," *Washington Post*, June 20, 1984, A1.

45. Quoted in David Gonzalez, "Trial of Salvadoran Generals in Nuns' Deaths Hears Echoes of 1980," *New York Times*, Oct. 21, 2000, A8.

46. O'Sullivan telephone interview.

47. William Ford, interviewed in Pellett, *Justice and the Generals*; Scott Greathead and Michael Posner, "Bill Ford, Remembered," *The Nation*, June 18, 2008, at https://www.thenation.com/article/bill-ford-remembered; Dennis Hevesi, "William P. Ford," *New York Times*, June 3, 2008, B8.

48. Robert Drinan and Teresa Kuo, "Putting the World's Oppressors on Trial: The Torture Victim Protection Act," *Human Rights Quarterly* 15, no. 3 (1993): 624. According to the Center for Justice and Accountability, the plaintiffs donated to charity most of what they received, which included $300,000 of Vides Casanova's personal assets—a fraction of the damages awarded. See Center for Justice and Accountability, "Human Rights Crimes under Salvadoran Ministers: *Romagoza Arce et al. v. Garcia and Vides Casanova*, Alien Tort Statute/Torture Victims Protection Act of 1991," n.d., at http://cja.org/what-we-do/litigation/romagoza-arce-v-garcia-and-vides-casanova/uscourt-ats-tvpa/.

49. Julia Preston, "Salvadoran General Accused in Killings Should Be Deported, Miami Judge Says," *New York Times*, Apr. 11, 2014, A13. See also Lalita Clozel, "Salvadoran Cites U.S. Backing of Violence in Deportation Appeal," *Los Angeles Times*, Feb. 6, 2014, at http://articles.latimes.com/2014/feb/06/nation/la-na-elsalvador-deport-20140207.

50. "Carlos Eugenio Vides Casanova Removal Proceedings," at 115, 81, 149–50.

51. Alfonso Chardy, "Deported Former Salvadoran Defense Minister Plans to Appeal His Removal," *Miami Herald*, Jan. 15, 2016, at http://www.miamiherald.com/news/local/crime/article54957610.html.

9. Human Rights City Initiatives as a People's Peace Process

1. Dia Da Costa and Philip McMichael, "The Poverty of the Global Order," *Globalizations* 4, no. 4 (2007): 588–602.

2. Immanuel Wallerstein, *World-Systems Analysis: An Introduction* (Durham, NC: Duke Univ. Press, 2004).

3. See Peter Uvin, "The Development/Peacebuilding Nexus: A Typology and History of Changing Paradigms," *Journal of Peacebuilding and Development* 1 (2002): 2–24; Roland Paris, "Peacekeeping and the Constraints of Global Culture," *European Journal of International Relations* 9 (2003): 441–73; and Isaac Kamola, "The Global Coffee Economy and the Production of Genocide in Rwanda," *Third World Quarterly* 28 (2007): 571–92.

4. See, for example, Saskia Sassen, *Globalization and Its Discontents* (New York: New Press, 1998); David Harvey, *Social Justice and the City* (Athens: Univ. of Georgia Press, 2009), and "The Right to the City," *International Journal of Urban and Regional Research* 27 (2003): 939–41; and Jackie Smith, "Globalization and Strategic Peacebuilding," in *Strategies of Peace: Transforming Conflict in a Violent World*, ed. Daniel Philpott and Gerard F. Powers (New York: Oxford Univ. Press, 2010), 247–70.

5. Thania Paffenholz and Christoph Spurk, "A Comprehensive Analytical Framework," in *Civil Society and Peacebuilding: A Critical Assessment*, ed. Thania Paffenholz (Boulder, CO: Lynne Rienner, 2010), 65–76, and *Civil Society, Civic Engagement, and Peacebuilding*, Social Development Papers: Conflict Prevention and Reconstruction (Washington, DC: World Bank, 2006); Thania Paffenholz, "Civil Society and Peacebuilding," in *Civil Society and Peacebuilding*, ed. Paffenholz, 43–64.

6. See, for example, Sabine Lang, *NGOs, Civil Society, and the Public Sphere* (New York: Cambridge Univ. Press, 2013).

7. Jackie Smith, Rebecca Burns, and Rachel Miller, "The World Social Forums as Transformative Peacebuilding," in *Globalization, Social Movements, and Peacebuilding*, ed. Jackie Smith and Ernesto Verdeja (Syracuse, NY: Syracuse Univ. Press, 2013), 207–34, esp. 207.

8. Jackie Smith and Ernesto Verdeja, introduction to *Globalization, Social Movements, and Peacebuilding*, ed. Smith and Verdeja, 12.

9. Stephen P. Marks, Kathleen A. Modrowski, and Walther Lichem, *Human Rights Cities: Civic Engagement for Societal Development* (New York: People's Movement for Human Rights Learning and United Nations Habitat, 2008), at http://www.pdhre.org/Human_Rights_Cities_Book.pdf.

10. Marks, Modrowski, and Lichem, *Human Rights Cities*.

11. See Jackie Smith, Marina Karides, Marc Becker, Dorval Brunelle, Christopher Chase-Dunn, Donatella della Porta, Rosalba Icaza Garza, et al., *Global Democracy and the World Social Forums*, 2nd ed. (Boulder, CO: Paradigm, 2014).

12. Washington, DC, became the first US Human Rights City in 2008, followed by Eugene, Oregon; Chapel Hill, North Carolina; Boston; Seattle; Pittsburgh; and most recently Jackson, Mississippi.

13. Marks, Modrowski, and Lichem, *Human Rights Cities*, 18.

14. Marks, Modrowski, and Lichem, *Human Rights Cities*, 146–47.

15. The American Friends Service Committee has been instrumental in other human rights cities as well, including Washington, DC.

16. My research on the US and World Social Forum process has informed this perspective because these spaces are organized around a similar intentionality. The forces that have shaped the Social Forums include groups that have been involved in articulating new practices for building just and equitable multiracial and multiclass

alliances. For instance, on the Pittsburgh Human Rights City Alliance's website (www.pghrights.org), we refer to the "Jemez Principles for Democratic Organizing" (1996), at https://www.ejnet.org/ej/jemez.pdf, as a guide to our work. And those helping to guide our initiative drew from the wealth of resources of the US Human Rights Network (https://www.ushrnetwork.org/), which works for a "people-centered human rights movement" that focuses on those most directly affected by human rights violations.

17. Harvey, "The Right to the City," 940–41.

18. Pittsburgh has among the highest rates of poverty among blacks, infant mortality, and unemployment in the country. The political marginalization of African Americans, moreover, has led to their significant displacement through ongoing processes of gentrification. See Center on Race and Social Problems, *Pittsburgh's Racial Demographics 2015: Differences and Disparities* (Pittsburgh, PA: Univ. of Pittsburgh School of Social Work, 2015), at http://www.crsp.pitt.edu/sites/default /files/Final%20version%20for%20publishing.pdf.

19. Joe [*sic*], "Washington, DC: A Human Rights City," *The Disorder of Things*, Aug. 25, 2013, at http://thedisorderofthings.com/2013/08/25/washington-dc-a-human -rights-city/.

20. Sacajawea Hall, "Reflections on the People's Summit on Climate Change and Our Climate Justice Movement," *Grassroots Global Justice Alliance Blog*, Jan. 15, 2015, at http://ggjalliance.org/ggj-blog, emphasis added.

21. See, for example, Nina Eliasoph, *Making Volunteers: Civic Life after Welfare's End* (Princeton, NJ: Princeton Univ. Press, 2011).

22. Sally Engle Merry, "Transnational Human Rights and Local Activism: Mapping the Middle," *American Anthropologist* 108 (2006): 42.

23. Amy C. Finnegan, Adam P. Saltsman, and Shelley K. White, "Negotiating Politics and Culture: The Utility of Human Rights for Activist Organizing in the United States," *Journal of Human Rights Practice* 2 (2010): 307–33.

24. Finnegan, Saltsman, and White, "Negotiating Politics and Culture."

25. American exceptionalism also promotes the myth that the United States is a model or beacon of human rights, and so allowing for critical reflection on the reality of human rights in this country disrupts the myth of US superiority, which is used to help justify US policies that undermine peace around the world.

26. The US Human Rights Network helps compile a "shadow report" (at http:// www.ushrnetwork.org/icerd-project, accessed Dec. 4, 2017) to bring together evidence from communities around the United States to compare with the official US report made under the Committee on the Elimination of Racial Discrimination review process.

27. Cities for CEDAW, n.d., at http://citiesforcedaw.org, accessed Dec. 4, 2017.

28. The report, "Pittsburgh's Human Rights City Alliance Hosts Event to Recognize Mother Earth Day," n.d., can be downloaded at http://wiki.pghrights.may first.org/index.php?title=File:Report_on_Mother_Earth_Day_2014.pdf.

29. "Pittsburgh Human Rights City Alliance Workshop at the 2015 Summit against Racism," n.d., at http://wiki.pghrights.mayfirst.org/index.php?title=File: Summit_Against_Racism_2015_REPORT_and_Agenda_Priorities.pdf, accessed Feb. 11, 2019; *Human Rights City Alliance Annual Report 2016* (2016), at http://wiki.pgh rights.mayfirst.org/index.php?title=File:Annual_Report_2016.pdf.

30. "Pittsburgh Human Rights City Alliance Human Rights Days of Action 2014," n.d., at http://wiki.pghrights.mayfirst.org/index.php?title=File:Action _Calendar_One_Pager.pdf, accessed Feb. 11, 2019.

31. "Police Reform," n.d., at http://wiki.pghrights.mayfirst.org/index.php?title =Police_Reform, accessed Feb. 11, 2019.

32. "How to Get Involved," n.d., at http://wiki.pghrights.mayfirst.org/index .php?title=How_to_get_involved, accessed Feb. 11, 2019.

33. "Human Rights City Action Plan," Dec. 10, 2014, at http://wiki.pghrights .mayfirst.org/index.php?title=Human_Rights_City_Action_Plan.

34. Human Rights City Alliance, "Making the Global Local: Human Rights Cities—Conference Summary Report," 2015, at http://wiki.pghrights.mayfirst.org /index.php?title=File:Conference_summary_-General_Version_3_2.pdf.

35. "Indigenous Peoples' Day," n.d., at https://en.wikipedia.org/wiki/Indigenous _Peoples%27_Day, accessed Dec. 4, 2017.

36. City of Pittsburgh, Council of the City of Pittsburgh, "Indigenous Peoples' Day: Will of the Council," 2014, at http://wiki.pghrights.mayfirst.org/index .php?title=File:Indigenous_Peoples_Day_Will_of_the_Council.pdf, accessed Feb. 11, 2019.

37. Lang, *NGOs, Civil Society, and the Public Sphere*, 209.

38. Mary Kaldor, *Global Civil Society: An Answer to War* (Cambridge: Polity, 2003), 96. See also Gillian MacNaughton and Mariah McGill, "Economic and Social Rights in the United States: Implementation without Ratification," *Northeastern University Law Journal* 4 (2012): 365–406, and Thomas Risse, Stephen C. Ropp, and Kathryn Sikkink, *The Power of Human Rights: International Norms and Domestic Change* (New York: Cambridge Univ. Press, 1999).

10. Is Ferguson the Same as Gaza?

1. For example, see Peter Beinart, "The Failure of the American Jewish Establishment," *New York Review of Books*, June 10, 2010, at http://www.nybooks.com /articles/archives/2010/jun/10/failure-american-jewish-establishment/; Steve Lipman, "U.S. Jews and Israel: On 'Different Paths,'" *Jewish Week*, Jan. 26, 2017, at http://

jewishweek.timesofisrael.com/u-s-jews-and-israel-on-different-paths/; Dov Wax-man, *Troubles in the Tribe: The American Jewish Conflict over Israel* (Princeton, NJ: Princeton Univ. Press, 2016); Michael N. Barnett, *The Star and the Stripes: A History of the Foreign Policies of American Jews* (Princeton, NJ: Princeton Univ. Press, 2016); Eric H. Yoffie, "AIPAC Is Feeling the Heat to Address Israel's 'Ayatollah' Judaism," *Haaretz*, July 13, 2017, at http://www.haaretz.com/opinion/.premium-1.801211; and Jewish Telegraphic Agency, "The More Americans Learn about Is-rael, the Less They Like It, Study Suggests," *Haaretz*, Jan. 7, 2017, at http://www.haaretz.com/us-news/1.798794.

2. Pew Research Center, Polling and Analysis, "A Portrait of Jewish Ameri-cans," Oct. 1, 2013, at http://www.pewforum.org/2013/10/01/jewish-american-beliefs-attitudes-culture-survey/.

3. Cecilie Surasky, at the time deputy director of JVP, provided the following information in a personal email correspondence from June 15, 2015: "In 2003 we had 2,000 online supporters. Today we have 200,000 . . . [and] over 9,000 donors. Our Facebook grew from 40,000 [followers] right before last year's attack on Gaza, to about 210,000 followers." By the time of the National Members Meeting of 2017, JVP reported 200,000 online supporters, more than sixty chapters, a youth wing, a Rabbinic Council, an Artist Council, an Academic Advisory Council, and an Advisory Board consisting of leading US intellectual and artists (see the membership numbers at the Jewish Voice for Peace website at https://jewishvoiceforpeace.org/membership/).

4. The site of LGBTQI activism often becomes a conflict zone where appar-ent progressivism of institutionalized Judaism on that front functions to pinkwash the occupation and thus turns into an activist conflict zone. See, for example, Judy Maltz, "Over 100 U.S. Rabbis Urge Hillel: Readmit LGBTQ Group Ousted for Teaming Up with Pro-Boycott Org," *Haaretz*, June 23, 2017, at http://www.haaretz.com/us-news/.premium-1.797457; Alissa Wise, "JVP: Reactions to Our Parade Protest Were 'Cruel,' 'Homophobic,' and 'Hyperbolic,'" *Forward*, June 7, 2017, at http://forward.com/scribe/374055/jvp-reactions-to-our-parade-protest-were-cruel-homophobic-and-hyperbolic/. See also note 44.

5. Jodi Melamed, "Non-violent Direct Action Can Be Our Big Tent," *Jew-school*, June 1, 2017, at https://jewschool.com/2017/06/79709/non-violent-direct-action-can-big-tent/.

6. See, for example, Erez Bleicher, "Why I Was Detained in Hebron Last Sum-mer and Why You Should Join Me This May," *TruthOut*, Nov. 23, 2016, at http://www.truth-out.org/speakout/item/38502-why-i-was-detained-in-hebron-last-summer-and-why-you-should-join-me-this-may.

7. Sami Awad, "Beyond Protesting Occupation, 'Sumud' Is Protecting Life," *+972*, July 6, 2017, at https://972mag.com/beyond-protesting-occupation-sumud-is

-protecting-life/128554/; Sophie Schor, "40 Days and 40 Nights: Building a New Reality in Sumud Freedom Camp," +972, July 3, 2017, at https://972mag.com/40 -days-and-40-nights-building-a-new-reality-in-sumud-freedom-camp/128500/.

8. See the *All That's Left Blog*, at https://allthatsleftcollective.com/.

9. I follow Yehuda Bauer in using the spelling "antisemitism" rather than "anti-Semitism" to denote that the latter form reflects the pseudoscientific use of the term to authorize racial hierarchies; see Yehuda Bauer, "A Note about the Spelling of 'Antisemitism,'" in *On Antisemitism: Solidarity and the Struggle for Justice*, ed. Jewish Voice for Peace (Chicago: Haymarket Books, 2017), xv.

10. The weekend following the violence in Charlottesville, Virginia, that resulted in the death of one antiracism protester, INN's speeches in a demonstration against white supremacy and antisemitism in Chicago underscored the need to reinforce an understanding of the intersectional nature of the struggle, wherein the fight against antisemitism is related to the struggles against racism in all its forms in the United States. See the video of the demonstration on Aug. 20, 2017, on INN's Facebook page at https://m.facebook.com/story.php?story_fbid=147140395627990 1&id=678900828863555.

11. For an important statement on antisemitism in the Left and the need to overcome it to deepen the Left's agenda, see April Rosenblum, *The Past Didn't Go Anywhere: Making Resistance to Antisemitism Part of All of Our Movements*, 2007, at https://engageonline.wordpress.com/2010/02/23/the-past-didnt-go-anywhere-making -resistance-to-antisemitism-part-of-all-of-our-movements/.

12. Colby Itkowitz, "'Every Person Deserves to Rest in Peace': American Muslims Raising Money to Repair Vandalized Jewish Cemetery," *Washington Post*, Feb. 21, 2017, at https://www.washingtonpost.com/news/inspired-life/wp/2017/02/21 /every-person-deserves-to-rest-in-peace-american-muslims-raising-money-to-repair -vandalized-jewish-cemetery/?utm_term=.8789d63833c1; Rachel Shabi, "Donald Trump Has Managed to Unite Muslims and Jews in a Way That Few Ever Managed to Do," *Independent* (UK), Feb. 14, 2017, at http://www.independent.co.uk/voices /donald-trump-muslims-jews-antisemitism-israel-palestine-neo-nazi-holocaust-unique -a7579861.html.

13. Asa Winstanley, "Watch: Registration Opens for World Social Forum Free Palestine in Brazil," *Electronic Intifada*, Oct. 10, 2012, at https://electronicintifada .net/blogs/asa-winstanley/watch-registration-opens-world-social-forum-free-palestine -brazil; BDS Movement Freedom Justice Equality, "Call for the World Social Forum Free Palestine, Nov. 2012 in Brazil," Jan. 19, 2012, at http://www.bdsmovement .net/2012/call-for-the-world-social-forum-free-palestine-nov-2012-in-brazil-8603.

14. See, for instance, the description of the annual conference of Students for Justice in Palestine in 2014: "Beyond Solidarity: Announcing the 2014 National SJP Conference at Tufts University," SJP National, posted Sept. 10, 2014, at http://

www.brooklynsjp.com/home/beyond-solidarity-announcing-the-2014-national
-sjp-conference-at-tufts-university.

15. Muriel Kane, "Report: Israeli Model Underlies Militarization of U.S. Police," *RawStory*, Dec. 4, 2011, at http://www.rawstory.com/rs/2011/12/report-israeli
-model-underlies-militarization-of-u-s-police/. See also Jewish Voice for Peace, "Deadly Exchange Campaign," n.d., at https://deadlyexchange.org/, accessed Mar. 27, 2018.

16. Max Blumenthal, "From Occupation to 'Occupy': The Israelification of American Domestic Security," *Modoweiss*, Dec. 2, 2012, at http://mondoweiss.net
/2011/12/from-occupation-to-occupy-the-israelification-of-american-domestic
-decurity.

17. See Movimiento Estudiantil Chican@ de Aztlan, "National M.E.Ch.A. Endorses Palestinian Boycott Call against Israel," Mar. 30, 2012, at https://bdsmove
ment.net/news/national-mecha-endorses-palestinian-boycott-call-against-israel. See also Adriana Maestas and Rania Khalek, "How Latino Activists Are Standing Up to the Israel Lobby," *Electronic Intifada*, Mar. 6, 2014, at https://electronicintifada
.net/content/how-latino-activists-are-standing-israel-lobby/13225.

18. See, for instance, coverage about Palestine-solidarity activists' direct action as a form of coresistance in "Operation Streamline," Oct. 11, 2013, at http://www
.latinorebels.com/2013/10/11/developing-story-immigration-activists-in-tucson
-block-deportation-buses/. See also Nora Barrows-Friedman, "Palestine Solidarity Activists Protest US Deportation Policies in Arizona," *Electronic Intifada*, Oct. 11, 2013, at https://electronicintifada.net/blogs/nora-barrows-friedman/palestine
-solidarity-activists-protest-us-deportation-policies-arizona.

19. Mitch Moxley, "Better Than a Wall: A New Detection System Can Help Monitor the U.S.–Mexico Border," *Popular Mechanics*, Jan. 28, 2016, at http://
www.popularmechanics.com/technology/security/a18622/border-control-integrated
-towers-system-invisible-wall/.

20. On these exchanges, see specifically the Jewish Voice for Peace hashtag #Deadly Exchange Campaign, launched in 2017 as a main area of focus, at https://
deadlyexchange.org/.

21. *The Economist*, "Binyamin Netanyahu Is Soft on Anti-semitism When It Suits Him," Aug. 24, 2017, at https://www.economist.com/news/middle-east-and-africa
/21726995-jewish-state-chooses-its-battles-carefully-binyamin-netanyahu-soft?fsrc
=FacebookInstant; see also Barak Ravid, "On Netanyahu's Orders: Israel's Foreign Ministry Retracts Criticism of Anti-semitism in Hungary and Slams George Soros," *Haaretz*, July 10, 2017, at http://www.haaretz.com/israel-news/1.800437.

22. See, for instance, Richard Spencer's speech "Facing the Future as a Minority," delivered at the American Renaissance Conference, Apr. 30, 2013, Nashville, TN, and Sam Kestenbaum, "The 'Alt-Right' Hates the Jews. But It Also Loves

Them—and Israel," *Forward*, Jan. 16, 2017, at http://forward.com/news/359889/the-alt-right-hates-the-jews-but-it-also-loves-them-and-israel/.

23. Judith Butler, keynote address at the Jewish Voice for Peace National Members Meeting 2017, Mar. 31–Apr. 2, Chicago.

24. Chandra Prescod-Weinstein, "Black and Palestinian Lives Matter: Black and Jewish America in the Twenty-First Century," in *On Antisemitism: Solidarity and the Struggle for Justice*, ed. Jewish Voice for Peace (Chicago: Haymarket Books, 2017), 33. See also the JOCSM blog at http://jocsm.org/unruly/.

25. One powerful articulation of this demand is in Leslie Williams, "White Jews: Deal with Your Privilege and Call Out Jewish Support for White Supremacy," speech given at the Stephen Douglas Monument on behalf of Resist, Reimagine, Rebuild, Aug. 19, 2017, Chicago, at https://crankylibrarian.wordpress.com/2017/08/19/white-jews-deal-with-your-privilege-and-call-out-jewish-support-for-white-supremacy/.

26. See Alissa Wise's explanation as to why the JVP decided to grapple with antisemitism despite the organization's main objective of Palestinian rights in "Building toward the New World," in *On Antisemitism*, ed. Jewish Voice for Peace, 207–12.

27. Helga Tawil-Souri, "Media, Globalization, and the (Un)Making of the Palestinian Cause," *Popular Communication* 13 (2015): 145–57; Atalia Omer, "Religion, Nationalism, and Solidarity Activism," in *The Oxford Handbook of Religion, Conflict, and Peacebuilding*, ed. Atalia Omer, R. Scott Appleby, and David Little (New York: Oxford Univ. Press, 2015), 613–58.

28. Omar Bargouti, *BDS: Boycott, Divestment, Sanctions: The Global Struggle for Palestinian Rights* (Chicago: Haymarket Books, 2011). See also Maia Carter Hallward, *Transnational Activism and the Israeli–Palestinian Conflict* (New York: Palgrave Macmillan, 2013).

29. Michelle Alexander, *The New Jim Crow: Mass Incarceration in the Age of Colorblindness* (New York: New Press, 2011).

30. Rana Baker, "Palestinians Express 'Solidarity with the People of Ferguson' in Mike Brown Statement," *Electronic Intifada*, Aug. 15, 2014, at https://electronicintifada.net/blogs/rana-baker/palestinians-express-solidarity-people-ferguson-mike-brown-statement.

31. Mark Molloy and agencies, "Palestinians Tweet Tear Gas Advice to Protesters in Ferguson," *Telegraph*, Aug. 15, 2014, at http://www.telegraph.co.uk/news/worldnews/northamerica/usa/11036190/Palestinians-tweet-tear-gas-advice-to-protesters-in-Ferguson.html.

32. Quoted in Annie Robbins, "'Protest in the Form of a Prayer': Dream Defenders Demonstration in Nazareth Makes Connections from Ferguson to Palestine," *Mondoweiss*, Jan. 15, 2015, at http://mondoweiss.net/2015/01/demonstration-connections-palestine.

33. Black for Palestine, "2015 Black Solidarity Statement with Palestine," 2015, at http://www.blackforpalestine.com/read-the-statement.html.

34. Quoted in Michaela Whitton, "Black Palestinian Alliance Emerges to Confront Global Violence and Racism," *Anti Media*, Oct. 15, 2015, at http://theantimedia .org/black-palestinian-alliance-emerges-to-confront-global-violence-and-racism/.

35. W. E. B. Du Bois, "The Negro and the Warsaw Ghetto," *Jewish Life*, May 1952, 14–15, reproduced in *The Oxford W. E. B. Du Bois Reader*, ed. Eric Sundquist (New York: Oxford Univ. Press, 1996), 469–73.

36. James Baldwin, "Negros Are Anti-semitic because They're Anti-white," *New York Times*, Apr. 9, 1967, at http://www.nytimes.com/books/98/03/29/specials /baldwin-antisem.html, and "On Being White . . . and Other Lies," *Essence*, Apr. 1984, 1–3, at https://ourcommonground.com/2016/11/14/on-being-white-and-other -lies-james-baldwin-essence-magazine-1984/.

37. See David Palumbu-Liu's interview with Cornel West, "'It's Ugly, It's Vicious, It's Brutal': Cornel West on Israel in Palestine—and Why Gaza Is 'the Hood on Steroids,'" *Salon*, Feb. 25, 2015, at http://www.salon.com/2015/02/25/its_ugly_it% E2%80%99s_vicious_it%E2%80%99s_brutal_cornel_west_on_israel_in_palestine _%E2%80%94_and_why_gaza_is_the_hood_on_steroids/.

38. See Angela Y. Davis, *Freedom Is a Constant Struggle: Ferguson, Palestine, and the Foundations of Movement*, ed. Frank Barat (Chicago: Haymarket Books, 2016), esp. 51–60.

39. Davis, *Freedom Is a Constant Struggle*, 48, 104.

40. Movement for Black Lives, "Invest–Divest," n.d., at https://policy.m4bl .org/invest-divest/.

41. See, for instance, Martin Shaw and Omer Bartov, "The Question of Genocide in Palestine, 1948: An Exchange between Martin Shaw and Omer Bartov," *Journal of Genocide Research* 12, nos. 3–4 (2010): 243–59.

42. Judith Butler, "Violence, Mourning, Politics," in *Precarious Life: The Powers of Mourning and Violence* (London: Verso, 2006), 20, 33.

43. See Hannah Weilbacher, "Public Jewish Communal Response to the Movement for Black Lives Platform," *Jewish Social Justice Roundtable*, Nov. 9, 2016, at http://jewishsocialjustice.org/blog/public-jewish-communal-response-movement -black-lives-platform.

44. See, for a foundational work, Jasbir Puar, *Terrorist Assemblages: Homonationalism in Queer Times* (2007; reprint, Durham, NC: Duke Univ. Press, 2017). See also Sarah Schulman, *Israel/Palestine and the Queer International* (Durham, NC: Duke Univ. Press, 2012); Gil Hochberg, "'Check Me Out': Queer Encounters in Sharif Waked's *Chick Point: Fashion for Israeli Checkpoints*," *GLQ: A Journal of Lesbian and Gay Studies* 16, no. 4 (2010): 577–98; Jasbir Puar, "Rethinking Homonationalism," *International Journal of Middle East Studies* 45, no. 2 (2013):

336–39, and "Citation and Censorship: The Politics of Talking about the Sexual Politics of Israel," *Feminist Legal Studies* 19, no. 2 (2011): 133–42; and Jasbir Puar and Maya Mikdashi, "Pinkwatching and Pinkwashing: Interpenetration and Its Discontents," *Jadaliyya*, Aug. 9, 2012, at http://www.velvetparkmedia.com/blogs/pinkwatching-and-pinkwashing-interpenetration-and-its-discontents.

45. For a methodical examination of these politicization processes, see Atalia Omer, *Days of Awe: Reimagining Jewishness in Solidarity with Palestinians* (Chicago: Univ. of Chicago Press, 2019).

46. Jewish Voice for Peace, "Stifling Debate: How Israel's Defenders Use False Charges of Anti-semitism to Limit the Debate over Israel on Campus," fall 2015, at https://jewishvoiceforpeace.org/wp-content/uploads/2015/09/JVP_Stifling_Dissent_Full_Report_Key_90745869.pdf.

47. See, in particular, the Defund Islamophobia Campaign launched by JVP-Chicago, described in Jewish Voice for Peace, "Defund Islamophobia: How the Jewish United Fund of Metropolitan Chicago Supports Anti-Muslim Hate Groups," Mar. 2017, at https://jewishvoiceforpeace.org/wp-content/uploads/2017/03/JUF-Defund-Islamophobia-Report-FINAL-3-22.pdf.

48. Jewish Voice for Peace, "Jewish Groups Stand in Opposition to Hate Speech and All Forms of Islamophobia," interfaith press release, Apr. 28, 2015, at https://jewishvoiceforpeace.org/jewish-groups-stand-in-opposition-to-hate-speech-and-all-forms-of-islamophobia/.

49. For an exposition of this frame, see Mahmood Mamdani, *Good Muslim, Bad Muslim: America, the Cold War, and Roots of Terror* (New York: Pantheon Books, 2004).

50. See Jewish Voice for Peace, *On Antisemitism*.

51. Eric K. Ward, "Skin in the Game: How Antisemitism Animates White Nationalism," *Political Research Associates*, June 29, 2017, at http://www.politicalresearch.org/2017/06/29/skin-in-the-game-how-antisemitism-animates-white-nationalism/#sthash.b3Woocy4.Lg2YquFS.dpbs; Ben Lorber, "Understanding Alt-Right Antisemitism," *Doikayt*, Mar. 24, 2017, at https://doikayt.com/2017/03/24/understanding-alt-right-antisemitism/.

52. Other churches deliberated or voted in favor of selective divestment, including the United Church of Christ (June 2015); the United Methodist Church rejected a vote (2012), as did the Evangelical Lutheran Church in America (2005).

53. For instance, Chris Leighton, "An Open Letter to the Presbyterian Church," Institute for Christian and Jewish Studies, Feb. 6, 2014, at https://icjs.org/articles/2014/open-letter-presbyterian-church.

54. "Another Jew Supporting Divestment: Reflections from the Presbyterian Divestment Vote," June 24, 2014, at http://sumogaza.tumblr.com/post/92874855655/another-jew-supporting-divestment-reflections.

55. "Another Jew Supporting Divestment."

56. "Another Jew Supporting Divestment."

57. The Mennonite Church USA resolution can be found at http://mennonite usa.org/wp-content/uploads/2017/01/IP-Resolution.pdf.

58. In email correspondence with me on Aug. 4, 2017 (at https://www.face book.com/fosnalive/videos/1698418443520241/), Jonathan Brenneman, a key staff person working on cultivating the passing of the resolution, highlighted that the main concerns regarding the failed resolution in 2015 were that it "appear[ed] one sided, non-reconciliatory, hypocritical, un-fair to Israel, and anti-Semitic." See also Mennonite Church USA, "Israel–Palestine Resolution: Summary of Delegate Comments," considered and tabled by delegates, July 1, 2015, at http://mennoniteusa .org/wp-content/uploads/2015/04/SummaryDelegateComments_IsraelPalestineRes olutions.pdf, and Mennonite Church USA, "'Jewish and Palestinian Voices for Peace Tour' Announced," Mar. 17, 2017, at http://mennoniteusa.org/news/jewish-palestinian -voices-peace-tour-announced/. The relation building and awareness raising also involved setting up a webinar titled "A Rabbi and a Pastor Walk through a Check-point," featuring Amy Yoder McGloughlin (a Mennonite pastor) and Rabbi Linda Holtzman (JVP) about "relating to Jewish neighbors while working for justice in Palestine." In addition, the coordinating committee launched a speaking tour high-lighting "Jewish and Palestinian voices for peace." The tour featured Jonathan Kut-tab, a Palestinian human rights lawyer closely affiliated with the Mennonites, in at least twenty locations, and each stop engaged local JVP representatives, who spoke about, among other things, how their own experiences of antisemitism led them to engage in justice work for Palestinians. Likewise, a video highlighted the perspec-tives of Mennonites of color about issues raised in the resolution. JVP representa-tives participated in the Mennonite convention. Anna Baltzer, an activist in the US Campaign for Palestinian Rights and a member of JVP, explained in a seminar set-ting her resentment of the suggestion that criticizing Israeli violation of human rights is antisemitic. In addition, Brant Rosen addressed the delegate body directly and thus wielded a strong influence on the final deliberation process.

59. Marc H. Ellis, "Exile and the Prophetic: The Interfaith Ecumenical Deal Is Dead," *Mondoweiss*, Nov. 12, 2012, at https://mondoweiss.net/2012/11/exile-and -the-prophetic-the-interfaith-ecumenical-deal-is-dead/.

60. Paul Lichterman, "Studying Public Religion: Beyond the Beliefs-Driven Actor," in *Religion on the Edge: De-centering and Re-centering the Sociology of Religion*, ed. Courtney Bender, Wendy Cadge, Peggy Levitt, and David Smilde (New York: Oxford Univ. Press, 2013), 115–36.

61. Jeffrey Stout, *Blessed Are the Organized: Grassroots Democracy in America* (Princeton, NJ: Princeton Univ. Press, 2010).

62. Henry Jenkins, *Textual Poachers: Television Fans and Participating Culture* (New York: Routledge Press, 1992), and *Convergence Culture: Where Old and New Media Collide* (New York: New York Univ. Press, 2006).

63. Jewish Voice for Peace, "JVP Guiding principles," n.d., at https://jewish voiceforpeace.org/.

64. Judith Butler also articulates this mode of relationality through a philosophical lens in *Parting Ways: Jewishness and the Critique of Zionism* (New York: Columbia Univ. Press, 2013).

65. Tzedek Chicago, "About," n.d., at http://tzedekchicago.org/about/, accessed Jan. 4, 2019.

66. Tzedek Chicago, "Welcome to Tzedek Chicago!" June 2015, at https:// tzedezchicago.files.wordpress.com/2015/06/member-welcome-kit-revised-10-04-15 -1.pdf.

67. See "In Support of Dyett Hunger Strikers: An Open Letter to Mayor Rahm Emanuel and the Chicago Board of Education from Members of the Chicago Jewish Community," Sept. 2015/Elul 5775, at https://docs.google.com/forms/d/1zJelsaoyM xwgmx9wYOCdmKxz6th4C9Unz_rBME9mPKg/viewform?c=0&w=1.

68. Tzedek Chicago, "About."

69. Quoted in Omer, *Days of Awe*, 171.

70. Jay Stanton, "What Will We Make Different This Year? A Guest Sermon for Erve Yom Kippur," *Shalom Rav: A Blog by Rabbi Brant Rosen*, Sept. 24, 2015, at http://rabbibrant.com/2015/09/24/what-will-we-make-different-this-year-a-guest -sermon-for-erev-yom-kippur-by-jay-stanton/.

71. Atalia Omer, *When Peace Is Not Enough: How the Israeli Peace Camp Thinks about Religion, Nationalism, and Justice* (Chicago: Univ. of Chicago Press, 2013).

72. Efrat Yerday spoke on a panel titled "Let's Talk about Zionism," JVP National Members Meeting, Apr. 1, 2017, Chicago.

73. Jewish Voice for Peace, "JVP's Approach to Zionism" n.d., https://jewish voiceforpeace.org/wp-content/uploads/2019/01/JVP%E2%80%99s-Approach-to -Zionism.pdf, accessed May 20, 2019.

74. Jakeet Singh, "Religious Agency and the Limits of Intersectionality," *Hypatia* 30, no. 4 (2015): 657–74.

75. See, for instance, Saba Mahmood, *Politics of Piety: The Islamic Revival and the Feminist Subject* (Princeton, NJ: Princeton Univ. Press, 2005); Rachel Rinaldo, "Pious and Critical: Muslim Women Activists and the Question of Agency," *Gender & Society* 28, no. 6 (2014): 824–46; Elizabeth Bucar, "Dianomy: Understanding Religious Women's Moral Agency as Creative Conformity," *Journal of the American Academy of Religion* 78, no. 3 (2010): 662–86.

76. See Nira Yuval-Davis, "Intersectionality and Feminist Politics," *European Journal of Women's Studies* 13, no. 3 (2006): 193–209, and Singh, "Religious Agency and the Limits of Intersectionality," 664.

77. Singh, "Religious Agency and the Limits of Intersectionality," 667.

78. See Chandra Talpade Mohanty, "Under Western Eyes: Feminist Scholarship and Colonial Discourse," in *Third World Women and the Politics of Feminism*, ed. Chandra Talpade Mohanty, Ann Russo, and Lourdes Torres (Bloomington: Univ. of Indiana Press, 1991), 51–80; Patricia Hill Collins and Sirma Bilge, *Intersectionality* (Cambridge: Polity, 2016); Kimberlé Crenshaw, "Mapping the Margins: Intersectionality, Identity Politics, and Violence against Women of Color," *Stanford Law Review* 43, no. 6 (1991): 1241–99; Elizabeth V. Spelman, *Inessential Woman: Problems of Exclusion in Feminist Thought* (Boston: Beacon Press, 1988).

79. Singh, "Religious Agency and the Limits of Intersectionality," 668.

11. Peacemaking at the Intersection of the Local and Global in Bali

1. For example, see Alexander Laban Hinton, ed., *Transitional Justice: Global Mechanisms and Local Realities after Genocide* (New Brunswick, NJ: Rutgers Univ. Press, 2010), and Rosalind Shaw and Lars Waldorf, with Pierre Hazan, *Localizing Transitional Justice: Interventions and Priorities after Mass Violence* (Stanford, CA: Stanford Univ. Press, 2010).

2. Erin Baines, "Spirits and Social Reconstruction after Mass Violence: Rethinking Transitional Justice," *African Affairs* 109, no. 436 (2010): 409–39; Lia Kent, "Local Memory Practices in East Timor: Disrupting Transitional Justice Narratives," *International Journal of Transitional Justice* 5, no. 3 (2011): 434–55.

3. Roger MacGinty and Pamina Firchow, "Top-Down and Bottom-Up Narratives of Peace and Conflict," *Politics* 36 (2016): 223–35.

4. Lauren Leve, "Cruel Optimism, Christianity, and the Post-conflict Optic," *Fieldsights—Hot Spots, Cultural Anthropology Online*, Mar. 24, 2014, at http://www.culanth.org/fieldsights/509-cruel-optimismchristianity-and-the-post-conflict-optic.

5. Severine Autesserre, *The Trouble with the Congo: Local Violence and the Failure of International Peacebuilding* (New York: Cambridge Univ. Press, 2010); Oliver Richmond, *A Post-liberal Peace* (New York: Routledge, 2011).

6. Leslie Dwyer, "A Politics of Silences: Violence, Memory, and Treacherous Speech in Post-1965 Bali," in *Genocide, Truth, Memory, and Representation: Anthropological Approaches*, ed. Alexander Laban Hinton and Kevin Lewis O'Neill (Durham, NC: Duke Univ. Press, 2009), 113–46.

7. Rangga Prakoso, Ezra Sihite, Bayu Marhaenjati, and Firdha Novialita, "AGO Rejects Komnas HAM Report on 1965 Massacres," *Jakarta Globe*, Nov. 10, 2012, at http://thejakartaglobe.beritasatu.com/archive/ago-rejects-komnas-ham-report-on-1965-massacres/.

8. Quoted in Jess Melvin, "LSF Moves to Silence *Senyap*," *Jakarta Post*, Jan. 10, 2015, at http://www.thejakartapost.com/news/2015/01/10/lsf-moves-silence -senyap.html.

9. See Ehito Kimura, "The Problem of Transitional Justice in Post-Suharto Indonesia," Middle East Institute, Jan. 17, 2014, at http://www.mei.edu/content /problem-transitional-justice-post-suharto-indonesia; Edward Aspinall and Fajran Zain, "Transitional Justice Delayed in Aceh, Indonesia," in *Transitional Justice in the Asia-Pacific*, ed. Renee Jeffery and Hun Joon Kim (New York: Cambridge Univ. Press, 2013), 87–124; and International Center for Transitional Justice (ICTJ) and Kontras (Commission for the Disappeared and Victims of Violence), *Derailed: Transitional Justice in Indonesia since the Fall of Soeharto* (New York: ICTJ, 2011), at http://www.ictj.org/sites/default/files/ICTJ-Kontras-Indonesia-Derailed-Summary -2011-English.pdf.

10. See Leslie Dwyer, "Building a Monument: Intimate Politics of 'Reconciliation' in Post-1965 Bali," in *Transitional Justice*, ed. Hinton, 227–48.

11. Gde Putra, "Time Bomb in Bali," *Inside Indonesia*, July–Sept. 2012, at http://www.insideindonesia.org/time-bomb-in-bali.

12. For an example of work from this project, see *"The Prison Songs*—Trailer," n.d., at https://www.youtube.com/watch?v=l2BkA8bMgyE, accessed June 18, 2019, and *"Si Buyung—The Prison Songs,"* n.d., at https://www.youtube.com/watch?v =axKWsh25GQU, accessed June 18, 2019.

13. See Degung Santikarma, "Monument, Document, and Mass Grave," in *Beginning to Remember: Historical Memory in Indonesia*, ed. Mary Zurbuchen (Seattle: Univ. of Washington Press, 2005), 312–23.

14. Johan Galtung, "An Editorial," *Journal of Peace Research* 1, no. 1 (1964): 1–4.

15. For more information, see Luh De Suriyani, "Greater Effort Needed to Oppose Benoa Bay Reclamation," *Jakarta Post*, Aug. 9, 2014, at http://www.thejakarta post.com/news/2014/08/09/greater-effort-needed-oppose-benoa-bay-reclamation .html, and Eve Tedja, "Save Bali from Drowning—We Reject the Reclamation of Benoa Bay," For Bali, Aug. 13, 2014, at http://www.forbali.org/save-bali-from -drowning-we-reject-the-reclamation-of-benoa-bay/?lang=en.

12. People's Peace at Stake

1. For further reading on *xanmiholi*, see Yasmin Saikia and Amit Baishya, eds., *Northeast India: A Place of Relations* (Cambridge: Cambridge Univ. Press, 2017).

2. In an editorial in the newspaper *Axamiya*, the Hindu–Muslim relationship in Assam is described as the relationship between siblings: *bhai-kokoi*. Cited in Uddipana Goswami, "Miyā or Axamiyā: The Politics of Assimilation in Assam," *Journal of Social and Policy Research* 1 (2010): 1–36.

3. K. Sreedhar Rao, *Wither Governance: Reflections of an Assam Civilian* (Delhi: South Asia Foundation, 2002), 98.

4. For more on this "we" community that became Assamese in British Assam, see Yasmin Saikia, *In the Meadows of Gold: Telling Tales of the Swargadeos at the Crossroads of Assam* (Delhi: Spectrum, 1997), and *Fragmented Memories: Struggling to Be Tai-Ahom in India* (Durham, NC: Duke Univ. Press, 2005).

5. Government of Assam, *Census Report and White Paper* (Guwahati: Government of Assam, 2012).

6. For further reading on this transformation, see Saikia, *Fragmented Memories*.

7. Other recurring descriptives are *freebooters*, *plunderers*, *treacherous tribe*, and *warlike frontier tribe*. See Albums and Scrapbooks of Oscar Mallite Bailey and Carter, British Library, Oriental and India Office Collection, London.

8. Moffat Mills, *Report on the Province of Assam* (Calcutta: Calcutta Gazette Office, 1854), 5. Also see appendix 1A: "Letter to Mills from A. H. Danforth" (missionary in Assam), Guwahati, July 19, 1853, in Mills, *Report*, xxviii; J. Butler, *A Sketch of Assam with Some Account of the Hill Tribes* (London: Smith, Elder, 1847), 127, and *Travels and Adventures in the Province of Assam during the Residence of Fourteen Years* (London: Smith, Elder, 1855), 223, 228, 250; and W. W. Hunter, *Statistical Account of Assam*, 2 vols. (London: Trubner, 1879), 235–39.

9. Abdul Mannan, *Infiltration: Genesis of the Assam Movement*, trans. Hasinus Sultan and Badrul Islam Baig (Guwahati, Assam: Ayna Prakashan, 2017), 13.

10. This pervasive feeling of *xanmiholi* is emphasized in Assamese literature. See the works of Lakhinath Bezbaruah, Medini Chowdhury, Imran Shah, Abdul Majid, Yese Dorji Thongsi, and Lummer Dai, among many others.

11. The Chinese word *ho p'ing* or *p'ing ho* refer to a similar concept of harmonious state of mind. See Takeshi Ishida, "Beyond the Traditional Concepts of Peace in Different Cultures," *Journal of Peace Research* 6, no. 2 (1969): 133–45.

12. Fred Dallmayr, "'Asian Values' and 'Global Human Rights,'" *Philosophy East and West* 52, no. 2 (2002): 173–89.

13. Neither Prime Minister Narendra Modi nor the BJP national president Amit Shah has provided a vision or plan for the Hindu *rashtra*, unlike Gandhi, who promoted the Hindu concept of Ramrajya for postindependent India. BJP's Hindu *rashtra* at present looks like dominance by militant and virulent Hindus silencing the minorities and Hindus who oppose them.

14. Christophe Jeffrelot, *The Hindu Nationalist Movement and Indian Politics* (London: C. Hurst, 1996).

15. I am grateful to Sanjiv Goswami for this information as well as for information on the RSS and BJP's involvement in Assam's politics.

16. According to the Red Cross International report for 1951, 320,000 Bengali Hindu refugees were settled in Assam in 1947–48 alone (files G 3/37/f and G 68/170, Government of India documents, Geneva). I consulted these documents and visual material at the International Red Cross Library and Archives in Geneva.

17. Homen Borgohain observes, "The problem of outsiders for many of the Assamese is the problem of Bengali Hindus. Because they believe that it is only from them that the danger to their culture could come" (*Bahiragatar samasya* [Guwahati, Assam: Kamal Malakar, 1979], 24, my translation).

18. Nabina Das, "Himango Biswas's Historic Peace Road Trip Comes Alive in Singer's Mission," *The Wire*, July 12, 2017, at https://thewire.in/156201/hemango -biswas-historic-peace-road-trip-comes-alive-in-singers-mission/.

19. Premkanta Mahanta, *Rajbhaganar para kalthokalaike* (Guwahati, Assam: Naba Gaurang Press, 1994), 98–99.

20. Chaitanya Kalbag, "Anti-election Fire Burns Assam as Indira Gandhi Tries to Impose Her Brand of Politics," *India Today*, Feb. 28, 1983, updated May 16, 2014, at http://indiatoday.intoday.in/story/anti-election-fire-burns-assam-as-indira -gandhi-tries-to-impose-her-brand-of-politics/1/372346.html. Samir Das refers to Hiranya Bhattacharyya's book *The Silent Invasion* about a survey conducted by Sudhakar Rao in the district of Marigaon, known for its high concentration of Bengali Muslims. According to Rao and Bhattacharyya, during the early 1980s, when the Assam movement was at its peak, as many as twenty-five (Bengali Muslim) villages of the district were "totally deHinduized." Seventy-four other villages, which were "exclusively Hindu villages until 1983" were "being taken over by the Muslim immigrants" (quoted in Samir Das, "Ethnicity and the Rise of Religious Radicalism: The Security Scenario in Contemporary Northeastern India," in *Religious Radicalism and Security in South Asia*, ed. Satu P. Limaye, Robert G. Wirsing, and Mohan Malik [Honolulu: Asia-Pacific Center for Security Studies, 2004], 264–65).

21. Sanjiv Goswami to the author, email message, July 31, 2017. Sanjiv Goswami has extensively studied the immigrant-versus-Assamese struggle in "Identity and Violence in India's Northeast: Towards a New Paradigm," PhD diss., Swinburne Univ., 2016.

22. Goswami email, July 31, 2017.

23. The issue of defining an Assamese is unresolved. If language is the marker, then everyone whose mother tongue is Assamese has to be included, such as the Bengali Muslims, while excluding members of the plains tribes such as the Bodos, Kacharis, Tiwas, and other Assamese political allies. The religious heterogeneity of the Assamese speakers poses another problem. The Assamese cannot be an exclusive Hindu community. In the meantime, the "foreigner" discourse serves to create fear and to identify the Assamese as not-Bangladeshi "outsiders." See Sanjib Baruah,

India against Itself (Delhi: Oxford Univ. Press, 1999), and Habib Fazlul Bashid, "The Assamese Language Issue: An Analysis from Historical Perspective," *International Journal of Humanities and Social Sciences* 6, no. 2 (2016): 125–33.

24. The Assam Sahitya Sabha was founded in 1917 to promote the culture of Assam and Assamese literature. In its inaugural session, a Bengali Muslim farmer, Osman Ali Sadagar, made a hefty contribution of 10 rupees (equivalent to $130 in 1917). The presence of the *miyah*s, or Mymensingh Muslims, in Assam has been recognized in the annual sessions of the Sahitya Sabha since then, and they have been embraced as an Assamese community, sometimes being referred to as "miyah-Asomiya," "na-Assamiya," "Pammua-Asmiya," and so on. They were not deemed "illegal" or "infiltrators," as later politics have made them out to be.

25. Rafiul Ahmed, "Anxiety, Violence, and the Postcolonial State: Understanding the 'Anti-Bangladeshi' Rage in Assam, India," *Perceptions* 19, no. 1 (2014): 55–70, reprinted in *Citizens Times*, ed. Atiqur Rahman Barbhuiya (Guwahati, Assam: Justice Forum, 2017), 49.

26. Jayanta Kumar Ray, *India's Foreign Relations, 1947–2007* (Delhi: Routledge, 2011), 376. Also see Sanjoy Hazarika, *India's North East and the Crisis of Migration*, paper no. 32 (New Delhi: Rajiv Gandhi Institute of Contemporary Studies, 1996); Rao, *Wither Governance*, 142.

27. Goswami, "Identity and Violence in India's Northeast," 113.

28. Anjuman Ara Begum and Diganta Sharma claimed online in 2009 that the RSS was involved in communalizing the agitation, and they cited an article by Partha Banerjee in *Onlooker* magazine. See Anjuman Ara Begum and Diganta Sharma, "Who Is Responsible for Nellie Massacre?" TwoCircles, Feb. 20, 2009, at http://twocircles.net/2009feb20/who_responsible_nellie_massacre.html.

29. Quoted in Dhiraj Kumar Sarma, "Rise of RSS in the Northeast," *Northeast Today*, May 4, 2016, at https://www.northeasttoday.in/rise-of-rss-in-northeast/. Also see Simantik Dowerah, "Rise of Hindutva in North East: RSS, BJP Score in Assam, Manipur, but Still Untested in Arunachal," *FirstPost*, Apr. 21, 2017, at http://www.firstpost.com/politics/rise-of-hindutva-in-north-east-rss-bjp-make-a-mark-in-assam-manipur-but-poll-waters-still-untested-in-arunachal-3391504.html.

30. Dowerah, "Rise of Hindutva." Also see Christophe Jeffrelot, "BJP's Assam Win Is Proof Hindutva Has Reached Areas Where It Was Marginal," *Indian Express*, June 11, 2016, at http://indianexpress.com/article/opinion/columns/bjp-sarbananda-sonowal-assam-assembly-elections-tarun-gogoi-congress-the-enigma-of-arrival-2846193/. Jeffrelot gives the count of 830 *sakha*s for Assam, but it seems the organization has grown since the election victory in 2016.

31. Ekalavya Schools and the current establishment of the Saraswati Shishu Mandirs communalize youth in Assam. These schools operate in sensitive areas, such as the Kokrajhar, Sonitpur, and Dibrugarh districts, where the Marwaris dominate

the commercial sector and plains tribes and immigrant Muslim communities live in proximity to one another.

32. C. S. Mullen, *Administrative Report on the Census of Assam 1931* (Calcutta: Government of India Central Publication Branch, 1932). These Assamese bureaucrats include Bhabani Bhuyan, H. N. Das, Bhaskar Barua, J. P. Rajkhowa, P. C. Sarma, and C. K. Das. For some, only local issues were important, whereas others, such as H. N. Das, became politically active and joined the BJP.

33. Government of Assam, *Census Report and White Paper*.

34. The tensions between the two groups became evident in 1925, when one of the first communal riots took place in Assam over a fishing dispute in Nowgong. An inquiry found the charges against the Assamese Muslims to be false. I have argued elsewhere that after this incident Assamese Muslims began to be erased, and only Bengali Muslims were left to be accounted for politically in Assam. See Yasmin Saikia, "The Muslims of Assam: Present/Absent History," in *Northeast India*, ed. Saikia and Baishya, 127. For further reading on the "line system" and the division of Muslim and Hindu politicians on this issue, see Bodhi Sattwa Kar, "The Immigration Issue, Line System, and Legislative Politics in Colonial Assam (1927–1939): A Historical Study," *Journal of Humanities and Social Science* 11, no. 4 (2013): 1–3.

35. "Immigration of Muslims into Assam," File 41-83/43-P, 1943, Government of India, E. H. L. Department, Food Production Branch, National Archives of India, New Delhi.

36. Rao, *Wither Governance*, 140.

37. The targeting of Muslim communities to vacate their land continued throughout the 1960s, and this issue was debated in both the Assam and East Pakistan Assemblies. Transcripts of these debates are available at the Nehru Memorial Museum and Library in New Delhi, India, as well at the National Documentation Wing in Islamabad, Pakistan.

38. Ahmed, "Anxiety, Violence, and the Postcolonial State," 49.

39. The level of poverty is shocking at a per capita monthly expenditure of 511 rupees, which is less than $8. See Mannan, *Infiltration*, 79.

40. *Alok* founder-editor Radhika Mohan Goswami had met with Keshav Baliram Hedgewar, founder of RSS, and was one of the earliest RSS activists in Assam.

41. Myron Weiner, *Sons of the Soil: Migration and Ethnic Conflict in India* (Princeton, NJ: Princeton Univ. Press, 1978). Interestingly, Homen Borgohain, who translated this book into Assamese and published it, was later ostracized by the Assamese press for his complaints regarding the press's role in sensationalizing the issue and abetting the violence during the Nellie massacre of 1983.

42. Shalim Hussain claims the derogatory term *miyah* for his community because he says he cannot be a "Bangladeshi" with divided loyalties to India. See Shalim M. Hussain, "Changing the Narrative: 'I Beg to State I Am Not a Bangladeshi, I

Am an Assamese Asomiya,'" *The Citizen*, May 2, 2016, at https://www.thecitizen.in/index.php/en/newsdetail/index/1/7587/changing-the-narrative-i-beg-to-state-i-am-not-a-bangladeshi-i-am-an-assamese-asomiya.

43. Nandana Dutta, *Questions of Identity in Assam: Location, Migration, and Hybridity* (New Delhi: Sage, 2012).

44. Madhurjya Kakati, "What Was the Assam Agitation or the Assam Movement in 1979 and How Did It Change the Politics of Assam?" *Quora*, n.d., at https://www.quora.com/What-was-the-Assam-agitation-or-the-Assam-movement-in-1979-and-how-did-it-change-the-politics-of-Assam, accessed Dec. 18, 20.

45. The choice of 1971 as the "cut-off" date for citizenship was connected to the war of 1971 between India and Pakistan for the creation of Bangladesh. India had encouraged Hindu Bengalis to migrate, and many settled in Assam.

46. Quoted in Samudra Gupta Kashyap, "'Choose Your Enemy, Hindu or Muslim Migrants': Assam BJP Minister Himanta Biswa Sarma," *Indian Express*, Nov. 16, 2016, at http://indianexpress.com/article/india/india-news-india/choose-your-enemy-hindu-or-muslim-migrants-bjp-assam-minister-himanta-biswa-sarma-3733080/.

47. See Sanjib Baruah, "Who Can Become an Indian Citizen?" *Indian Express*, Nov. 28, 2016, at http://indianexpress.com/article/opinion/columns/who-can-become-an-indian-citizen/.

48. According to Carola Lorea, of the 4 million noncitizens in Assam, 1.5 million are Matuas, who came to India after 1947 ("Matua, Hindu, or Foreigner? Shifting Identities in Bengali-Speaking Borderlands," paper presented at the South Asia Annual Conference, Oct. 11, 2018, Madison, WI). Another group of noncitizens in Assam are the Gorkhas; see "The Gorkhas of Assam, India Explained," *Indian Express*, Oct. 15, 2018, at http://epaper.indianexpress.com/1857209/Delhi/October-15,-2018#page/8/2.

49. BJP supporters in Assam use the rhetoric of persecution in Bangladesh and Pakistan to justify their "return" to India. Nava Thakuria is a vocal proponent of this approach. See, for example, his message "Is the Government's Aim to Integrate Neighbouring Minority Asylum Seekers Hindu-Centric?" #*Swarajya*, Oct. 15, 2016, at https://swarajyamag.com/politics/from-india-to-bharat-government-seeks-to-integrate-neighbouring-minority-asylum-seekers.

50. In rallies in Rajasthan and Delhi, Amit Shah has referred to the Muslim Bengalis as "termites." On these references, see Rohan Venkataramkrishnan, "The Daily Fix: When Amit Shah Says Immigrants Are Termites, He Is Actually the One Undermining India," *Scroll.in*, Sept. 24, 2018, at https://scroll.in/article/895567/the-daily-fix-when-amit-shah-says-immigrants-are-termites-he-is-actually-the-one-undermining-india.

51. Quoted in "What Amit Shah as Home Minister Means for the Power Situation at the Center," *NDTV News*, June 1, 2019, at https://www.ndtv.com/india-news

/amit-shah-pm-narendra-modi-cabinet-with-home-ministry-amit-shah-is-formally
-no-2-in-government-2045928?pfrom=home-topstories.

52. For details of how this bill could transform India into a Hindu *rashtra* and its
anti-Muslim politics, see Darshan Mitra, "Hindus Angry at Trump's Ban on Muslim
Refugees Should Look at What Modi Is Doing," *The Wire*, Jan. 1, 2017, at https://
thewire.in/104236/indians-angry-trumps-new-travel-ban-muslims-look-modi/.

53. See Haider Hussain's passionate recrimination of the Vishwa Hindu Parishad's religious politics in Assam: "Hindutva Rabble Rousing in Assam," *RAIOT*,
July 26, 2017, at http://raiot.in/hindutva-rabble-rousing-in-assam/.

54. Naresh Mitra, "Indigenous Groups Oppose Inclusion of Refugees in NRC,"
Times of India, Aug. 19, 2018, at https://timesofindia.indiatimes.com/city/guwahati
/indigenous-groups-oppose-inclusion-of-refugees-in-nrc/articleshow/65458368.cms.

55. Pranjal Barua, "Assam NRC: Shunned by Families, Citizenship of Many
Transgender Individuals at Stake as They Fail to Secure 'Legacy Data," *First Post*,
Aug. 28, 2018, at https://www.firstpost.com/india/assam-nrc-shunned-by-families
-citizenship-of-many-transgender-individuals-at-stake-as-they-fail-to-secure-legacy
-data-5062251.html.

56. R. Dutta Choudhury, "Politicians, Bureaucrats Involved: Panel," *Assam
Tribune*, July 27, 2017, at http://www.assamtribune.com/scripts/detailsnew.asp?id
=jul2717/ato62.

57. ECC Library Platform, "Violence over Land in Assam," n.d., at https://
library.ecc-platform.org/conflicts/assam-violence-india, accessed Dec. 16, 2018.

Conclusion

1. Nikos Kazantzakis, *Saint Francis*, trans. P. A. Bien (1962; reprint, Chicago:
Loyola Press, 2005), selected quotations provided in "*Saint Francis* Quotes," n.d.,
at https://www.goodreads.com/work/quotes/921820.

2. Ziauddin Sardar, *Desperately Seeking Paradise: Journeys of a Sceptical
Muslim* (London: Granta, 2004), 339.

3. Naguib Mahfouz, *The Journey of Ibn Fattouma*, trans. Denys Johnson-
Davies (New York: Anchor Books, 1993).

4. Wendy Brown, *Regulating Aversion: Tolerance in the Age of Identity and
Empire* (Princeton, NJ: Princeton Univ. Press, 2006).

5. Domenico Losurdo, *Liberalism: A Counter-History*, trans. Gregory Elliott
(London: Verso, 2011).

6. Martha Nussbaum, *Human Capabilities: The Human Development Approach* (2011; reprint, Cambridge, MA: Belknap Press of Harvard Univ. Press, 2013).

7. Laura F. Edwards, *The People and Their Peace: Legal Culture and the
Transformation of Inequality in the Post-revolutionary Era* (Chapel Hill: Univ. of
North Carolina Press, 2009), 4.

Bibliography

"5 Salvadorans Are Found Guilty in Slaying of U.S. Churchwomen." *New York Times*, May 25, 1984, A1.

Abu-Nimer, Mohammed. *Dialogue, Conflict Resolution, and Change: Arab–Jewish Encounters in Israel.* Albany: State Univ. of New York Press, 1999.

Abu-Nimer, Mohammed, Amal Khoury, and Emily Welty. *Unity in Diversity: Interfaith Dialogue in the Middle East.* Washington, DC: United States Institute of Peace Press, 2007.

Achrati, Ahmed. "Deconstruction, Ethics, and Islam." *Arabica* 53, no. 4 (2006): 472–509.

Ackerman, Peter, and Christopher Kruegler. *Strategic Nonviolent Conflict: The Dynamics of People Power in the Twentieth Century.* Westport, CT: Praeger, 1994.

Ahmed, Raful. "Anxiety, Violence, and the Postcolonial State: Understanding the 'Anti-Bangladeshi' Rage in Assam, India." *Perceptions* 19, no. 1 (2014): 55–70. Reprinted in *Citizens Times*, edited by Atiqur Rahman Barbhuiya, 45–54. Guwahati, Assam: Justice Forum, 2017.

Alejandre, Juan Antonio, and María J. Torquemada. *Palabra de hereje: La Inquisición de Sevilla ante el delito de proposiciones.* Seville: Univ. of Seville, 1998.

Alexander, Michelle. *The New Jim Crow: Mass Incarceration in the Age of Colorblindness.* New York: New Press, 2011.

Alger, Chadwick F. "Peace Studies at the Crossroads: Where Else?" *Peace Chronicle* 12, no. 6 (1987): 117–27.

Ali, Abdullah Yusuf. *The Holy Qur'an: Text, Translation and Commentary.* Lahore: n.p., 1934.

Alsaleh, Asaad, ed. *Voices of the Arab Spring: Personal Stories from the Arab Revolutions.* New York: Columbia Univ. Press, 2015.

Amembassy, San Salvador. "Threats against U.S. Citizen Nuns Working in Chalatenango." Dec. 11, 1980. US Department of State El Salvador Declassification Project. At http://foia.state.gov/Search/Collections.aspx.

Anderson, Gary A. *Charity: The Place of the Poor in Biblical Tradition.* New Haven, CT: Yale Univ. Press, 2013.

———. "How Does Almsgiving Purge Sins?" In *Hebrew in the Second Temple Period,* edited by Steven Fassberg, Moshe Bar Asher, and Ruth A. Clements, 1–14. Leiden: Brill, 2013.

———. *Sin: A History.* New Haven, CT: Yale Univ. Press, 2009.

Anderson, Gordon L. "The Elusive Definition of Peace." *International Journal on World Peace* 2, no. 3 (1985): 101–4.

Andrejc, Gorazd. "Small Steps: Youth Interfaith Work in Post-conflict Bosnia-Herzegovina." *Perspectives,* Winter 2014–15, 10–13. At http://www.academic.edu/9550196/Small_Steps_Youth_Interfaith_Work_in _Post-Conflict_ Bosnia-Herzegovina.

"Another Jew Supporting Divestment: Reflections from the Presbyterian Divestment Vote." June 24, 2014. At http://sumogaza.tumblr.com/post /92874855655/another-jew-supporting-divestment-reflections.

Apologia de la intolerancia religiosa. Caracas, Venezuela: Juan Baillio, 1811.

Appleby, R. Scott. *The Ambivalence of the Sacred: Religion, Violence, and Reconciliation.* Lanham, MD: Rowman and Littlefield, 2000.

Arendt, Hannah. *On Violence.* New York: Harcourt, Brace and World, 1970.

Asad, Muhammed, trans. *The Message of the Qur'an: The Full Account of the Revealed Arabic Text Accompanied by Transliteration.* Explained by Muhammed Asad. Transliterated by Ahmed Mustafa. 1980. Reprint. Britton, UK: Book Foundation, 2003.

Aspinall, Edward, and Fajran Zain. "Transitional Justice Delayed in Aceh, Indonesia." In *Transitional Justice in the Asia-Pacific,* edited by Renee Jeffery and Hun Joon Kim, 87–124. New York: Cambridge Univ. Press, 2013.

Augustine of Hippo. *The City of God.* Translated by Marcus Dods. New York: Random House, 1950.

Autesserre, Severine. *The Trouble with the Congo: Local Violence and the Failure of International Peacebuilding.* New York: Cambridge Univ. Press, 2010.

Awad, Sami. "Beyond Protesting Occupation, 'Sumud' Is Protecting Life." +972, July 6, 2017. At https://972mag.com/beyond-protesting-occupation-sumud-is-protecting-life/128554/.

Baines, Erin. "Spirits and Social Reconstruction after Mass Violence: Rethinking Transitional Justice." *African Affairs* 109, no. 436 (2010): 409–39.

Baker, Rana. "Palestinians Express 'Solidarity with the People of Ferguson' in Mike Brown Statement." *Electronic Intifada*, Aug. 15, 2014. At https://electronicintifada.net/blogs/rana-baker/palestinians-express-solidarity-people-ferguson-mike-brown-statement.

Baldwin, James. "Negros Are Anti-semitic because They're Anti-white." *New York Times*, Apr. 9, 1967. At http://www.nytimes.com/books/98/03/29/specials/baldwin-antisem.html.

———. "On Being White . . . and Other Lies." *Essence*, Apr. 1984, 1–3. At https://ourcommonground.com/2016/11/14/on-being-white-and-other-lies-james-baldwin-essence-magazine-1984/.

Bargouti, Omar. *BDS: Boycott, Divestment, Sanctions: The Global Struggle for Palestinian Rights*. Chicago: Haymarket Books, 2011.

Barnett, Michael N. *The Star and the Stripes: A History of the Foreign Policies of American Jews*. Princeton, NJ: Princeton Univ. Press, 2016.

Barrows-Friedman, Nora. "Palestine Solidarity Activists Protest US Deportation Policies in Arizona." *Electronic Intifada*, Oct. 11, 2013. At https://electronicintifada.net/blogs/nora-barrows-friedman/palestine-solidarity-activists-protest-us-deportation-policies-arizona.

Bartkowski, Maciej, and Mohja Kahf. "The Syrian Resistance: A Tale of Two Struggles." *openDemocracy*, Sept. 23, 2013. At https://www.opendemocracy.net/civilresistance/maciej-bartkowski-mohja-kahf/syrian-resistance-tale-of-two-struggles.

Barua, Pranjal. "Assam NRC: Shunned by Families, Citizenship of Many Transgender Individuals at Stake as They Fail to Secure 'Legacy Data.'" *First Post*, Aug. 28, 2018. At https://www.firstpost.com/india/assam-nrc-shunned-by-families-citizenship-of-many-transgender-individuals-at-stake-as-they-fail-to-secure-legacy-data-5062251.html.

Baruah, Sanjib. *India against Itself*. Delhi: Oxford Univ. Press, 1999.

———. "Who Can Become an Indian Citizen?" *Indian Express*, Nov. 28, 2016. At http://indianexpress.com/article/opinion/columns/who-can-become-an-indian-citizen/.

Bashid, Habib Fazlul. "The Assamese Language Issue: An Analysis from Historical Perspective." *International Journal of Humanities and Social Sciences* 6, no. 2 (2016): 125–33.

Bauer, Yehuda. "A Note about the Spelling of 'Antisemitism.'" In *On Antisemitism: Solidarity and the Struggle for Justice*, edited by Jewish Voice for Peace, xv. Chicago: Haymarket Books, 2017.

Bayat, Asef, and Eric Denis. "Who Is Afraid of Ashwaiyyat? Urban Change and Politics in Egypt." *Environment and Urbanization* 12 (2000): 185–99.

BDS Movement Freedom Justice Equality. "Call for the World Social Forum Free Palestine, Nov. 2012 in Brazil." Jan. 19, 2012. At http://www.bdsmovement.net/2012/call-for-the-world-social-forum-free-palestine-nov-2012-in-brazil-8603.

Begum, Anjuman Ara, and Diganta Sharma. "Who Is Responsible for Nellie Massacre?" TwoCircles, Feb. 20, 2009. At http://twocircles.net/2009feb20/who_responsible_nellie_massacre.html.

Beinart, Peter. "The Failure of the American Jewish Establishment." *New York Review of Books*, June 10, 2010. At http://www.nybooks.com/articles/archives/2010/jun/10/failure-american-jewish-establishment/.

Benecke, Chris. *Beyond Toleration: The Religious Origins of American Pluralism*. Oxford: Oxford Univ. Press, 2006.

Berenskoetter, Felix. "'Friends, There Are No Friends': An Intimate Reframing of the International." *Millennium: Journal of International Studies* 35, no. 3 (2007): 647–76.

Bethencourt, Francisco. *História das Inquisições*. Lisbon: Circulo de Leitores, 1994.

———. "A Inquisição." In *História religiosa de Portugal*, 3 vols., 2:95–131. Lisbon: Circulo dos Leitores, 1998–2000.

"Beyond Solidarity: Announcing the 2014 National SJP Conference at Tufts University." SJP National, posted Sept. 10, 2014. At http://sjpnational.org/.

Bhabha, Homi. *The Location of Culture*. London: Routledge, 1994.

Black for Palestine. "2015 Black Solidarity Statement with Palestine." 2015. At http://www.blackforpalestine.com/read-the-statement.html.

Blanke, Svenja. "Civic Foreign Policy: Human Rights, Faith-Based Groups, and U.S.–Salvadoran Relations in the 1970s." *The Americas* 61, no. 2 (2004): 217–44.

Blázquez, Miguel J. *La Inquisición en Albacete*. Albacete, Spain: Instituto de Estudios Albacetences, CSIC-CECEL, 1985.

Bleicher, Erez. "Why I Was Detained in Hebron Last Summer and Why You Should Join Me This May." *TruthOut*, Nov. 23, 2016. At http://www.truth-out.org/speakout/item/38502-why-i-was-detained-in-hebron-last-summer-and-why-you-should-join-me-this-may.

Blumenthal, Max. "From Occupation to 'Occupy': The Israelification of American Domestic Security." *Modoweiss*, Dec. 2, 2012. At http://mondoweiss.net/2011/12/from-occupation-to-occupy-the-israelifica tion-of-american-domestic-decurity.

"Bodies of 4 American Women Are Found in El Salvador." *New York Times*, Dec. 5, 1980, A3.

Bolton, Nell, and Myla Leguro. *Local Solutions to Land Conflict in Mindanao: Policy Lessons from Catholic Relief Services*. Baltimore: Catholic Relief Services, Oct. 2015. At https://www.crs.org/sites/default/files/tools-research/local-solutions-to-land-conflict-in-mindanao.pdf.

Bondurant, Joan V. *Conquest of Violence: The Gandhian Philosophy of Conflict*. Rev. ed. Princeton, NJ: Princeton Univ. Press, 1988.

Borgohain, Homen. *Bahiragatar samasya*. Guwahati, Assam: Kamal Malakar, 1979.

Boyarin, Daniel. *Carnal Israel: Reading Sex in Talmudic Culture*. Berkeley: Univ. of California Press, 1993.

Bramon, Dolors. *Contra moros y judíos*. Barcelona: Península, 1986.

Brinton, William M., and Alan Rinzler, eds. *Without Force or Lies: Voices from the Revolution of Central Europe in 1989–90*. San Francisco: Mercury House, 1990.

Brown, Francis, S. R. Driver, and Charles Briggs. *Hebrew and English Lexicon of the Old Testament*. Boston: Houghton Mifflin, 1907.

Brown, Judith M. *Gandhi: Prisoner of Hope*. New Haven, CT: Yale Univ. Press, 1989.

Brown, Wendy. *Regulating Aversion: Tolerance in the Age of Identity and Empire*. Princeton, NJ: Princeton Univ. Press, 2006.

Bucar, Elizabeth. "Dianomy: Understanding Religious Women's Moral Agency as Creative Conformity." *Journal of the American Academy of Religion* 78, no. 3 (2010): 662–86.

Buhaug, Halvard, Jack S. Levy, and Henrik Urdal. "50 Years of Peace Research: An Introduction to the *Journal of Peace Research.*" *Journal of Peace Research,* anniversary special issue 51, no. 2 (2014): 139–44.

Bush, Ray, and Habib Ayeb. Introduction to *Marginality and Exclusion in Egypt,* edited by Ray Bush and Habib Ayeb, 3–13. Cairo: American Univ. in Cairo Press, 2012.

———, eds. *Marginality and Exclusion in Egypt.* Cairo: American Univ. in Cairo Press, 2012.

Butler, John. *A Sketch of Assam with Some Account of the Hill Tribes.* London: Smith, Elder, 1847.

———. *Travels and Adventures in the Province of Assam during the Residence of Fourteen Years.* London: Smith, Elder, 1855.

Butler, Judith. Keynote address at the Jewish Voice for Peace National Members Meeting 2017, Mar. 31–Apr. 2, Chicago.

———. *Parting Ways: Jewishness and the Critique of Zionism.* New York: Columbia Univ. Press, 2013.

———. "Violence, Mourning, Politics." In *Precarious Life: The Powers of Mourning and Violence,* 19–49. London: Verso, 2006.

Byrnes, Timothy. *Reverse Mission: Transnational Religious Communities and the Making of U.S. Foreign Policy.* Washington, DC: Georgetown Univ. Press, 2011.

Cahill, Lisa Sowle. *Global Justice, Christology, and Christian Ethics.* Cambridge: Cambridge Univ. Press, 2013.

Capéran, Louis. *Le probleme du salut des infidels.* 2 vols. Toulouse: Grand Séminaire, 1934.

"Carlos Eugenio Vides Casanova Removal Proceedings." US Department of Justice, Executive Office for Immigration Review, Dec. 17, 2012. Center for Justice and Accountability. At http://cja.org/downloads/Vides%20Casanova%20Removal%20Proceedings.pdf.

Caro Baroja, Julio. *De la superstición al ateísmo.* Madrid: Taurus, 1974.

Carter Hallward, Maia. *Transnational Activism and the Israeli–Palestinian Conflict.* New York: Palgrave Macmillan, 2013.

Ceadel, Martin. *Thinking about Peace and War.* New York: Oxford Univ. Press, 1987.

Center for Justice and Accountability. "Human Rights Crimes under Salvadoran Ministers: *Romagoza Arce et al. v. Garcia and Vides Casanova.*

Alien Tort Statue/Torture Victims Protection Act of 1991." N.d. At http://cja.org/what-we-do/litigation/romagoza-arce-v-garcia-and-vides -casanova/uscourt-ats-tvpa/.

Center on Race and Social Problems. *Pittsburgh's Racial Demographics 2015: Differences and Disparities.* Pittsburgh, PA: Univ. of Pittsburgh School of Social Work, 2015.

Chapman, William. "Plea to Restore Aid to Salvador Does Not Persuade Congress." *Washington Post*, June 12, 1982, A6.

Chardy, Alfonso. "Deported Former Salvadoran Defense Minister Plans to Appeal His Removal." *Miami Herald*, Jan. 15, 2016. At http://www .miamiherald.com/news/local/crime/article54957610.html.

Chaudhuri, Jean, and Joyotpaul Chaudhuri. *A Sacred Path: The Way of the Muscogee Creeks.* Los Angeles: American Indian Studies Center, Univ. of California at Los Angeles, 2001.

Chenoweth, Erica, and Kurt Schock. "Do Contemporaneous Armed Challenges Affect the Outcomes of Mass Nonviolent Campaigns?" *Mobilization: An International Quarterly* 20, no. 4 (2015): 427–51.

Chenoweth, Erica, and Maria J. Stephan. "How the World Is Proving Martin Luther King Jr. Right about Nonviolence." *Monkey Cage, Washington Post* blog, Jan. 18, 2016. At https://www.washingtonpost.com /news/monkey-cage/wp/2016/01/18/how-the-world-is-proving-mlk -right-about-nonviolence/?utm_term=.f7a9f7b3f811.

———. *Why Civil Resistance Works: The Strategic Logic of Nonviolent Conflict.* New York: Columbia Univ. Press, 2011.

Choudhury, R. Dutta. "Politicians, Bureaucrats Involved: Panel." *Assam Tribune*, July 27, 2017. At http://www.assamtribune.com/scripts/details new.asp?id=jul2717/ato62.

Christin, Olivier. *La paix de religion: L'autonomisation de la raison politique au xvi siècle.* Paris: Seuil, 1997.

City of Pittsburg, Council of the City of Pittsburgh. "Indigenous Peoples' Day: Will of the Council." N.d. At http://wiki.pghrights.mayfirst.org /index.php?title=File:Indigenous_Peoples_Day_Will_of_the_Council .pdf. Accessed Feb. 11, 2019.

Clozel, Lalita. "Salvadoran Cites U.S. Backing of Violence in Deportation Appeal." *Los Angeles Times*, Feb. 6, 2014. At http://articles.latimes .com/2014/feb/06/nation/la-na-elsalvador-deport-20140207.

Coll, Steve. *Ghost Wars: The Secret History of the CIA, Afghanistan, and Bin Laden, from the Soviet Invasion to September 10, 2001.* New York: Penguin Books, 2004.

Corkran, David H. *The Creek Frontier, 1540–1783.* Norman: Univ. of Oklahoma Press, 1967.

Cortright, David. *Peace Works: The Citizen's Role in Ending the Cold War.* Boulder, CO: Westview Press, 1993.

Crenshaw, Kimberlé. "Mapping the Margins: Intersectionality, Identity Politics, and Violence against Women of Color." *Stanford Law Review* 43, no. 6 (1991): 1241–99.

Cross, Harry. "Commerce and Orthodoxy: A Spanish Response to Portuguese Commercial Penetration in the Viceroyalty of Peru." *The Americas* 35, no. 2 (1978): 151–67.

Da Costa, Dia, and Philip McMichael. "The Poverty of the Global Order." *Globalizations* 4, no. 4 (2007): 588–602.

Dadson, Trevor. *Los Moriscos de Villarubia de los Ojos (Siglos XV–XVIII): Historia de una minorìa asimilada, expulsada y reintegrada.* Madrid: Iberoamericana-Vervuert, 2007.

———. *Tolerance and Coexistence in Early Modern Spain: Old Christians and Moriscos in the Campo de Calatrava.* Woodbridge, UK: Tamesis, 2014.

Dahl, Elizabeth S. "Oil and Water? The Philosophical Commitments of International Peace Studies and Conflict Resolution." *International Studies Review* 14, no. 2 (2012): 240–72.

Dallmayr, Fred. "'Asian Values' and 'Global Human Rights.'" *Philosophy East and West* 52, no. 2 (2002): 173–89.

Darweish, Marwan. "Israeli Peace and Solidarity Organization." In *Conflict, Transformation, and the Palestinians: The Dynamics of Peace and Justice under Occupation*, edited by Alpaslan Ozerdem, 229–46. New York: Routledge, 2016.

Das, Nabina. "Himango Biswas's Historic Peace Road Trip Comes Alive in Singer's Mission." *The Wire*, July 12, 2017. At https://thewire.in/156201/hemango-biswas-historic-peace-road-trip-comes-alive-in-singers-mission/.

Das, Samir. "Ethnicity and the Rise of Religious Radicalism: The Security Scenario in Contemporary Northeastern India." In *Religious Radicalism and Security in South Asia*, edited by Satu P. Limaye, Robert G.

Wirsing, and Mohan Malik, 245–71. Honolulu: Asia-Pacific Center for Security Studies, 2004.

Davis, Angela Y. *Freedom Is a Constant Struggle: Ferguson, Palestine, and the Foundations of Movement*. Edited by Frank Barat. Chicago: Haymarket Books, 2016.

De Certeau, Michel. *The Practice of Everyday Life*. Translated by Steven F. Randall. Berkeley: Univ. of California Press, 1984.

Deming, Barbara. *Revolution and Equilibrium*. New York: Grossman, 1971.

Derrida, Jacques. *Margins of Philosophy*. Translated by Alan Bass. Chicago: Univ. of Chicago Press, 1982.

———. *Of Hospitality: Anne Dufourmantelle Invites Jacques Derrida to Respond*. Translated by Rachel Bowlby. Stanford, CA: Stanford Univ. Press, 2000.

De Sandoval, Alonso. *Un tratado sobre la esclavitud*. Edited by Enriqueta Vila Vilar. Madrid: Alianza, 1987.

Dickens, Roy S., Jr. *Archaeological Investigations at Horseshoe Bend National Military Park, Alabama*. Moundville: Alabama Archaeological Society, 1979.

Domínguez, Pablo. "Los progresos de la tolerancia religiosa en el mundo vista desde la España del siglo XVIII." *Hispanic Research Journal* 15 (2014): 120–36.

———. "Reformismo Cristiano y tolerancia en España a finales del siglo xviii." *Hispania Sacra* 65, extra no. 2 (2013): 113–72.

———. "Tolerancia religiosa en la España afrancesada." *Historia y Política* 31 (2014): 195–223.

Dowerah, Simantik. "Rise of Hindutva in North East: RSS, BJP Score in Assam, Manipur, but Still Untested in Arunachal." *FirstPost*, Apr. 21, 2017. At http://www.firstpost.com/politics/rise-of-hindutva-in-north -east-rss-bjp-make-a-mark-in-assam-manipur-but-poll-waters-still -untested-in-arunachal-3391504.html.

Drinan, Robert, and Teresa Kuo. "Putting the World's Oppressors on Trial: The Torture Victim Protection Act." *Human Rights Quarterly* 15, no. 3 (1993): 605–24.

Du Bois, W. E. B. "The Negro and the Warsaw Ghetto." *Jewish Life*, May 14–15, 1952. Reproduced in *The Oxford W. E. B. Du Bois Reader*, edited by Eric Sundquist, 469–73. New York: Oxford Univ. Press, 1996.

Dutta, Nandana. *Questions of Identity in Assam: Location, Migration, and Hybridity*. New Delhi: Sage, 2012.

Dwyer, Leslie. "Building a Monument: Intimate Politics of 'Reconciliation' in Post-1965 Bali." In *Transitional Justice: Global Mechanisms and Local Realities after Genocide*, edited by Alexander Laban Hinton, 227–48. New Brunswick, NJ: Rutgers Univ. Press, 2010.

———. "A Politics of Silences: Violence, Memory, and Treacherous Speech in Post-1965 Bali." In *Genocide, Truth, Memory, and Representation: Anthropological Approaches*, edited by Alexander Laban Hinton and Kevin Lewis O'Neill, 113–46. Durham, NC: Duke Univ. Press, 2009.

Ebaugh, Helen Rose. "Vatican II and the Revitalization Movement." In *Religion and the Social Order: Vatican II and U.S. Catholicism*, edited by Helen Rose Ebaugh, 3–19. Greenwich, CT: JAI Press, 1991.

ECC Library Platform. "Violence over Land in Assam." N.d. At https://library.ecc-platform.org/conflicts/assam-violence-india. Accessed Dec. 16, 2018.

The Economist. "Binyamin Netanyahu Is Soft on Anti-semitism When It Suits Him." Aug. 24, 2017. At https://www.economist.com/news/middle-east-and-africa/21726995-jewish-state-chooses-its-battles-carefully-binyamin-netanyahu-soft?fsrc=FacebookInstant.

Edwards, John. "Religious Faith and Doubt in Late Medieval Spain: Soria circa 1450–1500." *Past and Present* 120 (1988): 3–25.

Edwards, Laura F. *The People and Their Peace: Legal Culture and the Transformation of Inequality in the Post-revolutionary Era*. Chapel Hill: Univ. of North Carolina Press, 2009.

Eggleston, George C. *Red Eagle and the Wars with the Creek Indians of Alabama*. New York: Dodd, Mead, 1878.

Eilberg, Amy. *From Enemy to Friend: Jewish Wisdom and the Pursuit of Peace*. Maryknoll, NY: Orbis Books, 2014.

Eisen, Robert. *The Peace and Violence of Judaism from the Bible to Zionism*. New York: Oxford Univ. Press, 2011.

El Feki, Shereen. *Sex and the Citadel: Intimate Life in a Changing Arab World*. New York: Pantheon Books, 2013.

Eliasoph, Nina. *Making Volunteers: Civic Life after Welfare's End*. Princeton, NJ: Princeton Univ. Press, 2011.

Ellis, Marc H. "Exile and the Prophetic: The Interfaith Ecumenical Deal Is Dead." *Mondoweiss*, Nov. 12, 2012. At https://mondoweiss.net/2012/11/exile-and-the-prophetic-the-interfaith-ecumenical-deal-is-dead/.

El-Mahdi, Rabab. "Against Marginalization: Workers, Youth, and Class in the 25 January Revolution." In *Marginality and Exclusion in Egypt*, edited by Ray Rush and Habib Ayeb, 133–47. Cairo: American Univ. in Cairo Press, 2012.

Engle Merry, Sally. "Transnational Human Rights and Local Activism: Mapping the Middle." *American Anthropologist* 108 (2006): 35–51.

Erickson Nepstad, Sharon. *Convictions of the Soul: Religion, Culture, and Agency in the Central America Solidarity Movement*. New York: Oxford Univ. Press, 2004.

Ethridge, Robbie. *Creek Country: The Creek Indians and Their World*. Chapel Hill: Univ. of North Carolina Press, 2003.

Evangelista, Matthew, ed. *Peace Studies: Critical Concepts in Political Science*. 4 vols. London: Routledge, 2005.

Fernández Sebastián, Javier. "Toleration and Freedom of Expression in the Hispanic World between Enlightenment and Liberalism." *Past and Present* 211 (2011): 159–97.

Ferris, Susan, and Ricardo Sandoval. *The Fight in the Fields: Cesar Chavez and the Farmworkers Movement*. Edited by Diana Hembree. New York: Harcourt Brace, 1997.

Finnegan, Amy C., Adam P. Saltsman, and Shelley K. White. "Negotiating Politics and Culture: The Utility of Human Rights for Activist Organizing in the United States." *Journal of Human Rights Practice* 2 (2010): 307–33.

First, Mitchell. "What Is the Origin of the Word *Mechilah*?" *Hakirah: The Flatbush Journal of Jewish Law and Thought* 18 (2014): 147–58.

Fitzpatrick Behrens, Susan. "From Symbols of the Sacred to Symbols of Subversion to Simply Obscure: Maryknoll Women Religious in Guatemala, 1953–1967." *The Americas* 61, no. 2 (2004): 205–16.

Fixico, Donald L. *The American Indian Mind in a Linear World: American Indian Studies and Traditional Knowledge*. New York: Routledge, 2003.

Foucault, Michel. *Discipline and Punish: The Birth of the Prison*. Translated by Alan Sheridan. 1977. Reprint. New York: Vintage, 1995.

Frank, Andrew. *Creeks and Southerners: Biculturalism on the Early American Frontier.* Lincoln: Univ. of Nebraska Press, 2005.

"Friar Ivo Markovic/Bosnia." Tanenbaum Peacemakers in Action Network, n.d. At https://tanenbaum.org/peacemakers-in-action-network /meet-the-peacemakers/friar-ivo-markovic/. Accessed Sept. 1, 2017.

Friedmann, Yohanan. *Tolerance and Coercion in Islam.* Cambridge: Cambridge Univ. Press, 2003.

Furman, Frida Kerner. "Religion and Peacebuilding: Grassroots Efforts by Israelis and Palestinians." *Journal of Religion Conflict and Peace* 4 (2011). At http://www.religionconflictpeace.org/volume-4-issue-2 -spring-2011/religion-and-peacebuilding-grassroots-efforts-israelis-and -palestinians.

Galeazzi, Giacomo. "Philippines: Communist Rebel Nuns Accused of Being Enemies of the Army." *Vatican Insider, La Stampa,* Apr. 10, 2015. At http://vaticaninsider.lastampa.it/en/world-news/detail/articolo/filippine -philippines-filipinas-suore-nun-monja-15315/.

Galtung, Johan. "An Editorial." *Journal of Peace Research* 1, no. 1 (1964): 1–4.

———. *Peace by Peaceful Means: Peace and Conflict, Development and Civilization.* Thousand Oaks, CA: Sage, 1996.

———. *Peace: Research, Education, Action.* Essays in Peace Research no. 1. Copenhagen: Ejlers, 1975.

———. "Twenty-Five Years of Peace Research: Ten Challenges and Some Responses." *Journal of Peace Research* 22, no. 2 (1985): 141–58.

———. "Violence, Peace, and Peace Research." *Journal of Peace Research* 6, no. 3 (1969): 167–91.

Gandhi, Mohandas K. *Hind Swaraj and Other Writings.* Edited by Anthony J. Parel. Cambridge: Cambridge Univ. Press, 1997.

———. "Working of Non-violence." *Harijan,* Feb. 6, 1939. Reprinted in *The Collected Works of Mahatma Gandhi,* 75 vols., 68:388–91. New Delhi: Publications Division, Ministry of Information and Broadcasting, Government of India, 1999.

García-Arenal, Mercedes. *Inquisición y Moriscos: Los procesos del Tribunal de Cuenca.* Madrid: Siglo XXI, 1978.

———. "Religious Dissent and Minorities: The Morisco Age." *Journal of Modern History* 88 (2009): 888–920.

García Fuentes, J. M. *La Inquisición de Granada en el siglo xvi*. Granada, Spain: Universidad de Granada, 1981.

Gereboff, Joel. "Talmudic Stories about Angry and Annoyed Rabbis." In *A Legacy of Learning: Essays in Honor of Jacob Neusner*, edited by Alan J. Avery-Peck, Bruce Chilton, William Scott Green, and Gary G. Porton, 82–109. Leiden: Brill, 2014.

Goldenberg, Robert. "The Deposition of Rabban Gamaliel II: An Examination of the Sources." *Journal of Jewish Studies* 23 (1972): 167–90.

Gonzalez, David. "Trial of Salvadoran Generals in Nuns' Deaths Hears Echoes of 1980." *New York Times*, Oct. 21, 2000, A8.

Gopin, Marc. *Between Eden and Armageddon: The Future of World Religion, Violence, and Peacemaking*. New York: Oxford Univ. Press, 2002.

———. *Holy War, Holy Peace: How Religion Can Bring Peace to the Middle East*. New York: Oxford Univ. Press, 2002.

———. "Judaism and Peacebuilding." In *Religion and Peace Building*, edited by Howard Coward and Gordon Smith, 111–27. Albany: State Univ. of New York Press, 2004.

"The Gorkhas of Assam, India." *Indian Express*, Oct. 15, 2018. At http://epaper.indianexpress.com/1857209/Delhi/October-15,-2018#page/8/2.

Gosse, Van. "'El Salvador Is Spanish for Vietnam': The Politics of Solidarity and the New Immigrant Left, 1955–1993." In *The Immigrant Left in the United States*, edited by Paul Buhle and Dan Georgakas, 302–30. Albany: State Univ. of New York Press, 1996.

Goswami, Sanjiv. "Identity and Violence in India's Northeast: Towards a New Paradigm." PhD diss., Swinburne Univ., 2016.

Goswami, Uddipana. "Miyā or Axamiyā: The Politics of Assimilation in Assam." *Journal of Social and Policy Research* 1 (2010): 1–36.

Greathead, Scott, and Michael Posner. "Bill Ford, Remembered." *The Nation*, June 18, 2008. At https://www.thenation.com/article/bill-ford-remembered.

Green, Michael D. "Alexander McGillivray." In *American Indian Leaders: Studies in Diversity*, edited by R. David Edmunds, 41–64. Lincoln: Univ. of Nebraska Press, 1980.

———. *The Politics of Indian Removal: Creek Government and Society in Crisis*. Lincoln: Univ. of Nebraska Press, 1982.

Grell, O. P., and Roy Porter, eds. *Toleration in Enlightenment Europe.* Cambridge: Cambridge Univ. Press, 2000.

Haefeli, Evan. *New Netherland and the Dutch Origins of Religious Liberty.* Philadelphia: Univ. of Pennsylvania Press, 2012.

Haers, Jacques, Felix Wilfred, Kristien Justaert, and Yves De Maeseneer, eds. *Reconciliation: Empowering Grace.* London: SCM Press, 2013.

Hahn, Steven C. *The Invention of the Creek Nation, 1670–1763.* Lincoln: Univ. of Nebraska Press, 2004.

Haines, Chad. "Dialogical Din and Everyday Acts of Peace: An Islamic Perspective." In *Women and Peace in the Islamic World: Gender, Agency, and Influence,* edited by Yasmin Saikia and Chad Haines, 43–68. London: I. B. Tauris, 2014.

Halbert, H. S., and T. H. Ball. *The Creek War of 1813 and 1815.* 1895. Reprint. Tuscaloosa: Univ. of Alabama Press, 1995.

Halbi, Rabah. *Israeli and Palestinian Identities in Dialogue: The School of Peace Approach.* New Brunswick, NJ: Rutgers Univ. Press, 2004.

Haleem, Muhammad Abdel, trans. *The Qur'an: A New Translation.* Oxford: Oxford Univ. Press, 2004.

Hall, Douglas John. *Imaging God: Dominion as Stewardship.* Grand Rapids, MI: Eerdmans, 1986.

Hall, Sacajawea. "Reflections on the People's Summit on Climate Change and Our Climate Justice Movement." *Grassroots Global Justice Alliance Blog,* Jan. 15, 2015. At https://ggjalliance.wordpress.com/2015/01/15/reflections-on-the-peoples-summit-on-climate-change-and-our-climate-justice-movement/.

Halperin, Eric. *Emotions in Conflict: Inhibitors and Facilitators of Peace Making.* New York: Routledge, 2015.

Hancock, Landon Edward. "Peace Studies and Conflict Resolution: Similarities, Differences, and Blurred Boundaries." International Studies Association, Jan. 8, 2014. At http://www.isanet.org/ISA/Sections/PEACE/News/ID/228/Peace-Studies-and-Conflict-Resolution-Similarities-Differences-and-Blurred-Boundaries.

Hany, Sara. "It Is Just . . . the Beginning." In *Voices of the Arab Spring: Personal Stories from the Arab Revolutions,* edited by Asaad Alsaleh, 67–70. New York: Columbia Univ. Press, 2015.

Harvey, David. *Rebel Cities: From the Right to the City to the Urban Revolution.* London: Verso Books, 2012.

———. "The Right to the City." *International Journal of Urban and Regional Research* 27 (2003): 939–41.

———. *Social Justice and the City.* Athens: Univ. of Georgia Press, 2009.

Havel, Václav. "The Power of the Powerless." In *Without Force or Lies: Voices from the Revolution of Central Europe in 1989–90*, edited by William M. Brinton and Alan Rinzler, 43–127. San Francisco: Mercury House, 1990.

Hazarika, Sanjoy. *India's North East and the Crisis of Migration.* Paper no. 32. New Delhi: Rajiv Gandhi Institute of Contemporary Studies, 1996.

Heer, Richard. *The Eighteenth-Century Revolution in Spain.* Princeton, NJ: Princeton Univ. Press, 1958.

Henderson, Charles P. "Organizations Working toward a Just and Lasting Peace in the Middle East." *Crosscurrents* 58 (2008): 227–443.

Hennelly, Alfred T. Introduction to *Liberation Theology: A Documentary History*, edited by Alfred T. Hennelly, xv–xxi. Maryknoll, NY: Orbis Books, 1990.

Hermann, Tamar. *The Israeli Peace Movement: A Shattered Dream.* New York: Cambridge Univ. Press, 2009.

Hevesi, Dennis. "William P. Ford." *New York Times*, June 3, 2008, B8.

Hezser, Catherine. "Seduced by the Enemy or Wise Strategy? The Presentation of Non-violence and Accommodation with Foreign Powers in Ancient Jewish Literary Sources." In *Between Cooperation and Hostility: Multiple Identities in Ancient Judaism and the Interaction with Foreign Powers*, edited by Rainer Albertz and Jakob Wöhrle, 221–50. Göttingen, Germany: Vandenhoeck and Ruprecht, 2013.

Hill Collins, Patricia, and Sirma Bilge. *Intersectionality.* Cambridge: Polity, 2016.

Hindawy, Maha. "My Egyptian Revolution." In *Voices of the Arab Spring: Personal Stories from the Arab Revolutions*, edited by Asaad Alsaleh, 75–78. New York: Columbia Univ. Press, 2015.

Hinton, Alexander Laban, ed. *Transitional Justice: Global Mechanisms and Local Realities after Genocide.* New Brunswick, NJ: Rutgers Univ. Press, 2010.

Hippler, Thomas. "Images of Peace." *New Centennial Review* 13, no. 1 (2013): 45–70.

Hochberg, Gil. "'Check Me Out': Queer Encounters in Sharif Waked's *Chick Point: Fashion for Israeli Checkpoints*." *GLQ: A Journal of Lesbian and Gay Studies* 16, no. 4 (2010): 577–98.

Hoffman, Scott. "The Evolution of the Concept of Repentance in Biblical, Second Temple, and Rabbinic Sources." PhD diss., New York Univ., 2012.

Holland Braund, Kathryn E. "Red Sticks." In *Tohopeka: Rethinking the Creek War and the War of 1812*, edited by Kathryn E. Holland Braund, 84–104. Tuscaloosa: Univ. of Alabama Press, 2012.

———, ed. *Tohopeka: Rethinking the Creek War and the War of 1812*. Tuscaloosa: Univ. of Alabama Press, 2012.

Hornblower, Margot. "Panel Votes Most of El Salvador Aid." *Washington Post*, May 12, 1983, A1.

———. "Rumbles of War Give Hill the Jitters." *Washington Post*, Mar. 8, 1982, A1.

"House Votes to Extend Curbs on Military Aid to Salvador." *Washington Post*, Oct. 1, 1983, A19.

Howard, Michael. *The Invention of Peace: Reflections on War and International Order*. New Haven, CT: Yale Univ. Press, 2001.

"How to Get Involved." N.d. At http://wiki.pghrights.mayfirst.org/index .php?title=How_to_get_involved. Accessed Feb. 11, 2019.

"Human Rights City Action Plan." Dec. 10, 2014. At http://wiki.pghrights .mayfirst.org/index.php?title=Human_Rights_City_Action_Plan.

Human Rights City Alliance. "Making the Global Local: Human Rights Cities—Conference Summary Report." 2015. At http://wiki.pghrights .mayfirst.org/index.php?title=File:Conference_summary_-Genera l_Version_3_2.pdf.

Human Rights City Alliance Annual Report 2016. 2016. At http://wiki .pghrights.mayfirst.org/index.php?title=File:Annual_Report_2016.pdf.

Human Rights Watch. "Syria: Events of 2016." In *Human Rights Watch World Report 2017*. New York: Human Rights Watch, 2017. At https:// www.hrw.org/world-report/2017/country-chapters/syria.

Hunter, W. W. *Statistical Account of Assam*. 2 vols. London: Trubner, 1879.

Hussain, Haider. "Hindutva Rabble Rousing in Assam." *RAIOT*, July 26, 2017. At http://raiot.in/hindutva-rabble-rousing-in-assam/.

Hussain, Shalim M. "Changing the Narrative: 'I Beg to State I Am Not a Bangladeshi, I Am an Assamese Asomiya.'" *The Citizen*, May 2, 2016. At https://www.thecitizen.in/index.php/en/newsdetail/index/1/7587

/changing-the-narrative-i-beg-to-state-i-am-not-a-bangladeshi-i-am
-an-assamese-asomiya.

Hyer, Marjorie. "Four Murders Trigger US Catholic Protests." *Washington Post*, Dec. 10, 1980, A38.

"Indigenous Peoples' Day." N.d. At https://en.wikipedia.org/wiki/Indigenous _Peoples%27_Day. Accessed Dec. 4, 2017.

Ingram, Catherine, ed. *In the Footsteps of Gandhi: Conversations with Spiritual Social Activists*. Berkeley, CA: Parallax, 1990.

"In Support of Dyett Hunger Strikers: An Open Letter to Mayor Rahm Emanuel and the Chicago Board of Education from Members of the Chicago Jewish Community." Sept. 2015/Elul 5775. At https://docs.google .com/forms/d/1zJelsaoyMxwgmx9wYOCdmKxz6th4C9Unz_rBME9m PKg/viewform?c=o&w=1.

International Center for Transitional Justice (ICTJ) and Kontras (Commission for the Disappeared and Victims of Violence). *Derailed: Transitional Justice in Indonesia since the Fall of Soeharto*. New York: ICTJ, 2011. At http://www.ictj.org/sites/default/files/ICTJ-Kontras-Indonesia -Derailed-Summary-2011-English.pdf.

Isaacs, Alick. *A Prophetic Peace: Judaism, Religion, and Politics*. Bloomington: Indiana Univ. Press, 2011.

Ishida, Takeshi. "Beyond the Traditional Concepts of Peace in Different Cultures." *Journal of Peace Research* 6, no. 2 (1969): 133–45.

Israel, Jonathan. *Radical Enlightenment: Philosophy and the Making of Modernity, 1650–1750*. Oxford: Oxford Univ. Press, 2001.

Itkowitz, Colby. "'Every Person Deserves to Rest in Peace': American Muslims Raising Money to Repair Vandalized Jewish Cemetery." *Washington Post*, Feb. 21, 2017. At https://www.washingtonpost.com/news /inspired-life/wp/2017/02/21/every-person-deserves-to-rest-in-peace -american-muslims-raising-money-to-repair-vandalized-jewish -cemetery/?utm_term=.8789d63833c1.

Jackson, Andrew. *The Papers of Andrew Jackson*. Vol. 2: *1804–1813*. Edited by Harold D. Moser and Sharon MacPherson. Knoxville: Univ. of Tennessee Press, 1980.

Jastrow, Marcus. *A Dictionary of the Targumim, the Talmud Babli and Yerushalmi, and the Midrashic Literature*. New York: Judaica Press, 1971.

Jeffrelot, Christophe. "BJP's Assam Win Is Proof Hindutva Has Reached Areas Where It Was Marginal." *Indian Express*, June 11, 2016. At http://indianexpress.com/article/opinion/columns/bjp-sarbananda -sonowal-assam-assembly-elections-tarun-gogoi-congress-the-enigma -of-arrival-2846193/.

———. *The Hindu Nationalist Movement and Indian Politics*. London: C. Hurst, 1996.

"Jemez Principles for Democratic Organizing." 1996. At https://www .ejnet.org/ej/jemez.pdf.

Jenkins, Henry. *Convergence Culture: Where Old and New Media Collide*. New York: New York Univ. Press, 2006.

———. *Textual Pouchers: Television Fans and Participating Culture*. New York: Routledge Press, 1992.

Jenkins, Loren. "Maryknollers Reconsider Role in El Salvador after Action by Priest." *Washington Post*, May 14, 1981, A15.

Jensen, Ove. "Horseshoe Bend: A Living Memorial." In *Tohopeka: Rethinking the Creek War and the War of 1812*, edited by Kathryn E. Holland Braund, 146–56. Tuscaloosa: Univ. of Alabama Press, 2012.

Jewish Voice for Peace. "Deadly Exchange Campaign." N.d. At https:// deadlyexchange.org/. Accessed Mar. 27, 2018.

———. "Defund Islamophobia: How the Jewish United Fund of Metropolitan Chicago Supports Anti-Muslim Hate Groups," Mar. 2017. At https://jewishvoiceforpeace.org/wp-content/uploads/2017/03/JUF -Defund-Islamophobia-Report-FINAL-3-22.pdf.

———. "Jewish Groups Stand in Opposition to Hate Speech and All Forms of Islamophobia." Interfaith press release, Apr. 28, 2015. At https:// jewishvoiceforpeace.org/jewish-groups-stand-in-opposition-to-hate -speech-and-all-forms-of-islamophobia/.

———, ed. *On Antisemitism: Solidarity and the Struggle for Justice*. Chicago: Haymarket Books, 2017.

———. "Stifling Debate: How Israel's Defenders Use False Charges of Anti-semitism to Limit the Debate over Israel on Campus." Fall 2015. At https://jewishvoiceforpeace.org/wp-content/uploads/2015/09/JVP _Stifling_Dissent_Full_Report_Key_90745869.pdf.

Joe [sic]. "Washington, DC: A Human Rights City?" *The Disorder of Things*, Aug. 25, 2013. At https://thedisorderofthings.com/2013/08/25 /washington-dc-a-human-rights-city/.

Johnson, Janell. "Between Text and Sermon: Genesis 1:26–28." *Interpretation* 59, no. 2 (2005): 176–78.

Johnson, L. Gunnar. *Conflicting Concepts of Peace in Contemporary Peace Studies*. Sage Occasional Paper no. 4. International Studies series. Beverley Hills, CA: Sage, 1976.

JTA. "The More Americans Learn about Israel, the Less They Like It, Study Suggests." *Haaretz*, Jan. 7, 2017. At http://www.haaretz.com/us-news /1.798794.

Kakati, Madhurjya. "What Was the Assam Agitation or the Assam Movement in 1979, and How Did It Change the Politics of Assam?" *Quora*, n.d. At https://www.quora.com/What-was-the-Assam-agitation-or -the-Assam-movement-in-1979-and-how-did-it-change-the-politics-of -Assam.

Kalbag, Chaitanya. "Anti-election Fire Burns Assam as Indira Gandhi Tries to Impose Her Brand of Politics." *India Today*, Feb. 28, 1983, updated May 16, 2014. At http://indiatoday.intoday.in/story/anti-election -fire-burns-assam-as-indira-gandhi-tries-to-impose-her-brand-of-politics /1/372346.html.

Kaldor, Mary. *Global Civil Society: An Answer to War*. Cambridge: Polity, 2003.

Kalmin, Richard. *The Sages in Jewish Society in Late Antiquity*. London: Routledge, 1999.

———. *Sages, Stories, Authors, and Editors in Rabbinic Babylonia*. Atlanta, GA: Scholars Press, 1994.

Kamen, Henry. "Inquisition, Tolerance, and Liberty in Eighteenth-Century Spain." In *Toleration in Enlightenment Europe*, edited by O. P. Grell and Roy Porter, 250–58. Cambridge: Cambridge Univ. Press, 2000.

———. "Toleration and Dissent in Sixteenth-Century Spain: The Alternative Tradition." *Sixteenth-Century Journal* 19 (1988): 3–23.

Kaminsky, Howard. *Fundamentals of Jewish Conflict Resolution: Traditional Jewish Perspectives on Resolving Interpersonal Conflicts*. Brighton, MA: Academic Studies Press, 2017.

Kamola, Isaac. "The Global Coffee Economy and the Production of Genocide in Rwanda." *Third World Quarterly* 28 (2007): 571–92.

Kane, Muriel. "Report: Israeli Model Underlies Militarization of U.S. Police." *RawStory*, Dec. 4, 2011. At http://www.rawstory.com/rs/2011 /12/report-israeli-model-underlies-militarization-of-u-s-police/.

Kaplan, Benjamin J. *Divided by Faith: Religious Conflict and the Practice of Toleration in Early Modern Europe*. Cambridge, MA: Harvard Univ. Press, 2007.

Kar, Bodhi Sattwa. "The Immigration Issue, Line System, and Legislative Politics in Colonial Assam (1927–1939): A Historical Study." *Journal of Humanities and Social Science* 11, no. 4 (2013): 1–3.

Karatnycky, Adrian, and Peter Ackerman. "How Freedom Is Won: From Civil Resistance to Durable Democracy." *International Journal of Not-for-Profit Law* 7, no. 3 (2005). At http://www.icnl.org/research /journal/vol7iss3/special_3.htm#_ednref1.

Kashyap, Samudra Gupta. "'Choose Your Enemy, Hindu or Muslim Migrants': Assam BJP Minister Himanta Biswa Sarma." *Indian Express*, Nov. 16, 2016. At http://indianexpress.com/article/india/india-news -india/choose-your-enemy-hindu-or-muslim-migrants-bjp-assam-min ister-himanta-biswa-sarma-3733080/.

Kazantzakis, Nikos. *Saint Francis*. Translated by P. A. Bien. 1962. Reprint. Chicago: Loyola Press, 2005.

Keck, Margaret, and Kathryn Sikkink. *Activists beyond Borders: Advocacy Networks in International Politics*. Ithaca, NY: Cornell Univ. Press, 1988.

Keeley, Theresa. "Reagan's Real Catholics vs. Tip O'Neill's Maryknoll Nuns: Gender, Intra-Catholic Conflict, and the Contras." *Diplomatic History* 40, no. 3 (2016): 530–58.

Kent, Lia. "Local Memory Practices in East Timor: Disrupting Transitional Justice Narratives." *International Journal of Transitional Justice* 5, no. 3 (2011): 434–55.

Kessler, Ronald. "Pocket Veto by Reagan Overturned." *Washington Post*, Aug. 30, 1984, A1.

Kestenbaum, Sam. "The 'Alt-Right' Hates the Jews. But It Also Loves Them—and Israel." *Forward*, Jan. 16, 2017. At http://forward.com/news/359889 /the-alt-right-hates-the-jews-but-it-also-loves-them-and-israel/.

Khan, Maulana Wahiduddin. "War and Peace in Islam." *New Age Islam*, Sept. 22, 2014. At http://www.newageislam.com/islamic-society/maulana -wahiduddin-khan/war-and-peace-in-islam/d/99197.

Kiel, Yishai. "Penitential Theology in East Late Antiquity: Talmudic, Zoroastrian, and East Christian Reflections." *Journal for the Study of Judaism in the Persian, Hellenistic, and Roman Period* 45 (2014): 551–83.

Kimura, Ehito. "The Problem of Transitional Justice in Post-Suharto Indonesia." Middle East Institute, Jan. 17, 2014. At http://www.mei.edu/content/problem-transitional-justice-post-suharto-indonesia.

King, Martin Luther, Jr. "Letter from a Birmingham Jail." In *A Testament of Hope: The Essential Writings and Speeches of Martin Luther King, Jr.*, edited by James M. Washington, 289–302. San Francisco: Harper San Francisco, 1991.

Konstan, David. *Before Forgiveness: The Origins of a Moral Idea*. Cambridge: Cambridge Univ. Press, 2010.

Konstan, David, and Charles Griswold, eds. *Ancient Forgiveness: Classical, Judaic, and Christian*. Cambridge: Cambridge Univ. Press, 2012.

Kosman, Admiel. "R. Johanan and Resh Lakish: The Image of God in the Study Hall: 'Masculinity' versus 'Femininity.'" *European Judaism* 43 (2010): 128–45.

Lacusta, Maxine Kaufman, and Ursula Franklin. *Israeli Nonviolent Resistance to the Israeli Occupation*. Reading, UK: Garnet, 2011.

Lambert, David. *How Repentance Became Biblical: Judaism, Christianity, and the Interpretation of Scripture*. New York: Oxford Univ. Press, 2016.

Lang, Sabine. *NGOs, Civil Society, and the Public Sphere*. New York: Cambridge Univ. Press, 2013.

LaReau, Renée. "Meet Myla, M.A. '10." Alumni Profiles, Kroc Institute, June 6, 2011. At https://kroc.nd.edu/profiles/myla-leguro-2010/?section=ma.

Laursen, John Christian, and Cary J. Nederman, eds. *Beyond the Persecuting Society: Religious Toleration before the Enlightenment*. Philadelphia: Univ. of Pennsylvania Press, 1997.

Lawrence, Bruce B. *The Koran in English: A Biography*. Princeton, NJ: Princeton Univ. Press, 2017.

Lawyers Committee for International Human Rights. *Justice in El Salvador: A Case Study*. New York: Lawyers Committee for International Human Rights, 1982.

Lecler, Joseph. *Histoire de la tolerance au siècle de la Réforme*. 2 vols. Paris: Aubier, 1955.

Lederach, John Paul. *Building Peace: Sustainable Reconciliation in Divided Societies*. Washington, DC: United States Institute of Peace, 1997.

Lefebvre, Solange. "Reconciliation through Creativity: Story-Telling and Music." In *Reconciliation: Empowering Grace*, edited by Jacques

Haers, SJ, Felix Wilfred, Kristien Justaert, and Yves De Maeseneer, 13–23. London: SCM Press, 2013.

Leguro, Myla. "The Many Dimensions of Catholic Peacebuilding: Mindanao Experience." Paper presented at the Fifth Annual Catholic Peacebuilding Network Conference, Univ. of Notre Dame, Apr. 2008. At http://cpn.nd.edu/announcements-media-and-past-events/annual-conferences/5th-annual-cpn-conference-at-the-university-of-notre-dame-april-2008/background-papers-about-catholic-peacebuilding/.

Leighton, Chris. "An Open Letter to the Presbyterian Church." Institute for Christian and Jewish Studies, Feb. 6, 2014. At https://icjs.org/articles/2014/open-letter-presbyterian-church.

LeoGrande, William. Our Own Backyard: The United States in Central America, 1977–1992. Chapel Hill: Univ. of North Carolina Press, 1998.

Lernoux, Penny. Hearts on Fire: The Story of the Maryknoll Sisters. Maryknoll, NY: Orbis, 1993.

Leve, Lauren. "Cruel Optimism, Christianity, and the Post-conflict Optic." Fieldsights—Hot Spots, Cultural Anthropology Online, Mar. 24, 2014. At http://www.culanth.org/fieldsights/509-cruel-optimismchristianity-and-the-post-conflict-optic.

Levin, Yigal, and Amnon Shapira, eds. War and Peace in Jewish Tradition: From the Biblical World to the Present. London: Routledge, 2011.

Levinas, Emmanuel. Otherwise Than Being or Beyond Essence. Translated by Alphonso Lingis. Pittsburgh, PA: Duquesne Univ. Press, 2011.

Lewis, Anthony. "Abroad at Home; Showing His Colors." New York Times, Mar. 29, 1981, E21.

Lewis, David, Jr., and Ann T. Jordan. Creek Indian Medicine Ways: The Enduring Power of Mvskoke Religion. Albuquerque: Univ. of New Mexico Press, 2002.

Li, Chenyang. "The Confucian Ideal of Harmony." Philosophy East and West 56, no. 4 (2006): 583–603.

Lichterman, Paul. "Studying Public Religion: Beyond the Beliefs-Driven Actor." In Religion on the Edge: De-centering and Re-centering the Sociology of Religion, edited by Courtney Bender, Wendy Cadge, Peggy Levitt, and David Smilde, 115–36. New York: Oxford Univ. Press, 2013.

Lipman, Steve. "U.S. Jews and Israel: On 'Different Paths.'" *Jewish Week*, Jan. 26, 2017. At http://jewishweek.timesofisrael.com/u-s-jews-and-israel-on-different-paths/.

Lorber, Ben. "Understanding Alt-Right Antisemitism." *Doikayt*, Mar. 24, 2017. At https://doikayt.com/2017/03/24/understanding-alt-right-antisemitism/.

Lorea, Carola. "Matua, Hindu, or Foreigner? Shifting Identities in Bengali-Speaking Borderlands." Paper presented at the South Asia Annual Conference, Oct. 11, 2018, Madison, WI.

Losurdo, Domenico. *Liberalism: A Counter-History*. Translated by Gregory Elliott. London: Verso, 2011.

Luria, Keith. *Sacred Boundaries: Religious Coexistence and Conflict in Early-Modern France*. Washington, DC: Catholic Univ. of America Press, 2005.

MacGinty, Roger, and Pamina Firchow. "Top-Down and Bottom-Up Narratives of Peace and Conflict." *Politics* 36 (2016): 223–35.

MacNaughton, Gillian, and Mariah McGill. "Economic and Social Rights in the United States: Implementation without Ratification." *Northeastern University Law Journal* 4 (2012): 365–406.

Maestas, Adriana, and Rania Khalek. "How Latino Activists Are Standing Up to the Israel Lobby." *Electronic Intifada*, Mar. 6, 2014. At https://electronicintifada.net/content/how-latino-activists-are-standing-israel-lobby/13225.

Mahanta, Premkanta. *Rajbhaganar Para Kalthokalaike*. Guwahati, Assam: Naba Gaurang Press, 1994.

Mahfouz, Naguib. *The Journey of Ibn Fattouma*. Translated by Denys Johnson-Davies. New York: Anchor Books, 1993.

Mahmood, Saba. *Politics of Piety: The Islamic Revival and the Feminist Subject*. Princeton, NJ: Princeton Univ. Press, 2005.

Maltz, Judy. "Over 100 U.S. Rabbis Urge Hillel: Readmit LGBTQ Group Ousted for Teaming Up with Pro-boycott Org." *Haaretz*, June 23, 2017. At http://www.haaretz.com/us-news/.premium-1.797457.

Mamdani, Mahmood. *Good Muslim, Bad Muslim: America, the Cold War, and Roots of Terror*. New York: Pantheon Books, 2004.

Manifesto da las variaciones de Europa, y de las vilezas y usurpaciones francesas. Mexico City: Mariano Ontiveros, 1810.

Mannan, Abdul. *Infiltration: Genesis of the Assam Movement*. Translated by Hasinus Sultan and Badrul Islam Baig. Guwahati, Assam: Ayna Prakashan, 2017.

Maoz, Ifaz. "Peace Building in Violent Conflicts: Israeli–Palestinian Post-Oslo People to People Activities." *International Journal of Politics, Culture, and Society* 17 (2004): 563–74.

Marks, Stephen P., Kathleen A. Modrowski, and Walther Lichem. *Human Rights Cities: Civic Engagement for Societal Development*. New York: People's Movement for Human Rights Learning and United Nations Habitat, 2008.

Martin, Joel W. *Sacred Revolt: The Muskogees' Struggle for a New World*. Boston: Beacon Press, 1991.

Martín Casares, A. "Cristianos, musulmanes, y animistas en Granada: Identidades religiosas y sincretismo cultural." In *Negros, mulatos, zambaigos*, edited by Berta Ares and A. Stella, 207–21. Seville: Escuela de Estudios Hispano-Americanos, 2000.

Marx, Tzvi. "Theological Preparation for Reconciliation in Judaism." In *Religion, Conflict, and Reconciliation: Multifaith Ideals and Realities*, edited by Jerald D. Gort, Henry Jansen, and Hendrik M. Vroom, 93–103. Amsterdam: Rodopi, 2002.

McCarthy, Colman. "The Maryknoll Order." *Washington Post*, Apr. 19, 1981, G1.

McCartney, Robert. "5 Salvadorans Get 30 Years for Killing Missionaries." *Washington Post*, June 20, 1984, A1.

Melamed, Jodi. "Non-violent Direct Action Can Be Our Big Tent." *Jewschool*, June 1, 2017. At https://jewschool.com/2017/06/79709/non-violent-direct-action-can-big-tent/.

Melvin, Jess. "LSF Moves to Silence *Senyap*." *Jakarta Post*, Jan. 10, 2015. At http://www.thejakartapost.com/news/2015/01/10/lsf-moves-silence-senyap.html.

Mennonite Church USA. "Israel–Palestine Resolution: Summary of Delegate Comment." Considered and tabled by delegates, July 1, 2015. At http://mennoniteusa.org/wp-content/uploads/2015/04/Summary DelegateComments_IsraelPalestineResolutions.pdf.

———. "'Jewish and Palestinian Voices for Peace Tour' Announced." Mar. 17, 2017. At http://mennoniteusa.org/news/jewish-palestinian-voices-peace-tour-announced/.

Menocal, Maria Rosa. *Ornament of the World*. Boston: Little Brown, 2002.

Mills, Moffat. *Report on the Province of Assam*. Calcutta: Calcutta Gazette Office, 1854.

Mindinao Peacebuilding Institute (MPI). *Annual Training Report: MPI 2014 Annual Peacebuilding Training*. Mindinao, Philippines: MPI, Oct. 2, 2014. At http://mpiasia.net/2014-annual-peacebuilding-training -report.html.

Minutii, Rolando. "Toleration in China and Siam in Late Seventeenth Century Travel Literature." In *Paradoxes of Religious Toleration in Early Modern Political Thought*, edited by John Christian Laurensen and María José Villaverde, 109–21. Lanham, MD: Lexington Books, 2012.

Mitra, Darshan. "Hindus Angry at Trump's Ban on Muslim Refugees Should Look at What Modi Is Doing." *The Wire*, Jan. 1, 2017. At https:// thewire.in/104236/indians-angry-trumps-new-travel-ban-muslims-look -modi/.

Mitra, Naresh. "Indigenous Groups Oppose Inclusion of Refugees in NRC." *Times of India*, Aug. 19, 2018. At https://timesofindia.india times.com/city/guwahati/indigenous-groups-oppose-inclusion-of-refugees -in-nrc/articleshow/65458368.cms.

Molloy, Mark, and agencies. "Palestinians Tweet Tear Gas Advice to Protesters in Ferguson." *Telegraph*, Aug. 15, 2014. At http://www.telegraph .co.uk/news/worldnews/northamerica/usa/11036190/Palestinians-tweet -tear-gas-advice-to-protesters-in-Ferguson.html.

Monsalvo Antón, María. "Herejía conversa y contestación religiosa a fines de la edad media: Las denuncias a la Inquisición en el obispado de Osma." *Studia Historica* 2, no. 3 (1984): 109–39.

Morgan, Michael. "Mercy, Repentance, and Forgiveness in Ancient Judaism." In *Ancient Forgiveness: Classical, Judaic, and Christian*, edited by David Konstan and Charles Griswold, 137–57. Cambridge: Cambridge Univ. Press, 2012.

Movement for Black Lives. "Invest–Divest." N.d. At https://policy.m4bl.org /invest-divest/.

Movimiento Estudiantil Chican@ de Aztlan. "National M.E.Ch.A. Endorses Palestinian Boycott Call against Israel." Mar. 30, 2012. At http:// www.nationalmecha.org/archives/2012/03/national_mecha_endorses _palestinian_boycott_call_against_israel.php.

Moxley, Mitch. "Better Than a Wall: A New Detection System Can Help Monitor the U.S.–Mexico Border." *Popular Mechanics*, Jan. 28, 2016. At http://www.popularmechanics.com/technology/security/a18622/border-control-integrated-towers-system-invisible-wall/.

Mullen, C.S. *Administrative Report on the Census of Assam 1931*. Calcutta: Government of India Central Publication Branch, 1932.

Murphy, Jeffrie G., and Jean Hampton. *Forgiveness and Mercy*. Cambridge: Cambridge Univ. Press, 1988.

Nagati, Omar, and Beth Stryker, eds. *Archiving the City in Flux: Cairo's Shifting Urban Landscape since the January 25th Revolution*. Cairo: CLUSTER, 2013.

Nehru, Jawaharlal. *Toward Freedom: The Autobiography of Jawaharlal Nehru*. New York: John Day, 1941.

Neusner, Jacob. *War and Peace in Rabbinic Judaism*. Lanham, MD: Univ. Press of America, 2011.

———. "War in the Halakhah, Peace in the Aggadah." *Review of Rabbinic Judaism* 14 (2011): 133–57.

Newman, Louis. "Balancing Justice and Mercy: Reflections on Forgiveness in Judaism." *Journal of Religious Ethics* 41 (2013): 435–56.

———. *Repentance: The Meaning and Practice of Teshuvah*. Woodstock, VT: Jewish Lights Press, 2010.

Niebuhr, Reinhold. *Moral Man and Immoral Society: A Study in Ethics and Politics*. 1932. Reprint. New York: Scribner's, 1960.

Nierenberg, David. *Communities of Violence*. Princeton, NJ: Princeton Univ. Press, 1996.

Nikolsky, Ronit, and Tal Ilan. "Mihatam lihacha, 'From There to Here' (b. Sanh. 5a): Rabbinic Traditions between Palestine and Babylonia: An Introduction." In *Rabbinic Traditions between Palestine and Babylonia*, edited by Ronit Nikolsky and Tal Ilan, 1–21. Leiden: Brill, 2014.

Noone, Judy. *The Same Fate as the Poor*. Rev. ed. Maryknoll, NY: Orbis Books, 1995.

Nussbaum, Martha. *Human Capabilities: The Human Development Approach*. 2011. Reprint. Cambridge, MA: Belknap Press of Harvard Univ. Press, 2013.

Omer, Atalia. *Days of Awe: Reimagining Jewishness in Solidarity with Palestinians*. Chicago: Univ. of Chicago Press, 2019.

————. "Religion, Nationalism, and Solidarity Activism." In *The Oxford Handbook of Religion, Conflict, and Peacebuilding*, edited by Atalia Omer, R. Scott Appleby, and David Little, 613–58. New York: Oxford Univ. Press, 2015.

————. *When Peace Is Not Enough: How the Israeli Peace Camp Thinks about Religion, Nationalism, and Justice*. Chicago: Univ. of Chicago Press, 2013.

Omer, Atalia, and Jason A. Springs. *Religious Nationalism: A Reference Handbook*. Oxford: ABC-CLIO, 2013.

"Operation Streamline." Oct. 11, 2013. At http://www.latinorebels.com /2013/10/11/developing-story-immigration-activists-in-tucson-block -deportation-buses/.

Paffenholz, Thania. "Civil Society and Peacebuilding." In *Civil Society and Peacebuilding: A Critical Assessment*, edited by Thania Paffenholz, 43–64. Boulder, CO: Lynne Rienner, 2010.

————, ed. *Civil Society and Peacebuilding: A Critical Assessment*. Boulder, CO: Lynne Rienner, 2010.

Paffenholz, Thania, and Christoph Spurk. *Civil Society, Civic Engagement, and Peacebuilding*. Social Development Papers: Conflict Prevention and Reconstruction. Washington, DC: World Bank, 2006.

————. "A Comprehensive Analytical Framework." In *Civil Society and Peacebuilding: A Critical Assessment*, edited by Thania Paffenholz, 65–76. Boulder, CO: Lynne Rienner, 2010.

Paiva, José Pedro, and Giuseppe Marcocci. *História da Inquisição Portuguesa, 1536–1821*. Lisbon: Esfera dos Livros, 2013.

Palumbu-Liu, David. "'It's Ugly, It's Vicious, It's Brutal': Cornel West on Israel in Palestine—and Why Gaza Is 'the Hood on Steroids.'" *Salon*, Feb. 25, 2015. At http://www.salon.com/2015/02/25/its_ugly_it%E2% 80%99s_vicious_it%E2%80%99s_brutal_cornel_west_on_israel_in _palestine_%E2%80%94_and_why_gaza_is_the_hood_on_steroids/.

Paris, Roland. "Peacekeeping and the Constraints of Global Culture." *European Journal of International Relations* 9 (2003): 441–73.

Peace, Roger. *A Call to Conscience: The Anti–Contra War Campaign*. Amherst: Univ. of Massachusetts Press, 2012.

"Peace." In *Encyclopedia Judaica*, 2d ed., vol. 15, 700–703. Detroit: Macmillan, 2007.

Pellett, Gail, dir. *Justice and the Generals*. Brooklyn, NY: First Run/Icarus Films, 2002. VHS.

Pérez, Lorenç, Leonard Muntaner, and Mateu Colom, eds. *El Tribunal de la Inquisición en Mallorca: Relación de causas de fe*. Palma de Mallorca, Spain: Miquel Font, 1986.

Peterson, Bill. "Reagan Plea Rejected, Senate Votes Terms for Salvadoran Aid." *Washington Post*, Sept. 25, 1981, A5.

Pew Research Center, Polling and Analysis. "A Portrait of Jewish Americans." Oct. 1, 2013. At http://www.pewforum.org/2013/10/01/jewish -american-beliefs-attitudes-culture-survey/.

Piker, Joshua. *Okfuskee: A Creek Indian Town in Colonial America*. Cambridge, MA: Harvard Univ. Press, 2004.

Pilario, Daniel Franklin. "Restorative Justice amidst Continuing Violence." In *Reconciliation: Empowering Grace*, edited by Jacques Haers, Felix Wilfred, Kristien Justaert, and Yves De Maeseneer, 64–73. London: SCM Press, 2013.

"Pittsburgh Human Rights City Alliance Human Rights Days of Action 2014." N.d. At http://wiki.pghrights.mayfirst.org/index.php?title=File :Action_Calendar_One_Pager.pdf. Accessed Feb. 11, 2019.

"Pittsburgh Human Rights City Alliance Workshop at the 2015 Summit against Racism." N.d. At http://wiki.pghrights.mayfirst.org/index.php ?title=File:Summit_Against_Racism_2015_REPORT_and_Agenda _Priorities.pdf. Accessed Feb. 11, 2019.

"Pittsburgh's Human Rights City Alliance Hosts Event to Recognize Mother Earth Day." N.d. At http://wiki.pghrights.mayfirst.org/index .php?title=File:Report_on_Mother_Earth_Day_2014.pdf. Accessed Feb. 11, 2019.

Polat, Necati. "Peace as War." *Alternatives: Global, Local, Political* 35, no. 4 (2010): 317–45.

"Police Reform." N.d. At http://wiki.pghrights.mayfirst.org/index.php?title =Police_Reform. Accessed Feb. 11, 2019.

Pope, Stephen J. *Human Evolution and Christian Ethics*. Cambridge: Cambridge Univ. Press, 2007.

Porter, Roy. *The Creation of the Modern World*. New York: Norton, 2000.

Prakoso, Rangga, Ezra Sihite, Bayu Marhaenjati, and Firdha Novialita. "AGO Rejects Komnas HAM Report on 1965 Massacres." *Jakarta*

Globe, Nov. 10, 2012. At http://thejakartaglobe.beritasatu.com/archive /ago-rejects-komnas-ham-report-on-1965-massacres/.

Prescod-Weinstein, Chandra. "Black and Palestinian Lives Matter: Black and Jewish America in the Twenty-First Century." In *On Antisemitism: Solidarity and the Struggle for Justice*, edited by Jewish Voice for Peace, 31–41. Chicago: Haymarket Books, 2017.

Preston, Julia. "Salvadoran General Accused in Killings Should Be Deported, Miami Judge Says." *New York Times*, Apr. 11, 2014, A13.

"*The Prison Songs*—Trailer." N.d. At https://www.youtube.com/watch?v =l2BkA8bMgyE. Accessed June 18, 2019.

Prosperi, Adriano. "America e Apocalisse: Note sulla 'conquista spirituale' del Nuovo Mondo." In *America e Apocalisse e altri saggi*, 15–65. Pisa, Italy: Istituti Editoriali e Poligrafichi Internazionale, 1999.

Puar, Jasbir. "Citation and Censorship: The Politics of Talking about the Sexual Politics of Israel." *Feminist Legal Studies* 19, no. 2 (2011): 133–42.

———. "Rethinking Homonationalism." *International Journal of Middle East Studies* 45, no. 2 (2013): 336–39.

———. *Terrorist Assemblages: Homonationalism in Queer Times*. 2007. Reprint. Durham, NC: Duke Univ. Press, 2017.

Puar, Jasbir, and Maya Mikdashi. "Pinkwatching and Pinkwashing: Interpenetration and Its Discontents." *Jadaliyya*, Aug. 9, 2012. At http://www.velvetparkmedia.com/blogs/pinkwatching-and-pinkwashing -interpenetration-and-its-discontents.

Putra, Gde. "Time Bomb in Bali." *Inside Indonesia*, July–Sept. 2012. At http://www.insideindonesia.org/time-bomb-in-bali.

Rabbis for Human Rights (RHR). "We Ask Forgiveness." Sept. 30, 2011. At https://rhr.org.il/eng/2011/09/we-ask-forgiveness/.

Rao, K. Sreedhar. *Wither Governance: Reflections of an Assam Civilian*. Delhi: South Asia Foundation, 2002.

Ravid, Barak. "On Netanyahu's Orders: Israel's Foreign Ministry Retracts Criticism of Anti-semitism in Hungary and Slams George Soros." *Haaretz*, July 10, 2017. At http://www.haaretz.com/israel-news/1.800 437.

Ray, Jayanta Kumar. *India's Foreign Relations, 1947–2007*. Delhi: Routledge, 2011.

"Reagan-Appointed Democrat Speaks Her Mind on World, Domestic Politics." *Tampa Tribune*, Dec. 25, 1980, A23.

Remini, Robert V. *Andrew Jackson and His Indian Wars*. New York: Viking Penguin, 2001.

Richmond, Oliver. *Peace in International Relations*. London: Routledge, 2008.

———. *A Post-liberal Peace*. London: Routledge, 2011.

Rinaldo, Rachel. "Pious and Critical: Muslim Women Activists and the Question of Agency." *Gender & Society* 28, no. 6 (2014): 824–46.

Risse, Thomas, Stephen C. Ropp, and Kathryn Sikkink. *The Power of Human Rights: International Norms and Domestic Change*. New York: Cambridge Univ. Press, 1999.

Robbins, Annie. "'Protest in the Form of a Prayer': Dream Defenders Demonstration in Nazareth Makes Connections from Ferguson to Palestine." *Mondoweiss*, Jan. 15, 2015. At http://mondoweiss.net/2015/01 /demonstration-connections-palestine.

Robert, Dana. "The Influence of American Missionary Women on the World Back Home." *Religion and American Culture* 12, no. 1 (2002): 59–89.

Roberts, David. "Beyond the Metropolis? Popular Peace and Post-conflict Peacebuilding." *Review of International Studies* 37, no. 5 (2011): 2535–56.

Robinson, Marilynne. *Lila*. New York: Farrar, Strauss and Giroux, 2014.

Roccu, Roberto. "David Harvey in Tahrir Square: The Dispossessed, the Discontented, and the Egyptian Revolution." *Third World Quarterly* 34, no. 3 (2013): 423–40.

Rodríguez Morel, Genaro. *Cartas de la Real Audiencia de Santo Domingo (1530–1546)*. Santo Domingo, Dominican Republic: Archivo General de la Nación, 2007.

Rohter, Larry. "4 Salvadorans Say They Killed U.S. Nuns on Orders of Military." *New York Times*, Apr. 3, 1998. At http://www.nytimes.com /1998/04/03/world/4-salvadorans-say-they-killed-us-nuns-on-orders -of-military.html.

Rosenblum, April. *The Past Didn't Go Anywhere: Making Resistance to Antisemitism Part of All of Our Movements*. 2007. At https://engage online.wordpress.com/2010/02/23/the-past-didnt-go-anywhere-making -resistance-to-antisemitism-part-of-all-of-our-movements/.

Rubenstein, Jeffrey. *The Culture of the Babylonian Talmud*. Baltimore: Johns Hopkins Univ. Press, 2003.

———. *Stories of the Babylonian Talmud*. Baltimore: Johns Hopkins Univ. Press, 2010.

Saffey, Thomas M., ed. *A Companion to Multiconfessionalism in the Early Modern World*. Leiden: Brill, 2011.

Sager, Mike. "25,000 Demonstrators March on the Pentagon." *Washington Post*, May 4, 1981, C1.

Saikia, Yasmin. *Fragmented Memories: Struggling to Be Tai-Ahom in India*. Durham, NC: Duke Univ. Press, 2005.

———. *In the Meadows of Gold: Telling Tales of the Swargadeos at the Crossroads of Assam*. Delhi: Spectrum, 1997.

———. "The Muslims of Assam: Present/Absent History." In *Northeast India: A Place of Relations*, edited by Yasmin Saikia and Amit Baishya, 111–34. Cambridge: Cambridge Univ. Press, 2017.

Saikia, Yasmin, and Amit Baishya, eds. *Northeast India: A Place of Relations*. Cambridge: Cambridge Univ. Press, 2017.

"*Saint Francis* Quotes." n.d. At https://www.goodreads.com/work/quotes /921820.

Santikarma, Degung. "Monument, Document, and Mass Grave." In *Beginning to Remember: Historical Memory in Indonesia*, edited by M. Zurbuchen, 312–23. Seattle: Univ. of Washington Press, 2005.

Sardar, Ziauddin. *Desperately Seeking Paradise: Journeys of a Sceptical Muslim*. London: Granta, 2004.

Sarma, Dhiraj Kumar. "Rise of RSS in the Northeast." *Northeast Today*, May 4, 2016. At https://www.northeasttoday.in/rise-of-rss-in-northeast/.

Sassen, Saskia. *Globalization and Its Discontents*. New York: New Press, 1998.

Satlow, Michael. "From Salve to Weapon: Torah Study, Masculinity, and the Babylonian Talmud." In *Religious Men and Masculine Identities in the Middle Ages*, edited by P. H. Cullum and Katherine Lewis, 16–27. Woodbridge, UK: Boydell and Brewer, 2013.

Saunt, Claudio. *A New Order of Things: Property, Power, and the Transformation of the Creek Indians, 1733–1816*. Cambridge: Cambridge Univ. Press, 1999.

Schell, Jonathan. *The Unconquerable World: Power, Nonviolence, and the Will of the People*. New York: Metropolitan Books, 2003.

Schmiechen, Peter. *Saving Power: Theories of Atonement and Forms of the Church*. Grand Rapids, MI: Eerdmans, 2005.

Schneider, Nathan. "Peace from the Ground Up: An Interview with Myla Leguro." The Immanent Frame: Secularism, Religion, and the Public Square, Oct. 12, 2010. At http://blogs.ssrc.org/tif/2010/10/12/leguro/.

Schor, Sophie. "40 Days and 40 Nights: Building a New Reality in Sumud Freedom Camp." +972, July 3, 2017. At https://972mag.com/40-days-and-40-nights-building-a-new-reality-in-sumud-freedom-camp/128500/.

Schulman, Sarah. *Israel/Palestine and the Queer International*. Durham, NC: Duke Univ. Press, 2012.

Schwartz, Stuart B. *All Can Be Saved: Religious Tolerance and Salvation in the Iberian Atlantic World*. New Haven, CT: Yale Univ. Press, 2008.

Sesboüé, Bernard. *Hors de l'Église pas de salut*. Paris: Desclée de Brouwer, 2004.

Shabi, Rachel. "Donald Trump Has Managed to Unite Muslims and Jews in a Way That Few Ever Managed to Do." *Independent* (UK), Feb. 14, 2017. At http://www.independent.co.uk/voices/donald-trump-muslims-jews-antisemitism-israel-palestine-neo-nazi-holocaust-unique-a7579861.html.

Sharp, Gene. *From Dictatorship to Democracy*. Cambridge, MA: Albert Einstein Foundation, 1994.

———. *The Politics of Nonviolent Action*. 3 vols. Boston: Porter Sargent, 1973.

———. *Waging Nonviolent Struggle: 20th Century Practice and 21st Century Potential*. Boston: Extending Horizons Books and Porter Sargent, 2005.

Shaw, Martin, and Omer Bartov. "The Question of Genocide in Palestine, 1948: An Exchange between Martin Shaw and Omer Bartov." *Journal of Genocide Research* 12, nos. 3–4 (2010): 243–59.

Shaw, Rosalind, and Lars Waldorf, with Pierre Hazan. *Localizing Transitional Justice: Interventions and Priorities after Mass Violence*. Stanford, CA: Stanford Univ. Press, 2010.

"*Si Buyung—The Prison Songs*." N.d. At https://www.youtube.com/watch?v=axKWsh25GQU. Accessed June 18, 2018.

Siddiqui, Mona. *Hospitality and Islam: Welcoming in God's Name*. New Haven, CT: Yale Univ. Press, 2015.

Singerman, Diane, ed. *Cairo Contested: Governance, Urban Space, and Global Modernity.* Cairo: American Univ. in Cairo Press, 2009.

Singh, Jakeet. "Religious Agency and the Limits of Intersectionality." *Hypatia* 30, no. 4 (2015): 657–74.

Smith, Jackie. "Globalization and Strategic Peacebuilding." In *Strategies of Peace: Transforming Conflict in a Violent World*, edited by Daniel Philpott and Gerard F. Powers, 247–70. New York: Oxford Univ. Press, 2010.

Smith, Jackie, Rebecca Burns, and Rachel Miller. "The World Social Forums as Transformative Peacebuilding." In *Globalization, Social Movements, and Peacebuilding*, edited by Jackie Smith and Ernesto Verdeja, 207–34. Syracuse, NY: Syracuse Univ. Press, 2013.

Smith, Jackie, Marina Karides, Marc Becker, Dorval Brunelle, Christopher Chase-Dunn, Donatella della Porta, Rosalba Icaza Garza, et al. *Global Democracy and the World Social Forums.* 2nd ed. Boulder, CO: Paradigm, 2014.

Smith, Jackie, and Ernesto Verdeja, eds. *Globalization, Social Movements, and Peacebuilding.* Syracuse, NY: Syracuse Univ. Press, 2013.

Smith, Jackie, and Ernesto Verdeja. Introduction to *Globalization, Social Movements, and Peacebuilding*, edited by Jackie Smith and Ernesto Verdeja, 1–18. Syracuse, NY: Syracuse Univ. Press, 2013.

Sobrino, Jon, SJ. *Christ the Liberator.* Maryknoll, NY: Orbis, 2001.

Sokoloff, Michael. *A Dictionary of Jewish Babylonian Aramaic of the Talmudic and Geonic Periods.* Ramat Gan, Israel: Bar Ilan Univ. Press, 2002.

Spelman, Elizabeth V. *Inessential Woman: Problems of Exclusion in Feminist Thought.* Boston: Beacon Press, 1988.

Spencer, Richard. "Facing the Future as a Minority." Speech delivered at the American Renaissance Conference, Apr. 30, 2013, Nashville, TN.

Splendiani, Anna Maria, et al., eds. *Cincuenta años de Inquisición en el tribunal de Cartagena de Indias, 1610–1660.* [Santafé de Bogotá]: Centro Editorial Javeriano, Instituto Colombiano de Cultura Hispánica, 1997.

Stanton, Jay. "What Will We Make Different This Year? A Guest Sermon for Erve Yom Kippur." *Shalom Rav: A Blog by Rabbi Brant Rosen*, Sept. 24, 2015. At http://rabbibrant.com/2015/09/24/what-will-we-make-different -this-year-a-guest-sermon-for-erev-yom-kippur-by-jay-stanton/.

St. Columbans Mission Society. "The Life and Death of Father Fausto Tentorio." Nov. 16, 2011. At http://www.columban.org.au/e-news/e-news -vol.-4-no.-10/the-life-and-death-of-father-fausto-tentorio.

Steinmetz, Devora. "Must the Patriarch Know *Uqtzin*? The Nasi as Scholar in the Babylonian Aggada." *AJS Review* 23 (1998): 163–89.

Stephan, Maria J., and Erica Chenoweth. "Why Civil Resistance Works: The Strategic Logic of Nonviolent Conflict." *International Security* 33, no. 1 (2008): 7–44.

Stout, Jeffrey. *Blessed Are the Organized: Grassroots Democracy in America*. Princeton, NJ: Princeton Univ. Press, 2010.

Stroumsa, Susan. *Freethinkers in Medieval Islam: Ibn al-Rawandi, Abu Bark at-Razi, and Their Impact on Islamic Thought*. Leiden: Brill, 1999.

Stryker, Beth, Omar Nagati, and Magda Mostafa, eds. *Learning from Cairo: Global Perspectives and Future Visions*. Cairo: CLUSTER, 2013.

Sullivan, Francis A. *Salvation outside the Church*. New York: Paulist Press, 1922.

Suriyani, Luh De. "Greater Effort Needed to Oppose Benoa Bay Reclamation." *Jakarta Post*, Aug. 9, 2014. At http://www.thejakartapost .com/news/2014/08/09/greater-effort-needed-oppose-benoa-bay-recla mation.html.

Swanton, John R. *Early History of the Creek Indians and Their Neighbors*. Bureau of American Ethnology Bulletin no. 73. Washington, DC: US Government Printing Office, 1922.

———. *The Social History and Usages of the Creek Confederacy*. Forty-Second Annual Report of the Bureau of American Ethnology. Washington, DC: US Government Printing Office, 1928.

Talpade Mohanty, Chandra. "Under Western Eyes: Feminist Scholarship and Colonial Discourse." In *Third World Women and the Politics of Feminism*, edited by Chandra Talpade Mohanty, Ann Russo, and Lourdes Torres, 51–80. Bloomington: Univ. of Indiana Press, 1991.

Taubman, Philip. "The Speaker and His Sources on Latin America." *New York Times*, Sept. 12, 1984, B10.

Tawil-Souri, Helga. "Media, Globalization, and the (Un)Making of the Palestinian Cause." *Popular Communication* 13 (2015): 145–57.

Tedja, Eve. "Save Bali from Drowning—We Reject the Reclamation of Benoa Bay." For Bali, Aug. 13, 2014. At http://www.forbali.org/save -bali-from-drowning-we-reject-the-reclamation-of-benoa-bay/?lang=en.

Thakuria, Nava. "Is the Government's Aim to Integrate Neighbouring Minority Asylum Seekers Hindu-Centric?" #*Swarajya*, Oct. 15, 2016. At https://swarajyamag.com/politics/from-india-to-bharat-government -seeks-to-integrate-neighbouring-minority-asylum-seekers.

Toribio Medina, José. *Historia del Tribunal del Santo Oficio de la Inquisición de Lima*. 2 vols. Santiago de Chile: Gutenberg, 1887.

Towner, W. Sibley. "Clones of God: Genesis 1:26–28 and the Image of God in the Hebrew Bible." *Interpretation* 59, no. 4 (2005): 341–56.

"Treaty with the Creeks, 1814." In *Indian Treaties, 1778–1883*, compiled and edited by Harold D. Moser and Sharon MacPherson, 107–10. New York: Interland, 1972.

Tyler, Harold. "The Churchwomen Murders: A Report to the Secretary of State." Dec. 2, 1983. Federal Bureau of Investigation Library, Gale World Scholar: Latin America and the Caribbean.

Tzedek Chicago. "About." N.d. At http://tzedekchicago.org/about/. Accessed Jan. 4, 2019.

———. "Welcome to Tzedek Chicago!" June 2015. At https://tzedezchicago .files.wordpress.com/2015/06/member-welcome-kit-revised-10-04-15-1 .pdf.

United Nations Commission on the Truth for El Salvador. *From Madness to Hope: The 12-Year War in El Salvador*. New York: United Nations, 1993.

Uvin, Peter. "The Development/Peacebuilding Nexus: A Typology and History of Changing Paradigms." *Journal of Peacebuilding and Development* 1 (2002): 2–24.

Van den Dungen, Peter, and Lawrence S. Wittner. "Peace History: An Introduction." *Journal of Peace Research* 40, no. 4 (2003): 363–75.

Van Heerikhuzen, Annemarie. "How God Disappeared from Europe: Visions of a United Europe from Erasmus to Kant." *European Legacy: Towards a New Paradigm* 13, no. 4 (2007–8): 401–11.

Venkataramkrishnan, Rohan. "The Daily Fix: When Amit Shah Says Immigrants Are Termites, He Is Actually the One Undermining India." *Scroll.in*, Sept. 24, 2018. At https://scroll.in/article/895567/the-daily

-fix-when-amit-shah-says-immigrants-are-termites-he-is-actually-the
-one-undermining-india.

Villiers Negroponte, Diana. *Seeking Peace in El Salvador: The Struggle to Reconstruct a Nation at the End of the Cold War.* New York: Palgrave Macmillan, 2011.

Wade, Christine J. "El Salvador: Contradictions of Neoliberalism and Building Sustainable Peace." *International Journal of Peace Studies* 13, no. 2 (2008): 15–32.

Walfish, Avraham. "Halakhic Confrontation Dramatized: A Study of Mishnah Rosh Hashanah 2:8–9." *Hebrew Union College Annual* 79 (2008): 1–41.

Waller, James. *Becoming Evil: How Ordinary People Commit Genocide and Mass Killing.* Oxford: Oxford Univ. Press, 2002.

Wallerstein, Immanuel. *World-Systems Analysis: An Introduction.* Durham, NC: Duke Univ. Press, 2004.

Walsh, Edward. "Reagan Gets First Public Opinion Backlash—on Salvador Policy." *Washington Post*, Mar. 27, 1981, A9.

Walsham, Alexandra. *Charitable Hatred: Tolerance and Intolerance in England, 1500–1700.* Manchester, UK: Manchester Univ. Press, 2006.

Walzer, Michael. *Just and Unjust Wars: A Moral Argument with Historical Illustrations.* 2nd ed. New York: Basic Books, 1977.

Wang, Yvonne Margareta. "How Can Religion Contribute to Peace in the Holy Land? A Study of Religious Peace Work in Jerusalem." PhD diss., Oslo Univ., 2011.

———. "Strategic Engagement and Religious Peace-Building." *Approaching Religion* 4 (2014): 71–82.

Ward, Eric K. "Skin in the Game: How Antisemitism Animates White Nationalism." *Political Research Associates*, June 29, 2017. At http://www.politicalresearch.org/2017/06/29/skin-in-the-game-how-antisemitism-animates-white-nationalism/#sthash.b3W00cy4.Lg2YquFS.dpbs.

Warner, Michael. *The Trouble with Normal: Sex, Politics, and the Ethics of Queer Life.* Cambridge, MA: Harvard Univ. Press, 1999.

Waselkov, Gregory A. *A Conquering Spirit: Fort Mims and the Redstick War of 1813–1814.* Tuscaloosa: Univ. of Alabama Press, 2006.

Wasow, Omar. "Do Protest Tactics Matter? Evidence from the 1960s Black Insurgency." Feb. 2, 2017. At http://www.omarwasow.com/Protests_on_Voting.pdf.

Waxman, Dov. *Troubles in the Tribe: The American Jewish Conflict over Israel.* Princeton, NJ: Princeton Univ. Press, 2016.

Weilbacher, Hannah. "Public Jewish Communal Response to the Movement for Black Lives Platform." *Jewish Social Justice Roundtable*, Nov. 9, 2016. At http://jewishsocialjustice.org/blog/public-jewish-communal-response-movement-black-lives-platform.

Weiner, Myron. *Sons of the Soil: Migration and Ethnic Conflict in India.* Princeton, NJ: Princeton Univ. Press, 1978.

Weixi, Hu. "On Confucian Communitarianism." *Frontiers of Philosophy in China* 2, no. 4 (2007): 475–87.

Wescott, Roger W. "Reflections on the Etymology of Some Words for 'Peace.'" *International Journal on World Peace* 7, no. 3 (1990): 94–97.

Whaley, Joachim. *Religious Toleration and Social Change in Hamburg, 1529–1819.* Cambridge: Cambridge Univ. Press, 1985.

"What Amit Shah as Home Minister Means for the Power Situation at the Center." *NDTV News*, June 1, 2019. At https://www.ndtv.com/india-news/amit-shah-pm-narendra-modi-cabinet-with-home-ministry-amit-shah-is-formally-no-2-in-government-2045928?pfrom=home-topstories.

Whitton, Michaela. "Black Palestinian Alliance Emerges to Confront Global Violence and Racism." *Anti Media*, Oct. 15, 2015. At http://the antimedia.org/black-palestinian-alliance-emerges-to-confront-global-violence-and-racism/.

Williams, Leslie. "White Jews: Deal with Your Privilege and Call Out Jewish Support for White Supremacy." Speech given at the Stephen Douglas Monument on behalf of Resist, Reimagine, Rebuild, Aug. 19, 2017, Chicago. At https://crankylibrarian.wordpress.com/2017/08/19/white-jews-deal-with-your-privilege-and-call-out-jewish-support-for-white-supremacy/.

Wink, Walter. *Engaging the Powers: Discernment and Resistance.* Minneapolis, MN: Fortress, 1992.

Winstanley, Asa. "Watch: Registration Opens for World Social Forum Free Palestine in Brazil." *Electronic Intifada*, Oct. 10, 2012. At https://electronicintifada.net/blogs/asa-winstanley/watch-registration-opens-world-social-forum-free-palestine-brazil.

Wise, Alissa. "Building toward the New World." In *On Antisemitism: Solidarity and the Struggle for Justice*, edited by Jewish Voice for Peace, 207–12. Chicago: Haymarket Books, 2017.

————. "JVP: Reactions to Our Parade Protest Were 'Cruel,' 'Homophobic,' and 'Hyperbolic.'" *Forward*, June 7, 2017. At http://forward.com/scribe/374055/jvp-reactions-to-our-parade-protest-were-cruel-homophobic-and-hyperbolic/.

Woodward, Bob. *Veil: The Secret Wars of the CIA, 1981–1987*. New York: Simon and Schuster, 1987.

Wooten, David. "Lucien Febvre and the Problem of Unbelief in the Early Modern Period." *Journal of Modern History* 60 (1988): 695–730.

Wright, J. Leitch, Jr. *Creeks and Seminoles: Destruction and Regeneration of the Muscogulge People*. Lincoln: Univ. of Nebraska Press, 1986.

Yoffie, Eric H. "AIPAC Is Feeling the Heat to Address Israel's 'Ayatollah' Judaism." *Haaretz*, July 13, 2017. At http://www.haaretz.com/opinion/.premium-1.801211.

Yuval-Davis, Nira. "Intersectionality and Feminist Politics." *European Journal of Women's Studies* 13, no. 3 (2006): 193–209.

Zagorin, Perez. *How the Idea of Religious Toleration Came to the West*. Princeton, NJ: Princeton Univ. Press, 2003.

Contributors

Lisa Sowle Cahill is the J. Donald Monan Professor of Theology at Boston College. She is an ethicist who focuses on questions of gender, peacebuilding, and bioethics, having earned her MA and PhD from the University of Chicago Divinity School. Her publications include *Blessed Are the Peacemakers: Pacifism, Just War, and Peacebuilding* (2019), *A Theology and Praxis of Gender Equality* (2018), *Global Justice, Christology, and Christian Ethics* (2013), *Theological Bioethics: Participation, Justice, and Change* (2005), and *Bioethics and the Common Good* (2004).

David Cortright is the director of policy studies at the University of Notre Dame's Kroc Institute for International Peace Studies. He is the author or editor of twenty books, including *Gandhi and Beyond: Nonviolence for a New Political Age* (2nd ed., 2009) and *Peace: A History of Movements and Ideas* (2008). Cortright has written widely on nonviolent social change, peace history, nuclear disarmament, and the use of multilateral sanctions and incentives as tools of international peacemaking. He has served as a consultant to member states of the United Nations Security Council and to many foundations and institutions. Cortright has a long history of public advocacy for disarmament and the prevention of war. As an active-duty soldier during the Vietnam War, he spoke against that conflict.

Leslie Dwyer is an associate professor and director of the Center for the Study of Gender and Conflict at the School for Conflict Analysis and Resolution at George Mason University. She is a cultural anthropologist (with a BA from the University of Pennsylvania and an MA and PhD from Princeton University) whose academic research focuses on issues of violence, gender, postconflict social life, transitional justice, and the politics of memory and identity. Her most recent project, supported by grants from the MacArthur Foundation, the H. F. Guggenheim Foundation, and the United States

Institute of Peace, is an ethnographic study of the aftermath of political violence in Indonesia, where she has worked for more than twenty years. Her book on this research, *"A World in Fragments": Aftermaths of Violence in Bali, Indonesia*, is forthcoming. She is also a documentary filmmaker working on a film, *The Black Highway* (forthcoming), that engages critically with postconflict peacebuilding practices in Aceh, Indonesia.

Donald L. Fixico is Shawnee, Sac and Fox, Mvskoke Creek, and Seminole. He is a Regent's and Distinguished Foundation Professor of History and Distinguished Scholar of Sustainability in the Wrigley Global Institute at Arizona State University. He previously was the Thomas Bowlus Distinguished Professor at the University of Kansas and held seven visiting professorships, including the John J. Rhodes Chair in Public Policy and American Institutions in the Barrett Honors College at Arizona State University. He has written and edited fifteen books on American Indians and the West and has worked on twenty documentaries.

Joel Gereboff is an associate professor of religious studies at Arizona State University. His research focuses on early rabbinic Judaism, American Judaism, Judaism and emotions, and Jewish ethics. His most recent publication is coedited volume *Qol Tamid: The Shofar in Ritual, History, and Culture* (2017, with Jonathan L. Friedman), to which he contributed the essays "The Emotional Resonance of the Shofar" and "Each One Blowing His Own Horn: Sounding the Shofar in American Machzorim."

Chad Haines is a cultural anthropologist and associate professor of religious studies and senior sustainability scholar at Arizona State University. He is the author of *Nation, Territory, and Globalization in Pakistan: Traversing the Margins* (2012) and a forthcoming book on Muslim modernities, urbanism, and everyday ethics in Cairo, Islamabad, and Dubai. He is also coeditor of *Women and Peace in the Islamic World: Gender, Agency, and Influence* (2014, with Yasmin Saikia). He earned MA degrees in South Asian studies and anthropology as well as a PhD in anthropology from the University of Wisconsin at Madison. Prior to teaching at Arizona State University, he was assistant professor of anthropology at the American University in Cairo.

Amanda Izzo is assistant professor of women's and gender studies at Saint Louis University. She is the author of *Liberal Christianity and Women's*

Global Activism: The YWCA of the USA and the Maryknoll Sisters (2018). She earned her MA and PhD in American studies from Yale University. Her research interests include women, faith, and transnational social action.

Bruce B. Lawrence is the Nancy and Jeffrey Marcus Humanities Professor Emeritus of Religion at Duke University. He is the author of more than fifteen books as well as editor and coeditor of a number of volumes on Islamic philosophy, Islam in South Asia, Sufism, religious fundamentalism, Islamic modernities, and Asian religions in the United States. His books include *The Koran in English: A Biography* (2017), *Who Is Allah?* (2015), and *Defenders of God: The Fundamentalist Revolt against the Modern Age* ([1989] 1995).

Atalia Omer is associate professor of religion, conflict, and peace studies at the Kroc Institute for International Peace Studies and the Keough School of Global Affairs at the University of Notre Dame. Her research focuses on religion, violence, and peacebuilding as well as on theories and methods in the study of religion. She is a 2017 Andrew Carnegie Fellow and the author of *Days of Awe: Reimagining Jewishness in Solidarity with Palestinians* (2019) and *When Peace Is Not Enough: How the Israeli Peace Camp Thinks about Religion, Nationalism, and Justice* (2013). She is also a coeditor of *The Oxford Handbook of Religion, Conflict, and Peacebuilding* (2015, with R. Scott Appleby and David Little).

Yasmin Saikia has held the Hardt-Nickachos Endowed Chair in Peace Studies since 2010 and is a professor of South Asian history at Arizona State University. She is the author of two award-winning books: *Fragmented Memories: Struggling to be Tai-Ahom in India* (2005) won the Srikanta Datta Best Book Award on Northeast India and the Social Sciences (2005) and *Women, War, and the Making of Bangladesh* (2010) was honored with the Oral History Association Biennial Book Award in 2013. *Women, War, and the Making of Bangladesh* is the first book to be published simultaneously in India and Pakistan. She is also the coeditor of *Northeast India: A Place of Relations* (2017, with Amit Baishya) and of *Women and Peace in the Islamic World: Gender, Agency, and Influence* (2014, with Chad Haines).

Stuart B. Schwartz is the George Burton Adams Professor of History at Yale University, the chair of the Council of Latin American and Iberian

Studies, and the former master of Ezra Stiles College. He is the author of a number of books, including *All Can Be Saved: Religious Tolerance and Salvation in the Iberian Atlantic World* (2008), which won a number of awards; *Slaves, Peasants, and Rebels* (1992); and *Sugar Plantations in the Formation of Brazilian Society* (1985).

Jackie Smith is professor of sociology at the University of Pittsburgh and editor of the *Journal of World-Systems Research*. She is a leading scholar of transnational social movements, and her most recent books include *Social Movements and World-System Transformation* (2016, coedited with Michael Goodhart, Patrick Manning, and John Markoff), *Global Democracy and the World Social Forums* (2014, co-written with multiple collaborators), and *Social Movements in the World-System: The Politics of Crisis and Transformation* (2012, cowritten with Dawn Wiest). Smith's work on the World Social Forum process has led her to examine how global analyses and models of action are "translated" to local settings. Her participant–observation research has included work with Pittsburgh's Human Rights City Alliance.

Index

Page numbers in italics refer to illustrative material.

375